GREAT DEPRESSION

Selected titles in ABC-CLIO's Perspectives in American Social History series

African Americans in the Nineteenth Century: People and Perspectives
American Revolution: People and Perspectives
Baby Boom: People and Perspectives
British Colonial America: People and Perspectives
Civil Rights Movement: People and Perspectives
Civil War: People and Perspectives
Cold War and McCarthy Era: People and Perspectives
Colonial America: People and Perspectives
Early Republic: People and Perspectives
Industrial Revolution: People and Perspectives
Jacksonian and Antebellum Age: People and Perspectives
Jazz Age: People and Perspectives
Making of the American West: People and Perspectives
Reconstruction: People and Perspectives
Vietnam War Era: People and Perspectives
Westward Expansion: People and Perspectives
Women's Rights: People and Perspectives

PERSPECTIVES IN

AMERICAN SOCIAL HISTORY

Great Depression

People and Perspectives

Hamilton Cravens, Editor
Peter C. Mancall, Series Editor

Santa Barbara, California • Denver, Colorado • Oxford, England

Library of Congress Cataloging-in-Publication Data
Great Depression: people and perspectives / Hamilton Cravens, editor.
p. cm. — (Perspectives in American social history)
Includes bibliographical references and index.
ISBN 978-1-59884-093-3 (hardcopy : alk. paper) — ISBN 978-1-59884-094-0 (ebook)
1. Depressions—1929—United States. 2. United States—Social conditions—1933–1945. 3. United States—Social conditions—1918–1932. 4. Popular culture—United States—History—20th century. I. Cravens, Hamilton.
E806.G833 2009
338.5′42—dc22 2009015602

13 12 11 10 09 1 2 3 4 5

This book is also available on the World Wide Web as an eBook.
Visit www.abc-clio.com for details.

ABC-CLIO, LLC
130 Cremona Drive, P.O. Box 1911
Santa Barbara, California 93116-1911

This book is printed on acid-free paper ∞

Manufactured in the United States of America

Contents

Series Introduction

Social history is, simply put, the study of past societies. More specifically, social historians attempt to describe societies in their totality, and hence often eschew analysis of politics and ideas. Though many social historians argue that it is impossible to understand how societies functioned without some consideration of the ways that politics worked on a daily basis or what ideas could be found circulating at any given time, they tend to pay little attention to the formal arenas of electoral politics or intellectual currents. In the United States, social historians have been engaged in describing components of the population that had earlier often escaped formal analysis, notably women, members of ethnic or cultural minorities, or those who had fewer economic opportunities than the elite.

Social history became a vibrant discipline in the United States after it had already gained enormous influence in Western Europe. In France, social history in its modern form emerged with the rising prominence of a group of scholars associated with the journal *Annales Économies, Sociétés, Civilisations* (or *Annales ESC,* as it is known). In its pages and in a series of books from historians affiliated with the École des hautes études en sciences sociales in Paris, brilliant historians such as Marc Bloch, Jacques Le Goff, and Emmanuel Le Roy Ladurie described seemingly every aspect of French society. Among the masterpieces of this historical reconstruction was Fernand Braudel's monumental study, *The Mediterranean and the Mediterranean World in the Age of Philip II,* published first in Paris in 1946 and in a revised edition in English in 1972. In this work Braudel argued that the only way to understand a place in its totality was to describe its environment, its social and economic structures, and its political systems. In Britain the emphasis of social historians has been less on questions of environment, per se, than in a description of human communities in all their complexities. For example, social historians there have taken advantage of that nation's remarkable local archives to reconstruct the history of the family and details of its rural past. Works such as Peter Laslett's *The World We Have Lost,* first printed in 1966, and the multiauthored *Agrarian History of England and Wales,* which began to appear in print in 1967, showed that painstaking work could reveal the lives and habits of individuals who never previously attracted the interest of biographers, demographers, or most historians.

Social history in the United States gained a large following in the second half of the 20th century, especially during the 1960s and 1970s. Its development sprang from political, technical, and intellectual impulses deeply embedded in the culture of the modern university. The politics of civil rights and social reform fueled the passions of historians who strove to tell the stories of the underclass. They benefited from the adoption by historians of statistical analysis, which allowed scholars to trace where individuals lived; how often they moved; what kinds of jobs they took; and whether their economic status declined, stagnated, or improved over time. As history departments expanded, many who emerged from graduate schools focused their attention on groups previously ignored or marginalized. Women's history became a central concern among American historians, as did the history of African Americans, Native Americans, Latinos, and others. These historians pushed historical study in the United States farther away from the study of formal politics and intellectual trends. Though few Americanists could achieve the technical brilliance of some social historians in Europe, collectively they have been engaged in a vast act of description, with the goal of describing seemingly every facet of life from 1492 to the present.

The 16 volumes in this series together represent the continuing efforts of historians to describe American society. Most of the volumes focus on chronological areas, from the broad sweep of the colonial era to the more narrowly defined collections of essays on the eras of the Cold War, the baby boom, and the United States in the age of the Vietnam War. The series also includes entire volumes on the epochs that defined the nation, the American Revolution and the Civil War, as well as volumes dedicated to the process of westward expansion, women's rights, and African American history.

This social history series derives its strength from the talented editors of individual volumes. Each editor is an expert in his or her own field who selected and organized the contents of his or her volume. Editors solicited other experienced historians to write individual essays. Every volume contains first-rate analysis complemented by lively anecdotes designed to reveal the complex contours of specific historical moments. The many illustrations to be found in these volumes testify too to the recognition that any society can be understood not only by the texts that its participants produce but also by the images that they craft. Primary source documents in each volume allow interested readers to pursue some specific topics in greater depth, and each volume contains a chronology to provide guidance to the flow of events over time. These tools—anecdotes, images, texts, and timelines—allow readers to gauge the inner workings of the United States in particular periods and yet also to glimpse connections between eras.

The articles in these volumes testify to the abundant strengths of historical scholarship in the United States in the early years of the 21st century. Despite the occasional academic contest that flares into public notice, or the self-serving cant of politicians who want to manipulate the nation's past for partisan ends—for example, in debates over the Second Amendment to the U.S. Constitution and what it means about potential limits to the rights of gun ownership—the articles here all reveal the vast increase in knowledge of the American past that has taken place over the previous half century. Social historians do not dominate history faculties in American colleges and universities, but no one could deny them a seat at the intellectual table. Without their efforts, intellectual, cultural, and political historians would be hard pressed to understand why certain ideas circulated when they did, why some religious movements prospered or foundered, how developments in fields such as medicine and engineering reflected larger concerns, and what shaped the world we inhabit.

Fernand Braudel and his colleagues envisioned entire laboratories of historians in which scholars working together would be able to produce *histoire totale*: total history. Historians today seek more humble goals for our collective enterprise. But as the richly textured essays in these volumes reveal, scholarly collaboration has in fact brought us much closer to that dream. These volumes do not and cannot include every aspect of American history. However, every page reveals something interesting or valuable about how American society functioned. Together, these books suggest the crucial necessity of stepping back to view the grand complexities of the past rather than pursuing narrower prospects and lesser goals.

Peter C. Mancall
Series Editor

Migrant workers, Oregon, 1939. Note the social security number tattooed on his arm. Photo by Dorothea Lange for the Farm Security Administration. (*Library of Congress*)

Introduction

The Age of the Great Depression

Most American historians would agree that the Great Depression spanned the years between the stock market crash of October 1929 and the Japanese attack on the U.S. Naval fleet at Pearl Harbor, in the Hawaiian Islands, on December 7, 1941. Yet a chorus of dissenters within the historical clan would argue that hard times really began in the mid-1920s in the Great Plains and on southern farms. Others would insist that hard times, however difficult for some, did not become general or "great" until after "Black Thursday," October 29, 1929, when the New York stock market collapsed. Still other historians would point out that the stock market's collapse did not lead to widespread hard times for a couple of years. This debate illustrates the fact that one of the greatest seismic shocks in our nation's history, about which one would think there would not be much disagreement, is a source of contention among historians, economists, and other social scientists who commonly describe, analyze, and interpret. What these arguments show is that the Depression's effects were not uniform but eccentric, diverse, and complex. Many Americans suffered serious economic privation in the several years before the stock market crash—especially farmers, laborers, women, and members of minority groups. Others had better experiences, and some were never touched by the Depression. But clearly those with fewer options, and those with restricted opportunities before the crash, had more difficult times than those who were more insulated from economic difficulties. Those who were more vulnerable experienced privation, tight budgets, and unemployment years before their more fortunate middle- and upper-class fellow citizens on Main Street—and Wall Street.

The stock market crash of 1929 triggered the Great Depression. U.S. participation in World War II, not the New Deal, finally lifted the nation out of the Depression. It is the 1930s in which we are interested and, therefore, in the epochal Great Depression—and the political response to that seismic phenomenon, the New Deal. Our mandate in this series and, therefore, in this work, was to focus on the *groups* of people who lived in the society and participated in its culture in these years. And we have done so, although the constraints of space, not to mention the availability of contributors, has meant that there were many groups about which essays could not be commissioned and completed. In short, it has not been possible to have essays or chapters on every conceivable group in America in those years. Many are missing. But we hope that our examples of social groups will illuminate larger themes, just as our interpretations of American culture will shed light on the larger society. We have summed up a significant amount of the accumulated scholarship, with crispness and authority.

Causes of the Great Depression

A serious worldwide economic depression occurred throughout the 1930s, and its effects in the United States were catastrophic and widespread. The extent of the Great Depression in the United States can be expressed in numbers. The nation's gross national product (GNP)—a measure of the total value of the economy—was $104.4 billion before the crash in 1929. By 1933 it had shrunk to $74.2 billion (expressed in 1929 prices). The GNP per capita in those same years plummeted from $857 to $590, the latter being lower than in the years 1907–1911, so that the economic growth since 1911 suddenly disappeared, as if by magic. Unemployment statistics are even more mind-numbing. By 1933—depending on the estimate upon which one consults (and there was an ideological twist to these figures that were, after all, *estimates*)—at least 20 percent, and more likely 25 percent, of able-bodied persons were unemployed and looking for work. For African Americans, the figures were much worse, at least two, and sometimes more than three, times as high as for whites. And there was much underemployment, that is, persons working for less pay at jobs below their skill levels. Our evidence here is more anecdotal than quantitative, but it is no less harrowing for that. For those with civil service or tenured positions, as in jobs with a local, state, county, or federal government institution, including schools, colleges, and the military, there were often reductions in pay, but because prices fell with the Depression, such individuals often saw their standard of living modestly improve as the 1930s wore on. In the countryside, farmers were especially hard-pressed as commodity prices fell some 61 percent from 1929 to 1933—and they had been deteriorating since the mid-1920s. The times were particularly rough for family farmers, especially those who had expanded their indebtedness during the rise in farm prices before and after World War I. Many farmers could not make enough money to pay their production costs. And bank failures everywhere made problems worse for consumers, workers, businessmen, and farmers—everyone. Savings evaporated as banks failed.

The question arises: Why was there a Great Depression in the first place? It should be understood that its causes and extent were worldwide, and that no telling of one nation's experiences can be the whole story, even when that nation had the largest economy—the United States. That said, we could isolate a number of factors that brought the nation to its knees, economically speaking. There was, in the first instance, a devastating crash in the stock market, in which hundreds of millions of inflated stocks lost their value. The reasons for the stock market crash are not hard to understand: There was an excess of investment capital, and people put it in certain stocks, hoping to make profits of several times their investment, which in turn drove stock prices up and up, in many cases far beyond the value of the company. Put another way, the stock market came to resemble a house of cards—without a firm foundation or structure. Too much money chased too little value in corporate stocks, leading to a bubble phenomenon, in which stocks were way overvalued. The stock market crash led to the Great Depression. We should think of the stock market crash, in this instance, as a trigger or a catalyst, even a match to kindling. Not all stock market speculative booms and busts will lead to such disastrous events as the Great Depression. Indeed, most have not. But this one did.

The reasons that the crash led to the Depression had to do with the unsoundness of the nation's economy in the decade or so after World War I. Business managers and owners kept up prices, thus inflating profits, while pressing down on wages and raw materials, which meant that farmers and workers could not have the benefits of increases in their own productivity. That in turn cut into the potential for mass consumption and purchasing power. Products came out of ever-expanding manufacturing plants in ever-increasing quantities, yet there was correspondingly less money in the hands of consumers to purchase the goods and keep the system of producing and consuming going at full tilt. The structure of income distribution was, in short, not able to maintain prosperity over the long haul. In short, the economy's structure was self-defeating. But there was more. All through the 1920s, managers and owners had saturated the economy by putting capital investment at high rates, thus expanding productive capacity beyond the capability of the economy to consume. The existing rate of capital formation was distorting the economy. Different government policies were needed to shift these funds from those who had too much money and who put it in savings, to those who had less—consumers, who would purchase goods and services if they could. And the deployment of the profits of technological innovation into speculation, transformed the stock market from a securities market into a casino. The federal government encouraged tax policies that led to oversaving, monetary policies that were expansive when prices were going up and constrictive when they fell, unnecessary protective tariff policies that mandated loans to foreign buyers as the only means of exporting American goods abroad, and antitrust policies that encouraged more and more concentration in business, placed rigidity into markets, and made the price system insensitive to the realities of consumer demand. Put simply, for a capitalist market to work, a continuous process of production and consumption is needed, and the more consumers can buy, the better off everyone will be. In short, there must be a buyer as well as a seller. And that is precisely what broke down in America in the decade following World War I, as ours became the world's creditor nation. Many nations now owed us money but could not purchase U.S. goods because of its self-destructive policies. And all of this came about because of the devotion of owners, managers, politicians, and many ordinary Americans to an outmoded form of laissez-faire economics. Adding fuel to the fire was the lack of government regulation, especially with regard to corporate debt, and the unwillingness of the relatively new Federal Reserve System to use any of the fiscal tools at its disposal to prevent disaster. Such a large and complex economic behemoth as the U.S. economy in the 1920s could not run without some rational, informed direction. And that, alas and alack, was not to be. Many millions had to make do, or do without, or stand in line for a daily bowl of soup, or not work for months or even years at a time. These were harrowing days, weeks, months, and years, certainly for peoples around the world, and clearly for Americans. We may turn to those experiences below. The essays in this book fall into two broad categories. First comes a series of portraits of some groups and their experiences—rural folk, adolescents, women, immigrants, families, and African Americans. Those seven essays are followed by four in which the contributors tell us, from seemingly different perspectives, what Americans thought of the society in which they lived, and how they regarded some of their modern technologies—not just dams, skyscrapers, and airplanes, but their most characteristic entertainment: film, especially Hollywood movies. It is interesting to see how much the essays in each section "speak to" one another and provide a kaleidoscopic view of the larger society and culture.

Perspectives on the Great Depression

In 1968, Cesar Chavez recalled his hardscrabble youth in the Depression for Studs Terkel, the famous interviewer of ordinary Americans. Chavez's family lived in the North Gila Valley, about fifty miles north of Yuma, Arizona, on land that his grandfather had homesteaded. In 1934, when Cesar was about six, the bank foreclosed rather than renewed their loan, because the bank's president wanted their land (his land surrounded theirs and this would complete his spread). Cesar remembered that they had to leave the land in a horsedrawn wagon, with their few possessions. A huge tractor came, knocked down all the buildings, and within a few days the landscape was totally changed. He "didn't like it as much." His family then began years of "following the crops," picking crops in the South and West as seasonal workers, often living hand to mouth, sleeping and living in their old jalopy, sometimes not being paid for their work, often told by waitresses that they did not serve Mexicans in their restaurants and coffee shops, and experiencing similar hurtful racist episodes.

The Depression was hard on Americans who lived in the countryside. Of that there was little doubt, as Derek Scott. Oden forcefully reminds us in the first chapter in his sober assessment of the difficulties of rural Americans in those years. Farmers simply could not do it on their own, without government help, recalled Oscar Heline, of Marcus, Iowa. During the

Depression, grain and corn were burned for heat instead of coal, as they were cheaper. In South Dakota, the county elevator listed corn at minus three cents: "If you wanted to sell 'em a bushel of corn, you had to bring in three cents." Oscar worked as a lobbyist for the state cooperatives in the thirties, so he fought for legislation to help farmers, instead of having to fight to survive on the family farm. He gave Henry A. Wallace, Roosevelt's secretary of agriculture, an enthusiastic "thumbs up" for letting farmers design their own farm program during the early New Deal (Terkel 1970, 53–56, 217–221).

Farmers constituted a huge and highly diverse group, yet as a group they did cohere—they experienced many of the same constraints, difficulties, and opportunities. The same may be said of the other groups in this book. Adolescents, women, families, immigrants, and persons of color—all played particular roles in society, and to a greater extent, perhaps, than in better times, these roles were scripted, fixed, held in by hard realities that constituted tight boundaries. The structure of the society in the Great Depression was hard, constricted—without the looseness one usually associates with more prosperous times, such as came starting a few years later with World War II and the Cold War.

In the next chapter, according to Kriste Lindenmeyer, adolescence became a definite stage in the life cycle of the individual in the interwar years, especially in the 1930s, defined, as she puts it, a distinct stage between being a child and an adult. An adolescent—a *teenager*, to use the term coined in the 1930s—was in an experimental time of life, attending full-time school, participating in a social life centered on other teens, and creating long-term financial dependency on adults. Among those circumstances that defined teenagers' experiences in the 1930s were extending one's education, often because the job market was so dismal, experiencing the explosion of popular culture aimed at teens—meaning radio, motion pictures, and special publications for this age-group, such as the magazine *Seventeen*, as well as various "hobby" publications for boys—and following new crazes in popular music and dance. There were other defining circumstances, too: diminished living circumstances occasioned by parental unemployment or underemployment, riding the rails looking for work (something that millions experienced in that decade), participation in New Deal programs for young people, such as the Civilian Conservation Corps, and various "official" attempts at moral regulation, such as raising the legal age for marriage, and even leaving school early to make money for one's family, especially if the male breadwinner was out of work. And there were other problems as well. In January 1930, the New York State Board of Labor finally persuaded the Long Island sea scallop industry to stop hiring teens under 14 in their sheds. And the Home Missions Council of North America announced in March 1931, that almost about 13.4 million American children lived in 10,000 villages that had no churches, obviously a matter of great concern to the Council. In July 1936, the New York City Park Department ran a sports competition in 28 sports for some 1,200 fortunate adolescents who qualified to compete. So the experiences of teenagers varied widely (*New York Times*, January 14, 1930; *St. Louis Post-Dispatch*,

March 9, 1931; *New York Times,* July 19, 1936). Lindenmeyer's rich essay packs an enormous amount of information into a small space and is worth careful reflection—and digestion.

In Chapter 3, as Jennifer Barker-Devine argues, for many adult American women in the 1930s, it was a matter of making do or doing without—these were pinched, difficult times, no doubt about it. That was not true for all American women. There were families and individuals who were sheltered from the worst effects of the Great Depression. Thus California-born Helen Wills Moody, a former world's women's singles tennis champion, and recently divorced, married also recently divorced Aidan Roark, a noted polo player and film writer, in the fall of 1939 in Las Vegas, Nevada, and went on to make their home in the exclusive community of Rolling Hills, near Los Angeles, California. Other women lived closer to the edge, although probably atypical was the experience of Mrs. Evelyn Morfesis, twenty-five years old, and with her husband, a partner in a New York City lunchroom, who was held up twice within three months by gunmen, the first time on a bus near 96th Street, near her home, for $500, and three months later, in May 1935, for $1,020 in the hallway of her home, on the second floor above the lunchroom. Frank Schwartz, thirty-four years old, convicted of the first robbery, was serving twenty years in Sing Sing Prison (*New York Times,* May 19, 1935; October 29, 1939). Women constantly found themselves the victims of institutionalized discrimination in employment and education, paid less by at least a third than men for comparable work, and blocked out of many careers or frozen at a certain level. Married women schoolteachers were often fired, so that the male breadwinners could have their jobs. Women talented at science and mathematics found themselves shunted to low-prestige jobs (when they could find employment at all) well below their levels of education and skill. Thus, women could be librarians, but not administrators of libraries, grade school teachers, but not principals, and so on—and in the working-class occupations, discrimination was, if anything, more severe.

The world of families and of the health they enjoyed, and the care they received, seems removed from our own technologically advanced times, in the telling of Philip L. Frana's enormously informative chapter 4. These were difficult times. In 1930, for example, the U.S. Public Health Service noted that the death rate from disease rose, and the birth rate fell; disease outbreaks especially notable included smallpox and influenza. In another sign of the times, in 1940, the U.S. Public Health Service established a new unit for the study of diseases of middle and old age; heretofore the emphasis of the medical profession had been on infectious and epidemic diseases, not those attributable to aging. This was a sure sign that the 1930s were a turning point in the history of American public health (*New York Times,* January 20, 1930; November 23, 1940). The experiences of ordinary Americans were still in what appears to us today as a horse-and-buggy era of medical care—family physicians still made house calls; clinics, when they existed, were small affairs, mainly laboratories, or offices for small partnerships, usually in the larger cities; and the age of physician specialization was just getting established in the land. Indeed, doctors were businessmen too, and they found it just as difficult in many ways to function in the marketplace as greengrocers, owners of lunch counters or even nightclubs, or anyone else involved in trade and commerce. Although the effectiveness of medical practice had improved by leaps and bounds in the last several decades, especially with the increasingly successful campaigns against various infectious diseases, there remained many problems. Three diseases, Frana tells us, were especially troublesome in the 1930s, because they threatened the family unit, commonly regarded as the basic unit of the society. The first was pulmonary tuberculosis, for which there was no cure before the discovery of the antibiotic streptomycin in 1943. And the antibiotic penicillin, the drug that would cure the other two fearsome diseases of the decade, lobar pneumonia and syphilis, was not widely available until after World War II. There were fairly strenuous government efforts to control these and other threats to public health, but the largest irony is that the greatest advances in public health, including the development of appropriate medicines and procedures, and their effective and extensive delivery, awaited the war, the enlistment or conscription of millions of Americans into the armed forces, and the development of military and civilian programs during the war and after to promote public health. The New Deal could only do so much, and no more. There were limits on the roles that government and politics as well as anything else.

With increasing frequency since the Civil War, various interests in American politics and society had campaigned to restrict immigration and to establish racial segregation. Our next three essays show the effects of these efforts in "social engineering," to reduce the flow of "undesirable" immigrants to our shores, with tragic consequences, as Roger Daniels expertly shows in chapter 5, and the successful campaign to create a racially segregated society, which became in fact an admired model among whites in South Africa who wished to establish the vicious segregationist regime of apartheid, which they did in the later 1940s. The American model, as Albert S. Broussard shows us in what makes painful reading in chapter 6, was the worst of times for African Americans in the 1930s. Many European refugees from Nazi persecution found safe havens often difficult to flee to after the rise of Adolf Hitler, and many died in the Holocaust. Those who made it to American shores included not only famous personages, such as Albert Einstein, but also humble refugees fortunate enough to be allowed to enter the country. And not all who made it to America's shores could stay. Thus Ignata Koos, a refugee from fascist Hungary, hanged himself in his Auburn, New York, cell in January 1930 rather than face deportation to his native land and certain death. Yet Anthony Sciacca received but a year's suspended sentence in July 1936 for having made a false oath when declaring he entered the country legally, when his entrance was actually illegal. Sciacca did not face deportation (*New York Times*, January 12, 1930; July 18, 1936).

And, so millions of American citizens, certainly African Americans—but, in reality, any group of Americans who could be defined as persons of color by the white majority—found themselves the victims of cruel, harsh practices, in law and in majority white attitudes and behavior, of segregation. Since 1896 "separate but equal" had been the law of the federal constitution, thanks to a famous U.S. Supreme Court decision, *Plesey v. Ferguson,* but in fact racial segregation existed as the consequence of emancipation. Thus as African Americans in the northern states were emancipated, a regime of racial segregation grew up around them, and this happened with the second Emancipation, following the Civil War. It was a system that was almost entirely consistent throughout the land, a statement for which there is overwhelming—and shameful—evidence. Further proof, if that were needed, of the effects of segregation on African Americans comes from the pen of Ben Keppel in chapter 7, who has used the testimony of contemporary social science to detail the structures of discrimination, poverty, and segregation abroad in the land in the America of the 1930s. Keppel even provides us with price levels of the 1930s translated to those of 2007, giving the reader an even more vivid, immediate picture of what it was like to be African American in that distant time. But Keppel goes further. Again using the evidence that African American social scientists collected on how members of the race viewed segregation, he presents strong evidence of the comprehensiveness and totality of white oppression of African Americans. If anything, the poverty of the Depression years made the segregation and discrimination even more overwhelming.

Part II begins with a pair of essays, the first discusses what the New Dealers thought they were doing, the second explains the approach a particular group of urban social scientists took toward social structure and urban issues more generally. After all, there were affinities between the ideas and goals of New Dealers and of social scientists. In a brilliant, arresting portrait of New Deal thinking and programs, George T. McJimsey shows in chapter 8 how the New Deal moved from early New Deal static conceptions of a "cooperative commonwealth," such as the National Recovery Administration, to what he dubs a "pluralistic democracy." This was the assumption that if government granted various social rights to different groups in society—such as industrial workers and farmers, among others—these actions would disseminate the American middle-class ideal. And it would be "democratic," McJimsey insists, for two reasons. First, groups of persons would vote to join programs and to create institutions that would advance their social status. And, second, they would become partners in furthering American democratic society; Americans would keep their distinct identities but also would have the rights of equal citizens, entitled to a secure existence and their country's protection and support. Of course, as the preceding several essays forcefully tell us, this was still a vision that included as its key citizens white, American-born males. It was left to later generations to expand that vision to include previously excluded groups—for example, African Americans from the protections of Social Security.

In Chapter 9, Alan I Marcus provides a portrait, locked in time, of how social scientists dealt with the problems of cities in the interwar years. As a group, they were a transitional lot as scholars who eschewed the use of quantification to depict urban phenomena. Ever since social science emerged as the scientific study of society in the early nineteenth century, social scientists, who were reformers at heart, used numbers to show their fellow citizens the sordid truth of social problems. Now in the interwar years, leading urban social scientists insisted that the city was a state of mind, a body of customs and traditions, each different from all others, and locked in time and place. Hence numbers would be misleading. They were not helpful for getting at the vital essence, the core, of what each city was about. Numbers would miss what was important and telling. The case study, the vignette, and the anecdote—these were the tools that the social scientist should use in studying, say, Middletown (Muncie, Indiana), or Little Italy in Chicago's near north side, or North Beach, in San Francisco. A succession of "urbanologists," including anthropologist Clark Wissler, historian Caroline Ware, and sociologist Robert M. Lynd, followed these dicta and published accounts that gained considerable notice at the time. They were also operating at a time in American culture, in which there was, among some social scientists, a belief in philosophical relativism, an antipositivist approach to the study of human society, which disparaged a mechanistic, scientific approach. But this climate of opinion was about to change. In the later 1930s, as Marcus notes, and well into the next several decades, there was a strong positivist movement in the social sciences, together with the sudden crystallization of various kinds of mathematical and quantitative methods, including game theory, econometrics, operations research, forecasting, and the new dynamic statistics of the 1930s and 1940s, much of which was derived during World War II, and all of which changed how social scientists and their clients in government and business thought and spoke and acted about social problems, with the sterile intellectual results that Marcus outlines. This was truly the triumph of an engineering approach to social problems—and was, once one stops to think about it, not unlike the resolution of the New Dealers' ideas.

The final two essays provide glimpses into Americans' dreams, hopes, and fantasies about their world and what was possible in it in the present and the future. Amy Sue Bix astutely outlines in chapter 10 Americans' love affair with the machine in all of its manifestations in that Depression decade. As spectacle, technology brought Americans massive engineering projects, whether of dams, bridges, or skyscrapers (for example), but also marvels of aviation, such as the Douglas Aircraft's all-metal monoplane, the DC-3, one of the most successful airliners ever, which literally made commercial passenger aviation feasible and profitable, but also the "China Clippers," with their luxurious accommodations and long flights. As symbol, technology became one of the New Deal's most promising assists in solving the Depression's problems, whether encouraging agricultural research, creating "Greenbelt towns," or constructing the Tennessee Valley Authority, a social, political, economic, cultural, and technological shot in the arm for a depressed area of the South. As a strain or producer of tensions, technology helped create fears—some quite justified—of automation, of technological unemployment in a decade in which there was already much more unemployment than most citizens could contemplate with serenity. And, finally, technology as showpiece meant a virtual avalanche of shiny consumer products, including automobiles with gutsy V-8 engines, hydraulic rather than mechanical brakes, streamlined designs, the spreading radio networks, and the development of sound and color in the movies, as well as in advertisements in the mass media and in such shows as the New York World's Fair of 1939, whose theme was "the world of tomorrow." Americans could see a bright, happy, prosperous future. Ever since the Civil War, America had been a nation racked by social conflict, increasingly difficult economic times with a tightening boom-and-bust cycle, and labor and racial unrest. Increasingly, Americans had become an industrial country with a large working class, a shrinking middle class, and more persons renting than owning their domiciles—hardly the dream of Thomas Jefferson and his minions for a country of the landed middle classes.

And so we can now see that Americans were poised on the cusp of change toward the kind of affluent world that we have known since World War II. Yet people always live in the present. The future is hard to see. And this contains important clues to the sparkling, perceptive essay that concludes the volume, on Americans at the movies. And here Charles M. Dobbs provides a sophisticated exploration in chapter 11 into how the movies interacted with American politics, with sustaining the status quo. Movies developed quite differently in Europe, essentially for an elite audience; indeed, to this day, for example, film in France is regarded as one of the fine arts. In the United States, on the contrary, the movies became what every cultural artifact in America had become: mass culture, an artistic product that is bought and sold in the marketplace and which seeks to gain the largest paying audience possible. That democratic take on "art" or "culture" is inherently conservative, by definition mainstream, for it is only by appealing to the common, the ordinary, the hackneyed, the familiar that an artifact of mass culture can succeed in the marketplace. For the promoter of a sports event, such as a boxing match, one needed a champion, a Joe Lewis, as well as a sophisticated public relations campaign—and luck. For the promoter of the motion picture during the Depression era, however, things were much more slippery and, to a considerable extent, it was difficult to figure out what would work. All manner of movies failed or were regarded as disposable. The men who ran the movie studios as businesses in the Depression decade were often immigrants who had made it up in a new industry. From their own marginal position in American society, they could cast a cold eye on the American public, and see what needed to be emphasized in story lines, plots, the development of "stables" of star actors and actresses, and the like. That they were successful was due in part to the cultural monopoly they held over studios and theaters—the entire business. But that they could understand their fellow citizens culturally in ways that their fellow citizens could not, was an advantage as well, and it helped contribute to the status quo by plumbing those deeply held democratic values. Not everyone living in America in the Depression decade experienced the benefits of American democracy equally, to be sure. But for the purposes of the men and women who made and acted in the movies, such considerations hardly mattered—or, in many cases, even registered.

Bibliography

This introduction is based on wide reading, especially in many standard histories of the New Deal and of the Depression, but the one book that is indispensable is Studs Terkel's *Hard Times* (1970). I have also culled literally thousands of newspaper stories, mainly from the *New York Times,* but from other newspapers and magazines of the times as well.

Acknowledgments

I thank the Honors Program of Iowa State University for having assigned one or two honors students per year over the last several years to help me with finding some of the original source materials on which I based my work. In particular I would like to praise Ms. Alissa Marie Struble, an honors student who worked with me above and beyond the call of duty, imaginatively and resourcefully digging out original sources relevant to the essays in this volume in the spring and summer of 2008, and the Honors Program for providing her with a grant to do research during the summer.

I also thank my editors at ABC-CLIO, especially Steven L. Danver and James Sherman, for their important assistance during the preparation of this volume.

Hamilton Cravens

References

New York Times, January 12, 1930.

New York Times, January 14, 1930.

New York Times, January 20, 1930.

New York Times, July 18, 1936.

New York Times, July 19, 1936.

New York Times, May 19, 1935.

New York Times, October 29, 1939.

New York Times, November 23, 1940.

St. Louis Post-Dispatch, March 9, 1931.

Terkel, Studs. *Hard Times: An Oral History of the Great Depression.* New York: Pantheon Books, 1970.

About the Editor and Contributors

Jennifer Barker-Devine received her doctorate in agricultural history and rural studies from Iowa State University in spring 2008. She is the author of several studies of rural women in the twentieth century and is assistant professor of history, Illinois College, Springfield, Illinois.

Amy Sue Bix, associate professor of history, department of history and program in history of technology and science, Iowa State University, is the author of two books and numerous articles in the history of technology and science in America.

Albert S. Broussard, professor of history, Texas A&M University, is the author of numerous books and articles on the history of Afro Americans in American life.

Hamilton Cravens, professor of history, department of history and program in history of technology and science, Iowa State University, has published numerous books and articles on the history of science and technology in American culture.

Roger Daniels, Taft Professor of History Emeritus, University of Cincinnati, has published widely and extensively on American immigration history.

Charles M. Dobbs, professor and chair, department of history, Iowa State University, has published numerous books and articles on American relations with East Asia.

Philip L. Frana, assistant professor of science studies, and assistant director, the honors college, University of Central Arkansas, has published scholarly studies of the history of public health and of bioinformatics.

Ben Keppel, associate professor of history, the University of Oklahoma, has published books and articles on American race relations in the twentieth century.

Kriste Lindenmeyer, professor and chair, department of history, University of Maryland, Baltimore County, is the author of books and articles on youth in twentieth-century America.

Alan I Marcus, professor and head, department of history, Mississippi State University, has published eleven books and many articles on the history of technology and science, mainly in the United States.

George T. McJimsey, professor emeritus, department of history, Iowa State University, has published four major studies of nineteenth- and twentieth-century American national politics, including two major studies of America during the New Deal.

Derek Scott Oden, assistant professor of history, Del Rio College, Corpus Christi, Texas, received his doctorate in agricultural history and rural studies from Iowa State University in December 2006. He has published several articles on rural life in twentieth-century America.

Chronology

1929

Politics and the Economy

October–November, Stock Market Crash On October 24 and October 29, severe slumps in stock market resulted in about 29 million shares sold. By November 13, about 30 billion in the market value of the stocks listed on the New York Stock Exchange had been eliminated.

The Arts, Sciences, and Invention

Ernest Hemingway, a novelist, published *A Farewell to Arms,* about war and love.

William Faulkner, a novelist, published *The Sound and the Fury,* the first of a series of novels of southern decadence.

Edwin Hubble, an astronomer, discovered that the galaxies are moving away from one another, thus indicating an expanding universe.

The American Academy of Motion Pictures held its first Academy Awards ceremony.

1930

Politics and the Economy

More than 1,300 banks closed because of the Great Depression.

The Arts, Sciences, and Invention

Clyde W. Tombaugh, an astronomer at the Lowell Observatory, Flagstaff, Arizona, discovered the planet Pluto.

Sinclair Lewis became the first American to win the Nobel Prize in Literature.

George and Ira Gershwin scored the Broadway musical shows *Girl Crazy,* which included the songs "I Got Rhythm" and "Embraceable You," and *Strike Up the Band,* which featured their song "I've Got a Crush on You."

1931

Politics and the Economy

September–October Unemployment was estimated at about 5 million persons; in September, 305 banks closed; in October, 522 shuttered their doors.

The Arts, Science, and Invention

The Empire State Building in New York City, 102 stories, was finished.

Hoagy Carmichael, composer, wrote "Georgia on My Mind", which became a famous jazz song.

Congress made "The Star Spangled Banner" the official United States anthem.

Ernest Goodpasture, a pathologist, grew viruses in chicken eggs, paving the way for the mass production of vaccines.

1932

Politics and the Economy

The Great Depression's new lows: monthly wages were 60 percent less than in 1929, industry operated at about half of its 1929 volume, more than 5,000 banks closed, and average monthly unemployment was 12 million.

November 8, Presidential Election Democrat Franklin D. Roosevelt, governor of New York, won the presidency; the Democrats increased control of Congress.

The Arts, Science, and Invention

Damon Runyan, journalist, published *Guys and Dolls*, a collection of short stories.

Cole Porter's song "Night and Day" was featured in the Broadway musical, *The Gay Divorcee*.

Radio City Music Hall opened in New York City.

Irving Langmuir, a chemist at the General Electric Company Laboratories, won the Nobel Prize for chemistry.

1933

Politics and the Economy

January 20–June 16, The Hundred Days and the New Deal President Roosevelt was inaugurated on January 20. He held Congress in session for "the Hundred Days" to enact sixteen laws aimed at national economic recovery.

President Roosevelt began his so-called fireside chats on radio, speaking directly to the American people.

The Civilian Conservation Corps (CCC) began to hire many unemployed men to improve roads, bridges, airstrips, national parks, and other parts of the national infrastructure. By 1942, the CCC had hired about half a million unemployed persons.

The Arts, Science, and Invention

Lincoln Edward Kirsten and George Balanchine, innovators of dance, founded the School of American Ballet in New York City.

Jimmy Dorsey, who played both the clarinet and the saxophone, teamed up with his brother, Tommy, a trombonist, to form a very successful jazz orchestra.

Choreographer Busby Berkeley introduced large-scale dance productions, using dozens of precision dancers, in the films *42nd Street, Gold Diggers of 1933*, and *Footlight Parade*.

In the film *She Done Him Wrong*, Mae West gave her classic line, "Come up and see me sometime."

Composer Harold Arlen wrote the tune "Stormy Weather."

Thomas Hunt Morgan, professor of genetics and zoology at California Institute of Technology, won the Nobel Prize for Physiology or Medicine.

Frequency Modulation (FM) radio broadcasting was first developed.

1934

Politics and the Economy

January 30 Congress granted the president the authority to regulate the dollar's value.

January 31 Congress enacted the Farm Mortgage Refinancing Act.

February 15 Congress passed the Civil Works Emergency Relief Act, which authorized 950 millions in direct relief and civil works projects to be spent forthwith.

June 6 Congress established the Securities and Exchange Commission to license and to regulate stock and bond markets.

June 19 The Communications Act created the Federal Communications Commission.

The Arts, Science, and Invention

Lillian Hellman, playwright, wrote the searing play, *The Children's Hour*.

Benny Goodman, the "King of Swing" and ace clarinetist, established one of the earliest swing bands, thus making jazz dance music very popular.

Harold Urey, associate professor of chemistry at Columbia University, was awarded the Nobel Prize in chemistry.

George Minot, professor of pathology, Harvard Medical School; William Murphy, professor of medicine, Harvard Medical School; and George H. Whipple, professor of pathology, University of Rochester, shared the Nobel Prize in Physiology or Medicine.

Wallace Carothers, a Du Pont chemist, synthesized nylon.

1935

Politics and the Economy

January 4 President Roosevelt announced in his annual message to Congress the Second New Deal, which outlined his social reform program with three major goals. These goals were security of livelihood through the wise use of natural resources; protection against unemployment, old age, illness, and dependency; and, finally, slum clearance and improved housing.

April 8 Emergency Relief Appropriations Act enacted, and thus transferred relief functions to the states and localities. The Works Progress Administration (WPA) was also established, with Harry Hopkins as administrator.

April 27 Soil Conservation Act established the Soil Conservation Service within the Department of Agriculture to control and prevent soil erosion.

May 11 President Roosevelt established the Rural Electrification Administration (REA) to create rural electrical cooperatives.

June 26 President Roosevelt created the National Youth Administration (NYA), by executive order.

July 5 Congress enacted the National Labor Relations Act, which legitimated collective bargaining by labor unions.

August 14 Congress enacted the Social Security Act, providing for unemployment compensation, old age pensions, and supported state efforts to help persons who could not work.

The Arts, Science, and Invention

George and Ira Gershwin completed the opera *Porgy and Bess.*

John Steinbeck, a California novelist, published *Tortilla Flat,* sympathetic toward Mexican Americans.

Clifford Odets, playwright, produced three plays: *Waiting for Lefty, Awake and Sing,* and *Paradise Lost.*

Arthur J. Dempster, professor of physics, University of Chicago, discovered U-235, an isotope of uranium.

Edward C. Kendall, professor at the Mayo Foundation, isolated a hormone, *cortisone.*

1936

Politics and the Economy

January 6 In *U.S. v. Butler,* the U.S. Supreme Court, by a 6–3 ruling, invalidated the Agricultural Adjustment Act (AAA) because it was a regulatory scheme not justified under the general welfare clause of the Constitution.

February 29 The U.S. Congress replaced the AAA with the Soil Conservation and Domestic Allotment Act, paying benefits for limiting production and promoting soil conservation.

November, Presidential Election Franklin Roosevelt carried every state but Maine and Vermont, 523 electoral votes to 8 for the Republican nominee, Kansas governor Alfred M. Landon, and the Democrats increased their margins in the U.S. Congress.

The Arts, Science, and Invention

Eugene O'Neill, playwright, won the Nobel Prize in Literature.

Margaret Mitchell, an Atlanta author, published *Gone With the Wind,* about the Civil War's passions and sacrifices.

Robert Frost, New England poet, won the Pulitzer Prize for Literature for his *A Further Range.*

George S. Kaufman and Moss Hart wrote *You Can't Take It With You,* which won the Pulitzer Prize for Drama.

Henry Luce, a media mogul, began the publication of a new magazine, *Life,* entirely devoted to photographic news and features.

Carl D. Anderson, assistant professor of physics, California Institute of Technology, won the Nobel Prize for Physics.

1937

Politics and the Economy

January 20 President Roosevelt pledged during his inauguration speech that he would again pursue his goals of social justice, saying, memorably, "I see one-third of a nation ill-housed, ill-clad, ill-nourished ."

The Arts, Science, and Invention

Artie Shaw, jazz clarinetist, formed an early swing band; the African American vocalist Billie Holliday became its lead singer.

Richard Rodgers and Lorenz Hart wrote the score for the Broadway show *Babes in Arms,* which included the songs "The Lady Is a Tramp" and "Johnny One Note."

Walt Disney, California film entrepreneur, produced the first feature-length cartoon, *Snow White and the Seven Dwarfs.*

Dr. Clinton J. Davisson, a researcher in physics at the Bell Telephone Laboratories, New York, shared the Nobel Prize in Physics, with George Thomson, an English physicist.

In San Francisco Bay, the Golden Gate Bridge was completed. Its main section was 4,200 feet long, making it the longest span bridge to date.

Joe Louis, the "Brown Bomber," son of poor southern sharecroppers, and African American boxer, won the heavyweight boxing championship.

1938

Politics and the Economy

February 16 Agricultural Adjustment Act enacted and revived the AAA in modified form.

June 25 Fair Labor Standards Act, applied to interstate commerce, establishing a minimum hourly wage and a maximum work week, and outlawed child labor.

November 8 The Congressional elections led to a new conservative coalition in Congress that blocked many of Roosevelt's social reform ideas.

The Arts, Science, and Invention

Pearl Buck, author, won the Nobel Prize in Literature, for her novel, *The Good Earth.*

Thornton Wilder, playwright, published *Our Town,* which won the Pulitzer Prize.

Ella Fitzgerald, African American vocalist, and the band, which drummer Chick Webb led, achieved celebrity status with the song "A-Tisket A-Tasket."

Ralph Rainger, composer, and Leo Robin, lyricist, wrote "Thanks for the Memories," which the actor and comedian Bob Hope later adopted as his theme song.

"Invasion from Mars," which actor, director, and producer Orson Welles produced as a radio play, was so realistic that it caused a national panic.

The Du Pont Company marketed its first nylon toothbrush.

1939

Politics and the Economy

January 4 In his annual address to the Congress, President Roosevelt stressed national defense, not social reform.

September 1 War broke out in Europe.

The Arts, Science, and Invention

John Steinbeck, novelist, published *The Grapes of Wrath,* his epic novel of the Dust Bowl.

Carl Sandberg's sprawling *Abraham Lincoln: The War Years,* won the Pulitzer Prize.

William Saroyan refused the Pulitzer Prize for his play *The Time of Your Life.*

Trumpeter Harry James hired vocalist Frank Sinatra as the lead singer for his newly formed jazz and swing band.

Coleman Hawkins, saxophonist, recorded the jazz *tour de force,* "Body and Soul."

The motion picture version of *Gone With the Wind* was released.

Ernest Lawrence, professor of physics at the University of California, won the Nobel Prize in Physics.

Leo Szilard, professor of physics at Columbia University, and refugee from Nazi Germany, proved that a chain reaction took place during nuclear fission, thus suggesting the possibility of atomic weapons.

Du Pont de Nemours Company first marketed nylon stockings for women.

Color television was first demonstrated.

References

Cattell, Jacques, ed. American Men of Science. A Biographical Directory. Lancaster, Pa: The Science Press, 1944.

Morris, Richard B, ed. *Encyclopedia of American History*. New York: Harper and Brothers, 1953.

Urdang, Laurence, ed. *The Timetables of American History*. New York: Simon and Schuster, 1981.

NOTE:
In addition to the reference accounts noted above, Hamilton Cravens compiled this chronology using news stories in the *New York Times* (digitalized version) among other reference works.

American Society and Culture in the Age of the Great Depression

Part 1

The Great Depression in the Countryside

1

Derek Scott Oden

Privation Down on the Farm

The Great Depression represents a peculiar epoch in the history of twentieth-century America. The nation's continuous march toward technological, political, and economic ascendancy stood still for a time. After the stock market crash of 1929, the country was sent into a painful tailspin as a mysterious illness infected and spread to its every organ. Americans spent a decade attempting to vanquish the malady; however, an effective medicine was delayed until the onset of World War II. Although it ushered in an era of unprecedented carnage, the conflict did finally end a depression that had gripped the nation for a decade. During the period, the crisis produced unemployment, poverty, and unrelenting want, which took a terrific toll upon Americans.

The peoples' suffering is graphically communicated by images depicting haggard unemployed waiting wearily for nourishment in long soup lines and abandoned farmsteads buried by a devastated region's desiccated and windblown soil, pictures that have been seared into the nation's collective memory. The era's atmosphere of desperation is also symbolized by photographs of individuals who by the thousands opted to ride the rails in search of work. Such circumstances bear witness to how hard times tested the fortitude of even the most hardworking and determined individuals. Although many Americans would enjoy the benefits of a reinvigorated economy during the 1940s, large numbers forever possessed the Great Depression's psychological scars, always fully aware of the transitory nature of prosperity.

The era represented not only a time of great economic misfortune and need, but also a period of profound change. During the 1930s, American society and culture underwent a highly significant transformation, including a considerable expansion of the federal government's power and influence, a reinvigorated Democratic Party that would have a profound impact on subsequent public policy, as well as the increased power of organized labor. Such consequences represent just a few of the many ways Americans were affected by the twentieth century's most widespread and severe economic collapse.

Peoples' words also bear witness to the great difficulties endured during the era. Some wrote the nation's leaders, including President Franklin D. Roosevelt and First Lady Eleanor Roosevelt regarding their plight. These letters vividly describe the stark and challenging situations in which many found themselves. A small livestock raiser from Sulphur Spring, Texas, told a typical tale of worry and woe caused by a brutal mixture of crushing debt, an unsympathetic landlord, and an impending winter. He wrote to President Roosevelt stating,

> I am in debt needing help the worst in the world. . . . I have done all I could to pay the note and have failed on everything I've tried. I fell short on my crop this time and he didn't allow me even one nickel out of it to feed myself while I was gathering it and now winter is here and I have a wife and three (3) little children, haven't got clothes enough to keep them from freezing. (McElvaine 1983, 72)

He, among thousands, lacked physical necessities for himself and his family. In the fall of 1935, a distressed Louisiana farm woman wrote to Eleanor Roosevelt explaining her predicament. She indicated that her family had recently lost their milk cow, had earned little money picking cotton, and were lacking the very barest of necessities.

Families who experienced the effects of such crippling poverty not only bore its physical and psychological pain, but also experienced anxiety when asking for help. A person's lack of suitable clothing appears to have been particularly humiliating. In 1935, a woman from Goff, Kansas, wrote Eleanor Roosevelt inquiring whether she had a new coat that she could wear to church. She stated, "My clothes are very plain so I could wear only something plain. We were hit very hard by drought and every penny we can save goes for feed to put in crop. Hoping for a favorable reply" (McElvaine 1983, 75). Thus letter writers revealed not only a yearning to communicate their desperation, but also a desire to maintain a sense of dignity. Another woman, this time from Aurelia, Iowa, articulated similar sentiments. She wrote to the first lady stating,

> I am coming to you for help please do not think this does not cause a great feeling of shame to me to have to ask for old clothing. I am a Lutheran Sunday School teacher. We are very poor. I know that we must not let our clothes keep us from church (neither do I), but sometimes I feel so badly when I see all the others dressed so nice. I don't care for swell clothes, but you know one feels awful in old clothes worn shiny and thread bare. (McElvaine 1983, 77)

Such requests for help illustrate the conflicting emotions which emerged when people faced circumstances beyond their control (McElvaine 1983, 77).

Mother and young children of a family of nine living in a field on U.S. Route 70 in Tennessee, March 1936. Photograph by Carl Mydans for the U.S. Resettlement Administration. (*Library of Congress*)

Although people living in cities and those living in the countryside both endured the hardships, their experiences were nonetheless distinctive. This rather obvious, but nonetheless important, point is supported by the recognition that Americans residing in urban settings and those who occupied the countryside faced dissimilar realities. Although the lives of both groups continued to intersect in many ways, important differences existed. For instance, during and following the Industrial Revolution urban dwellers labored in a dizzyingly diverse range of occupations. Employment included a variety of professional endeavors such as engineering and law, managerial and secretarial vocations, as well as semiskilled and low-skilled factory work. While in the countryside, agriculture in its many and diverse forms dominated. Furthermore, urban Americans usually enjoyed modern conveniences such as running water, electricity, and paved roads long before such amenities were available in the countryside. These and other factors contributed to a rural experience that was distinct from that in metropolitan areas.

In the 1920s, a person's social, economic, and cultural realities were deeply shaped by one's place of residence. Although the nation's overall financial health declined briefly following World War I, most economic sectors quickly recovered. Automobile manufacturing, electrical appliances, new communication technologies, and other emerging commercial ventures contributed greatly to the decade's prosperity. Furthermore, advertisers employed increasingly sophisticated marketing practices that enticed consumers to purchase items. Additionally, Americans dove headlong and hurried into consumerism's alluring pleasures, enticed by new payment methods such as monthly payment programs. Although often overstated, the expanding popularity of motion pictures and less constrained sexual practices also contributed to the decade's boisterous metropolitan image.

Rural Americans generally experienced a more anxious decade; not only did they react negatively to cultural change, but they also endured a recession. They felt uneasy about what they viewed to be the morally corrupting influence of automobiles, jazz, and the motion picture industry. The Ku Klux Klan reemerged as an organization whose members identified specific religious groups, technologies, and social trends as threats. Such reactionaries aimed their animosity toward new musical forms such as jazz, their children's use of automobiles, and the rise of Catholic and Jewish immigration. Although the organization's rebirth was brief and faced resistance from more moderate rural dwellers, it nonetheless demonstrated that many people felt anxious about what they believed to be cultural threats. Farm families also suffered low commodity prices and a decreased demand for their products. Farmers who had hastily expanded their land holdings and purchased new equipment during the prosperous war years were particularly vulnerable. Thus, farmers had been left out of the affluent 1920s and were generally weakened and in some cases disillusioned by the time of 1929 stock market crash. Unfortunately, this momentous event signaled the onset of even bleaker times. Many small town businesses also experienced hardship since their livelihoods shrank as pocketbooks constricted. The decline of rural industries such as bituminous coal mining and textile mills, particularly in Midwestern and Southern towns, further amplified the hinterland's financial woes.

Despite such differences, both urban and rural Americans were affected by an economic collapse that plunged the nation into the depths of hard times. The signs of a weakening economy were emerging throughout 1929; however, it would not be until Thursday, October 24, that the stock market plummeted and confidence was shattered. Overly optimistic analysts' predictions that the nation's fortunes would quickly improve proved to be disappointingly inaccurate. Instead, the financial system continued to unravel as the productivity of the nation's factories constricted, banks failed by the thousands, and throngs of unemployed added to the resulting the human wreckage. The nation's gloom further descended as Europe's economy also faltered. Farmers' economic situations also grew exceedingly bleak, because their compensation for commodities was in many cases cut in half and in others slashed even more severely. The nation's cotton growers received exceptionally low compensation for their crops being paid only $0.16 per pound in 1929 and spiraling downward to a paltry $0.05 during the first two years of the 1930s. In 1932, farmers who cultivated wheat or raised cattle also received comparatively low compensation for their commodities. New England dairy farmers were suffering greatly, as evidenced by the fact that Vermont dairymen received only half of what they had been given for their milk three years earlier. Agricultural economist Willard Cochrane has surmised that diminishing incomes greatly affected how much farmers were able to invest in their operations, indicating that devaluation outpaced capital outlays into their operations in the first five years of the decade.

Agrarian families were almost universally affected by the era's farm crisis; however, the economic pain was by no means equally distributed. Such factors as geographic location, an operator's financial reserves, and even chance all determined one's odds of economic survival. Although distressed, New England farmers found themselves less desperate than their Midwestern and Western counterparts. For instance, some small-scale New England Farmers were less troubled than their agricultural brethren on the Plains who watched their wheat wither during the unrelenting drought or Southern sharecroppers whose continued prospects in agriculture often became completely unfeasible. Additionally, some Midwestern farmers who owned their land and entered the Depression in relatively healthy financial shape also had a better chance of keeping their farms. However, for some the pressure and struggles to survive proved to be overwhelming. In the spring of 1936, Elmer G. Powers, a prosperous Iowa farmer and diarist, recorded a particularly tragic incident. He stated,

> A middle-aged man committed suicide by hanging himself in his barn. He was well known, much liked, a good farmer and had a nice family. He was about to lose his farm to the mortgage company and I suppose that is what drove him to commit such a rash act. (Grant and Purcell 1976, 99)

People appear to have rarely starved, but they did go hungry and many were forced to go without very basic necessities, including clothing, medication, and proper housing. These realities meant that parents sometimes had to limit the amount of food their children consumed, send them to school in tattered clothes, or pray that they could overcome an illness without medical aid. Individuals were also sometimes required to endure the most extreme conditions that nature could produce. Great Plains residents faced particularly trying circumstances. In 1933, Lorena Hickok, a seasoned reporter, discovered one North Dakota family whose household conditions were exceptionally challenging. They lived on a farmstead located on the Canadian border, huddling together inside a flimsy shack, wearing threadbare clothing, while the thermometer dipped to twenty below zero.

Farm families faced such climatic extremes in addition to those challenges brought about by low farm prices. Although the Great Plains were particularly affected by lack of rainfall, a number of areas were affected by the era's unusually widespread and severe drought conditions. People in the Northern Plains, the South, and even portions of the eastern United

States experienced such circumstances. In December 1930, A. B. Sawyer, Jr., the Kentucky Farm Bureau Federation president, stated, "Few people outside of Kentucky have any conception of what Kentucky farmers have gone through and are still facing." He went on to state, "In Jefferson County the fiscal court is financing the distribution of water from the Louisville water works to farmers of the Louisville area. Huge tank trucks are busily engaged hauling the precious fluid into rural areas and people are counting every drop" (American Farm Bureau Federation Weekly Newsletter 1930, 4). Farmers encountered similar situations throughout the era but frequently demonstrated the desire to provide mutual assistance to their neighbors in a time of need.

In the case of the Kentucky drought, fellow New York Farm Bureau members extended a helping hand to brethren by marshaling a vigorous aid effort. In the spring of 1931, the national American Farm Bureau (AFB) president applauded the efforts of New York AFB members. They were deserving of the praise since they had collected and sent more than fifty railroad cars of emergency aid to Southern farm families. The Red Cross also assisted the Farm Bureau in its rural drought relief efforts. Despite such frequent and admirable demonstrations of generosity, the era often presented people with situations that overwhelmed both human stamina and local resources. This was particularly the case for those who struggled to adapt to the deteriorating conditions on the Great Plains.

The Terrors of the Dust Bowl

Residents of the Southern Plains in particular endured a traumatic ordeal as evidenced by the region's Dust Bowl identification. This great expanse encompassed an approximately oval-shaped portion of Colorado, New Mexico, Kansas, Oklahoma, and Texas, and was an area particularly affected by a disastrous combination of drought, wind, and dislocated topsoil. The calamity was principally caused by the absence of rainfall, which prevented wheat and other crops from protecting the region's dirt. This amalgamation of drought, high winds, and airborne soil produced dust storms of legendary proportions. Such dark and ominous tempests left previously fertile wheat fields barren and fence-rows buried and, in the end, consumed dreams by the thousands. Thus, farm families in significant numbers decided to flee the relentless ravages of dust, withering crops, and financial distress. In 1935, the exodus from the region began in earnest and persisted throughout the period, adding approximately a quarter of a million people to the California's expanding populace. Nevertheless, the majority in many locales stayed and bravely struggled to survive.

Although people's suffering on the upper plains is less publicized, it was no less severe. A large portion of North Dakota farmers were forced to adapt to the fact that they received approximately half of the usual precipitation during the first four years of the decade. The state's residents also bore some of the most severe temperature extremes as evidenced by a 121 degree Fahrenheit reading in Steele, North Dakota, on July 6, 1936. South

Power farming displaces tenants from the land in the western dry cotton area, Childress County, Texas Panhandle, June 1938. Photograph by Dorothea Lange. (*Library of Congress*)

Dakota newspaper writers reported that area residents sometimes experienced heat exhaustion or even death while working in such conditions. These circumstances exacted a terrible toll on the state's agricultural production. In 1937, Work Progress Administration employees Francis Cronin and Howard Beers summarized the appalling toll that nature had exacted upon North and South Dakota's agricultural production. They indicated that a majority of farmers in both states had grown about half of what they usually produced during the first five years of the 1930s. They also verified that this represented one of the most severe regions of crop loss in the entire nation. Nevertheless, some Dakotans could still find humor in such situations as did two young girls who successfully "grilled a cheese sandwich on a sidewalk" in Grafton, North Dakota (Stock 1992, 20, 25). Unfortunately, these unusual diversions probably represented only a brief respite from nature's seemingly rancorous mood.

Residents also endured dust storms that sometimes assumed biblical proportions. On May 9, 1934, a particularly brutal tempest hit the Dakotas, leaving dust-covered rooms, dead livestock, and feelings of hopelessness in its wake. The incessant gales sent the dirt high into the atmosphere and dumped it hundreds of miles away in the eastern United States. Another ferocious storm occurred approximately one year after the Dakota disaster. On April 14, 1935, southwestern Kansas residents experienced a storm that they soon remembered as "Black Sunday." The thick clouds of dust made day appear to be night, forced drivers off the road, and convinced others that Judgment Day had arrived. The finely pulverized wind-borne earth further degraded drought-withered fields, drastically increased household cleaning duties, and even threatened human health. Livestock also suffered; South Dakota reporters commented on the fact that cattle feed had become contaminated and inedible by the dust. For Euro-American residents, it must have appeared that nature was fulfilling the desires of the Native Americans who had joined the Ghost Dance in hopes of forever vanquishing the invaders from their land.

Plains dwellers also had to occasionally endure the grasshopper onslaught, which consumed what little crops had survived the drought. The insects seemed to thrive especially well in the era's hot and grimy conditions, adding to the era's deteriorating circumstances. Some farmers reported that their fields became animated by the hopper infestations by appearing to be a single crawling, flying, ravenous organism. Gladys Leffler Gist, a farm resident of Lyman County, South Dakota, remembered that "the earth was alive with them ... even the leaves of the trees were stripped ... there was so many piled dead in our potato patch that they stank" (Nelson 1992, 119). Dakotans' attempts to rid themselves of the insects seemed futile because little survived the relentless assault. The devastation included both families' crops and gardens, with the pests indiscriminately destroying both their money crops and table food. Grasshoppers even invaded the region's towns and denied residents of their beatification efforts. During the summer of 1933, a *Kadoka Press* writer stated, "They have practically destroyed all the gardens and flowers in town" (Stock 1992, 147). In the same year, the Van Schaak family, who resided in Mellettte County, South Dakota, faced the prospects of watching their cattle starve to death as the hoppers had consumed their livestock forage.

Even in Iowa, where nature usually behaved more cooperatively, grasshoppers and drought fully manifested themselves. In 1931, Dr. Carl J. Drake, an Iowa State insect specialist, surmised that pest infestations were severe and next year's prospects were also bleak. On July 19, 1936, Elmer G. Powers, a prosperous Iowa farmer, commented on conditions in the nation's agricultural heartland. He stated,

> It is becoming quite generally admitted that the drought is the most serious that our country has ever suffered. In Carroll and western counties farmers are said to be harvesting their corn fields with grain binders because regular corn binders will not handle the short crop. We have corn in our community that will not make fodder. And many of the fields that we had hoped a rain would benefit are being found to be fields of almost all barren stalks. (Grant and Purcell 1976, 116)

These depressing observations reconfirm both the severity and pervasiveness of the era's drought.

Coping with Adversity

Despite such expressions of pathos, people usually clung to optimism and persisted through the difficult times. For instance, Powers sometimes expressed hopefulness about the future stating, "Nothing can take the place of experience and nothing else can give one the necessary confidence in the future. We will come out of these dark, troublesome days again" (Grant and Purcell 1976, 22). Farm families' courageous and determined actions bear witness to such statements. Historian Pamela Riney-Kehrberg revealed that even during the worst of times some Kansas residents maintained the belief that rain and high prices would eventually return, which they did in the 1940s. Particularly resolute individuals even discovered ways to adapt and benefit a bit from the grasshopper onslaught. In August 1931, Colorado farmers reacted creatively to the grasshopper plague by driving cars fitted with water filled-troughs through their fields. After collecting the insects, they dried them and used them for chicken feed. One Farm Bureau writer indicated that "[o]ne farmer is reported to have gathered 30 bushels on an acre by this 'harvesting' method" (Riney-Kehrberg 1994, 117). The fact that divorces did not increase in places of extreme stress such as in southwestern Kansas also could be taken as an expression of hopefulness. Although this might not have been the case—few could afford to split up—the possibility exists that in such challenging circumstances families served as a way to buffer the era's difficulties.

In the absence of jobs and adequate aid, rural Americans employed a variety of strategies to clothe and feed themselves. This included expanding their gardens, incorporating more inexpensive kinds of foods into their diets, as well as finding a variety of other creative ways to make-do. Americans also relocated to other regions which promised improved conditions or returned to former places of origins in hopes of alleviating suffering. Women who were members of a local Grange, Parent-Teacher Association, or other organizations produced impressive results. Charlotte M. Temple, a *Farm Journal* contributor, praised the efforts of such club women, revealing that they canned garden produce to feed their families through the winter as well as transformed raw commodities into finished products to sell or for family use. Such activities included Arkansas club women in 37 counties making 1,225 mattresses out of surplus cotton, 5,000 Kansas women producing 18 tons of soap from lard, and their Maine counterparts collecting feed and fertilizer bags for clothing.

Rural folk short on money also turned to the simple tools of soil and seed as a simple way of meeting their families' needs. Women canned garden bounty and provided much-needed sustenance for their husbands and children. In the early 1930s, many Appalachian coal-mining families depended on such horticultural ingenuity to feed themselves. The Red Cross and other aid organizations frequently provided the seed required for such plots. These practices were particularly important in the early years of the Depression before the introduction of more substantial relief programs. Civic leaders in southwestern Kansas provided small-town residents with sections of property, seed, and other resources necessary for subsistence gardening. Unfortunately, the region's severe environmental challenges complicated such activities. Despite such exceptions, members of the agricultural press continued to praise gardening benefits.

Farm women also experimented with creative food choices and concocted recipes designed to enliven even the most unappealing foods. They demonstrated their culinary creativity by stuffing peppers with meat leftovers and making use of dry bread in pudding. Women created cheaper entrees whose primary ingredients consisted of cornmeal and other inexpensive products. Although such dishes might sound unappealing to contemporary readers, husbands and children were probably thankful for such simple foods. Home demonstration agents also assisted those engaged in the ever-present challenges of making-do. The female staff of county extension programs provided rural women with menu options that were both affordable and relatively nutritious. Although some homemakers probably found their situations discouraging, many took pride in their ability to make-do. In 1935, one farm woman stated, "I get a real thrill out of this depression—in keeping all my loved ones healthy and happy—even though I haven't much to do it with" (Howe 1935, 7).

The economic catastrophe also affected peoples' decision to move or return to their former home. The Dust Bowl exodus might be the most well known and significant of the era's migration streams; however, it was by no means the only one. Americans in other rural regions opted to move in search of better conditions and improved economic opportunities. Farm families left East Texas's Black Land Prairie in significant numbers, permanently abandoning the region's cotton fields for the allure of the state's urban centers. In the East Texas County of McLennan, which includes the midsize city of Waco, the number of tenant farmers decreased from 4,752 in 1930 to 2,518 a mere ten years later. Although the number of migrants appears to be relatively large, many of the state's other cotton-producing regions appear to have experienced significant population loss. Such long-suffering individuals appear to have left the Texas cotton fields due to a combination of the effects of New Deal programs and the attraction of city life.

Large growers usually benefited most from the Agricultural Adjustment Administration's (AAA's) subsidy programs, which used such resources to modernize their operations. Thus, their acquisition of tractors further contributed to a large number of tenants abandoning their bleak prospects for the hope of a better life. Furthermore, the young in particular became increasingly sensitive to the view popularized in the media regarding the superiority of urban living. Such conveniences as indoor plumbing, good housing, and electricity were a powerful draw for people raised amid a cotton farm's unrelenting hardships. The spectacular growth of Austin, Dallas, and San Antonio attest to Blacklanders' affirmation of such a view. Some observers were worried about this continued exodus from the land. In 1934, Alice Margaret Ashton, a *Farm Journal* contributor, cautioned parents againstcontinually telling their children about the farm's financial difficulties because it only encouraged them to leave. She indicated that "farm children have heard and discussed each disappointment and each setback, have heard all about father's discouragement and mother's dissatisfactions. I wonder if this does not cause many country children to decide they will try something besides farming" (Ashton 1934, 26).

Unfortunately, for some, their decision to leave sharecropping and tenancy only resulted in more hardship. Some sharecroppers who resided in the Deep South had faced the dual ravages of the boll weevil and plummeting cotton prices, and found few options except to join the agricultural migrant stream to the East. Growers' conversion of the Florida's Everglades into a rich farming region had created an insatiable appetite for the cheap labor required to harvest the region's fruits and vegetables. The thousands of dislocated sharecroppers who relocated to the state greatly assisted growers in keeping their labor costs down. These unfortunate but resilient souls supplemented their employment in Florida in the winter by laboring in New Jersey and other eastern states during the summer. Most eastern migrant laborers were African American, and usually encountered such abysmal living conditions as insufficient shelter, restroom facilities, and nourishment.

Some locales experienced the opposite of the rural-to-city migration as industrial jobs evaporated and were replaced with soup lines. A brief interruption and in some cases reversal of the southern migration to the northern industrial centers represented such a situation. For years before the Depression, large numbers of rural southerners had opted to leave an existence often mired in grinding poverty to secure jobs in Cleveland, Detroit, Chicago, and other Midwestern urban centers. By the close 1920s, the city of Detroit, Michigan contained 66,000 southern white migrants, Chicago had 50,000, and Indianapolis had 30,000. Many of the Midwest's smaller cities also had high numbers of such immigrants. African Americans moved to such industrial centers in large numbers. For instance, in the 1920s alone more than 800,000 blacks left the South in the hope of finding better prospects (Berry 2000, 31–33; Gregory 2005, 15).

Nevertheless, many southern transplants opted to return during the early Depression years. The fact that factory owners responded to declining consumer demand by issuing massive layoffs meant that the major reason for coming northward had dissolved. This bleak situation led to greatly reduced employment opportunities among both whites and blacks. However, the situation was particularly difficult for southern black migrants because factory owners often dismissed African Americans first and rehired them only after reemploying whites. The fact that blacks returned to the South in fewer numbers is probably related to that fact that more whites had relatives who were property owners. This meant that Caucasians usually had a greater incentive to return to the South than African Americans.

Orbie Berry, a former resident of Wayne County, Tennessee, located in south-central Tennessee (approximately 100 miles southwest of Nashville), typified those southerners who returned home. As the economy worsened, Berry recollected his observations, remembering the scene at one Flint, Michigan, auto plant stating, "Everything was standing-there was no machines a-moving." Many southerners faced such bleak scenes and returned to more familiar surroundings to survive the hard times. Although Berry never departed northward again, many of his southern comrades did return once the worst of the Depression had ended. The southern migration to the North

In August 1932, Sheriff Charles F. Keeling, of Polk County, Iowa, and a farmer, was grumpy at the so-called "Farmers Holiday Association." Its colorful leader, president Milo Reno, of the National Farmers Union, had declared a farmers' strike against all who would depress farm prices below the cost of production. And Reno mobilized Corn Belt farmers, insisting that if they did not strike, they would go broke, losing everything, to the last squealing piglet and the fusty old crocheted tablecloth.

The Depression hit farmers in the Corn Belt hard. In the early 1920s, they overextended themselves; when prices fell they were devastated. A thousand bushels of corn would have fetched $1,436 in 1920; twelve years later, a farmer was lucky to get $120! Foreclosures turned proud owners into discouraged tenants. The Farm Holiday Association fed on such miseries. In May 1932, more than 2,000 farmers from all over attended an emergency meeting in Des Moines, Iowa. By striking, they hoped to raise prices for their crops. They

resumed once the economy improved and increased drastically once more with the onset of World War II. Historian Chad Berry has surmised,

> By 1935, the blip on the migration scale was gone, and thousands again faced the difficult choice of whether to leave the South for the North. The Great White Migration was flowing again, though still not as voluminously as in the 1920s. It would take a massive economic mobilization for another world war to get surplus southerners to go northward again en masse. (Berry 2000, 35, 32)

A Fierce Discontent

Although many rural Americans stoically endured their difficulties, some agricultural workers, farmers, and sharecroppers were less peaceful in their response. Throughout the 1930s, farmworkers in such geographically disparate states as California and New Jersey protested their appalling pay and working conditions by attempting to unionize and organize strikes. However, the nation's growers usually possessed superior social, political, and financial weapons in their struggle to maintain cheap labor. As Carey McWilliams, one of the era's greatest farm worker advocates, stated, "The established pattern has been somewhat as follows: to bring in successive minority groups; to exploit them until the advantages of exploitation have been exhausted; and then to expel them in favor of more readily exploitable material" (McWilliams 2000, 305–306). Nevertheless, even individuals in far more stable situations occasionally acted confrontationally. In August of 1932, Northwest Iowa Farmers, organized under the Holiday Association, exhibited an unexpected outburst of passionate action. Farmers became inspired by Milo Reno's ardent rhetoric, armed themselves, blockaded highways leading to Sioux City, and protested low prices by pouring milk on the side of the road. The following year, they almost lynched a magistrate, symbolizing both the movement's climax and subsequent decline. In 1934, northern Arkansas sharecroppers also responded militantly to their expulsion by large absentee land owners.

despaired of any help from government. By August, violence was widespread as farmers tried to stop the flow of farm commodities to market and intimidate bankers intent on foreclosing farm mortgages. Sheriff Keeling provided deputies as escorts for trucks entering Des Moines to sell commodities. Soon deputies were slugging pickets; at least one driver cleared his way through a mob brandishing a gun. Sheriff Keeling sympathized with the striking farmers, but as sheriff he could not side with them. A local cooperative organized more than fifty armed men to allow trucks through. The Farm Holiday Association's tactics and strategies ultimately failed. Trains could easily transport what blockaded trucks could not. In the fall, with declining daily temperatures, the movement dissipated, and the general election attracted more attention. The farmers' structural economic problems remained unchanged, symptomatic of the Great Depression's distresses.

SOURCE: *New York Times*, May 4, August 15, 16, 30, 31, 1932, February 12, 1933.

They rallied under the banner of the Southern Tenant Farmers Union (STFU). By 1935, the organization's membership had swollen to approximately 25,000 people. Despite such fervent efforts, both attempts for economic equality failed, in the case of the Farm Holiday Association, farmers were not able to organize for their common interests, while the efforts of the STFU members crumbled due to landowners' often-violent resistance.

Agricultural groups and individual farmers were not universally supportive of those who responded radically to their tribulations. In February 1931, an *American Farm Bureau Weekly News Letter* writer commented on those who had participated in a food riot in the town of England, Arkansas, a small town near Little Rock. The author stated,

> The Red Venom of Communism is making itself more vivid in each report received at national headquarters of the AFBF on alleged food riots in Arkansas. Proof that communism is playing its dastardly part in inciting drought stricken farmers is now directly traced to activities of such persons as Ella Reeve Bloor. (*American Farm Bureau Letter* 1931, 2)

The author identified additional individuals he viewed to be communist agitators, stating that, "Farm Bureau officials should be on guard against radicals of like ilk…." (*American Farm Bureau Letter* 1931, 2). Although less caustic, Elmer G. Powers nonetheless disapproved of what he believed to be drastic and unwise actions. On April 6, 1933, he commented that the actions of Farm Holiday participants were "a very serious mistake," and added that, "[h]aving contact with nature as farmers do they should know that there are times when one must 'bow to the powers that be' whatever they are" (Grant and Purcell 1976, 31).

The New Deal and Rural Folk

In the end, the federal government would prove to be a major tool of aid and hope. Such centralized power had played a role in agriculture since

Mexican workers during the 1933 cotton strike led by the Cannery and Agricultural Workers Industrial Union in Corcoran, California. (*Library of Congress*)

the U.S. Department of Agriculture's (USDA's) establishment in the early 1860s; however, the farm crisis of the 1930s precipitated a much expanded involvement. In the 1920s, the trend for a more vigorous agricultural policy was already under way; the congressional farm block had successfully secured such legislation such as the Capper-Volstead Act and the Agricultural Credits Act of 1923. However, their efforts to achieve even more energetic action through such legislation as the McNary-Haugen bill proved to be ineffectual. Legislators had sought to return farmers to price parity by adjusting farm prices through direct interference in market; nevertheless, both the Coolidge and Hoover administrations opposed such government activism. Thus, the nation's farm families were left to languish in the cost price squeeze throughout the 1920s.

In spite of this government inertia, President Roosevelt's more interventionist approach and the desperate state of American farming coalesced in shifting political momentum to more vigorous action. Roosevelt's New Deal agenda established a variety of new administrative agencies such as the AAA and the Rural Electrification Administration to meet such challenges as overproduction, rural poverty, and poor farm practices head-on. These agencies produced policies that resulted in myriad changes regarding farmers' relationship to the government, their overall quality of life, and even the natural environment. Farmers' increased dependence on government subsidy programs and their improved living conditions resulting from the dissemination of electrical power can be traced to expanded federal power. Furthermore, the rural landscape was altered by the emergence of additional national forests and grasslands. Such sweeping changes demonstrated how the New Deal laid the groundwork for the future federal agricultural policy. Not all Americans enjoyed the benefits of new federal programs equally, however, because large farmers generally received the largest subsidy payments.

In May 1933, Congress enacted the Agricultural Adjustment Act, which represented one the New Deal's first and more significant pieces of farm legislation. Farmers who agreed to reduce their production of milk, hogs, rice, tobacco, cotton, and wheat in return received government payments. Henry A. Wallace, the Iowa genius, provided much of the direction for such measures aimed to restore farm families' buying power. Food processors met the cost of paying for the program by paying a tax. Many farmers owed their survival to the federal payments and were gracious for the compensation; nevertheless, some bitterly opposed the effort. In 1935, William H. King, a Utah senator, voiced a particularly harsh critique stating, "The AAA legislation, while new to our country, plagiarized from the pages recording the efforts of autocratic governments to control industry and restrict the activities of individuals" (King 1935, 6). He criticized the government's practices of destroying excess commodities in a time of great want as especially egregious.

The Supreme Court's declaration of the AAA's unconstitutionality represented a high point in the resistance to FDR's agricultural policy; some observers even surmised that AAA was "on the brink of disaster" (Nourse 1935, 5). Despite such a gloomy forecast, the passage of the Soil Conservation and Domestic Allotment Act by Congress effectively replaced the Agricultural Adjustment Act. The measure ended the practice of funding the program through a processing tax, and instead reduced production by paying farmers for their conservation efforts. In 1938, the AAA's third installment entrenched farmers' growing reliance on the federal government. Additionally, the Roosevelt administration developed a host of other programs in its attempts to raise farm prices and lower production. The Commodity Credit Corporation provided loans to farmers if they participated in crop-reduction agreements, thus similar to the AAA, and contributed to cementing a close relationship between the farmer and the federal government.

New Dealers not only desired to raise crop prices, but also to improve rural Americans' quality of life especially through the miraculous power of electricity. Although most small-town dwellers possessed electricity, many of their rural counterparts lived without it. Observers hailed the benefits of making electricity accessible to rural Americans and predicted that it would soon be within reach of those living in the countryside. In 1931, the comments of Howard S. Russell, the Massachusetts Farm Bureau Secretary, were particularly verbose regarding its advantages. He compared the role of electricity in the modern era to be that of the slave in antiquity, stating,

> Because electricity, the modern slave, is ready at his command to saw wood, turn the grind stone, whirl the cream separator or hoist the hay. It will fill silo, milk the cows, cool their milk, light the barn yard, and do a hundred tasks that Cato, the famous farmer of Roman times, was unable to get his slaves to do. (*American Farm Bureau Weekly* June 1931, 1)

"I arrested these Negroes because they were loafing around town," testified Paul D. Peacher, City Marshall of Earle, Arkansas, at his trial on charges of violating the Federal antislavery law of 1866, on November 24, 1936. "I have known them all for years," he continued, "they were loafers and a honkey-tonk bunch." Peacher justified his arrests of the seven African American men as "official acts," and the men had "regular trials," after which they were fined $25.00 and sentenced to thirty days for vagrancy. They were imprisoned for three days without food and then dispatched to Peacher's plantation, where they did hard labor for no pay. Peacher told the court that he had an oral agreement with his county for working prisoners on his plantation, and that he had filled all the requirements for a valid contract.

The prosecution's first witness, Winfield Anderson, described how Peacher arrested him. He said he was self-supporting; he owned his own home and had a steady income. He was not allowed to testify on his own behalf. The six others told very similar stories. Earle's mayor sentenced the seven

Dr. E. A. White, a rural electrification expert, spoke at a meeting of the American Society of Agricultural Engineers in Ames, Iowa. He stated, "It is probable that 10 years hence the farm without electric service will be looked upon as lacking essentials for economic production and desirable living standards" (*American Farm Bureau Weekly* July 1931, 4).

Dr. White's assessment proved to be overly optimistic since only 50 percent of the nation's farm families possessed electricity by the conclusion of World War II. The Rural Electrification Administration and the Tennessee Valley Authority (TVA) aided in electrifying the countryside much more rapidly than otherwise would have occurred. For years, private utility corporations had hesitated to serve rural populations with life-improving electricity. The TVA's accomplishments in creating a system of hydroelectric dams providing a less costly source of electricity than private companies particularly demonstrates the government's success. Despite the government's achievements in disseminating the spread of this modern convenience, it was ineffective in stemming the tide of the continued urban mass migration.

Political leaders also attempted to address the nation's emergency needs, unemployment, and persistent ill of rural poverty. Resettlement Administration officials acquired marginal lands, converting them into national forests or public grasslands. Federal employees provided monetary relief to families, some of whom faced shortages of basic necessities; however, attempts to offer such impoverished farmers with new farming opportunities rarely materialized. People benefited from the New Deal's conservation efforts both through improvements in their local environment as well as new employment opportunities. Regions of the country with a solid tradition of conservation profited greatly from these programs. Vermont's state commissioner of forestry was particularly pleased by the Civilian Conservation Corps' (CCC) contributions, particularly regarding how it aided in the development a modern and strong forestry service. CCC workers poured their energies into flood prevention measures as well as enhancing the state's recreational areas.

men, and twelve others, to work on Peacher's plantation, based on his word that all were vagrants.

Justice in the depression-era rural South was swift, because it was in a federal court and concerned violation of federal statute. The jury swiftly found Peacher guilty of all seven counts of falsely arresting the men and forcing them to work on his farm. The judge imposed a two-year jail sentence and a fine of $3,500 but offered probation if Peacher paid the fine. The defendant smiled—or perhaps he smirked—when the verdict was read. But later, when he was waiting for bail to be arranged, Peacher shouted at reporters and U.S. Justice Department officials, "Get away from here and don't mess with me. I don't want to talk to anybody else now." He blamed his conviction on "outsiders"—the Southern Tenant Farmer's Union and the followers of the Socialist Party of America presidential candidate Norman Thomas.

SOURCE: *New York Times*, November 25, 26, 1936, pp. 46 and 1.

Vermonters also noticed that the men employed in such projects earned money, gained weight, and elevated their spirits. People in other states made similar positive comments regarding the CCC.

However, rural Americans, in areas as diverse as New England, the Great Plains, and the U.S. West sometimes viewed the New Deal programs negatively. Some landowners believed that the Federal Emergency Relief Administration (FERA) and other relief programs reduced their access to inexpensive labor and undermined people's work ethic. Yet others argued that the government's practice of destroying hogs or plowing under a cotton crop was both wasteful and irrational. Eddie Wegner, a Texas cotton grower, stated, "I remember we had to plow out an acre or two. I can still see the stuff. You took a plow and just jerked it out. It layed [*sic*] there along that furrow—the beautiful white bolls laying there—it made me sick. The thing is, we dearly needed that cotton" (Hurt 2002, 85–87). Additionally some small-town newspapers viewed government programs as overly lenient and bureaucratic. A writer for the *Vermont Brattleboro Reformer* commented derisively on the Soil Conservation and Domestic Allotment Act of 1936, which "promised gravy for everyone and the usual red tape" (Judd 1978, 39).

Historians have pointed many shortcomings of the New Deal, including unequal treatment according to race and farm size. They have also stressed that the Roosevelt administration failed to solve the overproduction issue, which constituted the main cause for low commodity prices. Agricultural leaders who were sympathetic to the struggles of African Americans identified a racial divide regarding the government's distribution of resources. African American land grant colleges received significantly less funding and there were few black extension agents. Additionally, the few existent black extension workers were given much less power than their white counterparts. White land grant college staff sometimes treated African Americans with the same racism that was prevalent in other aspects of the society. The New Deal disproportionately favored large farmers who were best adapted to commercial agriculture. Such farmers used their benefit payments to acquire the latest agricultural innovations and thus displaced sharecroppers from the countryside. Moreover, the problem of excess production remained until insatiable needs brought about by World War II brought prosperity back.

The Great Depression era not only witnessed farmers' changing relationship to the government, but also more subtle changes in agriculture. Because farmers faced extreme conditions during the era, they were encouraged to expand their use of hybrid corn as well as new varieties of other crops such as sorghum. Before the Great Depression, farmers in the Corn Belt had held back some of their seed to use the following year; however, they sometimes experienced a shortage of seed due to drought. Additionally, New Deal crop acreage reduction programs encouraged farmers to seek additional ways to make their land as productive as possible They solved this challenge by purchasing seed from such emerging commercial seed companies as Pioneer Hybrid. Once farmers experienced the increasing yields produced by such commercial varieties, they abandoned old practices, and by the end of the decade, farmers in states such as Iowa had almost completely made the transition to commercial seed corn. The transition from open pollinated to hybrid corn was rapid. A survey conducted by the Brookings Institution of 700 Iowa farmers discovered that the numbers using hybrids between 1934 and 1935 almost doubled. In other cases, such as the sorghum crop, farmers purchased new varieties due to the special needs created by the demands of mechanical harvesting. The Oklahoma and Kansas agricultural experiment stations and the USDA jointly cooperated in disseminating sorghum varieties whose height was suitable for mechanical harvesting. This included the Periconia and other varieties that contributed to the fact that the crop became one of the most dominant crops in Texas. Such new developments fully demonstrate the myriad ways in which rural America would be forever changed by the 1930s.

Despite such interesting details, a more important story seems to emerge from an examination of rural America in the Great Depression, a story of rural Americans' dogged determination, tremendous resiliency, and in most cases amazing ability to reconstruct their lives. A proper appreciation and understanding of this momentous historical event cannot be achieved without acknowledging how Americans so often responded to tough times with a reservoir of courage, creativity, and undying loyalty to friends and family. Perhaps, the Great Depression provided the testing ground for a generation journalist Tom Brokaw has termed the "Greatest Generation." Whether any age bracket can be considered greater than another is far from certain; however, it is not difficult to imagine that a group of Americans who grew up amid the impoverishment of the 1930s were uniquely prepared for the immense sacrifices required to defeat totalitarianism. Although other important themes such as the federal government's greater involvement in the lives of farm families, the continued exodus of rural Americans from the land, and the reduction of smaller, less-progressive farmers represent historical trends of great consequence, the drama of admirable people facing difficult odds is a most compelling one.

References

American Farm Bureau Federation Weekly Newsletter 1930.

American Farm Bureau Letter 10 February 2 (no. 6) 1931.

American Farm Bureau Weekly June 1931.

American Farm Bureau Weekly July 1931.

Ashton, Alice Margaret. 1934. Are we raising farmers? *The Farm Journal,* March, 26.

Berry, Chad. *Southern Migration, Northern Exiles.* Urbana: University of Illinois Press, 2000.

Grant, H. Roger, and L. Edward Purcell, eds. *Years of Struggle: The Farm Diary of Elmer G. Powers, 1931–1936.* Ames: Iowa State University Press, 1976.

Gregory, James N. *The Southern Diaspora: How the Great Migrations of Black and White Southerners Transformed America.* Chapel Hill: The University of North Carolina Press, 2005.

Howe, Eleanor. 1935. Seven budget recipes. *The Farm Journal.* February, 7.

Hurt, R. Douglas. *Problems of Plenty: The American Farmers in the Twentieth Century.* Chicago: Ivan R. Dee, 2002.

Judd, Richard M. *The New Deal in Vermont: Its Impact and Aftermath.* New York: Garland Publishing Co., 1978.

McElvaine, Robert S. ed. *Down and Out In the Great Depression. Letters from the ''Forgotten Man.''* Chapel Hill: The University of North Carolina Press, 1983.

McWilliams, Carey. *Factories in the Field: The Story of Migratory Labor in California,* 4th ed. Berkeley and Los Angeles: University of California Press, 2000.

Nelson, Paula M. 1996. *The Prairie Winnows Out Its Own: The West River Country of South Dakota in the Years of Depression and Dust.* Iowa City: University of Iowa Press, 1996.

Nourse, Edwin G. 1935. Is the AAA doomed? *The Farm Journal,* August, 5.

Riney-Kehrberg, Pamela. *Rooted in Dust: Surviving Drought and Depression in Southwestern Kansas.* Lawrence: University of Kansas Press, 1994.

Stock, Catherine McNicol. *Main Street in Crisis: The Great Depression and the Old Middle Class on the Northern Plains.* Chapel Hill: The University of North Carolina Press, 1992.

Coming of Age in the 1930s

2

Kriste Lindenmeyer

A New Stage in the Life Cycle

The 1930s was a significant decade in the economic and political history of the United States. It also resulted in important social and cultural changes, especially for the generation that came of age during such difficult years. For adolescents growing up during the 1930s, the question, "How old are you?" held a much greater significance than it had for earlier generations of young Americans. Among adolescents, by 1940, attending and graduating from an age-graded high school became not only the prescribed normative experience, but also a practice adopted by the majority of young Americans for the first time in U.S. history. School, rather than wage labor, became the work of adolescence. In addition, although going to college was still not a common experience, it was no longer viewed as a luxury attainable only by young people from wealthy families. As the prescription for school-based and age-level graded education expanded to eighteen year olds, the 1935 Social Security Act recognized a federal responsibility to protect the welfare of adolescents through high school graduation. In return, Americans gave up some of the autonomy and independence possessed by most individuals in earlier generations.

The important shift extending dependency through adolescence that occurred in the 1930s happened in a perfect storm that mixed public policy, popular culture, economics, and a shift of public opinion about teens in an America that seemed increasingly removed from its past. The economic crisis of the Great Depression resulted in changes that universalized ideas about American adolescence stirring for several decades. By the early 1940s, the term *teenager* was a part of American culture and defined a distinct period of life separated by chronological age from childhood and adulthood. Being identified as a teenager assumed that a young person was in a transitional time of experimentation, attended full-time school-based education, enjoyed a social life centered on peers, and extended financial dependency on adults.

Until the 1930s, most adolescents spent more time working for wages, laboring as an apprentice, or putting in long hours on the family farm than in school. *Youth* was a fluid term used to describe the period of life between childhood dependence and the independence of adulthood, but it was not specifically defined by age. A young American's transition from childhood to youth was linked to physical capacity. For boys, the ability to do men's work moved them into the transitional stage most commonly known as youth. For girls, the ability to have children noted their new status. Marriage generally marked the transition from youth to full adulthood, with females reaching that stage earlier than males.

The idea that adolescence was a special period of life that needed special protections from adult responsibilities grew in importance first among middle-class urban parents in the mid-nineteenth century. The urban middle class grew in size and influence during the balance of the nineteenth century, but only a minority of teens went to high school. Secondary education seemed an unnecessary and impractical luxury for many young Americans.

By the early twentieth century, child welfare experts began to push for a more universal definition of adolescence built on the middle-class ideal. Psychologist G. Stanley Hall published an influential two-volume work in 1904, *Adolescence: Its Psychology and Its Relations to Physiology, Anthropology, Sociology, Sex, Crime, Religion, and Education.* According to Hall, adolescence was a distinct period of life defined by biology. He argued that this transitional period required special protections and restrictions, because ignoring these needs would hinder an individual young person's successful transition to healthy adulthood. Hall criticized adults for celebrating adolescent precociousness; a practice that had been common in the past. He maintained that the teen years were a period of awkwardness, confusion, vulnerability, and eccentricities exaggerated by dramatic physical change. Not all experts agreed with Hall, but his theories soon dominated the twentieth century's cultural definition of adolescence.

Public policies that influenced the lives of young Americans were slower to reflect the new definition. However, the economic upheaval of the 1930s called many public policies into question that encouraged the extension of dependency in adolescence. For example, as noted earlier, for most of American history, the majority of teens spent more time working than in the classroom. This practice changed for more than a majority of teenagers in the 1930s. More education seemed essential for getting a job and a secure future as an adult in a world in which jobs were scarce. In addition, most people agreed that the limited pool of jobs should be reserved for men supporting families. The lack of jobs, public pressure to build greater access to a quality high school education, and shifting opinions about the importance of going to school among parents and teens contributed to a dramatic rise in secondary education. In 1929, less than 20 percent of all Americans had earned a high school diploma. Most young people left school before or immediately after completing the eighth grade. Over the next ten years, the rate of fourteen through seventeen year olds still in school full time rose 43 percent, and the number of high school graduates in the population doubled, from 667,000 to 1,221,000. For the first time in American history, staying in school long enough to earn a high school diploma became the norm rather than the exception. At the same time, full-time employment rates among teens dropped, and attending college or some form of post–high school education was more common.

The identification of teens as a distinct group paralleled the rapid growth of radio. Advertisers faced with falling consumer markets quickly recognized radio as a new marketing tool that could reinvigorate business. The vast appeal of radio that also enabled broadcasters to target specific markets quickly exposed adolescents as a desirable and distinct group of consumers. At the same time, movies provided a visible stereotype of the ideal American adolescent. Public policy was another important factor that fueled the nation's transition to an ideal that defined teenagers as a generation that shared extended dependency, emotionalism, the need for experimentation, and the necessity for quality school-based education through at least age eighteen.

Hard Times and America's Adolescents

The onset of the Great Depression hit younger Americans especially hard. Unemployed and underemployed parents left many children and teens without even the basic necessities. Individuals coming of age during the 1930s shared the experience of growing up during a time when opportunities for their future seemed limited. Natural disasters, such as the floods that struck parts of Arkansas, Kentucky, and Tennessee in 1931; similar events in 1937 along the Ohio River and its tributaries; and drought that hit the nation's Dust Bowl from 1934 through 1936 only made matters appear worse. National unemployment rates rose dramatically and reached a height of 25 percent by the winter of 1932–1933. Despite federal efforts to turn the tide, unemployment rates remained in the double digits until the United States entered World War II. The problem was especially acute for young Americans. The U.S. Department of Labor estimated that unemployment was twice as high among teens seeking full-time work. This was a special burden since by the early 1930s, 28 percent of American households did not include a single wage earner.

In this atmosphere, adult job-seekers made it difficult for teens looking for paid work. In 1932, sixteen-year-old Duval Edwards decided that quitting school and finding a job would be a good way to help his parents. In Bossier City, Louisiana, Edwards saw a sign that read, "Dishwasher Wanted—only college graduates need apply." A high school dropout, Edwards asked about the job anyway. The owner responded, "We mean it, sonny. We are helping those who have finished college and can't find any other work" (Edwards 1992, 31).

Margaret Montgomery, 18 years old in the summer of 1936, was been working hard to live down her earlier reputation—as a child motion picture star known as 'Baby Peggy'. Time was when she was a top child actress, earning at one point in 1923, when she was but three and a half years old, an estimated $1,500,000 per year. To be sure, her contract had been made with her parents, Mr. and Mrs. Jack Montgomery, of Owensmouth, California. Within six months, she was the star of her own production company. She was often referred to in the entertainment press as a talented actress, as "weirdly expressive," and a "winning little three-year old". She took the leading role in her 1923 film *Whose Baby Are You?* Her director, King Baggott, declared that so talented was Peggy that she never required more than two rehearsals, even in her many comedic films.

In the mid-1930s, Margaret worked very hard to make a comeback in the new world of sound and color films. When she grew too gangling for the silent screen in the later 1920s, her parents enrolled her in elementary and secondary school and tried to

The lack of jobs and a viable future for teens like Edwards was part of what some policymakers and activists began to call "America's Youth Problem." On July 4, 1936, members of the American Youth Congress (AYC), a volunteer organization made up of high school and college-age youth, passed a manifesto they called, "A Declaration of the Rights of American Youth." The document outlined what members of the AYC believed was the lamentable situation of young Americans. They asked that adolescent dependency be extended for young Americans to have time to adequately prepare for adulthood. Members of the AYC argued that special circumstances in the 1930s demanded new strategies: "Today our lives our threatened by war; our liberties threatened by reactionary legislation; and our right to happiness remains illusory in a world of insecurity" (American Youth Congress 1936). The AYC declared that young Americans had a right "to a useful, creative, and happy life ... the guarantees of which are: full educational opportunities, steady employment at adequate wages, security in time of need, civil rights, religious freedom, and peace" (American Youth Congress 1936). Careful to showcase their loyalty to the United States, the AYC continued,

> We look at this country of ours. We love it dearly; we are its flesh and marrow: Therefore, we the young people of America reaffirm our right to life, liberty and the pursuit of happiness.... To those ends we dedicate our lives, our intelligence and our unified strength. (American Youth Congress 1936)

Such ideas were popular. By 1939, the organization claimed 4,697,915 members and had the influential ear of First Lady Eleanor Roosevelt.

Like Eleanor Roosevelt, many adults shared the AYC's fears and sentiments about the insecure future facing young Americans. In 1932, the U.S. Children's Bureau, a federal agency dedicated to investigating and lobbying on behalf of the nation's children and adolescents, released a prepare her in other ways for a life outside the entertainment industry. But Margaret would not surrender her dream. In addition to her schoolwork, she took lessons in voice, drama, and dance. As an adolescent she had stage roles at the Pasadena, California, Community Theater, that incubator of actors and actresses for Hollywood. And she devoted a year to acting on the vaudeville stage, to polish her technique and to prove that she could handle roles in variety shows.

But the times were tough for all Americans, including former child prodigies. These were the years of the Great Depression, when jobs were scarce, doubly so in the acting business. She declared that she had been working hard to overcome her reputation as a child actress, so that the movie moguls would take her seriously as an adult thespian. Only small roles have come her way, most recently as one of a hundred pretty young women in a Fox picture, *Girls' Dormitory*. In time, she did not make her comeback.

SOURCE: *New York Times*, July 19, 1936.

report outlining the special problems brought on by the Great Depression. As evidence of a national crisis, the bureau noted that an estimated 250,000 homeless young people were hitchhiking the nation's roads and hopping its freight trains. Most were boys and youth from thirteen to twenty-five years old. The bureau made it clear that unlike earlier times when most Americans believed that transients became hobos by choice or immorality, the current army of young was not composed of irresponsible runaways, drug addicts, juvenile delinquents, or illiterates. Instead, most were simply adolescents and young people in their early twenties looking for work. Far from illiterate, many had spent at least some time in high school or college. Sociologist Kingsley Davis echoed the bureau's findings in another publication and reminded Americans that the generation coming of age in the 1930s faced a world with circumstances quite different from those in the past. "The last frontier disappeared some forty years ago," Kingsley remarked.

> When young men now want to move on, they find there is no place to go.... The machinery by which young people are drawn into the work of the nation had broken down; and youth, bearing the burden of this breakdown were seeking blindly for some way out. (Davis 1935, 8, 29)

For Davis, rising crime rates and even revolution were inevitable if something was not done to help the nation's adolescents and youth.

The Media and America's Youth Problem

By the fall of 1933, newspapers, magazines, and movies also began to pay attention to "America's Youth Problem." The fall 1933 release of Warner Brothers' *Wild Boys of the Road* raised public debate about society's responsibility for young transients. The movie's director, William A. Wellman,

Young hobo in Westmoreland County, Pennsylvania, July 1935. Photo by Walker Evans for the Farm Security Administration. (*Library of Congress*)

hoped the film would act as a cautionary tale for boys and girls considering hitting the road. He also wanted to highlight the costs of ignoring the vulnerability of American adolescents and youth during the Great Depression.

The film starred sixteen-year-old Frankie Darro as "Eddie Smith." Eddie was an honest and optimistic teenager from an unidentified town in the Midwest. He lives with his middle-class parents and attends high school. Eddie's best friend, "Tommy," played by a young-looking twenty-year-old Edwin Philips, is not as lucky. Tommy does not have a father in his life and his mother makes a poor living taking in boarders. Tommy has always struggled, but the Great Depression also hits Eddie's family when his father is laid off from a job at the local cement plant. Wanting to help, Eddie sells his "jalopy" car for $22.00, but it is not enough to help his devastated parents. Eddie convinces Tommy that the two friends should hit the road in search of jobs. The boys hop a freight train and soon see that they are not the only young Americans on the road in search of work. They soon team up a freckle-faced "boy" who turns out to be a girl named "Sally," played by another young-looking nineteen year old, Dorothy Coonan.

The three friends experience difficulties at every turn. Eddie, Tommy, and Sally are happy to find friends and companionship among the other young wanderers. However, they also face violence and sexual abuse from older transients, police, and railroad authorities. The film's drama rises as the trio settles in with young squatters in a railroad yard in Columbus, Ohio. Local authorities violently clear the area and Tommy's leg is cut off by a passing train as he tries to flee. Tommy is hospitalized and survives, but he is unable to buy a prosthetic leg that will help him continue to travel with his friends. In response, Eddie breaks into a local prosthetics store and steals an artificial leg. The honest and earnest all-American boy has become a criminal and feels justified in his crime.

In the movie's final scenes, Eddie, Tommy, and Sally make their way to New York City. They are fooled into committing a crime and arrested. All three are charged with "vagrancy, petty theft, resisting police, breaking and entering and hold-up" and are sent to juvenile court. They refuse to give their full names, stating that they cannot go home because their parents are too poor to care for them. "What good will it do for you to send us home to starve?" Eddie asks the judge. "You say that you've got to send us to jail to keep us off the streets. Well, that's a lie. You're sending us to jail 'cause you don't want to see us; you want to forget us," Eddie argues. "Well, you can't do it 'cause I'm not the only one. There's thousands like me and there's more like me hitting the road every day!" Eddie's tough exterior unravels as he breaks into uncontrollable sobs. Aware that the tough young man is really a sympathetic teen, the judge wants to help. He tells him that "Things are going to be better now." Franklin Roosevelt's election means that "unemployed parents would be going to go back to work soon." The assumption for the audience is that the teens would soon be able to resume their normal places in society—a place where adolescents live with their parents, experience relatively carefree lives, and attend high school fulltime in preparation for adult independence (Wellman 1933).

Like Wellman, Thomas Patrick Minehan also wanted to stir Americans to do more to help the younger generation. A graduate student in sociology at the University of Minnesota, Minehan undertook a study of transients from 1931–1933. He went undercover and conducted 1,465 interviews (1,377 boys and 88 girls) and documented 509 case studies (493 boys and 16 girls) with other young people on the road. Minehan published his finding in a 1934 book, *Girl and Boy Tramps of America.* The young people in Minehan's sample were primarily in their teens and early twenties. Of the 548 individuals identified by age, 291 were thirteen through sixteen year olds, 282 were seventeen through twenty-one year olds, and only four were under thirteen. All twenty-nine girls in the study were less than nineteen years of age. Ninety-five percent of the transients in the sample were born in the United States and most claimed to be Protestant, Catholic, or Jewish. Sixty-two identified themselves as "nonbelievers." Only twenty-seven had earned a high school diploma, but more than half had graduated from at least the eighth grade, and twenty-five had attended a few college classes. Most had been on the road more than six months but less than two years. As further evidence of the widespread nature of the problem, they came from both rural and urban America in thirty different states and looked to many adults like the girl and boy next door (Minehan 1934, 253–262).

"Hard times" was the most frequent reason young transients gave for leaving home. Some admitted they sought adventure. Ina Máki left her home in rural Minnesota for a summer of hopping trains because "there was little else to do" (Uys 2003, 9–30), and a few simply hated school. "Nothing I ever did ever satisfied anybody in school," one girl told Minehan. Some ran away to escape abusive parents or guardians. Asked "if he ever got a licking at home," a boy named Nick told Minehan, "That's all I ever got. The old man would lick me if I did something. The old lady if I didn't" (Minehan 1934, 35, 48, 51).

Minehan concluded that being on the road was not good for the young people he met or for the future of the nation. The longer the boys and girls stayed on the road, the more likely they were to develop attitudes and behaviors contrary to mainstream American values. A boy nicknamed Happy Joe said that when begging for food it was a good strategy to lie. "Tell them you got a sick mother and a lot of younger kids at home hungry.... That way you get more and will have a nice lunch for later" (Minehan 1934, 77–78). Young transients stole from anyone and did not seem to feel guilty about their behavior. A few even talked openly about injuring others or even killing someone. Many talked about sex in ways that shocked adults. In one incident, Minehan tried to help a sixteen-year-old girl having sex with men in a freight train boxcar. Asked by a railroad brakeman if she was alright, the girl "came to the door a little bit drunk and very undressed." Cursing and yelling at the brakeman, "You big fat fool. You Y.M.C.A. dummy. Why do you have to spoil it all? Why can't you let a girl alone when she isn't hurting you? Everything was fine, all right, and now you've spoiled it all" (Minehan 1934, 141–142). Through his study, Minehan warned Americans that such circumstances left the nation in danger of corrupting an entire generation and thereby shaking the foundation of the nation's future.

A New Deal for Youth

Calls by advocates such as Minehan contributed to Franklin Roosevelt's efforts to address America's youth problem as part of his administration's New Deal. On March 30, 1933, members of Congress approved the selection of enrollees for the president's new Civilian Conservation Corps (CCC). The CCC was designed as a work relief program for unmarried males age eighteen to twenty-six from families receiving aid and for unemployed veterans of the Great War of any age. It also evolved into a modest education program and expanded to seventeen year olds in 1935. Some CCC recruits earned their General Education Diploma (GED) as part of the program. Before ending in 1943, the CCC established camps in Hawaii, Alaska, Puerto Rico, and the Virgin Islands as well as throughout the continental United

States. During its existence, approximately 3 million unmarried teens and youth spent time as ''Soil Soldiers'' in ''Roosevelt's Tree Army.'' The average CCC enrollee was a teen who had just reached his eighteenth birthday. He had completed the eighth grade, but read at only a sixth-grade level. His health was good, but he was probably malnourished and underweight. Sixty percent of CCC recruits came from rural areas and small towns. Most were native-born whites, because black enrollment was limited to 10 percent; the same proportion of African Americans as in the general population. It should be noted that this was much lower than poverty rates among black families in the United States. The CCC added special units for American Indian recruits on reservations and about 80,000 served.

The popularity of the CCC program encouraged the creation of the similar program for girls in 1934. This effort that became known as the ''She-She-She'' was much smaller and short lived. Only 8,000–10,000 adolescent girls and young women took part, ending in 1937. Many Americans did not support the idea of sending daughters away from their families; even to gender-segregated camps. In addition, most Americans did not view unemployment among girls as a danger to the nation's future. In an era of strong gender-based stereotypes, the failure and lack of support for a CCC-type effort among girls is not a surprise.

The seventeen-year-old minimum age requirement and rule that CCC enrollees come from families on relief also limited the program's effectiveness for males. Young male transients under seventeen were ineligible, and those who were did not have families did not qualify. Another problem was that the program's emphasis on work over education made it

Young Civilian Conservation Corps recruits transplant beaver from a ranch location where they were damaging crops to a forest watershed where they will help to conserve the water supply, Salmon National Forest, Camp F-167, Idaho. (*Franklin D. Roosevelt Presidential Library*)

somewhat inconsistent with the model for American teens that emphasized high school education.

Despite its shortcomings, the CCC was a very popular New Deal program, even among most recruits. Camps operated under rules similar to military service. Recruits earned $30 per month in exchange for forty-hour workweeks on conservation projects. Of a recruit's earnings, $25 per month went home to his family. One mother of a CCC recruit explained to a Federal Writers' Project interviewer that her son's CCC pay saved his family from starvation. Still, when the boy's father was unable to find work, the boy had to give up returning to high school his senior year.

President Roosevelt tried to address such dilemmas by taking the CCC idea further with Executive Order No. 7086, released in June 1935. Roosevelt entitled his new program for young Americans the National Youth Administration (NYA). It included girls as well as boys and lowered the age of eligibility to sixteen with an upper limit of twenty-five. In another important shift, the NYA emphasized full-time education over work relief and required participants to live at home with their parents or a guardian. NYA participants received stipends similar to today's work-study programs. An NYA youth from Pittsburgh wrote Eleanor Roosevelt in 1937 praising the program: "Words cannot express my gratitude to our President who has made this possible for me and thousands of others, and I trust that you and the President will continue your good work and remain at the White House for a 'long time'" (Cohen 2002, 158). Another NYA participant, an eleventh-grader from Des Moines, Iowa, noted that he had stayed in school because of the program. "When I started school in September, I did not know whether I was going to continue to go or not.... When I got my first check I was so tickled I could have shouted." He explained that the money enabled him to go "to town that evening and [get] some bread for my brothers' and sisters' and my own lunches.... Next I got some shoes. Even if they weren't high priced, I was proud of them, because I had bought them with my own money" (Cohen 2003, 158).

During its existence, the NYA enrolled 1.5 million high school students and 600,000 college recruits. An additional 2.6 million unemployed teens and young people in their early twenties who had already left school also participated in NYA training programs. The NYA's director, Aubrey Williams, saw the effort as not only practical, but also as a social experiment promoting civil rights and greater social equality. As part of that vision, Williams named African American reformer Mary McLeod Bethune to head a special NYA division for black youth. For Williams and Bethune, access to high-quality school-based education and vocational training for all young Americans was the key to leveling the playing field for a generation that faced special difficulties linked to the Great Depression. It could also help to eliminate historical inequities connected to racism, socioeconomic class, and ethnic prejudice.

Other New Deal efforts also contributed to efforts designed to level America's playing field. For example, the federal government channeled money into ailing schools through a wide range of New Deal programs. Work relief efforts paid for new school construction or the renovation of existing facilities. These efforts coupled with an acceptance of the idea among the general public that school-based education through high school graduation was a necessity for success as an adult. As noted earlier, in the 1930s, the majority of high-school-age teens attended high school for the first time in American history. The irony is that, during the first years of the Depression, many school districts closed or cut short the academic year because of a loss of tax revenue. For example, authorities from Chicago's public schools testified before Congress in 1933 that the system was bankrupt and teachers had not been paid in eight months. Students and teachers protested by marching in the streets. About the same time, many school districts in the rural South failed to open at all, even for limited three-month terms.

The Roosevelt administration responded by sending federal funds to schools through a variety of New Deal programs. The FERA paid teachers' salaries and offered work-relief employment for parents so that teenage sons and daughters could stay in school. In addition, bolstered by an influx of federal funding, states and local communities across the United States constructed new schools and consolidated small schools into state-of-the-art education facilities. Consolidated schools offered broader curriculums than the small schools of the past. The idea was to keep all young Americans in school through graduation; even those not planning to attend college. The transition to large multipurpose high schools that ran both traditional academic programs and vocational education curriculums had occurred in most cities by 1930. The influx of federal money sent to the states as part of the New Deal helped to bring the change to rural America as well. Not every community benefited, but for the first time in history, a majority of adolescents had the opportunity to attend high schools with a more diversified curriculum within a reasonable distance of their homes.

The changes in New London, Texas, during the mid-1930s were a good example of the trend favoring consolidated schools. Families in the area were drawn by jobs in the region's recently tapped oil fields. The influx of families strained the region's tiny and outdated schools, which rarely accommodated students over fourteen years of age. The new $1 million consolidated school that opened in the fall of 1936 housed modern facilities and offered an up-to-date curriculum for students from the first grade through high school. Although most parents did not have a high school diploma themselves, they believed that extended education opportunities were good for their own children and the community's future.

A massive explosion at the school during its first year rocked the New London community and the nation. The *New York Times* reported that on March 19, 1937, natural gas used to heat the New London campus ignited resulting in a massive explosion, collapsing the building's walls and the ceiling. Tons of debris came crashing down on the 700 children and forty teachers inside the facility before they could escape. The building was fireproof, so there was little fire, but the explosion's concussion and falling debris killed most of those inside. Approximately 10,000 area residents quickly gathered at the disaster site, witnessing the call of victims still buried under the rubble. Some students and teachers were saved; by nightfall, the school's powerful stadium floodlights revealed a sad scene composed of grief-stricken parents, relatives, and onlookers next to a lengthening row of bodies covered by white bed sheets. In the end, more than 500 students and teachers were killed. Approximately 200 individuals escaped with minor to serious injuries. Fifteen-year-old Doris Derring told a *New York Times* reporter that she witnessed "100 of her classmates blown from their desks into the schoolyard" (*New York Times*, March 21, 1937).

Before the heartbreaking disaster, the New London consolidated school campus served as an important source of community pride. It showed the working-class parents' and community leaders' commitment to providing quality education opportunities for the area's children and adolescents. An investigation after the blast, however, showed that even high-minded goals could include costly shortcomings. To save on long-term utility costs, planners used natural gas in an unsafe manner to heat the building and hot water supply. News of the disaster led some Americans to question the wisdom of putting so many children together in large, consolidated schools under any conditions. But even in the midst of such fears, the trend toward consolidated schools continued. As an article in the *New York Times* three days after the explosion concluded, larger modern schools allowed for expanded curriculums and better opportunities for students. In addition, even with the risk of disasters, modern school buildings were safer than the old-fashioned wooden structures of the past. New schools are

> made of sand and stone," explained the *Times*. They "have stairways of slate and cement, and are classed as fireproof. Broad corridors, fire towers, fire escapes, sprinkling systems are provided. They furnish a striking contrast to the wooden firetraps still used as schools. No structure, however built, when converted into a holder for inflammable gas ... can be made to resist explosion. (*New York Times*, March 24, 1937)

The rapid spread of consolidated schools marked the end of an era in American education. During the 1930s, a combination of federal, state, and community funds shifted the emphasis on schools in the American countryside from small one- and two-room facilities to grade-level and age-based programs for students in the elementary grades through high school. In 1916, 200 of every 1,000 schools in the United States employed only one teacher. Further progress was made in cities during the 1920s. By 1940, only 114 of every 1,000 schools employed only one teacher. By 1960, such tiny schools virtually disappeared from the landscape as viable education alternatives, even in rural America.

Besides broader curriculums and more modern facilities, larger schools also redefined the experience of being an adolescent in America. As part of the effort to keep young people in school through graduation, school authorities also paid more attention to extracurricular activities. Schools used sports for boys and girls, as well as special interest clubs to engage teens in their education outside the classroom. These activities put teens, for greater parts of their day, under the supervision of adults other than their own parents. High schools across the United States sponsored dances and made junior and senior proms a rite of passage among older adolescents. Even rural high schools organized football teams, sometimes with only six players on the field at a time, and published yearbooks as a way to build school pride. Peer pressure could have been used to keep teens in school, but it also might have had negative consequences. Many young Americans expressed increasing dismay at not being able to afford the clothing, carfare, or other expenses associated with going to high school. For example, frustrated and depressed teens wrote Eleanor Roosevelt asking for money and hand-me-down clothing that would help them keep up with their peers. Physically handicapped youngsters found little accommodation to their special needs in most schools. Racial segregation and economic disparity linked to a schools' surrounding community persisted. Despite such hurdles, school attendance increased. What was called "quitting school" before graduation in the 1930s, transformed to the more negative "dropping out" as earning a high school diploma grew into the expected norm for all American teenagers.

Adult-monitored recreational activities outside schools also adopted the school-based model and increased in the 1930s as by-products of the New Deal. The Works Progress Administration (WPA) alone constructed 770 community swimming pools and 5,598 athletic fields as part of the federal government's $750 million spent for recreational facilities throughout the United States. Such places created safer environments for teens to gather. For example, in New York City after the opening of ten WPA pools in 1936, drowning deaths in the city fell from 450 in 1934 to less than 300. Schools and public recreational facilities helped focus the social world of adolescents into more adult-controlled environments. Churches, synagogues, and other religious institutions copied the school- and community-based model as well. School and social life built around age-based activities, even outside schools, rose along with the expansion of adolescence through age eighteen.

Still, even with these dramatic changes, the playing field was not level for all American adolescents. Fourteen-year-old Margaret Williams and Lucille Scott attended Colored School 21, a racially segregated one-room school house in Cowdensville, a small community of African Americans located in Baltimore County, Maryland. At the end of the 1934–1935 school year, Williams' and Scott's teacher recommended them, along with a male classmate, for promotion to the eighth grade. A school board official denied the request, saying he saw, "no reason to pass the girls, because by the time [they] were fifteen or sixteen years old, [they] would be having babies" (Orser 1937). Williams and Scott also had to overcome the problem that in racially segregated Baltimore County, no high school admitted black students. Beginning in 1926, under pressure to make an accommodation for ambitious African American students, the county offered to pay the tuition of "qualified" black students to attend Baltimore City's all-black junior and senior high schools. The privilege included the requirement that black students pass a test, but no white students had to face a similar requirement to attend the county's

Young adults at the Greenbelt, Maryland, swimming pool, circa 1939. Greenbelt was a federal housing project built under the Resettlement Administration. The pool opened in 1939 and was the first in the Washington, D.C., area. (*Library of Congress*)

white-only high schools. Lucille Scott and Margaret Williams took the test, but they failed to get a score high enough to qualify for the tuition program.

Just before the start of the new school year in 1935, a National Association for the Advancement of Colored People (NAACP) lawyer, Thurgood Marshall, met with Margaret Williams' and Lucille Scott's parents to discuss the situation. He urged them to try and attend the high school nearest their homes. They tried, but the school principal told them that the matter was out of his hands because policy dictated that black students could not attend the white-only high school. Marshall filed a lawsuit on the girls' behalf, *Williams v. Zimmerman,* demanding that the court require the Baltimore County School Board to admit Margaret Williams to the high school nearest her home. The judge rejected Marshall's argument and decided the case in favor of the county.

Lucille Scott eventually retook the county's required examination and passed. Finally eligible for the tuition program, Scott attended Baltimore City's Booker T. Washington Junior High School and graduated from Frederick Douglass High School in 1941. Margaret Williams did not go to public school, but she earned a high school diploma from St. Frances Academy, a comprehensive elementary through secondary school run by the Oblate Sisters of Providence (a Roman Catholic Order of African American nuns founded in Baltimore in 1829).

The *Williams v. Zimmerman* case highlights the hurdles that still blocked many teenagers from accessing a level playing field centered on a high school education and a social life centered on school-based activities. However, another outcome of the case shows that times were changing. Fearing another expensive lawsuit, the Baltimore County School Board opened three "separate but equal" secondary school facilities for black students at the start of the 1938–1939 academic year. Williams and Scott were not able to take advantage of the change in policy, but their bravery set the stage for change. Learning from his failed suit in Baltimore County, over the next fourteen years, Thurgood Marshall successfully constructed a more aggressive argument that won in the 1954 *Brown v. Board of Education, Topeka, Kansas* case.

Adolescents and Work

The growth of high schools and new emphasis on recreation reflected new attitudes about how teens should be spending the majority of their time. Since the late nineteenth century, child welfare advocates promoted local and state compulsory school attendance laws as a good strategy for curbing exploitive child labor practices. The early focus centered on children under age of fourteen, but over time, advocates also called for changes that regulated the work of adolescents as well. In 1918, the U.S. Supreme Court declared the first attempt at federal regulation of the issue unconstitutional. Congress then passed a constitutional amendment regulating child labor, but the necessary number of states never ratified the measure. As an alternative, advocates worked for the inclusion of federal child labor guidelines in the National Recovery Administration's (NRA) codes that were passed as part of the early New Deal. The U.S. Supreme Court declared the NRA unconstitutional in 1935, however, and nullified those protections. Strikes by adolescent textile workers in Pennsylvania in 1933 highlighted the continued exploitation of young workers. Testimony before a state sweatshop commission revealed cases of sexual harassment, work for no or little pay, and unsafe and unhealthy working conditions.

Finally, passage of the Fair Labor Standards Act in 1938 (FLSA), and its eventual acceptance by the Supreme Court, put child labor regulations into federal law. President Roosevelt said the legislation "end[ed] child labor" in the United States. The president overstated the law's consequences, but the FLSA signaled an important shift and remains the foundation of labor regulations for adolescents in America today. The law prohibited the employment of individuals less than sixteen years of age in industries engaged in interstate commerce or deemed hazardous by the U.S. Department of Labor. The legislation also connected school attendance to work by prohibiting working past 10:00 P.M. on school nights for sixteen and seventeen year olds. The FLSA included restrictions on employing adolescents in the sugarbeet industry. This restriction was a specific response to a study conducted on that industry by the U.S. Children's Bureau. The specific mention failed to protect other young agricultural workers and made no mention of domestic service. Both agriculture and domestic work touched many young Americans, but strong resistance among adults to regulating such work, linked to traditional family responsibilities, were not included in the FLSA. Another loophole was the fact that fourteen and fifteen year olds could apply for special work permits. While the FLSA did not eliminate child labor, it created an atmosphere in which school was recognized by the federal government as the most important work of childhood *and* adolescence. In addition, the special regulations for sixteen and seventeen year olds emphasized adolescence as a transition period to adulthood. Entrance into World War II somewhat reversed this trend among adolescents, but in the years immediately following the conflict, children under sixteen were virtually eliminated from the paid labor force and most sixteen and seventeen year olds only worked part time in a subgroup distinct from adults.

Robert Omata of Hanford, California, began serving customers at the meat counter of his family's grocery business at age twelve in 1933. Despite his responsibilities to his family, Omata attended middle and high school, excelled in his studies, and qualified for the National Honor Society. He even found time to play football for Hanford Union High School and earned a diploma in 1938. Likewise, fifteen-year-old Jasper Harrell had family responsibilities. He lived with his single mother in Marion County, South Carolina. No one in Harrell's family had ever graduated from high school and his two older brothers quit school in the sixth grade. Harrell went to school each morning and worked at a local grocery each day from 3:00 P.M. to 6:00 P.M. In the early evening, a neighbor helped Harrell with his schoolwork, but he returned to the grocery every night at about 8:30 P.M. so that he could help clean up and close the business for the day. For his efforts, Harrell earned from $2.00 to $3.00 a week. He used the money to pay for school supplies and other expenses.

Andy Hardy's America

The movies, radio, and advertisers also provided messages that encouraged adolescents like Robert Omata and Jasper Harrell to stay in school. In the late 1930s, Hollywood child-star Mickey Rooney became the most visible symbol of the modern American teenager through his role in the very successful *Andy Hardy* film series. Rooney's fictional character, Andy Hardy, shared his days in high school with same-age friends from happy and stable middle-class families in small-town America. Rooney first appeared as Andy Hardy in the 1937 MGM film, *A Family Affair*. By the series' fourth film, *Love Finds Andy Hardy* (1938), Rooney was the major character and symbolized modern American teens. Young female screen actors such as Judy Garland and Lana Turner also had roles in the series. They provided the stereotypical sweater girl model that framed the stereotype of female adolescence in America's high schools. In the world according to Andy Hardy, the teen years were a period focused on same-age peers, school, self-exploration in a safe environment guided by wise adults and romantic experimentation limited to what became known as puppy love. There was no mention of the Great Depression or hard times. Some Hollywood films, such as the *Dead End Kids* (released in 1937), showed a more class-conscious and troubled adolescence, but the *Andy Hardy* series far surpassed such examples in popularity and staying power. Andy and his fictional friends lived lives that Americans wanted for teens and that many adolescents apparently wanted for themselves.

Radio provided another commercial avenue that spread the American adolescent ideal. At the start of the decade, less than half of all American households included a radio. In 1940, more than 80 percent owned at least one radio. Families often listened together to radio broadcasts, but teens also heard programs in isolation that connected them to their generation. Radio precipitated the rapid spread of information, cultural norms, and especially music for adolescents coming of age in the 1930s.

Swing defined teen music by the mid-1930s. In 1932, the elegant African American bandleader and composer Duke Ellington coined one of his most popular tunes, "It Don't Mean a Thing (If It Ain't Got That Swing)." Ellington did not invent Swing music, but his song proved a name for the sound that became known as Swing. Two years later, twenty-five-year-old Benny Goodman was working as the leader of a twelve-piece band in New York City. He and his group joined NBC radio's Saturday night broadcast, *Let's Dance*. The Goodman band's segment did not air until the program's last hour from 12:30–1:30 A.M. Although there was only a small audience by this hour, it was generally young and larger on the West Coast because of the time difference. Goodman's band's offerings included music arranged by Fletcher Henderson, the most successful African American jazz bandleader of the 1920s. In 1935, they went on a road tour and found their biggest success in California among the young fans of *Let's Dance*. Goodman's hometown of Chicago gave him a similar response and likewise labeled the new sound Swing. In June 1936, the CBS network aired a radio program entitled *Saturday Night Swing Session* featuring Benny Goodman and his band. Hollywood also noted the group's popularity and the Goodman band made two films: *The Big Broadcast of 1937* and *Hollywood Hotel*.

Swing bands usually included a piano player, trombones, coronets, saxophones, clarinets (also known as "licorice sticks"), and various drums and percussion instruments that formed the basis of the sound's syncopated four-beat rhythm. Fans expressed their enthusiasm through spontaneous shouts and applause as well as raucous dances such as the Lindy Hop, Suzy Q, and the Big Peach—collectively known as Jitterbug. Radio shows spread Swing's sound, and dance venues celebrating the style sprang up throughout the United States. Harlem, New York's Savoy Ballroom was the Mecca for young Swing fans. The Savoy attracted both blacks and whites. Such integrated settings were rare, but pointed to the racial mixing that became part of rock 'n' roll culture and controversy in a later generation. Record companies in the 1930s took advantage of teens' love for Swing music, but no avenue was more important to the genre's success than radio. Some adults worried that Swing music encouraged

Verna Mimosa

In 1935, the National Piano Teachers Guild's judges at its annual piano tournament unanimously declared nine-year-old Verna Mimosa the newest piano prodigy. The only daughter of an unemployed hotel dishwasher living in Harlem, Verna had competed the previous year in the Guild's tournament in its less daunting New York division, attracting the attention—and patronage—of a professional pianist, who instantly saw that Verna had raw talent that could be developed in a big way.

On the big day, Verna presented herself for the competition. A very small child for her age, with "a gentle face too old for her body," she was shy before the audience and judges. At the piano, she was a highly confident and professional concert musician. Dressed in a pleasing gingham, with long, brown curls peeking out of her teensy straw bonnet, she began with scales in C sharp, and then jumped to two of the more difficult Bach "Inventions" before throwing herself into a most demanding program, including the allegro and andante movements of Mozart's "Sonata in C Major," Chopin's "Prelude in A Major," then Grieg's taxing "Nocturne," and closing with Moszkowski's "Scherzo," which

antisocial sexual behavior among teens. Despite such concerns, the music prospered and radio made it impossible to stop Swing's appeal among young Americans across the United States.

Advertisers recognized that the teen market could make up losses in adult buying power. Comic books, first published in 1933, were directly marketed to adolescents. Advertisers such as Charles Atlas used psychology to appeal to teenage boys who were insecure about the physical changes they were experiencing in adolescence. Atlas sold a body-building method and health program that he said would turn any "97 lb. weakling" into "a new man." For girls, companies such as Breck shampoo sold the idea that "ordinary girls" could be models if they used the right products. The "Breck Girl" was one of the most successful advertising campaigns of the mid-twentieth century. The desire for healthy skin and elimination of acne also drew the teen market. Sanitary napkins and other female products were marketed in schools. Teens were told that the road to successful adulthood included improvements in their physical appearance as well as their education achievements.

Extending American Adolescence through Dependency

Hindsight provides a perspective highlighting the important shifts in the 1930s that had long-term consequences influencing ideas about adolescence in the United States. By the end of the decade, Americans exchanged some of the autonomy adolescents had traditionally held for new protections that extended their dependency. New federal labor laws limited teens' access to the job market, but provided legal protections for her judges found technically brilliant. Her tone was judged "excellent"; in phrasing, rhythm, pedaling, dynamics, style, and technique, her judges gave her a superior rating, and she got a general rating of 96, save for a missed beat on the Grieg piece, for which she received a still respectable 85. She showed "pronounced talent" and was "very sensitive," in the words of her judges.

Veronica—as she came to be called—continued with her musical education and career throughout the Depression and war years. Veronica continued to study and to hold recitals and performances. Thus, in 1941, at age fifteen, she performed as soloist with the New York Philharmonic, playing the Saint-Saens concerto in G minor to praiseworthy plaudits in the press, and performed again in 1943 at Carnegie Hall, and again with the Philharmonic at Lewisohn Stadium. Since 1940, she had studied at the Manhattan School of Music with Harold Bauer. Then, like so many talented but unlucky musicians, her career gradually melted away.

SOURCE: *New York Times*, May 14, 15, 1935, June 29, 1941, June 30, 1943.

young workers. Compulsory school attendance laws regulated by state governments required most adolescents to stay in school until they reached at least sixteen years of age. New attitudes about adolescents emphasized this period of life as a time that should be absent the full range of adult responsibilities.

This shift is perhaps most clearly evident in moves by states that raised minimum-age-at-marriage laws. Beginning in the 1880s, states raised minimum-age-of-sexual-consent laws from as low as age eight to at least sixteen. Such laws meant that any male having sex with a female younger than the specified minimum age could be charged and convicted of rape, even if the girl had consented to intercourse. The Women's Christian Temperance Union led the effort to raise the minimum age of consent as part of a broad purity crusade. By the early twentieth century, child welfare advocates, psychologists, and morality crusaders generally agreed that adolescents were too immature, both physically and emotionally, to indulge in most adult vices (such as tobacco, alcohol, and gambling). They turned to states to pass laws restricting such behaviors to adults. Engaging in sexual intercourse and having children were viewed as the most important signals that someone had reached adulthood. Like age of consent, the minimum age of marriage was a legal marker regulated by the states. In the 1920s, attempts to pass a federal marriage law included raising and standardizing the minimum age of marriage, but the effort failed. By the mid-1930s, most states had altered their marriage laws to include prohibitions against adolescent marriage before age eighteen, without parental consent, although some states provided for girls to marry at younger ages if their parents approved.

The extension of adolescent dependency, however, has not been uniform. Americans continue to harbor some ambivalence about the status and autonomy of teens. Attending and graduating from college is now viewed as even more important than in the past, but accessibility to college remains a hurdle for many. High school graduation rates are up to 89 percent, but there is great disparity in the quality of the education. Eighteen year olds were eligible for military service during World War II and thereafter, but eighteen, nineteen, and twenty-year olds did not receive the right to vote until 1971. Juvenile courts generally accept seventeen as the maximum age of individuals under their jurisdiction. The idea became fairly uniform among states by the late 1930s, but in recent years some states have reversed longstanding practices. Many states now try teens accused of murder as adults. At another level, more teens die in car accidents than from any other cause, but sixteen year olds may drive in all fifty states. Only recently have some reformers linked graduated drivers' licensing to protecting the lives of young Americans. Purchasing and consuming alcohol, however, is restricted to those twenty-one and over in the United States, but it is lower in most European countries. Eighteen-year-olds may buy cigarettes in all fifty states, but most adults who smoke admit they started at much younger ages. The U.S. Supreme Court upholds the right of states and the federal government to restrict access to birth control and abortion by females under age eighteen at the same time that the average age when girls start menstruating has declined to eleven. These are just a few examples of the contradictions concerning American adolescents imbedded in public policy. Perhaps keeping in mind that such policies and opinions are shaped by a combination of public attitudes, popular culture, economics, public policy, and biology will help Americans to make wiser decisions that influence the lives of young Americans.

The dramatic economic crisis of the 1930s established an atmosphere that established a strong foundation for extending adolescence as a distinct period of life that should be available to all young Americans. Inequities and unevenness remained, but by 1940 Americans shared the idea that during the teen years education outweighed all other responsibilities as preparation for adulthood. Respect for individual differences and the elimination of racial, ethnic, and gender stereotypes persisted. Still, calls by the American people for the federal government to do something to end the economic crisis of the 1930s resulted in new public policies that intentionally and sometimes unintentionally reshaped American adolescence for that decade and the balance of the twentieth century. Members of the generation that came of age during the 1930s expected a more level playing field for their own children.

References

American Youth Congress. 1936. The declaration of the rights of youth. July 4, 1936. From Robert Cohen, personal collection, reprinted on the New Deal Network, New York University. Available at http://newdeal.feri.org/students/age.htm; accessed April 20, 2007.

Cohen, Robert, ed. 2002. *Dear Mrs. Roosevelt: Letters from Children of the Great Depression*. Chapel Hill, NC: University of North Carolina Press.

Davis, Kingsley. 1935. *Youth in the Depression,* Chicago: University of Chicago Press.

Edwards, Duvall. 1992. *The Great Depression: A Teenager's Fight to Survive*. Gig Harbor, WA: Red Apple Publishing.

Minehan, Thomas. 1934. *Boy and Girl Tramps of America.* New York: Farrar and Rinehart.

Orser, W. Edward. 1937. Neither separate nor equal: Foreshadowing Brown in Baltimore County 1935–1942." *Maryland Historical Magazine* 92, Spring.

New York Times, March 21, 1937.

New York Times, March 24, 1937.

Uys, Errol Lincoln. *Riding the Rails: Teenagers on the Move during the Great Depression.* New York: Routledge, 2003.

Wellman, William, director. 1933. *Wild Boys of the Road* Warner Brothers.

"Make Do or Do Without": Women during the Great Depression

3

Jennifer Barker-Devine

Welcome to Hard Times

In 1933, the first year of Franklin Roosevelt's presidency and one of the worst years of the Great Depression, First Lady Eleanor Roosevelt found that the economic crisis affected all American women regardless of their age, income, or location. In that year alone, she received more than 300,000 letters from ordinary Americans, mostly women, who sought the First Lady's aid and advice, vented their frustrations, or expressed admiration for her strength. The letters indicated that for most American women, the Great Depression did not begin in October 1929, but rather it crept into their lives as they or their fathers or their husbands fell on hard times. Few women lost great fortunes or found themselves desperate and homeless, subsisting in Hoovervilles. Yet for nearly all women, life had become uncertain, and they had to find creative ways to cope with less.

In their letters to the First Lady, people wrote about the shame of unemployment and their reluctance to accept relief, or the loss of the family breadwinner to illness, death, or abandonment. They wrote of their inability to find work, or of jobs that simply did not pay enough. For many of those who wrote letters, time-honored family recipes, traditions, leisure activities, and material aspirations had suddenly become too expensive. Women who could not afford clothing asked Eleanor Roosevelt for her old garments. Others wanted work to fulfill their personal dreams. With good jobs scarce, many found it impossible to marry or start a family. If they cared for small children, or found themselves expecting a child, they worried that they could not afford to raise them. And they each asked Roosevelt to do *something*, ranging from personal favors to persuading her husband, the president, to pass new legislation.

In response, Eleanor Roosevelt reached out to the American public through newspaper and magazine articles, and through the radio. In 1933, she published a book, *It's Up to the Women*, in which she outlined the many ways women could cope with hard times. She urged women to become less dependent on material items for their happiness, to set up a family budget, to prepare modest, but nutritious meals, to pursue an education, become politically active, and most important, to strengthen community and family relationships. She believed American women were up to task and, citing women's important roles throughout history, she wrote, "The women know that life must go on and that the needs of life must be met and it is their courage and their determination which, time and again, have pulled us through worse crises that this one" (Roosevelt 1933, ix).

For the majority of American women, life during the Great Depression meant hard work, getting by with less, and living by the old adage, "use it up, wear it out, make it do, or do without" (Westin 1976). Most adult women during these years worked within the home as wives and mothers, caring for families and children, and making the most of a husband's limited income. More often than not, men retained their jobs but usually took a significant pay cut or a reduction in hours. Throughout the 1930s, more than half of American families subsisted on an annual income between $500 and $1,500. In 1935 and 1936, the median family income in the United States was $1,160 per year, well below the $2,500 considered necessary for a comfortable standard of living. The median income allowed families approximately $22 per week to pay for food, clothing, housing, and other necessities. Although most families did not live in dire poverty, many lived on the brink, in fear that one illness, accident, or catastrophe would spell the difference between making do and doing without.

Nonetheless, many women, both single and married, sought employment to support themselves and family members. Throughout the 1930s, women accounted for approximately one-quarter of the workforce and were usually employed in unskilled, low-wage occupations such as domestic service or clerical and retail work. They also continued to dominate the professions of nursing and teaching. Women found their options limited due to traditional notions of what was appropriate "women's work," and also because most Americans believed that jobs should first go to men supporting families. Working women often faced discrimination and false cultural stereotypes that portrayed women as dependents rather than breadwinners. A 1937 Gallup Poll revealed that 82 percent of Americans objected to women working outside of the home if their husbands were employed, and 67 percent supported a ban on hiring married women if their husbands earned an adequate salary (Ware 1982, 27).

Corporations, as well as state and federal laws, restricted the hours, locations, and occupations in which women could work. It was further reflected in their wages. In 1937, the Social Security Administration reported that women's average annual salary was just $525, compared with $1,027 for men. Yet the fact that women worked in traditionally female occupations actually may have saved them from unemployment, because men rarely demanded jobs that paid little, commanded no status, and could be demeaning to the men who took them. In other words, the Depression did not affect women's employment to the extent that it

Diana Morgan

The Depression hit women even harder than men, because for the most part, before the Crash, they had the less secure and remunerative situations. Diana Morgan, who grew up in a small North Carolina town, lived comfortably before the Depression. Her father was a cotton merchant and owned a general store. She was raised to think that she was better than others; her family had servants. Her elegant home was a century and a half old. In the early 1930s, she attended college.

When Diana came home for Christmas in her junior year, she realized that hard times had hit the family. Her father was ill; he was broke; he had to dismiss the servants. And he had to sell the family home for back taxes. When friends came to call, there was no ice for their water, for they had no electric refrigerator, and ice was not affordable. Finally, a family friend got Diana an appointment as a social worker with a local branch of a New Deal relief agency. When she first reported for work, she was appalled by the long lines of destitute people, mainly African American, but also white. She never forgot the shock of seeing impoverished people in desperate circumstances, anxious beyond description for a scrap of food and a clean, dry place in which to sleep, if not to live. Finally, with the relief program's end approaching, Diana moved to New York City to study at the New York School of Social Work, which led to a career and marriage, and a return home in a more secure professional and personal situation. In 1934, she and her husband moved to Washington, DC, where they lived until 1945. Diana never forgot her memories of the Depression—of poverty, of ostentation, of conspicuous consumption.

SOURCE: Studs Terkel, *Hard Times: An Oral History of the Great Depression* (New York: Pantheon Books, 1986), 153–58.

affected men's opportunities, and throughout the decade, women's participation in the labor force actually increased.

Women across the country coped with the economic crisis in a variety of ways, and for most women, this meant adapting how they ran households and cared for their families. Family, for better or for worse, played a central role in the lives of American women during the Great Depression. They experienced this era as wives, daughters, and sisters, as members of families struggling to "make do" in hard times. Personal circumstances and challenges depended on a woman's support network, her ethnicity and social class, where she lived, whether her father or husband was employed, whether she could even afford to marry or continue with her education, and how many children or siblings she had in her care. For every decision she made, a woman had to weigh the impact her personal desires would have on her family members.

In *It's Up to the Women*, Eleanor Roosevelt observed that the family was a "powerful force." She wrote, "Of course, the real advantage in having little money is that families draw closer together; they have to depend on each other and they have to do things for and with each other and the result is that the clan spirit grows" (Roosevelt 1933, 8). She encouraged women, as wives and as daughters, to keep family spirits high by finding enjoyment in simple pleasures, as well as inner strength. Roosevelt concluded, "If [women] can learn to make it a game to get the most out of their dollars and above all spend to spend their money for those things which they really want, then they will have real success" (Roosevelt 1933, 8).

As members of families, most women had to find, in the words of Eleanor Roosevelt, "endless little economies" to make ends meet (Roosevelt 1933, 8). By the 1930s, managing a household was vastly different than it had been just a generation before. More than half of American homes had electricity that powered such appliances as irons, toasters, washing machines, vacuum cleaners, and refrigerators. Furthermore, women could take advantage of new foods, like Jell-o™ and dry cereals, as well as canned soups, vegetables, and precooked meals like Heinz™ spaghetti. Whereas women formerly sewed clothing for all family members, by this period, ready-made clothing was widely available. Yet while these products and technologies made life easier in some ways, they were expensive and out of reach for many families.

Typical of a young wife's efforts to "make do" were those of Vivian Raymond Weston, who lived in Logan, Utah, with her husband. As Weston's husband worked his way through college as a night watchman, earning just $15 per month, she did odd jobs, such as picking potatoes. She also kept house in a small attic room they rented for $6 per month. They counted every nickel and dime, finding creative ways to get by. The couple could not afford a refrigerator, so Weston simply hung a washtub outside of the window during the winter where she stored meat, milk, and other perishable foods.

Economizing often meant skimming all extra expenses out of the family budget to pay for the necessities of food, clothing, and housing. What they could not buy, women had to make or trade. By the mid-1930s, the median family income in the United States was $1,160 per year, or about $22 per week. Certainly, many families lived on much less and, depending on the types of work available, some faced seasonal differences in income and could not depend on steady paychecks. As a family's income wavered, they sometimes canceled magazine and newspaper subscriptions, or they shared with neighbors. They terminated telephone services, limited their use of gas by cooking several dishes at once, and used the radio and electric lights for only a few hours in the evening. Women and families also sought out inexpensive ways to spend their leisure time. Church attendance went up, while board games and playing cards surged in popularity. Instead of going out to dances or dinner, families hosted simple parties in their own homes, or turned on the radio for music and entertainment. Families also saved money by moving to smaller homes or living together with extended family members. Rather than buying new items, women repaired shoes, relined old coats, and altered worn clothes.

Kathryn Haskell Perrigo, a farmwife from Boone County, Missouri, recalled how she sewed all of her children's clothing. "It's absolutely surprising the number of things a woman can do to manage," she said. "I made my boys pants out of old coats, and a ten-pound flour bag was a pair of training pants when they were babies" (Westin 1976, 51). This practice of using flour sacks to make children's clothing was actually common, and became so popular that many companies sold flour in sacks made from printed fabric. This appealed to women because they could make appealing, stylish clothes for their children without the expense of purchasing new materials.

Likewise, Fern Yowell, from Anthony, Kansas, joined a rural women's club called Community Helpers where she learned to reupholster old furniture using gunnysacks, the thick, rough material used for bagging seed and feed on the farm. She said, "We'd take them and bleach them until they were soft and just the most beautiful beige color. Sometimes we'd cross stitch them" (Westin 1976, 27). In 1935, members of the Community Helpers won first prize at the Kansas State Fair for their display of an entire living room upholstered and decorated with gunnysacks.

As consumers, seamstresses, and cooks, women were responsible for spending 80 percent of the family earnings and usually had to find creative means to stretch their budget. Mary Grace McKenna Monahan, a young wife from Pittsburg, recalled that rather than going to a salon, she and her friends would cut and style one another's hair. "It must have looked awful," she said. "But we used to put it up in coffee can curlers and think we looked like Joan Blondell," referring to a famous movie star of the era (Westin 1976, 273).

Federal guidelines recommended that families spend 33 percent of their income on housing, set aside 32 percent for clothing, transportation, education, recreation, and emergencies, and spend the remaining 35 percent on food. In urban areas and small towns, many women found it possible to feed a family of six on $5 per week. Stores sold milk at $0.10 a quart, bread at $0.07 a loaf, butter for $0.23 a pound, and two pounds of hamburger for $0.25. Yet this provided a limited diet, and women still struggled to make appetizing and nutritious meals with just a few staple items. The recipes handed down by their mothers and grandmothers called for too many expensive ingredients, such as meat, butter, sugar, lard, and cream, which proved impractical during hard times.

To save money on groceries, women purchased day-old bread and inexpensive cuts of meat, or they grew large gardens, canned their own produce, and baked their own bread. Erma Gage, a wife and mother of three, found a job near her home in a grocery store that allowed her to buy food at a discount. While she worked at the store, Gage could make "good" meat and cheese sandwiches for her children's lunches. Otherwise, her children ate "bean sandwiches," or mashed up beans spread over bread. Gage's family started a large garden in the backyard and grew a variety of vegetables, including pole beans, squash, tomatoes, and potatoes. Nonetheless, the family still found it necessary to economize and to sacrifice many of their favorite foods. Gage recalled, "We ate lots of macaroni and spaghetti and I could make three pounds of hamburger go a long way" (Westin 1976, 33).

Food, Glorious Food

Nutritionists and cooks at the General Mills' Betty Crocker Kitchens in Minneapolis, Minnesota received thousands of letters from women asking

Wife and son of a tenant farmer prepare a meal, Mississippi, 1931. Because of a drought, they've been given food by the Red Cross. Photo by Lewis Hine for the Works Progress Administration. (*Library of Congress*)

for recipes suitable for families on tight budgets. The staff at the Betty Crocker Kitchens complied, and drew up a number of wholesome menus that won the acclaim of nutritionists and social workers. Women across the country tuned into the *Betty Crocker Cooking Hour*, a popular weekly radio show, to get these recipes. These menus suggested that women use inexpensive meats, or find alternative protein sources such as skim milk, eggs, and beans. A typical daily menu for a family of six living on relief consisted of the following:

> Breakfast: Oatmeal, milk, bread, and molasses, milk for children, coffee for adults
> Lunch: Potato soup, crackers, scrambled eggs on toast, orange gelatin pudding, milk for children
> Dinner: Macaroni with cheese and tomatoes, onions and bacon strips, raw carrot strips, bread and peanut butter, prune pudding with sauce, milk for children. (Westin 1976, 42)

Because sugar and spices were usually at the bottom of the shopping list, dessert was often a luxury, although women also found it possible to make sweet treats with limited resources. Lois Farley, a young farm wife during the 1930s, could not afford much sugar to make desserts for her family. Instead, she baked "milk pudding." Farley said,

> I'd put a container of whole milk in the oven early in the morning. It was a good wood stove, so a small fire was kept burning all day. After twelve hours or so, it had formed the consistency of pudding and the milk sugar after this slow heating process had become very sweet. I'd take it out and grate a little lemon over it or sprinkle a little cinnamon on top. Delicious! (Westin 1976, 58)

Economizing and "making do" often proved easier for farm women than it did for those in urban areas. Even before the Depression, farm women generally enjoyed fewer conveniences than urban women, and they were more accustomed to having little cash for consumer goods. In 1930, only 34 percent of American farms had telephones and just 13 percent had electricity (though this climbed to 33 percent by 1940 due to the efforts of the Rural Electrification Administration). Indoor plumbing was an expensive luxury that the majority of farm families did not enjoy. During the 1930s, however, many farm women took pride in their homemaking skills because they could be more self-sufficient, escaping many of the hardships faced by urban women. They could also contribute to the family economy by working on the farm, and they did not have to worry about unstable jobs, cash wages, and uncertain hours. And although they worried about unstable crop and livestock prices, they generally did not need to worry about layoffs, unemployment, or lost wages.

Most farm women still grew large gardens and canned the produce as part of their regular work routine. Many women also had the benefit of living in the countryside, where wild game often took the place of expensive meats. Kathryn Haskell Perrigo, the farmwife from Boone County, Missouri, recalled that hunting became a favorite family activity during the Depression. "We just learned to eat squirrel, rabbit, wild ducks, fish, all those," Perrigo said. "We ate just whatever nature provided. There was really no point in sitting down and crying 'cause you didn't have any fresh meat, while there was wild meat out there running loose" (Westin 1976, 58).

Most important, farm women took charge of dairy operations and raised poultry. "Egg money," or the cash and credit women earned by selling eggs to local merchants, often made the difference between success and failure for many farm families during this era. Women took the eggs into town once or twice each week and sold them to the local grocer, who in turn gave women credit to purchase the materials they desired. Enterprising farm women also sold black walnuts, berries, and herbs gathered from their land, as well as seedlings for others to start gardens, or tomato, pimento, and celery plants. They relied on their unique skills to make braided rugs, quilts, baked goods, or clothing, which they sold at a small profit. Other farm women offered their cooking, baby sitting, or mending services to make extra money.

The seemingly small jobs of farm women actually had a tremendous impact on the family income. In the Midwest, women who sold eggs reported annual average earnings between $120 and $150 per flock. In 1935 and 1936, about one-quarter of American farm homes had an income of less than $500, and half had incomes of less than $1,000.

Women's egg money and profits from home-produced goods represented a sizable percentage of these family income figures and could amount to several hundred dollars in available cash for the household. Typically, farm families had little cash because any profits from crops and livestock went to pay off debts and farming expenses. Women's egg money and profits from home-produced goods often paid for clothing, children's education, items for the home, and home improvements. Many women also set their earnings aside and saved to purchase additional land, automobiles, or modern farming equipment to make their family's farm more profitable.

Difficult Choices

While all of these "endless little economies" affected how both rural and urban women cared for their families, the conditions of the Great Depression also resulted in a significant demographic shift that further illustrates how women's lives changed during this period. The national birth, marriage, and divorce rates all fell during the early part of the decade. During these bleak years, couples opted to have fewer children. In 1930, for the first time in American history, the national birth rate fell below replacement level, from 21.3 live births per 1,000 persons, to 18.4 per 1,000 in 1933. For many families, children were seen more as a burden than a blessing.

In January 1935, an expectant mother in Troy, New York, wrote a desperate letter to Eleanor Roosevelt. Because her husband was out of work, she could not afford to buy new baby clothes or pay the doctor's bills, and she would not accept public assistance. "It is very hard to face bearing a baby we cannot afford to have," she wrote. "And the fact that it is due to arrive soon, and still there is no money for the hospital or clothing, does not make it any easier ... somehow we must manage—but without charity." The mother enclosed a list of simple baby clothes and asked that the First Lady provide these items until the family could repay the loan. As collateral, the mother enclosed two rings of sentimental value. She concluded, "If you will get these [baby clothes] for me, I would rather no one knew about it. I promise to repay the cost of the layette as soon as possible" (McElvaine 1983, 63).

Another reason for the decline in the birth rate was the fact that fewer couples could afford to marry. In 1929, the marriage rate stood at 10.14 per 1,000 persons, but by 1932, it had fallen to 7.87 per 1,000. Couples without the means to marry postponed their marriages until prosperity returned, though quite often, postponements became permanent.

Ann Marie Low, a rancher's daughter in North Dakota, often wrote in her diary about her many dates but bleak prospects for marriage. In 1934, Low graduated from college and began working as a rural school teacher, sending most of her wages to her sister and brother who were still in college. She received numerous proposals from the men she dated, but always refused because she would lose her job if she married. In July

1936, she wrote, "One of the many things I'm fed up with is men who get ideas of getting married!" Then, six months later, following yet another proposal from a man she truly admired, she turned him down because he did not earn enough to support them both. She wrote, "And what in the billy-blue-blazes would we live on?" (Low 1984, 100, 150).

On the other hand, marriage was often a woman's only option if she could not support herself. In 1937, Ann Marie Low quit her teaching job when her ailing parents asked that she come home and help run the family's ranch. A year later, when her parents no longer needed her help, she was unable to find work as a teacher and finally accepted a marriage proposal from a long-time boyfriend. She wrote that with no job prospects and "with no money, I would be dependent on Dad for support in a purposeless life." Marriage seemed "the only future" (Low 1984, 182).

Most women were careful in their decisions to marry because they viewed marriage as a permanent decision. Divorce was expensive, and many unhappy couples who could not afford the legal fees, or the cost of supporting themselves and dependent children, remained together out of economic necessity. The national divorce rate fell from 1.66 per 1,000 in 1929 to 1.28 in 1932, although in some areas this was much more pronounced. With work hard to find, families found it easier to support themselves if they pooled their resources, even if they were living in a less-than-ideal family situation.

A common cause of marital discord was a husband's unemployment or underemployment. The effect of joblessness on men was a subject studied extensively by scholars and often commented on in the media. Sociologist Mirra Komarovsky, in her study of unemployed, blue-collar working men near New York City, found that men often became depressed when they were unable to find work. Ashamed that they could not secure a good job, men blamed themselves rather than economy. While some men actually took responsibility for household chores and childcare, unemployment led some men to become listless, irritable, and disconnected from their families; for others, unemployment led to alcoholism, physical and verbal abuse, or abandonment.

Ella Weesner recalled how her husband changed during the Depression and constantly worried about money. "All that worrying made him spiteful," she said.

> I remember he'd be listening to the radio and I'd call him for dinner, and he'd just ignore me. He'd hear me all right, and that's when we'd get into it. But I'd always give in. It seems I had to give in to keep peace. There weren't any divorces in my day. (Westin 1976, 77)

And like many Americans, Weenser's husband refused to accept relief or charity of any kind because he believed to do so would be a sign of personal failure (Westin 1976, 77).

Several of the couples in Komarovsky's study argued about how to spend money, how to spend leisure time, what types of food to buy, whether the husband should drink alcohol, how to spend money on the children, who should perform housework, whether the husband should continue to look for work, and most important, whether the wife should seek paid employment. One unemployed husband believed so strongly that women should not work, he said, "I would rather turn on the gas and put an end to the whole family than let my wife support me" (Komarovsky 1940, 76).

Work Outside the Home for Pay

This reaction, however, was extreme. Most men, even if they were unhappy about the decision, recognized that their wives needed to work for the family to make ends meet. During the 1930s, it was economic necessity rather than personal and professional aspirations that compelled most women to find employment. By 1930, approximately 11 million women—or 24 percent of adult women in the United States—were employed, and about 90 percent of these women worked in only a few occupations: domestic service, nursing, teaching, clerical work, and retail work. These figures were much different for African American women, 40 percent of whom worked outside the home for wages. And of these, nine out of ten worked in either domestic service or agriculture. In general, women's jobs commanded little status, did not usually offer opportunities for advancement, and did not pay adequate wages.

Women clerics transfer information on punch card machines at the U.S. Census Bureau in Washington, D.C., circa 1939. (*Library of Congress*)

African American woman ironing, 1933. Photograph by Doris Ulmann. (*Library of Congress*)

Domestic and personal servants, or 30 percent of all working women in 1930, felt the effects of the Depression most severely. Every week, on average, these women worked fifty to seventy hours or more, earned just $5 or $6, and they did not enjoy protections under the New Deal that guaranteed minimum wages, unemployment benefits, and union protection. Typically, domestic service jobs went to immigrant and monitory women who had been barred from other occupations on the basis of race. Quite often, working in private homes was the only option. For example, 60 percent of African American women who worked held domestic service positions. Wages were not regulated and varied by family, city, and region. Most striking was the regional difference between the North and South. In 1932, a domestic servant in Philadelphia could earn between $5 and $12 per week, whereas a survey of domestic servants in Mississippi revealed an average wage of just $2 per week.

Throughout the decade, domestic servants found it increasingly difficult to find work because families that formerly hired servants and domestic help could no long afford their services. Some families even fired their current help to hire someone else willing to work for less. Furthermore, homemakers who now had vacuum cleaners, electric refrigerators, and washing machines, as well as irons, stoves, and other conveniences, found domestic help unnecessary. Like many other jobs, the number of available positions for domestic servants dwindled.

Yet the decline of domestic service jobs was actually indicative of a changing workforce and the new demands of a modern society. During the Great Depression, the identity of the typical worker changed tremendously. At the turn of the century, most female workers were young, under twenty-five, unmarried, and either ethnic minorities, immigrants, or the daughters of immigrants. By the 1930s, however, more married and educated women sought work, and they found a variety of new opportunities open to them. The expanding municipal agencies, as well as state and federal bureaucracies, required a large clerical staff, while the programs of the New Deal needed administrators and social workers. This decade also saw the expansion of hospitals and the growth of the nursing profession. The number of professionally trained nurses increased from 228,737 in 1930 to 362,897 in 1940.

Still, working women faced considerable discrimination. By the 1930s, Americans accepted the idea of unmarried women pursuing careers, but most were not entirely convinced that married women should work. A 1936 poll in *Fortune* magazine asked the question, "Do you believe that married women should have a full-time job outside the home?" Only 15 percent of respondents approved, 48 percent disapproved, and 37 percent gave conditional approval. In general, Americans objected to married women working because they simply believed women should care for their homes and families first, especially if they had children. Others believed that working women took good jobs that should otherwise go to men. Though several laws and corporate policies had banned or limited married women from working for decades, the conditions of the Great Depression accentuated the demand for greater regulation.

In 1932, for example, Section 213 of Herbert Hoover's National Economy Act prohibited more than one family member from holding a civil service job. Though this act did nothing to alleviate unemployment, many women who earned less than their husbands were forced to give up their jobs. Many companies followed suit, and in 1931 the New England Telephone and Telegraph Company, the Northern Pacific Railway, and the Norfolk and Western Railway fired their married female employees. By 1939, a survey by the National Industrial Conference Board revealed that 84 percent of insurance companies, 65 percent of banks, and 63 percent of public utilities restricted the hiring of married women—although, again, such policies did little to help male jobseekers. For example, when King County, Washington, officials voted to ban married women from local government jobs, they created only fifty vacancies. This was of little help to the 83,000 unemployed persons in King County alone.

Women teachers, in particular, found their jobs threatened by discriminatory policies. Married women had long been barred from holding teaching positions, and it was not unusual that a 1930 National Education Association survey found that 77 percent of school districts did not hire married women, and 63 percent of districts dismissed women if they married.

During the Depression, however, these rules became even more stringent. As many school districts faced budget cuts, they dismissed teachers, and between 1930 and 1940, the number of women teachers fell from 853,976 to 802,264. This was not entirely due to discriminatory policies however. Many schools required teachers to meet higher educational standards, which usually meant holding a college degree. Unable to afford a college education, many women were then unable to attain teaching positions.

In 1930, when Elizabeth Baker's husband died, the rural Virginia homemaker was left with three young children. In 1931, she moved with her children to Newark, New Jersey, where she hoped to find work as a school teacher. Before she married at age twenty-seven, she had attended college for a few semesters and taught in several rural schools. Baker moved in with relatives and planned to stay only until she could afford a home of her own. When she sought work, however, school administrators told her she was not qualified to teach in the large city schools, and even if she was, school boards could not afford to hire new teachers. Baker eventually gave up the idea of teaching, but still could not find work. She sought positions in department stores, factories, and offices, but did not find a steady job for more than two years. Only then was she hired at a commercial laundry establishment for a mere $11 per week (Baker 1982, 98).

Though Baker was not happy with her job, and she continued to aspire to a better life, she did not question whether she should continue working at the laundry. Her job, no matter how difficult, was essential to her family. In dire economic times, most working women felt fortunate to have steady work and did not challenge poor working conditions or questionable treatment at the hands of superiors. Margaret O'Donnell Paladino, who worked at a variety of clerical jobs, said,

> As bad as some of them were, we hung on to our little jobs like they were life rafts. I did not spout obscenities at the boss or go on strike. I did everything possible to keep the axe from falling … anything to keep the paycheck coming. (Westin 1976, 211)

Still, many women who desired better working conditions found strength in unions. The 1935 National Labor Relations Act, also known as the Wagner Act, strengthened labor unions across the nation. Eleanor Roosevelt strongly advocated the organization of working women to attain safer working conditions, fair wages, and better benefits. In *It's Up to the Women,* Roosevelt dedicated an entire chapter to women and the National Recovery Act. She encouraged women, even homemakers, to support fair industrial practices and buy goods only from companies in compliance with the law, because this would guarantee good wages and quality consumer products. Furthermore, even if women did not hold jobs, they should be willing to speak out on behalf of workers and actively urge companies to adopt fair policies.

Hadassah

On October 29, 1939, just one month after the Nazi defeat of Poland, Mrs. Tamar de Sola Pool was unanimously elected president of Hadassah, the national Zionist women's organization, in New York City. Born in Jerusalem in 1898, she came to America when she was six and became an academic star at Hunter College, the University of Paris, and Columbia University, In 1917, she married the prominent rabbi David de Sola Pool and threw herself into political causes, including Zionism. In the 1930s, she involved herself deeply in Zionist activities. Especially alarmed by the rise of National Socialism in Germany, she firmly believed that only a Jewish homeland in Palestine would save world Jewry. In the early 1930s, she served as the president of the New York chapter of Hadassah. She was constantly involved in its activities, not merely as a leader or spokeswoman, but also as a foot-soldier at its various functions and campaigns.

At Hadassah's 1939 national meeting in late October, four thousand delegates attended, half from the New York state chapter, and half state delegates from other parts of the country. This national meeting's purposes were to deal with the crisis of Jewish persecution in Europe and Palestine, and to promote American democracy. Important dignitaries, including President Franklin Delano Roosevelt, New York governor Herbert Lehman, and New York City mayor Fiorello LaGuardia, praised their work. Dr. Solomon Goldman, president of the Zionist Organization of America, offered a bleak analysis of the Jewish situation in Palestine and in Europe. American Jews had to speak up in the capitals of London, Paris, and Washington on behalf of world Jewry and to promote American democracy at home. The Polish tragedy, he continued, had made the Palestinian question ever more important. As Hadassah's president, Mrs. Pool vigorously pledged the organization to carry out these goals. Mrs. Pool served as national president of Hadassah until 1943, when she retired from active service with the organization, but not with Jewish affairs.

SOURCE: *New York Times*, October 25, 30, 1939, June 2, 1981.

New Deal legislation and the sentiments of Roosevelt provided encouragement to organizations such as the Women's Trade Union League (WTUL). Founded 1903, the WTUL brought together women in industrial and nonindustrial occupations, and it sought benefits including better working conditions, competitive wages, and shorter working hours. Its membership increased from approximately 250,000 in 1929 to 800,000 in 1939. Likewise, the International Ladies Garment Workers Union (ILGWU) experienced a surge in membership. In 1933, citing debt and economic hardship, membership had dwindled to just 40,000 members, down from 105,000 members in 1920. Two years later in 1935, however, following the passage of the National Industrial Recovery Act that allowed for collective bargaining, the ILGWU organized a membership drive in sixty cities and signed up 200,000 members.

Organized labor offered many women an opportunity to take on leadership positions and become activists. Rose Pesotta was a Russian Jewish immigrant who arrived in the United States in 1912 and found work in the garment industry. Over time, she became interested in union activities and, in 1933, was fired from her job in a Los Angels garment factory as a result of her efforts at organizing the workers. Not discouraged, she began organizing women in cities around the country, including San Francisco, Boston, and Seattle. She served three full terms as the vice president of the general executive board of the ILGWU, becoming the first woman to do so.

Dorothy Bellanca immigrated from Latvia in 1900 and worked in the garment industry. By 1914, she also had become interested in trade unions and organizing workers, particularly women who worked making men's clothing. During the 1930s, she was active with the Amalgamated Clothing Workers of America (ACWA), and between 1932 and 1934, she organized 30,000 shirt workers in the northeast. Bellanca worked closely with the National Consumers' League and the WTUL to ensure that industries met the standards established by the National Recovery Act. In 1934, like Pesotta, she, too, became the first woman vice president on the executive board of the ACWA.

Though these women acted nationally, unions offered similar opportunities at the community level as well. During the 1930s, Kate Pemberton worked in a Westinghouse lamp plant in Fairmont, West Virginia, where she joined the United Electrical Workers, under the Congress of Industrial Organizations (CIO). Though her employers discouraged unions, she and her fellow workers had heard that women working in other plants earned $1 per hour while they made just $0.40. Pemberton considered this unfair and found unionization to be the answer. Within a short time, women were elected to leadership positions within the union, and Pemberton became the business agent, or chief negotiator, at the plant. This was extremely unusual for a woman, however, and local newspapers and radio stations reported Pemberton's election. She recalled, "I was considered aggressive by some of the other women. But it seemed natural to me ... There was a change in the late thirties, especially among union women. We started considering ourselves capable of exerting authority" (Westin 1976, 204).

Even domestic servants, whose occupation was notoriously difficult to organize, attempted to form labor unions to set standard working conditions and wages. Because domestic servants tended to negotiate individual contracts according to regional circumstances, women organized only locally. Some formed small groups to demand certain wages or conditions within a neighborhood. These informal efforts did not go unrecognized, and many employers were compelled to honor demands if they wished to retain their servants. Even the First Lady encouraged women to use fair employment practices when hiring domestic servants. In 1933, Eleanor Roosevelt wrote about a friend who allowed her maid to work for only eight hours each day because she wanted her maid to be happy and to provide good service, rather than coming to work tired and worn out.

A few labor unions for domestic servants did materialize often with the support of the Young Women's Christian Association, the Urban League, the National Consumer's League, and other labor organizations. In 1934, for example, African American and white women formed the New York Domestic Workers Union, and urged domestic servants to abandon long working hours in favor of two five-hour shifts, six days per week. They also insisted upon "no window washing." Though the New York Domestic Workers Union had the support of the Building Service Union Local 149, a subsidiary of the American Federation of Labor, they struggled to find financial resources and to build membership. By 1938, there were only 1,000 members out of a potential 100,000 domestic servants working in the city.

Whether they joined unions or simply accepted their working conditions, women did what they could to retain their jobs because, if they became unemployed, they did not necessarily enjoy the benefits of New Deal programs. Approximately 2 million women lost their jobs and sought relief during the Depression, and compared to the programs offered for men, women found their options limited. Administrators for federal and state relief programs assumed that women had husbands or fathers to support them. Any woman seeking assistance had to prove that she was the head of household and provided sole support for her family. A married woman could not apply for relief on her own, and she did not qualify if her husband was ill or injured and unable to find work, if he refused to apply for relief or federal work programs, or if he was simply unwilling to work. Even if a woman's husband applied for relief, she did not necessarily enjoy access to that money he earned. In 1935, one frustrated wife from Nashville, Tennessee, whose husband worked for the Works Progress Administration (WPA), wrote to Franklin Roosevelt and asked him to have WPA wages mailed directly to the family. When he picked up his wages, her husband spent most of the money on whiskey before she had an opportunity to buy food and necessities for their children (McElvaine 1983, 127).

Part of the problem was that many of the federal work programs provided heavy construction jobs considered unsuitable for women. The Civilian Conservation Corps (CCC), for example, was a New Deal program that employed 2.5 million young men to work on reforestation and soil conservation projects. When critics asked for a similar program for women, the government sponsored only a short-lived, limited program that enrolled just 8,000 women. Hilda Worthington Smith, the director of the women's camps, complained while the CCC camps operated on large budgets and provided men with education, work, and travel opportunities, she could not provide similar experiences for the women. The program lasted only a short time before it was suddenly ended in 1937.

The WPA was perhaps the most popular New Deal program. Between 1935 and 1943, it provided nearly 8 million Americans with jobs, primarily in the construction of roads, federal buildings, parks, and other public works. At its peak in 1938, 3.3 million Americans held WPA jobs, but only 405,700 of these went to women, and women never made up more than 18 percent of all WPA workers. Under the WPA many women were employed to do research and clerical work, or to establish programs at libraries and community centers. They started programs in nutrition, health, recreation, and canning to teach other families in the community how to survive with less.

Many women also benefited from cultural WPA projects, known as Federal One, which hired writers, actors, photographers, musicians, and artists. Those who participated in these programs established community

Works Progress Administration artist painting a mural, circa 1933–1941. (*Library of Congress*)

theaters and held classes, or put on performances and exhibits. They created works of art for government buildings, collected oral histories, and wrote state-by-state travel guides. Women played a key role in administering these projects, including Ellen Sullivan Woodward and Florence Kerr, who oversaw Federal One, and Hallie Flanagan who headed the Federal Theater Project. Famous participants in Federal One included poet and playwright May Swenson, as well as author Zora Neale Hurston. Several women artists also benefited from the programs, including sculptor Louise Nevelson and Lee Krassner. The WPA provided many young artists and writers with unprecedented opportunities, and it often gave women a chance to display their work alongside that of male artists.

Jean Gates Hall, an artist from Hollywood, California, worked as an inker for more than two years at Walt Disney's studio when she realized the impossibility of advancing her career simply because the studios did not promote women. In 1938, however, Hall applied to the Federal Art Project and became an easel artist. She received $80 per month, enjoyed the freedom of painting any subject she wished, and described it as "the most wonderful year of my life." Her paintings were displayed in public buildings, and she was even able to create enough pieces for her own art show at the Paul Edder Gallery in San Francisco. She had the opportunity to send her work to the Corcoran Art Gallery in Washington, D.C., where two of her paintings sold for $35 apiece. Hall remembered, "That was big money and a feather in my cap. I thought I was really on my way'' (Westin 1976, 124).

Despite their popularity, opportunities for women to participate in community and cultural projects were limited to the women who had the skills to carry out the programs. Even by the 1930s, most American women did not have the appropriate education or job training to carry out community projects, and they demanded jobs suitable to their skills and experiences. As a result, more than half of all women who worked for the WPA worked in sewing rooms. One WPA official equated these sewing rooms with the public works projects for men when she said, ''For unskilled men we have the shovel, for unskilled women we have only the needle'' (Ware 1982, 40). The women who worked in sewing rooms repaired old garments or sewed new clothing items from surplus materials, which were then given out to needy families (Ware 1982, 40).

Vera Bosanko, a wife and mother in Texas, sought a WPA job following the sudden death of her husband. Even though she raised her own garden and did laundry for others, it was not enough to make ends meet. When she first started working for the WPA, Bosanko canned vegetables, then found a better WPA job in a high school library. Her WPA jobs paid more than doing laundry, but she still found life to be very uncertain.

She said,

> [The job at the library] paid forty-two dollars a month. But about every few months they'd come in and say they just didn't have no more money for this project. I'd go home, and there'd come a telegram in the evening mail telling me to go back to work the next day 'cause they got a bit more money. That went on for about six years. Well, it was kind of scary. I never knowed where the job was going [*sic*]. (Westin 1976, 206)

Still, for many of those women whose husbands found work with the WPA, his additional earnings often made a significant addition to the family budget and helped them weather hard times. During the 1930s, women, like men, were often hesitant to rely on relief and programs like the WPA. Most families expected relief and WPA jobs to be temporary, and they hoped for better days ahead.

Days of Hope, Years of Sacrifice

The Great Depression was the most severe, prolonged economic crisis in American history. It displaced thousands of families, created hardships for millions of people, shaped an entire generation, and reshaped the way Americans viewed the role of their government. For American women, the 1930s was a decade characterized by uncertainty. Elsa Ponselle, an elementary school principal in Chicago, typified women's experiences when she said, ''The Depression was a way of life for me, from the time I was twenty to the time I was thirty. I thought it was going to be forever and ever and ever. That people would always live in fear of losing their jobs. You know, *fear*'' (Terkel 1970, 390).

On the other hand, Ponselle recalled those years as "a lot of fun," because she and other educators had to find easy, inexpensive solutions to their problems. Ponselle pointed out that few people actually felt depraved or poor because few families had money. Everyone knew what it meant to "make do or do without" (Terkel 1970, 390).

In 1933, when Eleanor Roosevelt encouraged American women to face the Great Depression head on in *It's Up to the Women*, she expressed confidence that women would find creative solutions to the economic crisis. And quite often, they did. Women "made do" in their own homes by economizing, finding new ways to prepare meals, and sacrificing luxuries. They found ways to support their families by working in the home, or going to work for wages. Erma Gage, the wife and mother who bought food at a discount by working at a grocery store, who grew a large garden, and who fed her family inexpensive and filling pasta dishes, agreed with Eleanor Roosevelt that women were resourceful and able in the face of adversity. Gage said, "I did what I had to do. I seemed to always find a way to make things work. I think hard times is harder on a man, 'cause a woman will do something. Women just seem to know where they can save or where they can help" (Westin 1976, 27).

References

Baker, Russell. 1982. *Growing Up*. New York: Signet Publishing.

Komarovsky, Mirra. 1940. *The Unemployed Man and His Family: The Effect of Unemployment Upon the Status of the Man in Fifty-nine Families*. New York: The Dryden Press.

Low, Ann Marie. 1984. *Dust Bowl Diary*. Lincoln: The University of Nebraska Press.

McElvaine, Robert S., ed. 1983. *Down and Out In the Great Depression. Letters from the "Forgotten Man."* Chapel Hill: The University of North Carolina Press.

Roosevelt, Eleanor. 1933. *It's Up to the Women*. New York: Frederick Stokes and Company.

Terkel, Studs. 1970. *Hard Times: An Oral History of the Great Depression*. New York: Pantheon Books.

Ware, Susan. 1982. *Holding Their Own: American Women in the 1930s*. Boston: Twayne Publishers.

Westin, Jean Eddy. 1976. *Making Do: How Women Survived the '30s*. Chicago: Follett Publishing.

Medicine and the Family in the 1930s

4

Philip L. Frana

Rx for an Ailing Nation

America was already deep into the Great Depression when Herbert Hoover relinquished the presidency in March 1933. As he exited office Hoover famously despaired, "We are at the end of our rope." The country was in shambles. The banking industry lay in ruins. Stockholders rendered suddenly penniless. Working men and women cut loose by factories that could no longer sell the goods they produced. Shiftless children and the elderly left without proper food, clothing, and health care. British economist Lionel Robbins in his book titled *The Great Depression* (1934) captured perfectly the mood of the public. The worries and anxieties of a world disrupted in turn by World War I, the Red Scare, gangster glamour, rebellious youth, and a racially motivated migrant and immigrant backlash had traumatized ordinary people. "We live," Robbins explained, "not in the fourth, but in the nineteenth year of the world crisis" (Robbins 1934, 1).

Hoover's successor, Franklin D. Roosevelt, reshuffled the priorities of government to provide a safety net for those wiped out by the crash and its aftermath and encouraged citizens to work together to restart the American economy. President Roosevelt also toiled to revive their foul spirits: "When you get to the end of your rope, tie a knot and hang on." It wasn't easy. Breadwinners, who lost sleep over dwindling finances, became bad-tempered and destroyed their happy homes. Consumer installment plans, which encouraged buyers to enjoy luxuries like cars, record players, and washing machines while continuing to make payments over long periods of time became the subject of gallows humor. Americans joked about the fleeting fortunes of the credit officer who, when asked about his frame of mind midway through a jump off the new Chrysler Building, replied, "All right, so far."

The Depression challenged both the mental and physical health of Americans. Stressed salesmen developed stomach spasms and perforated guts. Men without prospects despaired of ever walking down the aisle and sometimes committed suicide. Newly divorced couples became demoralized and suffered nervous breakdowns. Many people experienced sustained tension headaches or drowned their sorrows in alcohol. Others became prone to bad habits like leaving children home alone for prolonged periods of time.

Married women, especially those without access to health care, feared accidental pregnancies. "Nobody wanted Jimmy, but he was born anyhow," read one caption on fliers distributed on the streets of Cincinnati by the Committee on Maternal Health. Jimmy lived only four months before surrendering to pneumonia (Bromley 1934). Half the women on contraceptives in the city had indicated their desire for birth control after explaining with sick worry that their husbands were unemployed. The economic crisis gave pause to many physicians reluctant on moral grounds to dispense such service. "Doc," a young father told Kansan Arthur Hertzler, "I would not take a million dollars for this baby, but I would not give fifty cents for another. Three is all we can afford." Hertzler was moved to agree: "It is easier to hoe corn when there are only three stalks than when there are a dozen and one avoids the nubbins" (Hertzler 1940, 149). Medical students began to study contraceptives in medical school classes for the first time ever, wives attended public lectures on the subject, and librarians stocked their shelves with texts offering birth control advice.

Desperate people resort to desperate acts: An ailing Polish American father, Mr. Slenski, leaves his family one last time in a frantic hunt for employment. He collapses in the street and is taken to a local hospital where he dies. It is soon discovered that his undiagnosed ulcers have ruptured. His widow now lives in a state of grief, and the children are thrust into the role of providers. Elsewhere, little boys and girls raise money for their families by selling their bodies to strangers. They become obsessed with the pursuit of material comforts: first candy and comics and then cigarettes and seductive clothing. Later they develop the characteristic chancres of syphilis.

Desperation led others to scapegoat the supposedly disreputable: ethnic minorities, flappers, the intemperate, and even the sick. Social conformity promoted both escapism and ostracism, which helps to explain the appeal of Superman, the era's improbably invulnerable comic book hero.

Blind fear became the primary emotion of the Depression. Fear of loss of financial security. Fear of loss of health. Fear of hunger and want. Fear of failure. Americans forced onto the relief rolls and into the soup kitchens brooded about debts, unsustainable obligations to family members, and scarce coal. They wept uncontrollably in front of bankers and social workers, but disguised their worries at home by pacing the floors at night.

Some of these fears were excessive. Healthy people became hypochondriacs with real symptoms of imaginary illnesses. One man had spots on his body that burned like molten copper. Another traveled from clinic to clinic complaining of invisible cancerous lesions. A third mentally ill man rejected the care of a physician, declaring that there was "nothing the matter that money wouldn't cure'' (Cavan and Renck 1938, 61). Overwrought mothers developed cases of hysterics marked by high blood pressure or too much giggling.

The high-strung, incorrigible ''nervous child'' became the era's classic syndrome. Jittery, maladjusted kids exploded into view as they dodged both authorities and automobiles on the streets, alleyways, and country roads of America. Malnutrition produced neurosis, the doctors claimed, but so did preoccupation with want. Almost any child, even the exceptional one, could be a nervous child. One child might be too easily frightened by loud noises. Another, when disciplined, might go into convulsions. They showed evidence for nervousness in twitches, facial tics, and poor posture. Placid, even-tempered children were seemingly in very short supply. Some nervous children, it was feared, could never be cured because they inherited their temperament from one or both of their parents. Most, however, could be helped by a change in diet, lifestyle, or surroundings.

The home visit terrified nervous children. The physician's traveling black bag contained, for them, infernal instruments of torture: stethoscope, blood pressure cuff, hypodermic needles, stinging antiseptics, scissors and scalpels, otoscope and ophthalmoscope, tongue depressors, and rectal thermometer. Trust was only grudgingly given to doctors who consoled their young charges in a style and purpose similar to Roosevelt's fireside chats. Physicians calmed fears by developing elaborate allegorical health tales about enemy lands occupied by coffee rivers, fly farms, and the shoals of too much supper. Some stories they told were misleading, like the tale of the pup whose growth depended less on the quality of food provided than on the bone structure of mama and papa dog.

Fear also directly infected the spirit of the physician, who was often a social leader in the community. Dr. Victor Marshall, who served as the director of a community bank in Appleton, Wisconsin, recalled how his anxiety grew as neighbors clasping deposit books paused in the street between his clinic and the depository (Marshall 1945, 192–195):

> There were housewives with coats slung hurriedly over print house dresses; there were old ladies in rusty black and high button shoes, relics of another and a happier era. There were farmers, bronze faces drawn with worry. I knew then that a bank failure means far more than a big institution closing its heavy doors. It means dozens of little failures, insignificant in themselves as seen from the outside; but, seen through the eyes of all those worried little people, those failures were tragedies. Money for an education of young Tom, who was so bright in high school and wanted to study law; money which meant secure old age and bright last years for old, lonely people.

Physicians feared most the diseases that inevitably attended populations weakened by hunger and neglect. The United Public Health Service (USPHS) confirmed these fears by demonstrating that the families with the greatest loss in income incurred the largest increases in Depression-era sickness. Industrial communities suffered disabling sickness rates up

50 percent over their more fortunate neighbors, and families without a primary wage earner saw rates climb two-thirds higher.

Patients postponed treatments, artificially depressing the clinic sick rolls, but increasing the seriousness of abdominal, heart, and hernia conditions. In Muncie, Indiana, people arrived at the hospital in lesser numbers, but vastly sicker. Out in Ropesville, Texas, doctors treating other illnesses detected decayed teeth in 70 percent of the adults, and malnutrition and rickets in 5–10 percent of the children. In the New York City neighborhood of Harlem, men and women vied with cats and dogs for fresh garbage. In St. Louis, people searched the city dump for table scraps. In Oklahoma, siblings were encouraged to eat on alternate days.

The human cost was incalculable. Ella May Wiggins, a loom tender in her twenties, recalled standing by helplessly as four of her five children succumbed to whooping cough because she had no safety net. "I asked the super to put me on day shift so's I could tend them, but he wouldn't," said Wiggins. "I don't know why. So I had to quit my job and then there wasn't any money for medicine, so they just died. I never could do anything for my children, not even to keep 'em alive, it seems" (Watkins 2000, 193).

Three Horses of the Apocalypse

The three emblematic diseases of these years of worriment and crisis were pulmonary tuberculosis, lobar pneumonia, and syphilis. All were considered enemies of the family unit. Tuberculosis alone represented a staggering economic loss to the country. So contagious was the disease that the afflicted were often removed to remote sanatoria. Understanding of the household or familial aggregation of tuberculosis helped physicians keep bacterial transmission rates below the threshold level necessary for its continued propagation in the community.

Physicians blamed the home environment and mode of living, complicated by industrial work, for the rapid spread of tuberculosis. Experts recommended careful temperature, dust, and humidity control at home and in the workplace. René Laennec, the early nineteenth-century inventor of the stethoscope, considered melancholy a predisposing factor in the disease and so it became known again in the 1930s. Though pulmonary tuberculosis could be diagnosed by X-ray examination, sputum study, and skin-reacting tuberculin testing, there was no cure before the discovery of antibiotic streptomycin in 1943.

Physicians also suspected that familial relationships, industrial work, and unhygienic home conditions somehow contributed to the spread of lobar pneumonia. The disease was prevalent on the Great Plains, where it was commonly referred to as "dust pneumonia," but the disease appeared to strike randomly. Today we know that nearly everyone is a carrier of one of four strains of pneumococcus—described as Type I, II, III, or IV—at some point in a typical year, but disease usually appears only after close contact with other infected people. Physicians puzzled over the disease's pathophysiology and epidemiology in the 1930s. "How does it happen that

Children of Oklahoma drought refugees on a highway near Bakersfield, California. Family of six; no shelter, no food, no money, and almost no gasoline. The child has bone tuberculosis, June 1935. (*Library of Congress*)

one particular person in a group develops pneumonia,'' asked Cornell physician Wilson Smilie, ''whereas the other members of his own family, of his own school class, of his own working group, or his immediate friends, remain well?'' (Smilie 1940, 79–88).

Common early symptoms of lobar pneumonia included chills and a high fever, coughing spells, rapid or difficult breathing, chest pain, and sometimes vomiting. Immunizing sera produced from horses exposed to killed cultures of pneumococci was helpful in treating Types I and II disease, but most often patients lay prostrate in bed for one or two weeks, at which point they either died or experienced the *crisis.* In the *crisis,* the patients' temperature rose to 106 degrees Fahrenheit, and then suddenly fell to normal. A full recovery from secondary complications like inflammation in the chest cavity or ear infection could take months.

Pneumonia became the subject of very public control programs. Surgeon General Thomas Parran made pneumonia a national priority in 1937, and directed the states to establish comprehensive pneumonia surveillance programs. In December of that year character actor Gilbert Emery starred

Sunday, January 19, 1930, was the coldest day of New York City's winter so far, a mere 10° above, and 14° below the average low for that day. Two vulnerable people perished, victims of the cold. John Armour, 44 years old, died, from exposure that night. Patrolman John Delehanty, who knew Armour on his beat, discovered him huddled in a doorway, curled up in a ball. Patrolman Delehanty knew that Armour usually walked with a cane and a crutch. He tried to awaken him, but he was dead. And a neighbor discovered Mrs. Agnes Sharkey, 70 years old, dead in her unheated apartment on that Sunday afternoon. Her son told authorities that his mother seemed fine Saturday night. Apparently, the coal stove had gone out before morning. Death resulted from exposure.

What to do about the poor and homeless in the Depression? The situation in New York City was, according to Urbain Ledoux, manager of an institution for the city's down-and-out, the worst it had been at any time since 1921. Supplies for the poor at "Mr. Zero's" establishment, known as "The Tub", were totally gone. This was because of a

in the short film *A New Day* as Dr. Mason, son of a mother stricken with pneumonia Type I. More than 17 million people saw the film, in which Mason saves his patient with serum. Lobar pneumonia became a much less threatening community concern after the 1939 introduction of sulfapyridine, an antipneumococcal sulfa drug, and the discovery of penicillin during World War II.

The third enemy of the family was syphilis, which could be acquired in the womb or from sexual activity. Sexually transmitted diseases provided evidence of the breakdown of moral habits attending the Depression crisis. Prostitution increased in 41 major American cities between 1928 and 1933, and the rate of illegitimate births rose some 20 percent. Venereal disease clinics throughout the 1930s were awash in patients seeking treatment for open lesions and chancres on the skin or in body cavities like the nose, throat, mouth, urethra, vagina, and rectum. Half a million Americans sought treatment in 1936 alone, while an estimated half million incautiously avoided treatment altogether. Within two years, the total number of clinic treatments rose an additional 40 percent. Rapid spread of the disease in the Depression prompted the passage of the LaFollette-Bulwinkle Act in 1938, which authorized grants-in-aid for venereal disease control. Physicians treated the drug with oxophenarsine and dichlorophenarsine, two organic arsenical compounds, and later with penicillin.

Despite the wages of death rooted in these diseases, the *overall* health of the population actually may have improved in the 1930s. USPHS statisticians reported that infant and maternal mortality, the total death rate, and tuberculosis mortality all declined over the decade. Health improved most in New England and the Midwest, and least in the South. Historian David Kyvig explains this anomaly as arising from the growing accessibility of citrus fruit, green vegetables, and milk and cheese from self-service groceries. Consumption of oranges alone soared 1,000 percent between 1918 and 1935. Middle-class Americans may also have benefited from near-riot that had developed the previous night when "Mr. Zero" began distributing a second pair of socks to any and all who wanted them as protection against the cold. Conditions were hardly more cheerful at other institutions for the homeless and the poor. Thus, the Municipal Lodging House accommodated 1,138 "guests," including fifteen women and four children; attendance was only slightly above the average for a bitter winter weekend. The Salvation Army hotel had 225 of its 250 beds occupied. Its neighbor, the Bowery Rescue Mission, four doors away, provided beds for 450 men and fed 1,000 persons.

Obviously, winter brought its share of woes to the poor and the homeless even relatively early in the Depression, just four months after the Stock Market Crash of October, 1929. And clearly, there were important implications for public health for city residents as the Depression worsened.

SOURCE: *New York Times*, January 20, 1930.

"Depression dieting" and smaller helpings of meat, both food-conserving and unintentionally health-promoting strategies. New attention to prevention and progress in public diphtheria immunization campaigns also may have had an effect on overall health.

Marginalized populations in dependent roles—rural and urban women and children, for example, as well as racial and ethnic minorities—suffered most in the health emergency of the Depression. In Mississippi, 500 white citizens died before they could be seen by a physician in 1937, compared with 3,000 African Americans. Hospital space was also scarce. New York's Harlem Hospital had an official bed capacity of 325 in the mid-1930s, but it regularly housed 400. Cots were laid in the halls to lessen the overcrowding. Lack of funds for medical training also fell particularly hard on these groups. The spiraling cost of attending medical school continued right through the Depression years, resulting in a 30 percent decline in black enrollment. Delays in training meant that one-third of all black medical students entered the profession in their forties, an age in which many white physicians began making preparations to retire.

Still, the Depression caught up with families of all kinds as, over time, their health troubles multiplied. The death rate is not always a good indicator of general health and well-being. Damage that accumulates over a decade or more may not show up in statistical tables until much later. And in America the doctor is summoned only after the harm is done.

In the 1920s, Hoover had noted that the slogan of progress is changing from the full dinner pail to the full garage. Over that decade car ownership had tripled, reaching 27 million vehicles by 1929. Four out of five families now possessed an automobile, profoundly reshaping the American landscape and society. Those who did not own cars were considered poor. Physicians outside urban areas viewed cars as a necessity to their practice because transportation reduced the time spent making house calls and increased the territory that could be serviced. Patients, in turn, felt more secure and less isolated.

Doctors quickly surmised that the garage was less expensive than the livery stable. Motor cars depreciated less quickly than horses and were more reliable. Following the lead of bankers and merchants, physicians preferred first the stylish curves of the Oldsmobile, and then traded up to a Buick, Cadillac, or Chrysler Airflow Desoto (the "silver chariot of the future"). Everyone else owned a Ford or Chevy. The physician's car-buying indulgence bred disrespect the way an expensive golf bag sometimes does today. The extravagance of purchases in the depths of Depression moved one physician to declare luxurious automobiles a "constantly circulating medium of affront" to patients (Brengle 1935, 318).

The automobile's ubiquity underscored the most salient feature of the human body as a prime mover. As Yale physician Howard Haggard, one of the most respected and popular healers of the time put it: "The human body is an energy-transforming machine" (Haggard 1938 [1927], 1). The body burned nutrients the way cars burned petroleum by breaking food down into its chemical components—carbon and hydrogen—and combusting them. Haggard carried his metaphor further in comparing the individual cells of the body to factory hands working together harmoniously. The organs formed mechanical contrivances not unlike the exhaust pipe on a car, a steam engine's governor, or a boiler's water pump. Together, these organs formed involuntary systems for circulation, digestion, respiration, and enervation, as well as a voluntary muscular system powering body movement. Water, vitamins, and minerals became known, respectively, as the lubricating oil, corrosion inhibitor, and material for replacing worn-out parts. The body, all told, was simply a system of systems, a network similar to (but more intricate than) Henry Ford's River Rouge, America's most modern industrial plant.

Balance and Proportion

In the 1930s the sputtering engine became a perfect emblem, then, not only for the U.S. economy but also for the health of its people. Sickness and disease stemmed from worn and broken body parts, or poor timing and lack of proper coordination between the parts. The central problem involved teasing out the complex mechanisms by which the human body protected, adjusted, and repaired itself. Maintaining the body's dynamic internal and external equilibrium, what the famous Harvard physiologist Walter Cannon termed homeostasis, became the aspiration of Depression-era doctors. They now understood disease to be a deviation from a normal state of self-regulation. The old notion of "perfect health," was dispensed with, replaced by the new goal of "normal health."

The quickening pace of modern industrial life, however, made normal health difficult to maintain. The most obvious sign of trouble was the rapid rise in automobile accidents. With more cars on the road, the number of car crashes mounted. Doctors saw more steering wheel injuries caused by blunt force trauma to the chest in sudden stops. Bruised ribs. Cracked cartilages. Cuts, bruises, and broken bones. Whiplash. Alcohol-fueled Tinseltown

An automobile accident on U.S. 40 between Hagerstown and Cumberland, Maryland, November 1936. Photo by Arthur Rothstein for the U.S. Resettlement Administration. (*Library of Congress*)

crashes featured prominently on the variety pages of newspapers. Cut down in their prime, actors Dorothy Dell and Junior Durkin died in separate accidents in June 1934 and May 1935. Both were only 19 years old. By 1940, 36,000 people died each year in automobile accidents, and 1 million were injured in collisions involving one in every twenty cars on the road. America had recklessly remade herself into a car crash culture.

Material progress had seemingly outstripped humanity's ability to adapt, bewildering even the most cunning capitalist and ruining human health. Industrial and market noise dulled the ears. Figures inscribed in mountains of paperwork degraded human eyesight. Even the invention of gastronomy in the culinary arts threatened human health. The so-called art and science of delicate eating endangered the gastrointestinal tract and the teeth by eliminating food that was simple and coarse, offering instead soft and sweet foods that lacked nutritive essentials.

It all made sense now. The go-go twenties had upset the delicate balance of human mental capacities and facilities, driving Americans to nervous derangements like insanity, feelings of inferiority, chronic worry, and sorrow. The new complexities of life had also led to overcompensation with the use of depressants like alcohol, opiates, dope, and painkillers, and stimulants like chewing gum, tobacco, coffee, and tea. These synthetic substances, which had fueled the jazz clubs, gambling houses, and gin joints of the last decade, contributed substantially to creating a wholly maladjusted, non-natural Depression man. Addiction had become a social safety valve, draining the loud-talking, drunken dance hall denizen of inventive genius and resourcefulness. How *could* such a man escape his own self-imposed incapacitation?

Medicine and the helping professions—public health, psychology, social work, and nursing—responded with a call for a new science of physiological hygiene. Proponents of physiological hygiene argued that human progress and security could only be achieved in a safe, sanitary civilization. The basic requirements included clean streets, uncontaminated air and water, independence from illicit drugs and patent medicines, eugenics, well-fitted casual clothing and shoes, and ergonomic furnishings. Guidance in mental self-discipline was also important in situations in which individuals endangered the well-being of members of their own family or the community, as when driving a car or using a shared-party telephone line. The 1930s saw the introduction of all sorts of control mechanisms: speed limits, safety first programs, employee counseling, student honor codes, prescribed dieting, and popular health education.

The family practitioner became part trained mechanic and part safety inspector. When the body sputtered and back-fired, the physician rolled up his sleeves and pulled out his diagnostic and surgical instruments. Dexterously handling the electrocardiogram, cotton swab, and reflex hammer, he adjusted the human carburetor, cleaned the headlights, and took the kinks out of the fenders until the body once again ran smoothly and silently. Specialists were called in to handle the major repairs, the human degenerative equivalents of broken motor mounts, worn valve seals, or wholesale transmission failure. The hospital was the final scrap heap for rusted-out bodies.

People were lucky in the depths of the Depression to have any kind of medical care. "We had just a family doctor," said Lafayette, Louisiana, housewife Bertha Andrews, "and he treated you for everything" (Arnold 1982, 12). Patients liked it this way. Having a doctor of one's own inspired trust. "I think it was a good thing because he understood the background," recalled Sophia Bigge of Hays, Kansas, "[the] possible diseases that might come up in the family" (Arnold 1982, 5).

Still, most people doctored themselves most of the time. Homemakers took care of the sick in their own homes, calling the doctor only for serious illnesses or to deliver babies, and relied on home remedies for health. Those who could afford them had thick combination cookbook-doctoring books. Once more, the welfare of the human race depended on the art of mothering: Poisonous jimson weed for wounds. Green walnuts, catnip tea, or calf slobbers—the foam found floating in the cattle tank—as ringworm vermifuge. Skunk grease, kerosene, and turpentine mixed with sugar, or sulfur and molasses were administered for bad colds. Peach bark or boneset tea soothed sore throats. A mustard or onion or antiphlogistine chest plaster was offered for pneumonia. And a red bottle of Watkins rubbing liniment worked for just about everything else.

Health also depended on exercise and replenishment. Children could be kept out of the repair shop by playing outside in the sunshine, which physicians recognized as a valuable source of vitamin D for strong bones. They were also encouraged to drink more fresh water—three or four glasses each day—as well as extra helpings of green vegetables, fruit, and whole-grain bread. Adults were enjoined to substitute joy for jealousy, the latter of which had been inspired by the open acceptance of consumer envy. All people were enjoined to follow the natural rhythms of the day, which included regular mealtimes, sleep periods, and even premeditated bowel movements.

The family, in its biological and social relations, was considered a natural group for study in the Great Depression. Indeed, health professionals often referred to the family as the most fundamental unit in their work. Health and disease were social processes that could be understood in their full complexity only when considered in terms of association or relation rather than as independent entities. The community coalesced around families engaged in activities promoting mutual self-benefit, explained the famed syphilis doctor Harry Solomon of Boston, MA. Families were members of the community, and that community could harm healthy families or itself suffer harm by unhealthy families. Ira Wile, a respected New York pediatrician, was moved to describe the family not in terms of its individual members, but rather as the product of equal parts biological heredity and social environment.

This new conception of family as the touchstone of American health progress demanded fundamental changes in health care. Scientific medicine not only had produced tremendous good, but also had unduly discounted social relations, psychological states, and psychiatric evaluations because they resisted quantification. Doctors had long attended to the illnesses of family members, but now they emphasized the *relationships*—between father and daughter, mother and grandmother, aunt and in-law—that influenced the health of family members. Physicians could wear the traditional badge of family practitioner with renewed pride, and they learned that medicine and society are like two streams, which while arising from different sources and flowing in parallel valleys, were now cutting away the sandy ridge between the two.

According to physicians, the healthy home stood as the centerpiece, the great accomplishment, of the family in the 1930s. The household stood at the apex of American civilization and helped determine the relative health of all citizens. During the Depression, physicians thought this message had been lost. Maintaining healthy homes demanded the assistance of medical authorities operating beyond individual control, and it required popular medical education.

Wile, who wrote extensively on the urban housing problem, professed disappointment in Americans who erected housing solely on economic grounds, with little thought of community or family health. Homes built without regard to basic sociological principles, without a basic understanding of the family, contributed heavily to the construction of unhealthy surroundings. Wile also blamed the technology that had robbed homes of their creative virtues and core values. Privacy, peace, light, ample toilet facilities, and attractiveness were all apparently unimportant considerations in modern building techniques. The house contributed to the physical and mental disorientation, disintegration, and deterioration of families and communities.

In 1940, the distinguished New York City physician Dr. George Baehr proposed a pilot program for prepaid health care for low-income persons. It would be located in a new public housing development on the Lower East Side, known as the Vladeck Houses, comprised of two dozen six-story buildings that covered some six city blocks. The plan provided general medical care at $3.00 per year per person, or $12.00 a year for a family of four or more. About 1,700 families, comprising about 6,200 persons, were eligible. A tenant association, jointly governed by caregivers and renters, administered the plan. Two local hospitals, a settlement house, and a visiting nurse service also belonged, as did most doctors and nurses in the neighborhood. Tenants had available many medical services, including maternal and emergency care. The program's fundamental idea, insisted its founder, Dr. Baehr, was to test the value, to the patient and to the doctor, of the patient-doctor relationship, as well as to prove that low-income persons

The new conception of the proper home as a shelter against modern life led vital statisticians to collect information illuminating the so-called social kinetics of families. They needed to collect data on human association in and out of equilibrium to understand the health effects of collective events like wars, natural disasters, and economic catastrophes.

Doctors began keeping their notes of office and home visits in family folders. Cross-examination in the home loosened the tongues of otherwise reserved individuals, and these folders often contained intimate details of family life. Social and religious contacts were inscribed on the cover sheet. Other pages were given over to descriptions of the situation of the family, including the condition of the house, any outbuildings, the privy, water supply, garbage dump, and sewer. Records were kept on insurance provisions, home ownership, and family occupations. Invasive, yes, but this was exactly the point. The social, emotional, and physical health of the individual was tied directly to the health of other family members. It was the whole Smith family after all that drank polluted water from the local stream, the Boyd clan that refused to seek treatment for venereal disease, and the old Johnson farm where the young were all malnourished.

The concept of family as community in microcosm reached deeper than recordkeeping. Physicians used family relationships to comprehend the epidemiological features of specific afflictions at a time when very little could be done to prevent or treat disease. It was discovered that diseases moved in families and could not be prevented or isolated simply by treating infections as they became known. It was like bailing out the kitchen without fixing the water pipe that had burst. Physicians insisted on treating the whole family and eliminating immoral social influences that encouraged disease. Protecting the health of the family had a satisfying prophylactic effect; it protected American society as a whole.

Medicine may have been strengthened by revisiting accepted wisdom on the role of the individual in health and disease, but it was not ready to scrap individual responsibility for the costs associated with sickness.

could pay for their care. Thus, the idea was not socialized medicine or mass treatment, but to show the integrity and workability of the individual patient—individual doctor system.

The plan's difficulties were, alas and alack, predictable. It was a pilot program, ginned up with a certain enthusiasm, but its policies and practices would not become integrated into the community's life, its habits and customs. The monies it generated were insufficient to break even. And it was swallowed up in the city's enormous scale, which had, as a newspaper editorial writer put it, approximately the population of Australia, with almost 30 percent foreign born, in which no more than half of its ill population paid for hospitalization, and in which half a million African Americans lived in substandard conditions. The program was simply swamped by its milieu.

SOURCE: *New York Times*, April 28, 1940, November 11, 1940, November 25, November 25, 1940, November 29, 1940, December 9, 1943.

Doctors were virtually united in their opposition to government schemes that abandoned private practice in favor of group practice and compulsory health insurance. Members of the powerful American Medical Association (AMA) cried out against ''Bolshevik'' tax-supported public medicine, fearing it would turn doctors into ham-fisted bureaucrats or corporate stooges. Only the Medical League for Socialized Medicine, a few salaried Mayo Clinic physicians, and the breakaway Committee of 430 stood against the AMA governing elite.

The AMA favored the status quo, by which it meant entrepreneurial individualism. The medical professional wanted autonomy in rendering its service, which could be secured only in a world functioning by desire, ambition, skill, and the profit motive. Physicians, of course, called it courage, vigilance, hard work, and responsibility. They objected to government or corporate service on the grounds that it would not only weaken the power of the professional, but also lead to impersonal patient-physician relationships, narrow the view of the specialist, and increase the costs of medical care through needless expense.

Average Americans saw things differently. They worried about paying their bills. Impoverished families watched their public medical assistance evaporate on the eve of the Depression as the Federal Maternity and Infancy Act expired by limitation in 1929. (It was not restored until passage of Title V of the Social Security Act in 1935.) And they observed the shameful behavior of the AMA House of Delegates, which repeatedly denounced the act. Americans were not concerned about losing their individuality or political freedoms. In polls conducted each year between 1936 and 1938, 70 percent or more of the people agreed that the government should help them pay for their medical care. These were the people who had forced passage of workmen's compensation laws, pensions for the elderly, and unemployment insurance. Why not state-supported health care? Occasionally, local leaders forced the issue. In the winter of 1932–1933, Muncie businessmen stepped in to reform a local medical monopoly, which had failed in its duty to self-police by abusing a relief payment system that favored house calls over office visits. Some physicians had nearly given up office calls to take advantage of the higher home visit rates.

Pressure was building on the government to do something more. Hoover had pioneered a moderate policy of government-business cooperation called associationalism. Associationalism sought to bring together competitors into partnerships for the common good. One example was the Committee on the Costs of Medical Care (CCMC). Between 1927 and 1932, private foundations like the Milbank Memorial Fund, the Rockefeller Foundation, and the Carnegie Corporation funded research on the health problems of the nation through the CCMC. Led by a former AMA president and member of Hoover's cabinet, Dr. Ray Wilbur, the CCMC uncovered unfairness in the distribution and cost of private medical service. The group recommended group health insurance, and possible government taxation, in redress of the problem. Despite a decade of debate, the AMA steadfastly denounced the CCMC's conclusions as pure "communism." Facing mounting criticism and the prospect of another global war, the CCMC proposals were eventually whittled down to the 1940 National Hospital Act, which provided a few million dollars in hospital construction grants.

Despite the failure of the CCMC, the Roosevelt administration scored some moderate successes in its New Deal with the American people. One was Roosevelt's 1933 extension of Hoover's Emergency Relief Act, which established the Federal Emergency Relief Administration (FERA) for work relief and rural home visits by doctors, nurses, and dentists. FERA funded basic school lunch programs in several states. Many of the AMA's county medical societies endorsed the act because it provided no dollars for hospitalization, which, they argued, might erode traditional family care-giving practices and the family physician-patient relationship. The act did much good, but did not prevent abuses like the following reported by journalist Lorena Hickok, FERA's clandestine investigator (Lowitt and Beasley 2000, 17):

> Now I know from personal experience, having several relatives in the profession, that doctors have been badly hit by the depression.... But nevertheless I don't think this sort of thing should happen: Major Turner [a FERA agent] was called at his home by someone from a neighboring county who wanted him to guarantee payment of a hospital bill for a woman, mother of eight children, who was about to die of acute appendicitis. He was told that she would live only a few hours unless she was immediately taken in for an operation. He explained that he was not permitted by the federal regulations to pay hospital bills, and that therefore he couldn't okay the bill. Whereupon, he said, he was told that he and the United States government would be responsible for that woman's death and for making those children orphans if he did not okay that bill! ... He said—and I agree with him—that any doctor who would refuse to take that woman into his private hospital, regardless of whether she could pay her bill or not, ought to be held criminally responsible if she died.

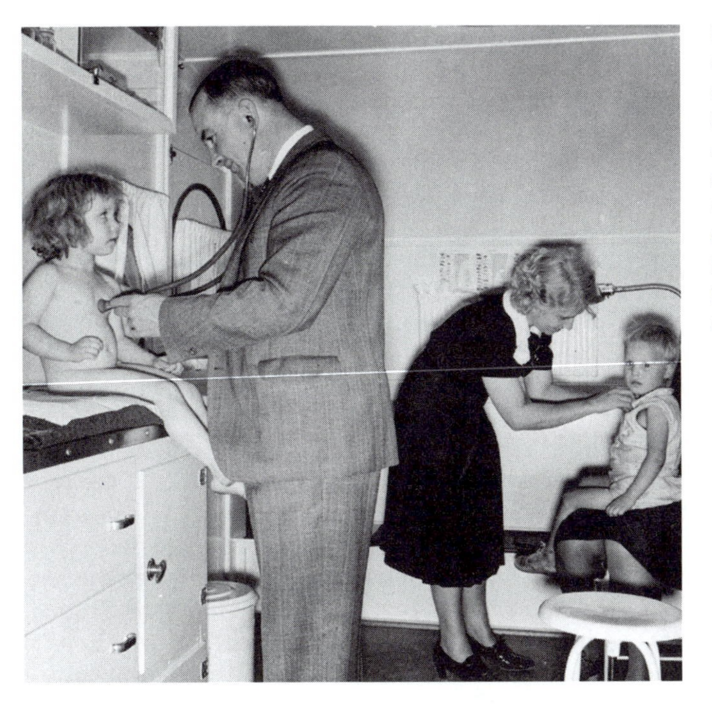

Doctor examines children in a trailer clinic at a Farm Security Administration mobile camp in Klamath County, Oregon, October 1939. Photograph by Dorothea Lange. (*Library of Congress*)

In 1937 another New Deal agency, the Farm Security Administration (FSA), began offering—in consultation with AMA state medical societies—group plans to rural families who pooled regular contributions into a common fund. Payments for medical services, including private physician care and hospitalization, came directly out of this fund. Patients chose their own doctors under the plan, and payments were fixed by the fund's trustee. In return for membership in the shared fund, families promised to retrofit their farms for cleanliness and safety by moving sewage pits away from drinking water sources and installing fly screens for doors and windows. Many plans also established family quotas for the canning of fruits and vegetables to reduce unhealthy rural diets of fat pork and potatoes. At its zenith in 1942, the medical rehabilitation program of the FSA covered 142,000 families across the United States, a small fraction of the total.

Chicanery in Medicine?

The federal government also attempted to follow the tenets of proper physiological hygiene by addressing the trade in patent medicines. Here, too, short-term political and economic interests had overridden common sense. "The doctor's job is not so much to help the patient," noted one city hospital intern, "as it is to make the patient feel that the doctor is earning his two dollars.... [H]e gives six prescriptions to prove that his knowledge is important" ("The Interne Remarks" 1939, n.p.). Homespun quackery was rampant in the Depression, even as sales of harmless but expensive commercial remedies like Listerine, Scott's Emulsion, and Lydia Pinkham's Vegetable Compound plummeted. Instead so-called medical charlatans ran amok, defrauding millions. In Los Angeles, fully 50 percent of the population received their primary medical care from osteopaths, chiropractors, Christian Science healers, or New Thoughtists rather than AMA-approved practitioners.

John Brinkley, the infamous Goat-Gland Doctor, purportedly restored the virility of men and women by transplanting into them testicles and ovaries harvested from farm animals. Almost unbelievably, Brinkley ran for governor of Kansas three times, receiving 30 percent of the vote each time. Brinkley was a pioneer in border blaster radio, setting up a high-gain antenna in Mexico that allowed him to broadcast his message of health across most of the continental United States. Yet his credentials as a licensed physician hinged mainly on his ability to pay for degrees from diploma mills.

Norman Baker, a former machinist and vaudevillian magician, ran the Baker Institute for cancer cure in Muscatine, Iowa. He made a name for himself by diagnosing illness and prescribing treatment over the airwaves on radio station KTNT. Baker claimed that physicians were out of touch with ordinary families, and explained that M.D. stood not for Medical Doctor but More Dough. He also argued that the University Hospital in Iowa City was nothing more than a "slaughterhouse" for duped rubes. For a time, Baker even had the ear of fellow Iowan Herbert Hoover. Baker got the president to buy into a scheme to start the presses of Baker's sensationalist *Midwest Free Press* by remote control over telegraph wires from Washington, D.C.

In 1930, Baker hired Harry Hoxsey, another self-taught cancer crusader from across the river in Illinois. Hoxsey extolled the virtues of his own cancer cure at the deceptively named National Cancer Research Institute and Clinic. He developed his clientele by directly opposing the AMA hierarchy, which he believed did not represent the popular sentiments of the American people.

All three of these quacks catered to a public nostalgic for pre–World War I agrarian ideals, especially the wisdom, virtues, and rights of ordinary folk. All of them proclaimed against the AMA trust, privileged bureaucrats, and haughty scientists, which they identified as the greatest threat to the family—and their practice—in the 1930s. None of these groups, Brinkley, Baker, and Hoxsey argued, offered anything to patients with diseases diagnosed as incurable. They, at least, offered therapeutic hope. Their audience also shared a suspicion of technoscientific rationalism, which conflicted with the sacramental ministries of the preacher. Never mind that radio, the high-tech medium of its time, helped both Brinkley and Baker spread their alternative gospels of health.

Sometimes commercial aspirations and the prevailing cult of American salesmanship got the better of otherwise sensible physicians. Sociologist Robert Lynd noted that, in Muncie, reputable doctors used publicity suggesting their services involved "no knife, no pain, no drugs, no danger" (Lynd and Lynd 1937, 396–397). In Marshall, Illinois, Dr. Edward Pearce got caught up in the rage over a supposed miracle cure called Crazy

Crystals, which were simply horse salt tablets mixed in water. Pearce opened a rival laboratory to produce a drug his promoter called Sane Crystals. Dr. Pearce's Sane Crystals were touted as a safe and reliable "family remedy" with no equal. Both products were said to cure most ailments, and although some consumers drank up to eight glasses for their maladies each day, their effect was mainly loose stools.

Regulation came to the patent medicine business only after tragedy struck in 1937. In that year, a chemist at a small pharmaceutical plant in Bristol, Tennessee, made a terrible error in preparing a liquid form of sulfa with the lethal solvent diethylene glycol. At least 107 were killed by Elixir Sulfanilamide, including scores of children. Death from diethylene glycol poisoning is prolonged (seven to twenty-one days) and agonizing. The Food and Drug Administration (FDA) tracked down nearly 2,000 pints of the deadly raspberry-flavored preparation, but could only prosecute the company on a technicality. All elixirs must have alcohol; Elixir Sulfanilamide did not. Thus, the only law that had been broken was that the product had been misbranded. The Bristol plant chemist committed suicide, but the owner—a physician himself—complained that the company should bear no guilt as the supplier of a prescribed drug. He paid a fine of $26,100.

Diethylene glycol is today used to make antifreeze, but in the golden age of malarkey, it was sprayed on tobacco to reduce the throat and lung irritation caused by cigarette smoking. Cigarette consumption skyrocketed in the 1930s, doubling in only ten years. By 1940, the average American adult lit up more than 2,500 times per year. Smoking soothed jangled nerves, the industry claimed, and reduced indigestion. Henry Ford had called the cigarette the "little white slaver" in 1914, but now women saw fit to augment their diet plans with cigarettes that suppressed the appetite. Thirty percent of Hollywood heroines smoked on screen, but only 3 percent of villainesses. Even physicians accepted tobacco's dubious science, allowing manufacturers to publish ads in their own medical journals. A classic 1930 advertisement read "20,679 Physicians say 'LUCKIES are less irritating.'"

Congress, outraged by the Elixir debacle, pushed through legislation including the Federal Food, Drug, and Cosmetic Act of 1938. The 1938 Act was long overdue. It replaced the archaic 1906 Food and Drugs Act, which had survived mainly on the popular point of view that an FDA with more power would turn into a powerful, sinister machine against the people's right to self-medicate. The new law required pharmaceutical manufacturers to list active ingredients, and to prove their drug's safety to the FDA before they could be sold.

Orthodox healers countered the quacks by inspiring the trust of the families they tended, and by impressing them with their growing armamentarium. The personality and training of the doctor was of preeminent concern in Depression-era medicine. In an age of anxiety, the most important feat of the physician was inspiring patient confidence. "Dr. S. M. Cotton was our country doctor in those days," remembered Beulah Grimsted of Sheridan, Indiana. "He delivered our first three children. He always wandered around the room and he would tell you tales—just sort of, I suppose, to keep you cheered up" (Grimsted 1981, 14).

Medical colleges sought candidates who radiated self-assurance themselves, and instruction moved away from the production of chilly, dispassionate personalities to the building of warm, buoyant ones. Physicians needed to present well in the clinical examination of the patient. "There's plenty hocus pocus in our profession," agreed Kings County (New York) Hospital resident physician Joseph Vogel:

> That's what's known as the bedside manner. It serves a psychological purpose.
>
> There's a visiting doctor comes to the hospital who knows as little about medicine as—we all think he's dumb. But you should see the manners he puts on. You would think he was the country's greatest doctor. He goes up to a patient, takes her hand and pats it, and says "Fine! You're improving wonderfully! You look fine today!" And sure enough you can see the patient actually improving. (Federal Writers Project 1939)

The doctor might even become what was once unthinkable: a "kindly, understanding friend" and "honorary member" of the family. True physicians were not carnival barkers, nor were they complainers. They were patient and kind. New doctors might cultivate their community for years without turning much of a profit beyond the meat and vegetables that came their way in trade. The most worthy physicians calmly faced the future, caring for families that had not paid for service in years in hopes that one day they might make payment in arrears.

In the depths of the Depression, the collection rate of Dr. Frank Brey of Wabasso, Minnesota, on all patient accounts was somewhere between 10 and 20 percent. The most common charges on the books involved the drainage of abscesses, immunization for diphtheria, incisions for treatment of mastoiditis, and tapping of the scrotum to relieve painful epididymitis (which often accompanied syphilis). Occasionally he performed other minor surgeries like office tonsillectomies and adenoidectomies. His patients did not complain of allergies, headaches, upper respiratory infections, or other benign illnesses that now form the bulk of private clinic practice.

The collection of equipment and methods used in the practice of medicine in the Depression was imposing. The physician needed to be comfortable with the mechanical helps of the modern office: electric sterilizers, equipment for calculating basal metabolism rate, an X-ray machine, the electrocardiogram, and various other physiotherapeutic and electromagnetic stimulators. Doctors used the X-ray machine to image broken bones, locate abnormal structures like an enlarged heart, or find foreign bodies accidentally swallowed or lodged in body tissues. X-rays also provided valuable treatment of cancers and other inflammations. They used high-frequency electromagnetic current to deliver heat to deep muscle injuries to reduce tenderness, increase blood flow, or tear down diseased tissue.

Scientific apparatus supplemented the doctor's already formidable "laboratory of personality." Doctors agreed that home visits gave patients a better sense of security than the office. Patients were comfortable at home. In the clinic, physicians attended to the minor comforts of their patients. Surfaces and walls were cleaned regularly. Cozy armchairs lulled patients into pliant states of mind. Physicians weighed carefully the question of whether the AMA popular monthly *Hygeia* inspired more confidence than *True Confessions* as a waiting room periodical despite the vast difference in circulation figures. Prominently placed and framed diplomas impressed patients, too.

The discovery of the role and function of the endocrine system helped physicians interpret the inner life of the sick. In the 1930s, the physiologists Walter Cannon and Hans Selye laid the groundwork for contemporary stress management and psychosomatic medicine in their studies of the sensitivity of the endocrine system in relation to physical and emotional trauma. There could not have been a better time for such research. Hormones secreted by the various endocrine glands, it appeared, determined patient personality types and the healthfulness of response to stress. Good doctors could size up the personality type of their patients in seconds. The thyroid type tended to be thin, slender, excitable, and emotional. The adrenal type was muscular, agile, and calm. The pituitary type tended to be ambitious, charming, and cerebral.

Family practice in the Great Depression was above all a down-to-earth cottage trade. The doctor expected to serve his injured patients in a manner paralleling the local garageman. The auto made him available for urgent care. He mastered all branches of the medical arts, including infectious disease, obstetrics, pediatrics, surgery, and radiology. He was a healer of mental as well as physical ailments. In complicated cases, he became a general contractor supervising the other health-building trades: nurses, social workers, and specialists. In his focus on personality and deportment, he saw the individual as a whole person, as a part of a family and, in turn, the greater community. And finally, safety and security formed his chief objectives—in a time and place characterized by neither one.

References

Arnold, Eleanor, ed. *Voices of American Homemakers Oral History Project*, 5 vols. Vale, Oregon: National Extension Homemakers Council, 1980–1985. Interviews of Beulah Grimsted, November 9, 1981; Bertha Andrews, March 30, 1982; Sophie Biggs, April 30, 1982.

Brengle, Deane. 1935. *Modern Office and General Practice*. Kingsport, TN: The Southern Publishers.

Bromley, Dorothy Dunbar. 1934. Birth control and the Depression. *Harper's Magazine*, 169 (October): 563.

Cavan, Ruth, and Katherine Renck. 1938. *The Family and the Depression: A Study of One Hundred Chicago Families*. Chicago: University of Chicago Press.

Federal Writers Project. 1939. *Oral Histories of the Folklore Project, 1936–1940*. Works Progress Administration (WPA), American Memory, Library of

Congress, Washington, DC. Interviews March 28, 1939, with Joseph Vogel, and June 19, 1939, "The Interview Remarks."

Haggard, Howard W. 1938 [1927]. *The Science of Health and Disease*, rev. ed., New York: Harper & Brothers.

Hertzlen, Arthur. 1940. *The Doctor and His Patients*. New York: Harper & Row.

Lowitt, Richard, and Maurine Beasley, eds. 2000. *One Third of a Nation: Lorena Hitchcock Reports on the Great Depression*. Urbana: University of Illinois Press.

Lynd Robert S., and Helen Merrell Lynd. 1937. *Middletown in Transition: A Study in Cultural Conflicts*. New York: Harcourt, Brace, and Company.

Marshall, Victor. 1945. *Doctor! Do Tell*. Appleton, WI: Nelson.

Robbins, Lionel. 1934. *The Great Depression*. London: MacMillan.

Smilie, Wilson. 1940. "The relationship of immediate family contact to the transmission of type-specific pneumococci." *American Journal of Hygiene* 32: 79–88.

Watkins, T. H. 2000. *The Hungry Years: A Narrative History of the Great Depression in America*. New York: Owl Books.

5 Immigration in a Time of Depression: The United States, 1931–1940

Roger Daniels

A Time of Decline

While every depression and even lesser economic downturns have negatively affected immigration to the United States, no previous—or subsequent—economic downturn affected immigration as did the Great Depression of the 1930s. And because the end of that Depression came after the outbreak of World War II, the fifteen-year period from 1930–1945 is a kind of Sargasso Sea in the surging history of American immigration. Total recorded immigration for the entire Depression decade was only 500,000 persons, the lowest decennial number since the 1820s. The average annual net immigration for the decade was 6,900; in 1914 more persons than that entered the country every two days. Nearly as many persons were recorded as leaving the country as entered it, so that officially calculated net immigration for the decade was only some 68,000 persons. Table 5.1 shows the official numbers.

It is now clear that these numbers understate the exodus that occurred in the early years of the Depression. The vast majority of the 460,000 listed emigrants in the decade were Europeans returning to their native lands. But we now know that an informal federal-state-corporate program—not recorded in the official statistics—sent perhaps 400,000 Mexicans back across the southern border, most from California, Texas, and Arizona, but with perhaps 50,000 coming from Midwestern industrial areas. (For a vignette of this later group see page 88)

This chapter will, after establishing the trend of immigration policy before the Depression, concentrate on what law and policymakers regarded as the three chief problems to deal with in immigration policy: reducing immigration from Mexico, ending the unchecked immigration from the Philippines, and altering the system to accommodate refugees,

Table 5.1 Immigration and Emigration, Continental United States, 1931–1940

Year	Immigration	Emigration	Net
1931	97,139	61,882	35,257
1932	35,576	103,295	−67,719
1933	23,065	80,081	−57,013
1934	29,470	39,771	−10,301
1935	34,956	38,834	−3,878
1936	36,329	35,817	512
1937	50,244	26,736	23,508
1938	67,895	25,210	42,685
1939	82,998	26,651	56,347
1940	70,756	21,461	49,295
Total	528,431	459,738	68,639

Note: Years are fiscal years beginning June 30 of indicated year.
Source: Historical Statistics, Series C 88–144.

predominantly Jewish, from Nazi Germany and, eventually, from the nations it overran.

Changes in Immigration Policy

To make sense of the immigration patterns of the Depression years, it is necessary to have an understanding of the radical transformation of immigration policy that took place in the 1920s. The two major immigration laws of those years, the so-called First Quota Act of 1921 and the National Origins Act of 1924, completed the initial restrictionist phase of American immigration policy that began with the Chinese Exclusion Act of 1882, the first of fifteen statutes that excluded Chinese persons. A succession of subsequent laws had, by 1917, restricted immigrant entry to the United States in eight major ways. By that time, laws had been enacted to keep out most Asians, contract laborers, convicted criminals, persons who failed to meet certain moral standards, people with certain diseases or disabilities, paupers, certain radicals, and illiterates. Yet, in those thirty-five years (1882–1917), total annual immigration to the United States had risen exponentially, reaching a peak in the years just before the outbreak of World War I: During the first fourteen years of the twentieth century, an average of 1 million immigrants a year came, almost three times the number of persons who had arrived in the last fourteen years of the nineteenth century.

Those favoring a general restriction, often called nativists, had placed their hopes on a literacy test, which, after three decades of struggle, was passed in watered-down form in 1917. The act had little effect that provided added force to the arguments of those nativists who were urging the general restriction of immigration that came about during 1921–1924. The basic method of restriction, which was added to those methods already in effect, was to establish an annual numerical limit, and then to allocate to each of the eligible nations, an annual quota based on the numbers of

Table 5.2 Immigration, 1925–1930, By Category

Year	Total	Quota	Family	New World	Other
1925	294,314	145,971	7,159	139,389	1,795
1926	304,488	157,432	11,061	134,305	1,690
1927	335,175	158,070	18,361	147,339	11,345
1928	307,255	153,231	25,678	123,534	4,812
1929	279,678	146,918	30,245	97,547	4,967
1930	241,700	141,497	32,105	63,147	4,951
Total	1,762,611	903,119	124,609	705,259	29,560

Source: Historical Statistics, Series C 139–151.

foreign-born persons of that nationality present in the United States. Under the 1921 Act, designated an emergency measure, the overall quota was set at 3 percent of the foreign born in the 1910 census—the latest available—resulting in an annual quota of nearly 400,000. But when Congress was writing the 1924 Act—which stayed on the books until 1952—its leaders discovered that applying the same formula to the now-available 1920 census figures would increase the quota spaces available for eastern and southern Europeans, who were considered by many as undesirable, and, concomitantly, would reduce the numbers available for the more favored British, Irish, German, and Scandinavian immigrants. For example, if the 1921 law's formula were applied using the 1920 census figures, a total quota of 270,000, with 42,000 spaces reserved for Italians and 31,000 for Poles, would result. Instead, Congress changed the formula and its base. The percentage was cut to 2 percent and applied to the 1890 census, producing an annual quota of 180,000 with slots for just 4,000 Italians and 6,000 Poles.

The quota numbers, often regarded as equivalent to total immigration, represented only just over half of it. Both the 1921 and 1924 laws had provisions for people who could enter as immigrants "without numerical limitation." For the period 1925–1930, quota immigrants were only 51 percent of those admitted. Most of the rest were "residents of the Western Hemisphere" (40 percent) and "family members" (7 percent). Table 5.2 gives the official numbers.

The New World provision, in the law because many southwestern and western legislators insisted that their regions needed Mexican agricultural labor, in its final version allowed immigration "without numerical limitation" of persons who had lived for five years in independent nations of the Western Hemisphere, plus Canada, Newfoundland and the Canal Zone. This did not mean that all could come: The previously enacted bars were still in place. For example, a Chinese person living in Canada, regardless of citizenship, would still be barred by the Chinese Exclusion acts, and a Mexican syndicalist would be barred by antiradical provisions.

Most Canadians and Mexicans could come and go relatively freely, however, and they were a growing proportion of contemporary immigration. Between 1910 and 1914 the 500,000 New World immigrants—almost

Mexican Repatriation from the Chicago Area

It is hard to imagine an exodus of 400,000 persons, but perhaps that many Mexicans were caught up in such a movement during the later years of the Hoover administration. These Mexicans were part of a repatriation program formed by private groups and state and local governments, which received the blessings of the federal government. Most came from California and other parts of the Southwest, but the program reached as far north as the Chicago area. It was supposedly voluntary, but as the following testimony, given years later, of a Mexican immigrant in Indiana Harbor, Indiana, shows, many if not most of those repatriated had no real choice. This is his oral history.

> We weren't asked voluntarily if we wanted to go. Your name was on the list of how many days you were working in the steel. Many were working only one day every two weeks to keep their names on the payroll of Inland Steel Company or Youngstown Sheet and Tube Company. The rest of the companies were either shut down or not available. Naturally you were put on welfare, very small amounts, food mostly. Well, when the trains became available to the Good Fellow Club, the welfare people

all from Canada and Mexico—had represented about 10 percent of all immigrants: This grew to 40 percent, as noted above, for the period 1925–1930.

In addition to those from the New World, persons eligible to enter outside the quota included wives and unmarried children of United States citizens under 18 years of age (husbands of United States citizens were added only in 1928, and then only if the marriage had taken place before June 1, 1928); previously admitted immigrants returning from a visit abroad; any minister of any religious denomination or professor of a college, academy, seminary, or university and his wife (but not husband) and unmarried children under eighteen; bona fide students; and women who had previously lost their citizenship by marriage or from the loss of citizenship by their husbands. And finally, the long-established rights of Chinese "treaty merchants" and their families to domicile within the United States were reaffirmed.

For the first time, all immigrants had to get visas and provide photographs, which involved the consular service of the Department of State directly in the regulation of immigration. There was a $9 charge for visas, which, added to the $9 head tax, meant an outlay of $18 to enter. While this sum was hardly a major deterrent to immigrants who were paying for an Atlantic passage, it was significant to Mexican immigrants, who were long used to casually crossing and recrossing the border. The act also required reentry permits at $3 each, for aliens leaving the country and wishing to return, which also encouraged Mexicans to come and go informally.

The statutory requirement of a visa that had to be obtained at an American consulate was felt to be most important by restrictionists. It was, in their terminology, a way of controlling immigration at the source and it gave considerable discretionary authority to individual consular officials. No thorough study examines how the consular service actually regulated came to your house and said: "Well, you're not making enough money to survive." Even though some people were staying in homes where they weren't paying one penny of rent because of the deplorable condition of the homes or the landlord didn't ask for money because there was no money available. So they told you, "You are making $7.00 or $8.00 per payday for your family. You can't feed them, you can't do nothing. So we are going to take you off welfare."

"Oh, God, what are you going to do, take us off welfare? We'll starve."

"No, no, you have an alternative ... go to Mexico. We have a train available. A train full of Mexican people. A train will stop at the corner of Michigan and Guthrie, on the Pennsylvania Railroad. And they will head for Mexico. In Mexico you will transfer and we'll take you where you come from, close, not actually there, but to the closest town."

So actually they weren't forcing you to leave, they gave you a choice, starve or go back to Mexico.

SOURCE: Lane and Escobar 1987, 13–14.

the issuance of visas, but it is quite clear that officials such as Wilbur J. Carr (1879–1942), who directed the consular service from 1909 to 1937, saw themselves as gatekeepers and that Carr and many if not most of his subordinates were nativists. Carr privately encouraged nativist members of Congress to raise bars to immigration with derogatory comments, such as the following: "[T]he great mass of aliens passing through Rotterdam ... are Russian Poles or Polish Jews of the usual ghetto type.... They are filthy unamerican [*sic*] and often dangerous in their habits" (Evans 1987).

Even before the onset of the Great Depression, the State Department instituted measures to reduce immigration from Mexico. In the last year of the Coolidge administration, it instructed American consular officials in Mexico to apply standards more stringently. Mexican visa applicants were faced with a "catch 22." Consular officials would ask if the applicant had a job waiting for him. If the answer was "yes," he could be barred as a contract laborer; if the answer was "no" and he could not demonstrate considerable assets, he could be barred under the "likely to become a public charge" clause, enacted first in 1882 to keep out paupers and persons unlikely to be able to earn a living. This cut immigration of Mexicans enabled by visas to 13,000 in 1928–1929 from 40,000 in the previous year. Herbert Hoover, in one of his earliest reactions to what became the Great Depression, ordered the State Department to apply the reinterpreted l.p.c. clause to all nonfamily immigrants who could not demonstrate substantial assets. This was, in the circumstances of the Great Depression, largely a useless precaution as European jobseekers soon learned about conditions in the United States and applications dropped accordingly. But later in the thirties, as Nazi Germany stepped up its persecutions of Jews, many, and perhaps most, American counsels continued to refuse the majority of visa applicants: Many of those Jews turned down were later slaughtered. Hoover wanted to have his administrative fiat written into the statute book, but Congress did nothing. In the closing years of his administration, as previously noted, trainloads of Mexican immigrants, including some American-born children, were sent across the southern border with the approval of the Mexican government, which made promises about looking after them and which it did not keep.

The New Deal and Immigration

The election of Franklin D. Roosevelt and the advent of his New Deal in 1933 forever changed many aspects of American life, but there was never a New Deal for immigration. Roosevelt did celebrate past immigration, most famously in his speech to the reactionary Daughters of the American Revolution in April 1938, he said: "Remember, remember always that all of us, and you and I especially, are descended from immigrants and revolutionists" (Rosenman 1938, 259).

But on most immigration questions, the father of the New Deal stood pat. His administration did stop the "voluntary repatriation" program to Mexico, but Hoover's admission policies for Mexicans were continued. Most conservative southwesterners had long supported bringing in Mexicans to pick the crops. Early in the century Hubert Howe Bancroft (1832–1918), the pioneer historian of California, welcomed Mexican labor under certain conditions: "[W]e want [them] for our low-grade work, and when it is finished we want [them] to go home and stay there until we want [them] again" (Bancroft 1918).

In the Depression era, many southwestern conservatives had similar views, as do many today. John Nance Garner, the Texas Congressman who became President Roosevelt's first vice president, argued that Mexicans in Texas "do not cause any trouble, unless they stay there and become Americanized" (*Immigration from the Western Hemisphere* 1930, 61).

For the entire Depression decade a total of 22,319 immigrants from Mexico, not all of who were Mexicans, are recorded as entering the United States. In the previous decade, the number had been 458,287. Informal border crossing continued in numbers that cannot be counted, but surely the totals were reduced as the Depression created large number of native-born migrant workers, like those photographed by Dorothea Lange and written about by John Steinbeck, who were desperate for any kind of employment.

To be sure, Secretary of Labor Frances Perkins was sympathetic to immigrants and did clean up some of the corruption and mismanagement that seems to be endemic in the immigration service. Even before the Depression, the Democratic Party's position on immigration was hardly distinguishable from that of the Republican's position. Although Al Smith, the Democratic candidate in 1928, was rightly regarded as a representative of the immigrant and urban masses, the Democratic platform that year pledged itself to preserving immigration restriction "in full force and effect," although it did favor more lenient provisions for family

Mexicans entering the United States, U.S. immigration station, El Paso, Texas, June 1938. Photo by Dorothea Lange. (*Library of Congress*)

reunification. Not one of the four platforms on which Franklin Roosevelt ran, 1932–1944, contained a word about immigration, and there would be no significant changes in immigration law until 1943.

Candidate Roosevelt had made his position clear in his 1932 Commonwealth Club address in San Francisco, arguing that "[o]ur industrial plant is built.... Our last frontier has long since been reached.... There is no safety valve in the form of a Western prairie.... We are not able to invite the immigration from Europe to share our endless plenty" (Rosenman 1938, 750).

This is not to say that had Hoover been reelected immigration policy would have been the same. Hoover wanted immigration restricted even further, while his successor wanted few changes. As Roosevelt put it in another 1932 campaign address, "[The President of the United States] says proudly that he has effectively restricted immigration in order to protect American labor. I favor that; but I might add that in the enforcement of the immigration laws too many abuses ... have been revealed" (Rosenman 1938, 854).

The New Deal did, however, treat resident aliens more generously than its predecessor. Instead of repatriation or deportation, the New Deal provided some relief. Deportations, which had risen steadily from 2,762 in 1920 to 19,865 in 1933, dropped to fewer than 9,000 the next year and

Filipinos cut lettuce, Salinas, California, 1935. (*Library of Congress*)

stayed at about that level for the rest of the decade. Federal relief regulations insisted on the eligibility of resident aliens, although local control of hiring usually discriminated not only against aliens but also against persons of color regardless of citizenship.

The first major immigration "problem" addressed by the Roosevelt administration concerned Filipinos. That the Asian Filipinos could enter the United States without significant restriction, was, of course, an anomaly, an unintended consequence of American imperialism that made their homeland an American possession. The federal courts had ruled that Filipinos were "American nationals" and thus not immigrants, and their entry could not be restricted because of their race. On the other hand, since they were neither white nor of African descent they were not eligible for naturalization. A few handfuls of Filipinos, brought to Mexico, had settled in Louisiana in the eighteenth century, and Jefferson's purchase of that vast entity made them Americans. After the United States conquered and annexed the Philippines, hundreds of students came to study at American colleges and universities, largely in the Midwest. But the overwhelming majority of Filipino immigrants arrived after the restriction of Japanese labor immigration in 1907–1908. In both Hawaii and on the American west coast, Filipinos filled the same low-skill niches in the labor force that Chinese and Japanese had filled before them. In

1930 the census counted some 63,000 in Hawaii and another 45,000 in the continental United States.

The Hawaiian Sugar Planters Association brought almost 120,000 Filipinos to Hawaii between 1909 and 1934, which previously had been responsible for bringing in Chinese and Japanese. More than 100,000 of them were men, nearly 9,000 were women, and 7,000 were children. Some came to the mainland after fulfilling their contracts in the islands; others went back to the Philippines. The California Filipino population was even more overwhelmingly male. In California in 1930 there were more than 28,000 males and fewer than 2,000 females.

A vigorous anti-Filipino movement arose in California in the late 1920s and early 1930s backed by a broad coalition of forces from organized labor to right-wing newspapers and politicians. While the basic cause was economic—during the Depression many whites were eager to get even the "stoop labor" jobs formerly left to assorted "foreigners"—there was also significant cultural conflict. Many middle-class Californians were aroused by what they regarded as the aggressive sexuality of Filipinos, large numbers of whom patronized "dime-a-dance" establishments. One Sunday feature story in the *Los Angeles Times* carried the following headlines:

> "Taxi-Dance Girls Start Filipinos on Wrong Foot"
> "Lonely Islanders' Quest for Woman Companionship Brings Problems of Grave National Moment"
> "Mercenary Women Influence Brown Men's Egos"
> "Minds Made Ripe for Work of Red Organizers" (*Los Angeles Times* 1930)

Similarly, David P. Barrows, president of the University of California, told a congressional committee that the state's "problems" with Filipinos stemmed from the latter's easily aroused sexual passions coupled with their natural propensity for vice and crime, all exacerbated by the deficiencies of modern American society:

> [The Filipino] usually frequents the poorer quarters of our towns and spends the residues of his savings in brothels and dance halls, which in spite of our laws exist to minister to his lower nature. Everything in our rapid, pleasure-seeking life, and the more or less shameless exhibitionism which accompanies it, contributes to overwhelm these young men who come, in most cases, only a few years removed from the even, placid life of a primitive native barrio. (Melendy 1977, 66)

This portrayal of Filipinos as people only a step from savagery was a misconception nurtured in part by the frequent exhibition of Igorots, a name given to several peoples of Luzon who had been largely unaffected by modern civilization, at American world fairs and even zoos in the decades after the annexation of the Philippines. The fact that the Filipino migrants were not Igorots and that many of them spoke two western languages (Spanish and English) as well as one or more of the many Philippine languages was irrelevant to the nativists.

A middle-class proponent of Filipino exclusion, Sacramento businessman C. M. Goethe, ignoring the lack of Filipino women in America, warned that the 10 million Negroes in the United States were descended from "an original slave nucleus of 750,000" and insisted that "Filipinos do not hesitate to have nine children ... [which means] 729 great grandchildren as against the white parents twenty-seven," and then, switching his point of attack, he argued that the Filipino tends to interbreed with near-moron white girls, producing an invariably undesirable hybrid. This ever-increasing brood of Filipino coolie fathers and low-grade white mothers may in time constitute a serious social problem (Goethe 1934, 354).

As ridiculous as all this now sounds, it was heady stuff to a generation that made best sellers of Oswald Spengler's *Decline of the West* and Lothrop Stoddard's *The Rising Tide of Color against White World Supremacy*. It was an era in which a leading liberal intellectual, Supreme Court Justice Oliver Wendell Holmes, Jr., could declare from the bench, while upholding a state statute permitting compulsory sterilization of women, that "three generations of imbeciles are enough" and equating the procedure with compulsory vaccination (*Buck v. Bell* 247, 207).

In addition, many Californians were startled to discover that the state's antimiscegenation laws, which forbade marriage between whites and African Americans and between whites and "Mongolians," could not be used to prevent marriages between whites and Filipinos. The legislature quickly passed a law making marriages between whites and "persons of the Malayan race" equally illegal.

There was also the traditional trade union argument. Even before the onset of the Depression the American Federation of Labor's national convention resolved in 1928 that:

> Whereas, the desire for cheap labor has acted like a cancer ... destroying American ideals and preventing the development of a nation based on racial unity; and Whereas ... this desire has exploited the Negro, the Chinese, the Japanese, the Hindus, as in turn each has been regulated and excluded; and
>
> Whereas, the Malays of the Philippines were in 1924 omitted from the general policy excluding all who cannot become citizens; and Whereas, there are a sufficient number of Filipinos ready and willing to come to the United States to create a race problem equal to that already here ... we urge exclusion of Filipinos. (American Federation of Labor 1928)

That same year, a California congressman introduced the first bill aimed at excluding Filipinos. Within two years, hearings were held and there was a congressional debate. The arguments against Filipino immigration were racial and economic. The chief opposition to restriction came from Hawaiian Sugar Planters, the War Department (which still administered the Philippines), and Filipino leaders. Most notable among the latter was Manual Roxas, speaker of the Philippine legislature, who was in the country as part of a delegation lobbying for independence. Filipino exclusion, according to Roxas, "has no precedent in the annals of colonization since the birth of time. No country, however imperialistic, however commercialistic in its policy in it dealings with its colonies, has ever prohibited the citizens of its colonies from migrating to the mother country" (*Exclusion of Immigration from the Philippine Islands* 1930).

Other Filipino spokesmen suggested that immigration and Philippine independence be tied together, an option that some American lawmakers quickly embraced. When in 1930 the restrictionists failed to get a simple Filipino exclusion clause added to an immigration bill, most of them jumped on the independence bandwagon. It was a nice irony: some of the most pronounced racists in Congress became, in effect, anti-imperialists. Hiram W. Johnson (1866–1945), the senior Republican senator from California and a long-time advocate of Asian exclusion, had a provision inserted into a 1932 bill granting independence that thereafter totally barred Filipinos as "aliens ineligible to citizenship." Hoover, however, who believed that the Filipinos were not ready for independence, vetoed that bill in January 1933 but stated that Filipino immigration should be restricted immediately. Congress overrode his veto, but the statute required the agreement of the Philippine Legislature, which was not forthcoming.

In 1934, with the support of the Roosevelt administration, a similar bill passed, was signed by the president, and was accepted by concurrent resolution of the Philippine Legislature. The Philippines were to become independent in 1945. The immigration aspects of the law were as follows: Instead of exclusion, Filipinos were to receive a quota of fifty spaces per year—half the size of the previous minimum quota. Although Filipinos remained ineligible for naturalization, the law specifically exempted Filipinos from the provisions of the 1924 law that excluded "aliens ineligible to citizenship" from immigration, and made it possible for the Territory of Hawaii to import more Filipino laborers if the secretary of the interior thought it advisable.

The basic Filipino "problem" had been solved, but many felt that the solution still left too many Filipinos in the country. In 1933, Samuel Dickstein (1885–1954), a Brooklyn Democrat who became chair of the House Committee on Immigration and Naturalization when his party took over in 1931, began to press for ways to get unemployed Filipinos sent back home. He supported legislation, enacted in 1935, to provide any Filipino who applied for it free "transportation and maintenance from his present residence to a port on the west coast of the United States and [subsequent] transportation and maintenance ... to Manila." In addition, the law forced any Filipino who received a free trip home to foreswear the right of return. In the event, only 2,190 persons applied for and received such a trip. Dickstein insisted that his motive was, in part, "humanitarian in behalf of these unfortunate Filipinos." One can imagine what Dickstein, an opponent of the quota system for Europeans, would have said if someone had proposed the same sort of arrangement for unfortunate immigrants from Europe. That an urban Democrat like Dickstein sponsored such a measure shows nicely the attitude that even liberal Congressmen had toward Filipinos. In 1946, at President Truman's urging, the bar against Filipino naturalization

The Voyage of the *St. Louis*

The Great Depression, which lasted until the prosperity associated with World War II, was hard on most working Americans, not just immigrants. But for one group of would-be immigrants, the mostly Jewish refugees from Adolf Hitler's Germany and some of the nations he conquered, even a Depression-era United States was a much-desired refuge. And, although the United States eventually took in more wartime refugees than any other nation, perhaps 150,000, many were turned away by officials in the U.S. State Department at home and abroad, who controlled the visas. Among those who did get in were distinguished scholars, artists, musicians, and writers who made important contributions to American life. Albert Einstein, the most important scientist since Isaac Newton (1642—1727), was the most illustrious, but there were so many others that historians speak of "the intellectual migration." Most enriched American culture, and a group of refugee physicists enabled the United States to win the race to develop an atomic bomb.

But many others were refused visas that might have saved their lives, or, as in one awful instance, these refugees were turned away from American shores. The *St. Louis* was a Hamburg Amerika luxury liner that sailed from Hamburg to Havana in May 1939 with 937 passengers, all but one of them Jewish refugees who had enough money to pay for their tickets. Most wanted to come to the United States and many had been approved for American visas but had to wait for their quota number to come up, so they were prepared to wait in Cuba. The Cuban government refused to let them land. The ship's captain then tried to take the ship to Miami, where he hoped that at least those who had been approved for later admission could land, but U.S. officials refused to allow the ship to enter the harbor. For a time the vessel waited off Miami Beach, close enough that passengers could hear the dance music being played at the resort hotels. One passenger had died on the west-bound voyage; twenty-eight were allowed to enter Cuba. The rest were returned to Europe. None had to go back to Germany. Britain took 288. The remaining 620 were admitted by the Netherlands, Belgium, and France. In spring 1940, those nations fell to the Nazis. By that time eighty-seven of the 620 had gone elsewhere.

was lifted, thus enabling wives and children to come in as nonquota immigrants.

No New Deal for European Refugees

The "problem" of refugees from Nazi Europe, refugees who were mostly Jewish, first arose as the Roosevelt administration began. Viewed through the horror of the Holocaust, the callous indifference of the United States and the other nations of possible asylum has become a scandal with an extensive literature. But it is not really useful to view the policies of the 1930s, as too many do, through the prism of the Holocaust. Some of the literature can induce one to believe that Franklin Roosevelt and even Rabbi Stephen S. Wise were somehow responsible for the Holocaust.

Jewish prisoners of the Sachsenhausen concentration camp in Germany on December 19, 1938. Prisoners of Sachsenhausen were forced to counterfeit millions of dollars in British and American currency. (*National Archives*)

Two hundred and fifty-four of the remainder died during the Holocaust, most murdered in the death camps of Auschwitz and Sobibór. Three hundred and sixty-five of the 620 survived the war. About half of the 937 passengers eventually got to the United States.

SOURCE: Ogilvie and Miller 2006.

Authors of phrases such as ''while six million died'' create the false notion that the United States, merely by changing its immigration policies, could have saved all or most of the Jews of Europe, a palpable impossibility. Nor is it accurate to assume that the Holocaust was inherent from the moment the Nazis came to power. By the time Americans learned about what Walter Laqueur has called the ''terrible secret'' of the Holocaust, the fate of most of the Jews of Europe was sealed. To be sure, even at that late date more could have been done. If one wishes to make a judgment, it is hard to improve on that of Vice President Walter F. Mondale, made in 1979: the United States and the other nations of asylum ''failed the test of civilization'' (Walter F. Mondale, text of speech, July 1979).

Any attempt to understand the pitiful refugee policy of the United States in the Nazi era must confront American traditions about asylum as well as contemporary political and social pressures. Many Americans share

President Jimmy Carter's belief that the United States was and always has been "a nation of refugees," but such a conclusion is unwarranted (James Earl Carter, speech, *New York Times*, July 29, 1979).

During most of the nineteenth century, few Americans voiced fears about political refugees, but despite the wide-open American door it was Britain that became the mecca for most European political exiles. The most significant exile activity in the United States was by Latin Americans, particularly Cubans who made a revolution against their Spanish overlords from bases in Tampa and New York. And almost as soon as the United States began systematic regulation of immigration, language was adopted so that "political offenses" could not be used as grounds for exclusion. In American immigration law, no distinction was made between refugees and other immigrants, and the word *refugee* does not appear in any immigration statute before 1934, although in 1923 a Near East Refugee Act did pass the Senate. The literacy provisions of the 1917 immigration act included a clause waiving the literacy requirement—but nothing else—for "aliens who shall prove ... that they are seeking admission to the United States to avoid religious persecution," but it is not clear that even one person gained admission because of that provision.

From the earliest days of his presidency, Franklin Roosevelt was aware of the Nazi persecution of Jews, trade unionists, socialists and others in Germany, and, as a humane liberal Democrat, he deplored and spoke out against it. But for years he did little or nothing to change American immigration policy, neither to restricting it further nor to liberalizing it, as many of his closest supporters wished him to do. When, for example, Felix Frankfurter and Raymond Moley urged him to send representatives to a 1936 League of Nations conference on refugees and appoint Rabbi Stephen S. Wise to the delegation, Roosevelt instead took the advice of the State Department and sent only a minor functionary. In an election year, he was willing to accept the narrow view of executive power set forth by Secretary of State Cordell Hull (1871–1955). This conservative Tennessee Democrat, whose wife was Jewish, told the president that the law left him "no latitude" even to discuss "questions concerning the legal status of aliens" (Nixon 1969, 3:278–280, 282–283).

Similarly, when his handpicked successor as governor of New York, Herbert H. Lehman (1878–1963), wrote him on two occasions in 1935 and 1936 about the difficulties German Jews were having in getting visas from some American consulates in Germany, the president sent replies drafted in the State Department. The letters assured Lehman of Roosevelt's "sympathetic interest" and claimed that consular officials abroad were carrying out their duties "in a considerate and humane manner." In addition, the governor was assured that a visa would be issued "when the preponderance of evidence supports a conclusion that the person promising the applicant's support will be likely to take steps to prevent the applicant from becoming a public charge" (Nixon 1969, 3:50–52, 64–66, 123–124, 341–343).

Roosevelt was notoriously distrustful of the State Department, and that he allowed its bureaucrats to draft his responses shows that he simply did not want to interfere or even to know what was really going on. Normally an activist president, he could be quite passive when it suited his purposes.

There is irrefutable evidence that many State Department officials consistently made it difficult for refugees in general and Jewish refugees in particular to gain asylum in the United States. One example involving just two individuals reflects a pervasive problem. Hebrew Union College (HUC) had a refugee scholars project that between 1935 and 1942 brought eleven refugee scholars and some of their families to its Cincinnati campus. Since there was no question of any of these persons becoming a public charge, most were able to enter under a provision of the 1924 act that exempted from quota restriction

> an immigrant who continuously for at least two years immediately preceding [his visa application] has been, and who seeks to enter the United States solely for the purpose of, carrying on the vocation of minister of any religious denomination, or professor of a college, academy, seminary or university, and his wife, and his unmarried children under 18 years age. (43 Stat. 153, 1924)

This provision must have seemed heaven-sent to the scholars that HUC, the premier American institution for training Reform rabbis, was trying to bring out. But, as Michael A. Meyer, the historian of the project, has demonstrated, the State Department, in the person of Avra M. Warren, head of the Visa Division, consistently created difficulties—difficulties that in some cases proved insurmountable.

Despite apparent *prima facie* qualifications, two German Jewish scholars whom HUC tried to rescue never managed to get to the United States. Albert Spanier had been Hebraica librarian at the Prussian State Library and then a teacher at the *Hochschule für die Wissenschaft des Judentums* in Berlin until he was sent to a concentration camp after *Kristallnacht* in November 1938, the notorious anti-Semitic pogrom all over Germany that marked a new stage of Nazi persecution of German Jews. The guaranteed offer of an appointment at HUC got him out of the concentration camp, but it could not get him an American visa. Avra Warren's Visa Division determined that the special provision did not cover librarians, and Spanier's teaching at the *Hochschule* did not count either. In 1934, the Nazis had demoted it—the leading institution for the study of Judaism in the world—from a *Hochschule* to the status of a *Lehranstalt* [institute]. An administrative regulation created by the Visa Division and not found in the statute held that the grant of a professorial or clerical visa to a scholar coming from a lower status institution abroad to a higher status one in the United States was impermissible.

Spanier and another refugee scholar invited by HUC, Albert Lewkowitz, managed to reach the Netherlands. It was assumed that Lewkowitz, at least, would get a visa because he had taught Jewish philosophy at the Jewish Theological Seminary in Breslau, an institution whose status the State Department did not question. But in May 1940, the Germans bombed Rotterdam destroying all of Lewkowitz's documents and American consular officials insisted that he get a new set from Germany. Five years earlier, in peacetime, Roosevelt had assured Lehman in a letter drafted by the State Department that

> consular officials have been instructed that in cases where it is found that an immigrant visa applicant cannot obtain a supporting document normally required by the Immigration Act of 1924 without the peculiar delay and embarrassment that might attend the request of a political and religious refugee, the requirement of such document may be waived on the basis of its being not "available." (Nixon 1969, 3:65)

No such waiver was made for Lewkowitz. Both he and Spanier were later rounded up and sent to the Bergen-Belsen concentration camp. Lewkowitz was one of the few concentration camp inmates exchanged and he got to Palestine in 1944. Spanier died in Bergen-Belsen.

As we have seen, actions by three presidents, Coolidge, Hoover, and Roosevelt, granted broad discretionary power to American consuls. Obviously, a wide range of attitudes and performance were represented within the consular corps. One American consul in Germany, Raymond Geist, actually went into concentration camps to help get individuals out; while another, John G. Erhardt, issued as few visas to refugees as possible. No historian has yet made a full-scale investigation of American visa policies, but as early as 1921, American Jewish leaders complained of the overt anti-Semitism of certain State Department officials, particularly, as noted previously, Wilbur J. Carr, and about the small number of Jews able to get appointments in the foreign and consular services. The published diary of Breckinridge Long (1881–1958), assistant secretary of state from January 1940 to January 1944, provides clear evidence of his anti-Semitism. One entry, for example, equated communism with Jewish internationalism and regarded Hitler's *Mein Kampf* as "eloquent in opposition to Jewry and to Jews as exponents of Communism and chaos" (Schwartz, *American National Biography*).

While it is rarely possible to connect a bureaucrat's personal anti-Semitism directly to his or her official decisions, it is not necessary to find the so-called smoking gun. When one finds a public official, in an era in which anti-Semitism is endemic, making anti-Semitic statements in his private correspondence *and* following policies that effect anti-Semitism, one should assume at least partial anti-Semitic motivation unless there is overwhelming evidence to the contrary. It is the conjunction that is crucial. Hiram W. Johnson, a governor of California and United States senator from 1917 to his death, is an example of the opposite tendency. There are vile anti-Semitic and anti-black references in his private papers at the Bancroft Library, but Johnson was, if anything, mildly philo-Semitic and pro-black in his public statements and policies.

Late in the 1930s the Roosevelt administration began to move on the refugee question, but its actions can best be characterized by the phrase that describes so much of western democracy's opposition to fascism, too little and too late. Shortly after the *Anschluss*, the German annexation of Austria in March 1938, Roosevelt created an Advisory Committee on Political Refugees under the chairmanship of James G. McDonald, former high commissioner for refugees of the League of Nations, and assigned an interdepartmental committee of government officials to work with it. Roosevelt also instructed Secretary Hull to try to arrange an international conference to "facilitate the emigration from Austria and presumably from Germany of political refugees," adding the caveat, "[N]o country would be expected or asked to receive a greater number of immigrants than is permitted by its existing regulations." He appointed Myron C. Taylor (1874–1959), former chairman of the U.S. Steel Corporation, to the rank of ambassador and named him to head the American delegation to the conference, which met in Evian, France, in July 1938. Its only accomplishment was to create an Intergovernmental Committee on Refugees, headquartered in London, under the chairmanship of George Rublee (1868–1957), an American lawyer. In mid-1939, Rublee did manage to negotiate a sub-rosa agreement looking toward the orderly emigration of 400,000 Jews over a five-year period, but the outbreak of war in 1939 made it nugatory.

In his note about those actions in his Public Papers, Roosevelt wrote things he never said to the American people in the crucial years of the refugee crisis, 1938–1939:

> For centuries this country has always been the traditional haven of refuge for countless victims of religious and political persecution in other lands. These immigrants have made outstanding contributions to American music, art, literature, business, finance, philanthropy, and many other phases of our cultural, political, industrial and commercial life. It was quite fitting, therefore, that the United States should follow its traditional role and take the lead in calling the Evian meeting....
>
> As this is written in June, 1941, it seems so tragically ironical to realize how many citizens of these various countries [which had been overly cautious in their attitude about receiving refugees] either are themselves now refugees, or pray for a chance to leave their native lands and seek some refuge from the cruel hand of the Nazi invader. Even the kings and queens and princes of some of them are now in the same position as these political and religious minorities were in 1938—knocking on the doors of other lands for admittance. (Rosenman 1938, 169–171)

When one compares this account with what the United States actually did and did not do in the months before war broke out in Europe, it is difficult not to believe that a guilty conscience lay behind his remarks, which later would be easy to describe as hypocritical. Of course, Congress and the American people were opposed to any dropping of our immigration barriers, as both Roosevelt and his ambassador, Myron Taylor, knew. The latter assured the American people in a November 1939 radio address:

> Our plans do not involve the "flooding" of this or any other country with aliens of any race or creed. On the contrary, our entire program is based on the existing immigration laws of all the countries concerned, and I am confident that within that framework our problem can be solved. (Divine 1957, 98)

His confidence, if it really existed, was sadly misplaced.

The American record, as opposed to its rhetoric and post-facto rationalizations, was dismal. Although we do not know how many actual visa applications by would-be German refugees there were (many refugees made multiple applications and one scholar says that there were more than 300,000 by June 1939), the fact is that between Hitler's coming to power and *Kristallnacht*, immigration from Germany was relatively light; more than half of the German quota spaces for the period, 1933–1940 went unused. Thus, a large portion of the Jews of Germany could have been accepted even within the relatively strict limits of the quota law.

The few attempts by sympathetic congresspersons to admit more refugees were forlorn hopes. The most notable of these was the so-called Wagner-Rogers bill of early 1939 that proposed bringing 20,000 German children to the United States outside of the quota system. Although sponsored by the New Deal's most prolific legislator, New York Senator Robert F. Wagner (Democrat), and a liberal Republican, Massachusetts Representative Edith Nourse Rogers, the bill never came to the floor for a vote. It had a great deal of support from prominent Americans, including Herbert Hoover, but was opposed by a sizable majority of ordinary Americans according to the public opinion polls. We do not know what would have happened had the White House tried to lead public opinion and put pressure on reluctant Democrats. Roosevelt refused to do so. He was willing to allow some administration officials—Secretary of Labor Frances Perkins and Children's Bureau Chief Katherine Lenroot—to testify in its favor. Other officials, such as Secretary of State Hull, took no stand but informed Congress of the numerous administrative difficulties the proposed law would create. Roosevelt even told his wife, in February 1939, that "it is all right for you to support the child refugee bill, but it is best for me to say nothing [now]." Now became never. In June, as the bill was dying, the president annotated a memo asking for his support, "File No Action, FDR." In addition, some of his personal and official family viciously opposed the bill: One of his favorite cousins, Laura Delano, wife of Commissioner of Immigration and Naturalization James Houghteling, told people at cocktail parties that the "20,000 charming children would all too soon grow up into 20,000 ugly adults" (Stewart 1982, 532).

In late 1938, Franklin Roosevelt did take one effective step by executive action: He "suggested" to Labor Secretary Perkins that the six-month visitor visas of "political" refugees be automatically extended and reextended for successive six-month periods as they ran out. This enabled about 15,000 persons to remain in the United States. Clearly, despite the president's 1941 claim, the vaunted "haven of refuge" did not function well. But perhaps 150,000 refugees, the overwhelming majority of them Jews, did manage to reach the United States before Pearl Harbor, a significantly larger number than was admitted by any other nation: Many thousands of others could have been saved by a more resolute policy.

References

American Federation of Labor. 1928. "List of Resolutions." *Proceedings.* Washington, DC.

Bancroft, Hubert Howe. 1918. *Retrospection: Political and Personal.* New York: Bancroft.

Carter, James Earl. Speech. *New York Times.* July 29, 1979.

Divine, Robert A. 1957. *American Immigration Policy, 1924–1952.* New Haven, CT: Yale University Press.

Evans, Patricia R. 1987. "Likely to become a public charge: Immigration in the backwaters of administrative law, 1882–1933." Unpublished doctoral dissertation, George Washington University.

Goethe, C. M. 1934. "Filipino immigration viewed as a peril." *Current History* January, 354.

Historical Statistics, Series C 88-144. 1975. Washington, DC: Government Printing Office. *Historical Statistics,* Series C 139–151. 1975. Washington, DC: Government Printing Office.

Kiser, George, and David Silverman. 1973. "Mexican repatriation during the Great Depression." *Journal of Mexican-American History* 3:21–42.

Lane, James B., and Edward J. Escobar, eds. 1987. *Forging a Community: The Latino Experience in Northwest Indiana, 1919–1975.* Chicago: Cattails Press.

Los Angeles Times, February 2, 1930.

Melendy, H. Brett. 1977. *Asians in America: Filipinos, Koreans, and East Indians.* Boston: Twayne.

Mondale, Walter F. Text of speech. July 1979.

Nixon, Edgar B., ed. 1969. *Franklin D. Roosevelt and Foreign Affairs.* Cambridge, MA: Harvard University Press.

Ogilvie, Sarah A., and Scott Miller. 2006. *Refuge Denied: The* St. Louis *Passengers and the Holocaust.* Madison: University of Wisconsin Press.

Rosenman, Samuel I. 1941. *Public Papers and Addresses of Franklin D. Roosevelt, 1938.* New York: MacMillan.

Schwartz, Donald. 1938. "Breckenridge Long." *American National Biography Online.* Available at http://www.anb.org/home.

Stewart, Barbara McDonald. 1982. *United States Government Policy on Refugees from Nazism, 1933–1940.* New York: Garland.

United States Congress, House Committee on Immigration and Naturalization. 1930. "Immigration from the Western hemisphere." Washington, DC: Government Printing Office.

The Worst of Times: African Americans during the Great Depression

6

Albert S. Broussard

A Daunting Time

The Great Depression represented a giant step backward for the majority of African Americans. As the nation fell into the worst and longest economic downturn in its history, African Americans from all economic classes and from every region of the nation struggled to find employment, to maintain shelter, and to provide even the most basic necessities for their families. Black workers, who lagged behind their white counterparts during the relatively prosperous decade of the 1920s, fell even further behind as the economy sank to unprecedented levels for more than a decade. Yet, through a succession of New Deal programs such as the Public Works Administration (PWA), the National Youth Administration (NYA), the Civilian Conservation Corps (CCC), Works Progress Administration (WPA), and the Farm Security Administration (FSA), many Africans Americans once again gained a foothold, albeit tenuous, in the workforce. Similarly, the policies of organized labor, particularly the Congress of Industrial Organizations (CIO) and the International Longshoremen's and Warehousemen's Union (ILWU), who organized unskilled and semiskilled workers in the mass production industries and on the nation's docks and seaports, benefited black workers in important ways. Finally, the liberal racial policies of the Communist Party, which worked to abolish all forms of racial discrimination and routinely elevated African Americans to leadership positions within some unions, advanced the cause of blacks in organized labor.

At the height of the Great Depression, an estimated 25 percent of the American workforce was unemployed. This dismal statistic alone, however, disguises the fact that millions of American workers were reduced to part-time work, were severely underemployed, or accepted any job, no matter how marginal or lowly, that they could find. The United States

Children of a turpentine worker near Cordele, Alabama, July 1936. The father earns one dollar a day. Photograph by Dorothea Lange. (*Library of Congress*)

Steel Corporation, one of the largest employers in the nation, with a workforce of 225,000, shifted entirely to part-time workers by 1933. For black workers, however, it appeared as if the bottom of the economy had dropped out altogether. The proportion of all persons in the nation on public assistance or relief was generally three times higher for African Americans as for white workers. In Detroit, for example, where blacks made up 4 percent of the population, they accounted for 25 percent of the relief cases. In St. Louis, blacks accounted for 60 percent of relief cases, although only made up 9 percent of the population. In Chicago, one-half of all black families were on relief. And in Norfolk, Virginia, African Americans accounted for 70 percent of all relief cases.

These stark figures underscore several critical points. African Americans worked the most marginal jobs in the economy, and these positions, generally unskilled or service oriented, were among the first to be eliminated. Second, when jobs were scarce, preference was given to white workers. In some areas of the nation, employers dismissed blacks to create jobs for whites. Black workers, as well as whites, were hit especially hard by the sharp decline in two industries, construction and coal mining, that suffered a catastrophic decline during the 1930s. Labor unions such as the American Federation of Labor (AFL) had systematically discriminated against black workers in every region of the nation. African American workers made up but 1 percent of all union membership in the nation in the early 1930s, and one-half of these black unionists belonged to the segregated Brotherhood of Sleeping Car Porters (BOSCP), the labor union of black railroad workers led by A. Philip Randolph. The lack of union protection within the AFL meant lower wages, fewer opportunities to move into supervisory or management positions, less seniority, and little, if any, job security during times of economic crisis. Finally, some cities exhausted their meager relief funds within several years, and others, such as Dallas and Houston, provided no relief funds whatsoever to African Americans or Mexicans. In Atlanta, white supremacist organizations demanded that all African American be terminated from the relief rolls to provide assistance to unemployed whites. Few cities went this far, although African Americans consistently reported greater difficulty obtaining relief than white workers. Black workers, who were no strangers to hard times or racial discrimination, were left to their own devices and ingenuity. Most managed to keep their heads above water, but the majority lived at the bare level of subsistence.

To no one's surprise, many African American voters welcomed a political change as the presidential election of 1932 drew near. Black voters, who had migrated from southern farms and cities to northern urban centers in unprecedented numbers between 1916 and 1930, had become an important political voice in a handful of northern industrial cities. Chicago serves as a case in point. The "Great Migration" (1916–1919) had brought about 500,000 African Americans southerners to northern industrial cities such as Chicago, Cleveland, Pittsburgh, and Detroit, the majority of whom were seeking factory jobs and a respite from the repressive violence in the South. The Chicago *Defender*, one of the leading black newspapers in the nation, initially welcomed these sojourners with open arms. Printing the most favorable train routes from the deep South to Chicago, the *Defender* called the migration the "Flight out of Egypt," and wrote that black migrants sang "Going into Canaan" as they arrived in northern cities.

Although black migrants had been prevented from voting in the southern states, their vote was actively courted in Chicago. Not only did African Americans vote in large numbers in the North, but they staunchly voted for the Republican Party ticket. In closely contested elections, such as the mayoralty election in Chicago, black voters were fiercely loyal to William Hale Thompson, and their votes helped to elect him to three terms as mayor. Thompson reciprocated by appointing black Chicagoans to a number of minor political posts and backing several others to important elective offices such as alderman, Republican committeeman, and a U.S. congressman. Indeed, as the venerable black leader Frederick Douglass had opined in the wake of slavery, when newly freed slaves were weighing their political options, the Republican Party "was the deck, and all else was the sea" (Meier 1963, 33). To be sure, black voters, despite some misgivings, had supported Republican President Herbert Hoover in both 1928 and 1932, but the number of black voters who had defected to the Democratic Party by 1932 was sizable. Hoover's policies had done little to end the suffering of unemployment for any group in American society, black or white, and more

African Americans, as well as many white Catholic and Jewish voters, were shifting to the Democratic Party between 1932 and 1936.

African Americans Shift Political Allegiances

As historian Nancy J. Weiss has written in her book, *Farewell to the Party of Lincoln*, the shift by African Americans from the Republican to the Democratic Party was complete by 1936, and for the first time since 1870, when black men were granted the vote as a result of the Fifteenth Amendment, they shifted their political allegiance to the Democratic Party, an allegiance that has remained intact until the present day. The Democratic Party juggernaut rolled throughout the nation's cities, as even the popular black Republican politician Oscar DePriest, formerly a Chicago alderman and the first black person to go to Congress from a northern district in 1928, was defeated by the black Democrat Arthur W. Mitchell. Little known outside of the city of Chicago, Mitchell, in 1934, became the first black Democrat ever elected to Congress. African Americans, who were initially either lukewarm or critical of Democratic President Franklin D. Roosevelt during his first term in office, were now solidly behind the president. Indeed, African Americans had a more positive relationship with Roosevelt than with any other U.S. president in the twentieth century except perhaps William Jefferson "Bill" Clinton.

Roosevelt's New Deal programs, which put millions of Americans of all races back to work and provided the bare minimum level of subsistence to survive, served as the principal reason for his broad-based appeal among black voters. Although the New Deal created no programs targeted specifically to alleviate the much higher unemployment rates among African Americans, many African Americans (and many white Americans) viewed Roosevelt as a Messiah because the New Deal put African Americans back to work. Moreover, this was a president who seemed to care about their problems. When Roosevelt came into office in the spring of 1933, approximately 3 million African Americans were on relief, three times the percentage of whites, and a solid indicator that blacks were feeling the sting of the Great Depression's wrath more severely than whites.

Yet unlike other twentieth-century presidents who have actively sought the black vote but disregarded the concerns of African Americans while in office in favor of more important constituencies, Roosevelt appealed to both the American sense of "fair play" and racial justice. Roosevelt, for example, was one of the few American presidents to ever publicly denounce lynching. This heinous crime, which had claimed more than 3,000 victims by the Great Depression, the vast majority of them African Americans, had been used widely throughout the Southern states as a mode of social control and as a means for white southerners to reassert their authority in the wake of Reconstruction. Although President Roosevelt had neither embraced the cause of civil rights nor compiled a substantial record fighting racial discrimination as governor of New York, he learned to become sympathetic to African Americans as a result of political

On an October evening in 1934, New York City patrolman Francis James took two drivers to the station. One was Joseph E. Priedolin, president of the National American University Fraternities; the other was Lewis B. Carrington, an African-American chauffer. Mr. Priedolin said that when he started his car, a small bus, driven by Carrington, hit its rear end. The bus's passengers were African Americans, all followers of "Father" Divine, whose "Kingdom" in Harlem offered solace, hot meals, and jobs to unemployed persons of all races. The passengers assembled around the two drivers at the station lieutenant's desk. The lieutenant turned to Mr. Carrington: "Where's your license?"

"I have no license," Carrington replied.

"Who owns this car?"

"It belongs to God, Lieutenant".

"What's that?" the lieutenant said.

"The bus belongs to God."

Strained silence reigned. And probably on cue, there was first, a low moaning and then, a soft crooning. The African-American passengers there chanted a prayer while they circled Carrington and Priedolin.

"Where did you leave your license?" the lieutenant asked against the holy din.

"Left it in The Kingdom, lieutenant."

"Can't you call The Kingdom?"

"I can't, no, sir!"

"Well, one of you go back to the Kingdom, wherever it is, and get that license. The rest of you will have to go outside."

The chorus filed out, still chanting, moaning, and praying. Ninety minutes later someone came from the Kingdom, license in hand. The lieutenant inspected it, found it proper, and released Carrington. The chorus walked back to the bus, Carrington first. He unlocked the vehicle, made sure all his passengers were accounted for, hoisted himself into the driver's seat, stepped on the starter, the engine turned over lustily, and away they went, to a camp meeting in Brooklyn, headlights blazing.

In the Depression, "Father Divine" attracted many followers thanks to his teaching of interracial harmony and faith in God.

SOURCE: *New York Times*, October 23, 1934, 11.

pressure and intense lobbying by black leaders. Prodded by First Lady Eleanor Roosevelt, his more racially egalitarian wife, Roosevelt stated in 1934 over a nationwide radio network that lynching was murder, "a deliberate and definite disobedience of the high command, 'Thou Shalt Not Kill.' We do not excuse those in high places or low who condone lynch law" (Sitkoff 1978, 63).

In spite of the U.S. Constitution and the nation's professed democratic beliefs, Roosevelt's denunciation of lynching represented a bold statement for a U.S. president, the majority of whom had refused to confront the racial problems that our nation faced. The respected black leader W. E. B. Du Bois wrote in the *Crisis Magazine*, the official organ of the National Association for the Advancement of Colored People (NAACP), that "[o]nly Franklin Roosevelt has declared frankly that lynching is murder. We all knew it, but it is unusual to have a President of the United States admit it. These things give us hope" (Sitkoff 1978, 63). Although the number of African Americans who were lynched had dropped significantly by the 1920s, lynching began to rise in the 1930s. Tuskegee Institute, which kept the most detailed figures on lynching and racial violence in the nation, reported that seven African Americans died at the hands of lynch mobs in 1929. However, the number had risen to twenty in 1930, nearly a threefold increase, and fifteen in 1934.

Roosevelt also made far better use of African Americans as presidential advisors than any previous president. In August, 1936, Roosevelt encouraged Mary McLeod Bethune, the president and founder of Bethune-Cookman Institute, a small black college in Daytona, Florida, and a prominent "clubwoman," to assemble a group of black leaders to advise the president on racial matters. This loosely coordinated group of twenty to twenty-five advisors became widely known as the "Black Cabinet," although none of these individuals had official cabinet status or would be permitted to sit in on the president's regular cabinet meetings. The Black Cabinet, nonetheless, brought into government service a larger group of highly talented African Americans than ever before. It allowed blacks for the first time to work within the government to directly influence federal policies on racial issues. The black leader Booker T. Washington had played a similar role with presidents William McKinley, Theodore Roosevelt, and William Howard Taft, but Washington had worked secretly and clandestinely within the government to shape racial policy.

The Black Cabinet's presence demonstrated to African Americans across the nation that the Roosevelt administration cared about them and their problems. This was revealed most dramatically in the presence of Bethune, the highest ranking African American in the New Deal and a black leader who had an open invitation to the White House. This formidable black woman had come from lowly origin to emerge as one of the most powerful African American women in the twentieth century. The daughter of an illiterate sharecropper and one of seventeen children, Bethune had attended Moody Bible Institute in Chicago. In 1923, she established Bethune-Cookman College in Daytona, Florida, shaping the small black college along the lines of Hampton Institute, Tuskegee Institute, and other black colleges that focused on industrial education, rather than the liberal arts. In 1935, Roosevelt appointed Bethune to head the Division of Negro Affairs within the NYA, a New Deal program designed to put high school and college-age students back to work. Although Bethune drew some criticism from black male leaders because of her gender, she proved to be an effective spokesperson for unemployed African Americans. Indeed, Bethune channeled important New Deal funds into black schools at all levels.

The presence and compassion of Eleanor Roosevelt also greatly enhanced President Roosevelt's appeal within black communities across the nation. Here was a First Lady who cared about the plight and suffering of African Americans, and unlike her more cautious husband, who had to be careful so as not to offend white southerners within the Democratic Party, for fear of political retaliation, Eleanor consistently crossed these racial boundaries and breached longstanding racial etiquette between blacks and whites. Eleanor visited many New Deal programs, reporting to her husband not only about the efficacy of these programs, but also about whether African Americans were treated fairly and received their fair share of jobs.

According to historian Harvard Sitkoff, Eleanor Roosevelt routinely invited black leaders to the White House and spoke long into the night about racial matters and the best strategies to confront discrimination within the New Deal and American society. The First Lady, for instance, persuaded her husband to increase the appropriation for both Howard University, the preeminent black university in the nation, and Freedmen's Hospital in the nation's capital. Despite the ire and horror of the white South, Eleanor Roosevelt also dined and mingled socially with African Americans, and permitted herself to be photographed with blacks in New Deal projects.

Eleanor Roosevelt maintained an intimate professional relationship with Mary McLeod Bethune, which no doubt proved a pivotal factor in Bethune's appointment as the NYA's head of Negro Affairs. But it was an even bolder move, though largely symbolic, that would forever endear Eleanor Roosevelt to African Americans during the 1930s and for decades to come. In 1939 Marian Anderson, the world-renowned black contralto, had been scheduled to present a concert in Washington, D.C., at Constitution Hall, but the Daughters of the American Revolution (DAR) announced that they would not permit Anderson, because of her race, to use their facility. Amid widespread public disapproval of the DAR's position, Eleanor

Eleanor Roosevelt presents African American opera singer Marian Anderson with the Spingarn Medal in 1939. J. E. Spingarn established the Spingarn Medal in 1915 to foster pride in African American accomplishments. (*Library of Congress*)

Roosevelt wrote in a newspaper column that she published regularly that she could no longer remain a member of the DAR in light of this incident. Amid some shrewd maneuvering, the federal government worked with the NAACP and other civil rights organizations to schedule a free public concert to be held at the Lincoln Memorial to focus on the hatred and bigotry of the DAR. An estimated 75,000 people turned out to hear Anderson sing in front of Lincoln's famous statute on a frigid Easter day, including many diplomats, congressmen, Supreme Court judges, and dignitaries. This episode demonstrated how Americans, when they possessed the will and commitment, could join together to defeat racial prejudice. But it demonstrated, too, that the president and the First Lady were willing to make a symbolic gesture in support of racial equality and a racially just society, a gesture that no previous president during the twentieth century had been willing to make.

A Segregated New Deal?

These symbolic gestures notwithstanding, the New Deal put many African Americans back to work who had been devastated by the Great Depression. African Americans benefited from every New Deal program to some degree, but some programs had a greater impact on both the morale and the purchasing power of black families than others. The CCC, established by Congress in March, 1933, was designed to provide relief to young men between the ages of eighteen and twenty-five through a variety of jobs in the nation's parks, forests, recreation areas, and soil conservation projects. Young men were sent to camps, where they were directed by army officers and foresters and worked under a strict military discipline. For their labor, they received the sum of $30 a month. The CCC enrolled 200,000 African Americans in their camps between 1933 and 1942, and, like the majority of New Deal programs, the camps were segregated. Even thought the CCC had a nondiscrimination clause, historian John A. Salmond noted, "it was never the policy of CCC officials to attempt to create a nationwide system of integrated camps" (Salmond 1967, 91, 93). In communities where the black population was relatively small or inconsequential, blacks and whites were integrated into the same camps. Yet segregation persisted even in these camps on occasion, as black newspapers reported numerous instances in which segregation existed. San Francisco's black press, for instance, attacked the CCC because it segregated African Americans in the dining facilities at some of its camps. The white residents of Contra Costa, California, also complained that the presence of a "Negro camp" in their town constituted a "menace to the peace and quiet of the community," although there is no evidence to substantiate their claim.

At a time when most African Americans resided in the southern states where life was brutal even under the best of circumstances, and when segregation was still the law of the land, it would have been remarkable if the CCC had maintained a nationwide system of integrated camps. On the whole, the 200,000 black youth who enrolled in these camps, stayed an average of fourteen months, learned a vocational skill, participated in the Corps academic training, were provided with adequate living conditions, and received better meals than they had access to prior to enrolling in the CCC. Although the majority of African Americans who left the Corps were placed in menial positions as janitors and waiters, some used their new-found skills to become cooks, gardeners, and poultry farmers.

African Americans fared less well under the Agricultural Adjustment Acts (AAA), which was signed into law in May 1933. These broad-based acts were designed to bring relief to the nation's farmers and reflected the Roosevelt administration's emphasis on centralized planning. They revolutionized American agriculture by providing government assistance to American farmers in the form of a subsidy, provided that farmers agreed to restrict their output. Yet black farmers were hurt severely by the AAA's policies.

Almost all black farmers (97 percent) lived in the southern states, but less than one in five owned their land. Many who did own land engaged in subsistence farming. Thus, when the AAA attempted to artificially raise the price of cotton, which had declined by two-thirds from 1929 to 1933, by restricting output, white farmers were the primary beneficiaries. Although the federal government advised landowners to distribute the cash payments fairly to those who worked the land, the AAA did not require landowners to show receipts for payments distributed to tenants, who worked their land. While the law stipulated that a landowner's benefits could have been terminated if he refused to follow this policy, it was never enforced. Black tenant farmers were also hurt when the AAA asked farmers to keep as much as 40 percent of their land out of production, reducing the need to hire tenant farmers or sharecroppers of any race to work their land. As many as 192,000 black farmers (and many whites as well) were removed from the land, representing about 15 to 20 percent of all sharecroppers. Many of these displaced farmers migrated to urban areas, swelling the already overburdened relief rolls in southern and northern cities.

The New Deal never adequately addressed the issue of rural poverty for either whites or African Americans. Indeed, one of the many ironies of the New Deal is that rural poverty actually worsened as the general state of agricultural improved between 1932 and 1935. During these years, farm income increased by 58 percent, part of it attributable to the AAA's policies and part to a devastating drought that reduced production and created the Dust Bowl migration. Yet the large number of displaced black and white farmers stimulated an interracial alliance that had not been seen since the Populist movement in the 1880s. In 1934, the Southern Tenant Farmers Union (STFU) was organized in Arkansas. This grassroots, interracial union was remarkable if for no other reason than for a brief moment black and white farmers shed their racial differences and attempted to improve their status along class, rather than racial lines. The union attracted 30,000 members, and had 200 locals spread across six states. Even more remarkably, black and white farmers worked together, no small feat in the South during the 1930s. African Americans were employed as STFU organizers, and E. R. McKinney, an African American, was elected vice president.

Evicted sharecroppers along Highway 60, New Madrid County, Missouri, 1939. Photograph by Arthur Rothstein. (*Library of Congress*)

The white labor leader H. L. Mitchell presided over this union, which attracted national attention and served mainly as a protest organization. The STFU demanded that the rental and parity payments that landowners received should be made directly to tenants and sharecroppers, rather than be funneled through landowners. The union also demanded that evictions from the land be halted. The STFU was unsuccessful in achieving either of these ambitious goals, but it succeeded greatly in focusing the national spotlight on the status of rural poverty and the dismal plight of the nation's tenant farmers and sharecroppers. The NAACP was so impressed with the work of the STFU that it provided limited financial support. Walter White, the NAACP's executive secretary, called the STFU the "most significant labor movement created in the United States in many years" (Wolters 1970, 49). Similarly, a number of liberal newspapers and magazines such as *The Nation* and the *New York Times* began to feature stories on the difficult plight that tenant farmers faced. While this union achieved few of its concrete goals, its very presence revealed that black and white farmers could temporarily put aside their racial grievances and prejudices to cooperate when it was in their economic interest.

Neither Congress nor President Roosevelt ever entertained the idea of creating a special program for black farmers, so their prospects would rise or fall depending on the success of broad-based programs to assist American farmers in general. In 1937, Congress created the Farm Security Administration (FSA), whose purpose was to provide low-interest loans to farmers. Headed by Will

Alexander, this program differed from earlier farm programs in that some of these loans were provided to sharecroppers and tenant farmers, essentially farmers who had not previously purchased land. With the help of Joseph Evans, a black administrative assistant, Alexander, despite the fiscal limitations of this program, attempted to address the wide disparity in land holding between blacks and whites. About 2,000 African Americans received tenant loans and another 1,400 were resettled in community projects where they were given the opportunity to purchase their land over a period of forty years. Many of these families were able to purchase land for the first time, were educated in modern farm techniques, and were introduced to new methods of production and marketing. One of these resettlement communities, Gees Bend, in rural Alabama, survives to the present day, and the African American women of Gees Bend are known nationally for their artistic quilting expertise. Indeed, the Gees Bend Quilting exhibition enjoyed a nationwide tour in 2006. White southerners expressed intense opposition to the liberal policies of the FSA as well as any New Deal program that suggested even a semblance of self-assertion or equality by African Americans. Southerners also balked at the prospect of resettling a substantial pool of cheap black labor.

The most successful New Deal programs not only put large numbers of African Americans back to work, but often employed black advisors or whites officials who were sensitive to the disproportionate number of unemployed black workers. The NYA serves as a case in point. When Roosevelt appointed Bethune to head the NYA's Division of Negro Affairs, African Americans succeeded in gaining a number of jobs that equaled their percentage in the U.S. population. In California and in every western state, the percentage of blacks who worked on NYA jobs was actually higher than the percentage of African Americans in the populations of those states. Although some African American leaders criticized segregation within New Deal programs, many others accepted or welcomed segregation because they believed that they would gain greater control over their own affairs in a segregated program.

The PWA and the WPA were highly responsive to the needs of African Americans. Established in 1933 with an initial appropriation of $3.3 billion, the PWA was created to build useful projects such as roads, schools, post offices, and government buildings. A number of PWA projects have stood the test of time, such as the Chicago subway system, New York's Triborough Bridge, and the Overseas Highway from Miami to Key West. The PWA was under the direction of Harold Ickes, a former president of the Chicago NAACP, Roosevelt's secretary of the interior, and an avid racial reformer. Ickes, for instance, had ended all segregation in the Interior Department and refused to hire whites who would not work with African Americans. As head of the PWA, he hired African Americans in skilled as well as unskilled positions. In an even bolder move, Ickes required that all PWA contracts include a clause stipulating that the number of blacks hired and their percentage of the project payroll be equal to their proportion in the general population. This form of quota, although derided by white southerners and many critics of the New Deal, would later be adopted in Affirmative Action programs during the 1960s and 1970s. The quota system remains as controversial today as it was when it was adopted by Harold Ickes in the 1930s.

Yet largely because of this quota and the leadership and commitment of Ickes, some African Americans saw a resurgence of construction in their communities. About $13 million was spent to build hospitals, community centers, and playgrounds. Ickes was equally concerned about the poor housing that many black families occupied. President Herbert Hoover had appointed a committee to study the state of African American housing in 1931 and the findings were gloomy. The committee concluded that less than half of the dwellings occupied by African Americans met modern standards. Thus the PWA constructed forty-nine low-rent housing projects and African Americans made up about one-third of the occupants of these units. Fourteen projects were built exclusively for African American occupancy, reinforcing the segregated housing pattern that had long existed in most American cities. However, one-third of these projects were designed for joint occupancy, permitting residents to cross racial boundaries. Whether segregated or integrated, thousands of African Americans for the first time were able to enjoy the modern conveniences of above-standard housing, such as gas, electric appliances, and indoor plumbing. The PWA's housing division was continued by its successor, the U.S. Housing Authority (USHA) in 1937. Like its predecessor, the USHA also favored the greater housing needs of African Americans, providing one-third of all units constructed to black families between 1937 and 1942.

Ickes deserves much of the credit for the success that African Americans received under the PWA, but the presence of Robert Clifton Weaver, a black advisor to Ickes, one of approximately forty-five who served as advisors in New Deal agencies, was also pivotal. Born in Washington, D.C., in 1907, this son of a postal clerk graduated from Dunbar High School and later earned a doctorate in economics from Harvard University in 1934. He was hired shortly thereafter by Ickes as the PWA's race relation's advisor. Weaver was a brilliant man. He was instrumental in helping Ickes develop the quota that required that black workers receive a certain percentage of the payroll of PWA projects. Weaver also served as a member of Roosevelt's Black Cabinet. His competence would lead to a succession of impressive appointments. Weaver left Washington, D.C., in 1944 to work for the United Nations. He taught later at Columbia and New York University, and in 1961 was appointed by President John Kennedy to head the Housing and Home Finance Administration, the highest federal position ever held by an African American. In 1966, Weaver was appointed by Lyndon Johnson to head the newly formed cabinet position of Housing and Urban Development (HUD), the first African American ever to hold cabinet rank.

While African American leaders and the black press lauded the PWA, the WPA proved the most effective New Deal agency in providing economic assistance to African American families. Roosevelt, however, issued an executive order in May 1935 stipulating that no discrimination shall exist in WPA projects. Harry Hopkins, who headed the granddaddy of all New Deal relief programs affirmed the president's commitment to nondiscrimination on two occasions by administrative orders from his office in Washington. The reality was quite different, for the white South had to be placated in the same manner as when Roosevelt spoke out forcefully against lynching but failed to push for antilynching legislation. Southerners insisted that the longstanding etiquette of race relations in their region, which required a separate and unequal status for African Americans, be maintained at all costs. Thus here, too, was a segregated New Deal program that paid African Americans in some regions of the country lower wages for similar work than whites. Blacks were dismissed en masse without cause from some WPA jobs to make additional room for whites and to ensure that white planters had adequate labor to pick crops during the harvest season. Black southerners in particular found it difficult to sign up for WPA jobs.

Yet for all of its bias, the WPA, according to Robert Weaver, represented a "godsend" for African Americans. "It made us feel like there was something we could do in the scheme of things," affirmed one black worker. As St. Clair Drake and Horace Cayton wrote in *Black Metropolis*, their classic study of African American life in Chicago, "Though the first few years of the Depression resulted in much actual suffering in Bronzeville, the WPA eventually provided a bedrock of subsistence which guaranteed food and clothing" (Drake and Clayton 1945; Drake and Clayton 1945, vol. 2, 386). This one New Deal program alone by 1939 provided the basic earnings for 1 million African Americans. It put black folks back to work, provided a basic and predictable income, and restored pride in many wage earners. Small wonder that the black press consistently lavished praise on Harry Hopkins for the fair-minded way in which he administered this program. In a number of cities such as New York and Chicago, African American workers received more than two or three times the proportion of WPA jobs as their percentage in the population.

The WPA also employed African Americans for many white-collar jobs and skilled positions in cities where these jobs had been either scarce or nonexistent. In Chicago, many black workers received their first experience in white collar and clerical jobs as a result of WPA employment. Many others were trained for the first time in skilled jobs. More than 5,000 African Americans, for instance, were employed throughout the nation as teachers and supervisors in the WPA education program, and hundreds of others, such as the black artists Jacob Lawrence and Sargeant Johnson, were employed in the WPA's Federal Art Project. The WPA's Federal Theatre Project, which contained a Negro Unit, employed African Americans to stage plays and dramatic productions, many of which had particular relevance to black history and the African American struggle for racial equality. The renowned black writers Ralph Ellison and Richard Wright were both employed by the WPA and published some of their earliest writings under the auspices of WPA programs. Historians owe a special debt of gratitude to the WPA, for its Federal Writers Project conducted approximately 2,300 interviews with former slaves, and this material ultimately transformed the way that modern historians and writers would interpret American slavery.

Scholarly and Political Challenges to Racism

The 1930s was also a time when scholars from a variety of academic disciplines began to challenge and undermine long-held scientific excuses and beliefs used to enforce white supremacy and racial inequality. As the historian Sitkoff wrote, a new intellectual consensus emerged that rejected the notion of innate black inferiority and, for the first time, stressed the damage done by racism to both African Americans and whites. Some scholars even depicted racial prejudice as a sickness, crippling the individual racist and the well-being of the nation. The fact that millions of whites had been displaced from work, and their unemployment had nothing to do with their inferiority or some innate racial characteristic was one factor. The rise of Nazism and the extreme racism against Jews that it inspired was perhaps more salient. Adolf Hitler had indeed given racism a bad name, although most white southerners would disagree. These changes in racial attitudes, which affected the general American population gradually, also transpired because new scientific information began to discredit old ideas and stereotypes (Sitkoff 1978, 190–192).

Franz Boas, a distinguished professor of anthropology at Columbia University, was one of the pivotal figures. Boas and his students, who included Margaret Mead, Ruth Benedict, and Ashley Montagu, concluded from their research that all mankind evolved from a single species, and there was no such thing as a "pure race." Instead, they maintained, racial intermixture had been continuous throughout human history. More important, Boas illustrated that previous data revealing that African Americans had higher mortality and morbidity rates than whites were unreliable, for whites died at higher rates than blacks from some diseases. Therefore, no creditable scientific evidence existed that African Americans constituted a lower order of species (Sitkoff 1978, 192).

An even more devastating blow to scientific racism was delivered by Otto Klineberg, a white social psychologist, who reexamined the results of World War I army intelligence tests, which had shown a large number of African Americans with test scores far below whites. Klineberg was interested in the effect that black migration to northern cities had on the intelligence scores of African Americans, and whether their scores would improve as their environment improved. In a pathbreaking study published in 1935, *Negro Intelligence and Selective Migration and Race Differences,* Klineberg found that the intelligence scores of individuals of different races changed according to their education and socioeconomic background. In a number of northern and midwestern cities, African Americans reported higher intelligence scores than both southern blacks and southern whites. The impact of Klineberg's findings were widely accepted in academic circles, although it took more than three decades for the majority of white southerners to agree that blacks were not innately inferior because of their race. These new studies also set the tone for future research on American race relations as well as illustrated the power that academics would have in shaping future public policy issues.

These changing racial attitudes were far more prevalent in the northern and western states, but racial inequality remained the defining feature of the American South. Although lynchings had declined significantly from their abysmal nineteenth-century figures, when two African Americans were murdered every week by white mobs, the South remained a rigidly segregated society. The *Plessy v. Ferguson* decision (1896), which affirmed the separate-but-equal principle in American law, regulated the races. Even minor transgressions of the southern racial etiquette could be dealt with harshly. Perhaps the greatest fear in the minds of white southerners was interracial sex, but only if it applied to black men and white women. Crossing this boundary, even if the relationship was consensual, could mean death to any African American male, no matter his reputation or economic standing in the community. Nine young black men, known as the Scottsboro Boys, would come face-to-face with this unyielding southern principle.

In 1931, as the Great Depression swept throughout the South, thousands of Americans of all races rode the rails in search of work. On one evening in 1931, a fight had broken out between groups of black and white men as one of these trains rode through the Alabama countryside. When the train reached the next town, nine African American boys were arrested and charged with raping two young white women who had been aboard the train. The Scottsboro Boys would spend the next two decades fighting for their freedom and defending themselves from these charges. Even though one of the women recanted her testimony and the medical evidence revealed that the women had not been sexually assaulted, the State of Alabama and indeed the entire white South saw this case as their duty to protect white womanhood and exercise racial control. The questionable character of these two women aside, the *Winston-Salem Journal* (North Carolina) expressed this position adamantly in 1932 when it wrote: "In the South it has been traditional ... that its white womanhood shall be held inviolate by an 'inferior race'" (Carter 1979, 105). If a white woman, any white woman, was willing to swear that she had been raped or sexually assaulted by an African American, "we see to it that the Negro is executed," stated another leading white southerner. In other words, the death penalty was the only punishment suitable for this crime.

The Scottsboro Boys were fighting both an entrenched and obstinate attitude, and the nation's leading civil rights organization, the NAACP, initially was reluctant get involved in the case for fear that the nine boys might be guilty as charged. After it became clear that the Scottsboro Boys did not have adequate counsel and the NAACP still was reluctant to take on this controversial case, the Communist Party agreed to defend the young men. Through its legal section, the International Labor Defense, the Communist Party supplied a highly capable defense for these men, saving them from certain execution. As Sitkoff wrote, "Communist propaganda transformed Scottsboro into the most searching indictment of Jim Crow yet to appear in the United States" (Sitkalf 1978, 147). This case is important for several additional reasons. The Scottsboro Boys attracted international support and attention, as thousands of prominent Americans and foreigners wrote letter to the president, the Supreme Court, and the governor of Alabama in support of the Scottsboro Boys. This case also resulted in a significant U.S. Supreme Court decision. In *Powell v. Alabama* (1931), the high court ruled that a victim is entitled to adequate counsel in capital cases. Failure to provide adequate counsel violated the Fourteenth Amendment's due process clause. The NAACP also conducted rallies and fundraisers for the Scottsboro Boys through their various branches, helping to defray their massive legal expenses. It was impossible for any African American to receive a fair trial in Alabama during the 1930s. In one of the greatest miscarriages of justice in American history, the nine Scottsboro Boys served more than 100 years in prison for a crime that they, in all likelihood, did not commit. The last Scottsboro Boy was released from prison in 1950.

Although less well known than the Scottsboro case, which attracted international attention, the Communist Party also supported Angelo Herndon, an articulate nineteen-year-old black coal miner from Birmingham, Alabama. Herndon, like many African Americans during the 1930s, was enticed by the liberal rhetoric and nondiscriminatory platform of the Communist Party, and joined the party in the early 1930s. Immediately, Communist Party officials recognized his leadership ability and persuaded him to work as an organizer, focusing particularly on the African American community in Georgia. The Communist Party was as feared in Georgia as in every other state. White southerners feared both the size of the crowds that Communist Party organizers could attract and the fact that the crowds were interracial. Thus radical activity would be combined with class solidarity and interracialism, the worse of all possible nightmares for white southerners. In July 1932, following a demonstration of Communists in Atlanta, two white detectives arrested Herndon after he retrieved his mail from a local post office. After he was booked at police headquarters on the charge of "suspicion," police wrote the word "Communist" across his name. Herndon was eventually charged with violating an 1869 Georgia insurrection statute. In other words, his presence at the Atlanta rally, the purpose of which was to persuade Atlanta city officials to appropriate more relief funds, was viewed not merely as threatening, but also as attempting to incite an insurrection or revolt. This charge was a capital crime in the state of Georgia. Following his trial, Herndon was sentenced to eighteen years in prison.

Similar to the Scottsboro case, the International Labor Defense sprang to Herndon's defense. Yet unlike the Scottsboro case, the Communist Party viewed Herndon's conviction as a serious threat to basic civil liberties, such as the rights of free speech and free assembly. After a costly five-year court battle, in 1937 the International Labor Defense's vigorous battle to free Herndon succeeded. In that year the U.S. Supreme Court declared the Georgia insurrection statute unconstitutional. The high court ruled by a five-to-four vote that Herndon had been deprived of the rights of all Americans guaranteed by the Fourteenth Amendment. The court's decision, writes Charles H. Martin, the definitive scholar on this case, also strengthened the principle established by Justice Oliver Wendell Holmes that free speech may not be curtailed because of a "dangerous tendency" to incite civil unrest, but only when a "clear and present danger" exists (Martin 1979).

The Left, Labor, and African Americans

These two cases, Scottsboro and the Angelo Herndon episode, reveal the important role that the Communist Party played in the civil rights struggle during the 1930s. The Communist Party proved far more radical in pushing for civil rights and racial equality for African Americans and the dispossessed than more traditional organizations such as the NAACP or the National Urban League. Taking the position that the racial conflict in America was part of a larger class struggle, the Communists adopted aggressive nondiscrimination policies within various CIO unions such as the ILWU, the National Maritime Union, and unions representing steel workers and packinghouse workers. If industrial unionism was going to succeed, racial discrimination, in their view, had no place. A white union leader such as Harry Bridges, who headed the ILWU, instituted a nondiscriminatory policy in all union affairs, including wages and supervisory positions. Indeed, the Communists went further than any other group or political party to place African Americans into leadership positions within industrial unions.

The United Auto Workers (UAW) had similar success by the late 1930s organizing African Americans in Detroit under the leadership of the CIO. Convincing African Americans that it was in their best interests to join the UAW was initially very difficult, as Henry Ford was held in high esteem by Detroit's black leadership. Ford had employed blacks in large numbers at several of his auto plants, accounting for nearly 12 percent of the total employees at the Ford Motor Company. Almost all of these workers, however, worked at the massive River Rouge plant. Henry Ford, although an openly avowed white supremacist and fiercely anti-Semitic, employed black autoworkers in all departments and positions, including foreman. Ford paid among the highest wages in the auto industry, and even though small wage differentials existed between blacks and whites, noted August Meier and Elliott Rudwick in their study of blacks and the UAW, African Americans earned more money at Ford than those employed in other industries (Meier and Rudwick 1979). As a consequence, black leaders in Detroit were solidly antiunion in the early 1930s. But the UAW ultimately convinced black autoworkers that it was in their long-term interest to affiliate with an industrial union that permitted no segregation. This strategy proved success, as African American autoworkers joined the UAW in large numbers. In return, the UAW became one of the staunchest supporters of the civil rights movement. They endorsed numerous campaigns of the NAACP for racial justice, including the Scottsboro Boys, as well as supported legislation to end the poll tax and to make lynching a federal crime. The UAW would also be included among a group of distinguished organizations and leaders who spoke in support of a federal civil rights bill in August 1963 when Dr. Martin Luther King, Jr., delivered his famous "I have a Dream" speech in the nation's capital.

African Americans were also the earliest group to equate southern racism with Adolf Hitler's racism against German Jews. Black journalists, in particular, took the lead in associating the trials and tribulations of the Scottsboro Boys, lynching, and Jim Crow with the Nazis' brutal treatment

U.S. Olympic athlete Jesse Owens, center, salutes during the presentation of his gold medal for the long jump on August 11, 1936, after defeating Nazi Germany's Lutz Long, right, during the 1936 Summer Olympics in Berlin. Naoto Tajima of Japan, left, placed third. Owens triumphed in the track and field competition by winning four gold medals in the 100-meter and 200-meter dashes, long jump and 400-meter relay. He was the first athlete to win four gold medals at a single Olympic Games. (*AP/ Wide World Photos*)

of Jews. They insisted, despite the protestations of white journalists to the contrary, that southern racism represented its own, but just as virulent, strain of Nazism. African American newspapers such as the *Chicago Defender* and the *Atlanta World*, among others, led the assault on Jim Crow, and were unrelenting in attempting to convince a skeptical white public that racism and Nazism were two sides of the same coin. As James Goodman noted in his book on the Scottsboro Boys, "Tales of Southern racism ran side by side with articles about Hitler's racism in Germany, and for many Northerners one story became an aid to understanding the other" (Goodman 1994, 151).

Jesse Owens's plight during the 1936 Olympics in Berlin, Germany, served further to drive home this point. The "Buckeye Bullet," as Owens was known, was an athletic marvel and arguably one of the greatest track and field athletes of his generation. A brilliant sprinter and broad jumper, Owens was just as talented in the low hurdles. At five feet, ten inches tall and weighing 160 pounds, sportswriters, wrote Jeremy Schaap, "often likened him to a big cat, or, alternately, to a thoroughbred" (Schaap 2007, 6). Representing the United States in four events, the 100- and 200-meter dashes, the broad jump, and the 4 x 100 meter relay, Owens set four Olympic records and two world records. Never before in the history of the Olympics had a track and

Health in Harlem

African Americans experienced much poorer health than did whites. So concluded Dr. Winifred B. Nathan, who conducted a five-year study for the New York Tuberculosis and Health Association. For example, the tuberculosis death rate for African Americans in Harlem was two and a half times that for whites elsewhere in the city. Dr. Nathan explained the disparity as the result of several factors in Harlem, including poor sanitary conditions caused by excessive population density, together with poor nutrition and living standards, themselves the product of poverty and ignorance. Association officials declared that the study showed that tuberculosis was the third most important cause of death among Harlem's denizens. Thus Harlem's death rate from tuberculosis was 193 per 100,000, whereas New York City's was but 81 per 100,000. The rate for African Americans increased in the later 1920s and 1930s, whereas that for the city as a whole remained stable.

Tuberculosis was hardly Harlem's only health problem. Pneumonia and heart disease ranked first and second, before tuberculosis. In the years under review, Harlem suffered more than 15,000 deaths, an annual average of 3,239, with heart disease averaging 541 deaths, pneumonia 489, tuberculosis 368, cancer 222, and accidents 175 deaths a year, on average. As for infant mortality during the five-year period of the study, the annual average was 111, or 57.6 percent higher than New York City's rate of 64. More than 30 percent of these Harlem babies died in the first seven days of life and another 10 percent within three weeks of birth. Maternal mortality was also twice as high for African-American new mothers in Harlem as for New York City as a whole. The greater the population density in Harlem, Dr. Nathan insisted, the higher the morbidity and mortality rates for infants and mothers, leading him to conclude that an ambitious and extensive program in health education was needed in the Harlem community, which meant the creation of a centralized institution to promote health awareness and sound living there—something that never happened in the years of the Great Depression.

SOURCE: *New York Times*, November 9, 1930.

field athlete dominated international competition with such ease. Hitler, the German *Fuehrer*, had personally greeted and congratulated each gold medal winner, but neither Owens nor any other black athlete would receive this honor. When he returned to the United States, however, Owens stated that it was President Roosevelt, not Hitler, who had snubbed him. "The president didn't even send me a telegram," he reported. This served as proof, in Owens's mind, that his own country did not respect his accomplishments because of his race.

Enduring Segregation and the New Deal

Owens's dissatisfaction with Roosevelt notwithstanding, the majority of African American voters continued to endorse the presidency of Roosevelt. They expressed their gratitude, in spite of segregation in New Deal programs, for the jobs and economic support that the president distributed to the black community. Roosevelt, however, increasingly faced critics within his own party as well as from black leaders who were dissatisfied that the New Deal never addressed the more critical employment needs of African Americans. The influential *Pittsburgh Courier*, which had endorsed Roosevelt during his first two terms, aligned with Republican Wendell L. Willkie in the 1940 presidential election. Similarly, the *Baltimore Afro-American* defected from the Democratic Party, critical of Roosevelt's accommodation to segregation within the CCC and other New Deal programs. The Afro-American also criticized the fact that several New Deal programs purposely excluded large categories of African American workers from wage and hour protections. When Congress passed legislation protecting the rights of workers in these areas, they purposely excluded farmworkers and domestics, both large categories of the African American workforce, particularly in the South. Nor did Congress provide Social Security benefits to these same workers when the Social Security Act, which Roosevelt referred to as the "cornerstone of the New Deal," was passed in 1935. African Americans made up 53 percent of all people engaged in agricultural labor in the nation in 1930. They represented 50 percent in 1940. The vast majority of these farmworkers were sharecroppers, who eked out the barest living imaginable, even in the best of times. Only a mere 10 percent of black farmers owned their own land, and their acreage, which averaged 63 acres in 1935, compared with 145 acres for white farmers, indicates the wide disparity between these two groups. Allison Davis accurately described the dismal plight of black farmers during the Great Depression when he wrote that "most [black] tenant families lived in semistaravation." Approximately two-thirds of the nation's African American population was not covered by the Social Security Act that Roosevelt signed in 1935. Not until 1954, when Republicans controlled the presidency and both houses of congress were these occupational exclusions eliminated.

One of the darkest episodes of the Great Depression involved the use of rural black southerners as human guinea pigs to test the long-range effects of syphilis on the human body if left untreated. This study, known as the Tuskegee Syphilis experiment, conducted by the U.S. Public Health Service in Macon County, Alabama, only came to public light in 1972. The study involved more than 600 black men, the vast majority of whom were illiterate and uneducated sharecroppers, tenant farmers, and unskilled laborers, who agreed to participate in the study, but were never told the truth. Rather than being informed that they had a serious venereal disease that could be fatal if left untreated, government doctors and nurses told them that they had "bad blood," a common euphemism for an array of illnesses used by rural blacks. The men were treated with vitamins and aspirin. Even after the drug penicillin was discovered in the 1940s and proved to be extremely effective against syphilis, the Public Health Service withheld treatment of the drug, a decision they had made at the start of this sordid experiment. Nor did it matter to government doctors that withholding medical treatment was a violation of Alabama state law. In 1972 after a reporter broke the story, the government agreed to compensate the victims and their families.

On balance, African Americans faired relatively well during the 1930s, even accounting for segregated New Deal policies and the exclusion of some categories of workers from the protection of social security. Those who succeeded in gaining employment on one of the public works projects of the PWA or the WPA faired best of all. Yet those African Americans who enrolled in the CCC or the NYA also found that the security of a monthly wage and a predictable income trumped unemployment every time. Given the choice between starvation and segregated employment, African Americans chose employment every time. Most African Americans, like the black leader W. E. B. Du Bois, were realists and understood that Roosevelt, even if he possessed the will, was powerless to change longstanding racial mores and attitudes against the wishes of a strong bloc of southern Democrats who insisted on segregation. "I feel without the slightest doubt that Franklin Roosevelt has done more for the uplift and progress of the Negro than any president since Abraham Lincoln," echoed Du Bois, as he supported Roosevelt's fourth term as president in 1944 (Katznelson 2005, 205). Du Bois and others were certainly aware that Roosevelt had failed to address numerous areas of inequality in American society. But in their political calculus, the good work of this president in the African American community and the widespread feeling that he cared about their problems far outweighed any negative assessment. Black Americans could point with pride to the number of African American advisors in New Deal agencies, the important role of Bethune in the NYA, the appointment of William Hastie as the first African American federal judge, and the appointment in 1940 of Benjamin O. Davis, Sr., as the first African American to hold the rank of general in the U.S. Army. These were much more than merely symbolic appointments in the black community. African Americans remembered all too well the indifference of previous presidents during the 1920s, and the cavalier manner in which Herbert Hoover had dismissed their suffering, as well as the massive unemployment that gripped the country.

Yet, in the final analysis, the New Deal failed to end the Great Depression or to bring about full employment in either the African American community or the nation. Only the massive demand for manpower as a result of the entrance of the United States into World War II would bring an end to the worse economic era in American history. Nor did any of the major civil rights organizations such as the NAACP, the National Urban League, or the National Council of Negro Women, established in 1935 and led by Bethune, possess the clout to force the president to address their problems in a more meaningful and decisive manner. Roosevelt, like every politician, listened to more powerful constituencies and organized blocs, and while he was sensitive to African Americans, he had to weigh their interest against a formidable group of white southern Democrats. Many important changes, nonetheless, transpired during the era of the Great Depression. The militancy of the NAACP, particularly the success of its legal campaign against racial discrimination, set the stages for more important victories during the 1950s and beyond, such as the historic *Brown v. Board of Education, Topeka* decision in 1954, outlawing segregation in public schools and overturning the 1896 *Plessy v. Ferguson* decision. This assertiveness would encourage African American leaders in both the North and South to demand a larger share of equality when the United States entered World War II, ultimately leading to the integration of the U.S. armed forces in 1948. That African Americans achieved as much as they did during the Great Depression was a testament to their ingenuity and their ceaseless struggle to achieve social and racial justice.

References

Carter, Dan T. 1979. *Scottsboro, A Tragedy of the American South*. Baton Rouge: Louisiana State University Press.

Drake, St. Clair, and Horace Cayton. *Black Metropolis: A Study of Negro Life in a Northern City*, 2 vols. New York: Harcourt Brace and Company, 1945.

Goodman, James. 1994. *Stories of Scottsboro*. New York: Pantheon.

Katznelson, Ira. 2005. *When Affirmative Action Was White*. New York: W. W. Norton.

Martin, Charles H. 1979. *The Angelo Herndon Case and Southern Justice*. Baton Rouge: Louisiana State University Press.

Meier, August. 1963. *Negro Thought in America: Racial Ideologies in the Age of Booker T. Washington 1880–1915*. Ann Arbor: University of Michigan Press.

Meier, August, and Elliott Rudwick. 1979. *Black Detroit and the Rise of the United Auto Workers*. New York: Oxford University Press.

Salmond, John A. 1967. *The Civilian Conservation Corps, 1933–1942: A New Deal Case Study*. Durham: Duke University Press.

Schaap, Jeremy. 2007. *Triumph: The Untold Story of Jesse Owens and Hitler's Olympics*. Boston: Houghton-Mifflin.

Sitkoff, Harvard. *A New Deal for Blacks: The Emergence of Civil Rights as a National Issue: The Depression Decade*. New York: Oxford University Press.

Weiss, Nancy J. 1978. *Farewell to the Party of Lincoln*. Princeton: Princeton University Press.

Wolters, Raymond. 1970. *Negroes and the Great Depression: The Problem of Economic Recovery*. Westport, CT: Greenwood Publishers.

The Scripts of Racial Segregation in New Deal America

7

Ben Keppel

The Segregated Social Sciences

This chapter uses social science research from the New Deal years to recapture what it meant to be black and live in the United States when it was a legally segregated society. The 1930s, in addition to their significance as the Depression Decade, are also important as the decade in which American social science began a long coming of age about race.

For many years before that time many social scientists, like other white Americans, believed that segregation reflected real differences between racial groups, although they might differ as to whether genetics or environment were the cause of these differences. By the 1930s and 1940s, however, the first doctorate-holding academic generation of any size was graduating and generally entering the social sciences through "Negroes Only" entrance provided by employment at a historically black college or university (As Jonathan Scott Holloway and I note in *Black Scholars on the Line: Race, Social Science and American Thought in the Twentieth Century*, 316 of the 384 doctorates to African Americans in *all of American history* up to 1943 were awarded after 1929).

Becoming an African American social scientist in the era of legalized racial segregation was not easy. According to the practice of that time, African Americans, especially if they lived in the South and border South (as most of them did), were locked out of higher education at the historically white institutions of the region. After receiving often excellent training at a far less financially endowed leading black college (such as Fisk, Atlanta University, or Howard), the deserving graduate might be permitted to pursue graduate work at a top-ranked historically white university (such as Harvard or the University of Chicago), only to find themselves ineligible for jobs at white schools.

John Hope Franklin

In the time of the Depression, John Hope Franklin was a young African American hoping to become a history teacher. Born in the rigidly segregated world of Tulsa, Oklahoma, in 1915, John Hope Franklin discovered his love of history while a student at Fisk University, where he was encouraged to attend Harvard for graduate work, which he did starting in fall, 1935. During three years at Harvard, he distinguished himself in his requirements and course work. For his dissertation, he chose the topic of free blacks in North Carolina 1790–1860. Yet it was as a budding African American social scientist that Franklin found his most challenging experiences as a scholar. He joined Harvard's History Club, a faculty and student discussion group devoted to his chosen field of American history. When he nominated for a club office Oscar Handlin, a fellow student from Brooklyn, he was shocked when other members of the club blackballed Handlin because he was a Jew. Franklin knew first hand the discrimination by whites against African Americans; only now did he realize that whites stigmatized other whites as well. He was a top student and most faculty treated him decently; but they never offered him a teaching assistantship, and in many

Historian Lorenzo J. Greene (1899–1988), a professor of history at Lincoln University for almost forty years, is best known for his pains-taking and perceptive study, *The Negro in Colonial New England* (1942). Of special interest here, however, is the diary Professor Greene wrote at the beginning of his career (1928–1933), as a valued researcher and representative for the Association for the Study of Negro Life in History and its founder, Carter G. Woodson. African American history was not part of the generally and historically white curriculum of this country until the civil rights movement forced a change. Long before that time, Greene went from school to school, primarily in the South and Southwest, selling both Woodson's textbooks and the idea of "Negro history" itself. Greene's notes convey the way in which segregation could vary by city and by state. Notes from a visit to Tulsa, Oklahoma, suggest that, in the aftermath of the devastating riot there in 1921, African Americans, armed with the ballot, were able to make "separate" a little more "equal." His treks during the hardest years of the Depression brought Greene face to face not only with how economic trauma turned certain laboring jobs from "Negro" to "white" but how it also provoked fierce competition between black and Mexican laborers. Greene took it all in, gaining the wisdom and compassion that come with age only by choice. Here was the experience of a very talented African American budding scholar.

The books under discussion here were not the first such efforts to study African American life with respect for the requirements of scientific inquiry—that distinction belongs to W. E. B. Du Bois's *The Philadelphia Negro* (1899). The white scholars and black scholars under discussion were taking work he had begun years earlier.

ways, by the time he left Harvard, Franklin had had his fill of the precious snobbery of so many Harvard students, not to mention segregation in the community. When he moved to North Carolina, to do his research at the state archives, he found himself in a segregated reading room, apart from the white patrons. Finally, he finished his dissertation—not before publishing an article in the distinguished journal *The New England Quarterly*—and found employment as a professor at St. Augustine College in North Carolina.

In the 1930s, Franklin struggled, as many aspiring African American social scientists did, against enormous barriers to their aspirations. Money was only part of the problem. There was also the twilight zone of American racial segregation, in which a person of color experienced cruel discrimination one moment, patronizing and condescending remarks the next, and the occasional delightful and civilized moment with a white person.

SOURCE: John Hope Franklin, *Mirror to America. The Autobiography of John Hope Franklin* (New York: Farrar, Straus, and Giroux, 2005), 3–102.

This chapter begins by exploring the material consequences of segregation for African Americans in Chicago and in the South. The balance of the discussion looks at the tense opposition between the rigidly observed script of southern segregation and the intense opposition to it expressed by blacks in their conversations with these researchers. The statements elicited are quite remarkable, especially if one considers the harsh punishments awaiting those believed to have spoken "out of place."

Dollars and Cents/Brick and Mortar

What did segregation cost those who were its targets in health, safety, and security? Whether one had migrated to Chicago during and after World War I, or chose to stay in the South, one had few dollars and thus could not well afford much brick and mortar. In an effort to translate these economic figures into their current values, I have converted major price and income figures to their 2007 equivalents using the Bureau of Labor Statistics' online Inflation Calculator (www.bls.gov/data/inflation_calculator).

St. Clair Drake and Horace Cayton report in the pages of *Black Metropolis: A Study of Negro Life in a Northern City* (1945), that "over 65 per cent of the Negro adults earn their bread by manual labor in stockyard and steel mill, in factory and kitchen, where they do the essential digging, sweeping and serving which make metropolitan life tolerable." When they break down the class structure of Chicago by race, Drake and Cayton finds that 67.9 percent of African Americans adults in Chicago earned annual incomes of under $1,000 (in 1935–1936) at the jobs described above (compared with 26.7 percent of native-born whites and 32.7 percent of foreign-born whites). In other words, almost twice as many African Americans earned below $14,960.36 (in 2007 dollars) as whites.

The African American members of Chicago's industrial working class formed the middle class of "Bronzeville" (Drake and Cayton's name for the Chicago Black Belt). According to a survey of 90,484 families, 484 workers in the iron and steel industry in Horace Cayton and George S. Mitchell's *The Black Worker and the New Unions* (1939), the national average for black workers was $0.55 an hour (about $8.35 in 2007 dollars) compared with $0.70 for white workers (about $10.55 an hour 2007 dollars). Whether they were white and earned an income of $20,256 (in today's dollars) or were black and making around $16,032, if they were supporting a family of four on that income alone, they would both fall below the 2007 federal poverty line of $20,650. The white worker would fall $394 below today's poverty line while the black worker would miss the line by $4,618—more than *ten times* as far. Being on the wrong side of the color line in this segregated society was expensive.

The wage ceiling under which these black workers were trapped was not only an economic one; they were also trapped in the hottest, most uncomfortable and most dangerous jobs. As one black worker in Clairton, Pennsylvania, reported to Cayton and Mitchell (1939, 32):

Electric phosphate smelting furnace used to make elemental phosphorus in a Tennessee Valley Authority chemical plant in the vicinity of Muscle Shoals, Alabama, June 1942. Photo by Alfred T. Palmer for the Farm Security Administration. (*Library of Congress*)

> The average job for the Negro is in the Coke Works—Battery Department and powdering steel. All are very hard jobs and very hot. The white worker will not work in the Coke Works ... or the Battery Department unless he is absolutely forced to hold his job.

The upper class of Bronzeville (5 percent of all African Americans in Chicago) was a small but unusually diverse group of professionals, including business people, lawyers, doctors, school principals, and teachers), none of whom made an annual income above $5,000 (1938 income in 2007 dollars: $73,740.78).

When the workday was done, African American workers returned home to overcrowded residences. "Negroes are not absorbed into the general population," wrote Drake and Cayton. "Black metropolis remains athwart the least desirable residential zones. Its population grows larger and larger, unable to either expand freely or to scatter" (Drake and Cayton 1945, 576). Symbolic of the Depression-era housing crisis in Bronzeville were the "kitchenettes," which became common in Bronzeville during the thirties. As houses and apartments in poorer areas of the Black Belt were being torn down between 1930 and 1938, landlords in the "better" sections would reconvert one six-room apartment into six "kitchenettes." In one case reported by Drake and Cayton, a six-room apartment renting in 1938 for $50 a month (2007 dollars: $737.41) became six kitchenettes, renting for a weekly rate of $8.00 (2007: $117.99) and generating for the landlord $192 a month.($2,831.65). Drake and Cayton describe the grim layout as follows: "For each one-room household [the landlord] provided an ice box, a bed, and a gas hot plate. A bathroom that once served a single family now served six. A building that formerly held sixty families now held three hundred" (Drake and Cayton 1945, 576).

Despite this clear evidence of institutionalized racism, it is also not difficult to understand why Drake and Cayton could conclude that Negroes found Chicago to be a positive change: "It was certainly different from slavery sixty years ago, or from the South today. Negroes liked [Chicago]" (Drake and Cayton 1945, 80).

Things were much worse in the rural South, where many had begun hardscrabble lives. In terms of gross income, life was hard for most small farmers, irrespective of race, but being an African American exacted a high price in terms of the economic bottom line. According to Arthur Raper's survey of Greene County Georgia in his detailed monograph, *Preface to Peasantry* (1936), African American annual farm family income (including the cash value of homegrown crops) was three-quarters that of white farm families in 1934. Within this average were African-American "owners" (12.1 percent of black families) who made between a top amount of $501.56 (compared with a top amount of $647.50 for the 40 percent of similarly situated white farmers) and a bottom amount of $111.86 for the 23.2 percent who worked as "wage hands" (white wage hands earned $216.69 and accounted for 12.5 percent of white farm families). Just under two-thirds of African American farm families made between $281.58 and $416.97 (compared with between $384.85 and $550.75 for the slightly less than half of white families who fall in the same laboring categories) (Raper 1936, 21, 33, 34, 35).

Converting these 1934 dollars to 2007 values, we can see why, even in the Great Depression, the South continued to symbolize acute poverty to a nation already on intimate terms with it. African American owners had an annual income of $7,783.50 compared with $10,048.28 for white owners. The vast majority of African American farm families made between $4,369.72 and $6,470.78 (compared with between $5,972.33 and $8,546.86 for white farm families earning a living in the very same wage categories). All of these families would be considered very poor by today's calculations, no matter what the size of the family.

In view of these figures, it should come as no surprise that, in housing, brick and mortar did not exist for these Americans. Charles S. Johnson, in his survey of 916 families in *Growing up in the Black Belt: Negro Youth in the Rural South* (1941, 55, 56), found that only sixty-nine of these families "lived in houses without a major physical defect." Johnson reported, "In over half the houses, the roof leaked; in nearly half the houses there were broken porches or steps and defective floors." Only 43 of these 916 families had an indoor toilet and only 191 "had a septic tank or sanitary pit outside."

The economic circumstances faced by Americans in the New Deal years only being to be comprehensible in today's terms by adjusting for the dramatic changes in the cost of living over the last seventy years, but it does not end there. In fact, standing alone, these numbers impart a false precision to a process of approximation. Before World War II, the United States was a traditional industrial working-class society in which home ownership and the most basic kind of economic security were far less easy to attain than they would become over the next thirty years. That achievement was made possible not only by new and substantial government support for home ownership and a college education (both aimed at returning veterans) but also by the negotiating power of the strong industrial unions that first exerted their strength during the thirties.

The two-income household so indispensable to making ends meet today also existed in these times, but to a far lesser degree. In Chicago, according to Drake and Cayton, almost half of the women who worked as "domestics" in 1940 were African Americans earning $2 for "day's work" and $20 for "week's work" (just under $300 a week today) (Drake and Cayton 1945, 242–43).

In addition, the truism that "times were simpler" actually makes sense: The modern consumer culture was in its earliest days—people made less, expected less, and were not disappointed with less. Another crucial separation between today and yesterday is the ubiquity of credit and debt of all kinds: Disparities in income are softened in the short term by too easy credit.

Land and Power/Past and Present

According to the intensive research of Allison Davis, Burleigh B. Gardner, and Mary P. Gardner contained in *Deep South: A Social Anthropological Study of Caste and Class* (1941), land ownership was rare and usually possible only on a small scale. In 1935, the authors report, just under 20 percent of the 2,000 "farm operators" in "Old County" (Natchez, Mississippi) were also landowners. Most of these fortunate few, whatever their race, owned very small plots. Land ownership was unevenly distributed among 400 families tied together by "extended kinship relations among the old planter families and by frequent intermarriage between collateral lines in the same family" (1941, 276–77). A majority of all land owned by this group was, in fact, held by of thirty-six people, of whom two were African American. Ninety-four percent of the 1,337 tenant farmers working in Old County in 1930 were African American. Among landowners, only 14.8 percent were African American, whereas 59 percent of whites could claim this status.

It is a common theme of the studies examined here that slavery cast a long shadow over the South of the 1930s. Most lasting was the hard mold into which economic and social relations were set for much of next century with the failure of Reconstruction. As Charles S. Johnson writes in *Shadow of the Plantation*,

> Patterns of life, social codes, as well as social attitudes, were set in the economy of slavery. The political and economic revolution through which they have passed has affected only slightly the social relationships or the mores upon which these relations have been based. The strength and apparent permanence of this early cultural set [*sic*] have made it impossible for newer generations to escape the. Influence of patterns of work and general social behavior transmitted by their elders. (Johnson 1934, 16)

Strong material evidence of this long shadow can be found by examining patterns of African American land acquisition and ownership laid out by Davis, Gardner, and Gardner. Among African American landowners, most of those holding the most valuable plots were either former slaves or the descendants of former slaves who purchased their land in the first few years after the end of legal slavery. Fourteen of the twenty-nine former slaves who purchased land acquired it from their former owners. All of this leads the authors to the conclusion that "there was less opposition to a colored man's buying land from a white landlord in the period of social and economic disintegration following the Civil War than there has generally been since 1875" (1941, 296).

Davis, Gardner, and Gardner also concluded that since none of the fourteen who purchased land from their master bought their land from the *same* master, a larger game of social control is being played in which *the sale* (not the gift) of land to selected former slaves was a way for former slave owners to reward "their 'favorite Negro', one ... who meticulously observed the caste sanctions and who, therefore, would not seek to make other colored workers on the plantation displeased with their landless condition" (1941, 296). Many of those who remained tenant farmers rented "from the same white family which owned their slave ancestors" (1941). This discussion underscores the idea that the failure to redistribute at least some significant portion of plantation lands to former slaves in compensation for their enslavement was possibly the most historically consequential mistake in all of American history.

The Great Depression did provoke a major federal intervention in agriculture in the form of the Agricultural Adjustment Act. This intervention hurt more than helped small farmers. Arthur F. Raper finds that, whatever the New Deal "Brains Trust" envisioned from Washington, implementation of the New Deal's agricultural stabilization efforts never had a chance to succeed. The politics of keeping the South a one-party region required that power remain in the hands of those who had always held power—men made powerful by their wealth and their whiteness. Thus, large landowners benefited overwhelmingly in comparison to small landowners, no matter on which side in the color line they lived. In addition, commodity price supports hurt the process of land acquisition by raising prices. Finally, very little federal aid reached African Americans because those who benefited from racial segregation administered the local programs. No less than

African American tenant farmer's family chops cotton near White Plains, Georgia, 1941. Photo by Jack Delano for the Farm Security Administration. (*Library of Congress*)

three research reports commissioned by specialized units of the U.S. Department of Agriculture (*Black Farmers and Their Farms, Social and Economic Environment of Black Farmers,* both published in 1986, and *Black Farmers in America, 1865–2000,* released in 2002) argued that discrimination against black farmers by its programs remains a significant issue. In addition, as late as 1979, the Delta Crop Region (parts of Arkansas, Louisiana, and Mississippi) remained an area in which the incidence of poverty was starkly divided by race: 56.3 percent of blacks lived below the poverty level compared with 15.9 percent of whites (Social and Economic Environment 2002, v).

For all of the hardships of life in the Chicago Black Belt, it is not at all hard to understand what pulled so many millions of African Americans north between the beginning of World War I and the late 1960s. Black teachers working in Chicago public schools made wages equal to those of their white colleagues, whereas in the South, Charles S. Johnson, in *The Negro College Graduate* (1938), found that African American teachers typically made between 25 percent and 50 percent less than white teachers (a gap that widened during the Depression years). For black Chicagoans, Drake and Cayton confirmed that New Deal assistance was more available, perhaps because African Americans in Chicago could vote and held real political power. The segregation regime in Chicago was rigid in housing and the economy—making the budget and the living conditions generally tight; nonetheless, there was more freedom of movement and a better living to be had (brought about by the nondiscriminatory industrial unions formed by the Congress of Industrial Organizations), all of which brightened the look of the future.

The Southern Script of Segregation

Fifty years ago, in *Blackways of Kent,* sociologist Hylan Lewis offered the most perceptive description of racial segregation's cultural dimension—the way in which it subtly regulates the behavior of all who come within its scope: "[T]he Negroes of Kent may be thought of as acting out a life drama in accordance with an imaginary 'script' that each person 'carries in his head'" (1955, 5).

Measuring human experience in dollars and cents provides some important answers about the nature of that experience, but it does not go inside that life to establish, as closely as possible, how one's circumstances are seen and understood by the people themselves. When we speak of a "script" of proper conduct, we are referring primarily to Southern society. While racial segregation definitely existed in Chicago, it was less scripted because it was less deeply rooted in that city's social relations. As Drake and Cayton observe:

> In the South, Negroes are constantly reminded that they have a "place," and that they are expected to stay in it. In [Chicago], they have a much wider 'freedom to come and go'. The city is not plastered with signs pointing COLORED here and WHITE there. On elevated trains and streetcars, Negroes and whites push and shove... with a common disregard for age, sex, or color. At

> ball parks, wrestling and boxing arenas, race tracks and basketball courts, and other spots where crowds congregate as spectators, Negroes will be found sitting where they please, booing and applauding, cheering and "razzing" with as little restraint as their white fellows in virtually all of the city's theaters and movie houses.... [B]ut there are public situations where an attempt is sometimes made to draw the color line. For instance, objections are frequently expressed to the presence of Negroes in certain elementary and high schools, and to their use of parks, and swimming pools in various sections of the city.... The very presence of a Black Belt leads the public to feel that Negroes should have their own recreational facilities, and should not "invade" those in other sections of the city. (Drake and Cayton 1945, 101–102)

Much has been written about the power of "tradition" in keeping segregation in force. That is acutely true if we are willing to include the threat of violence as a primary tradition. Typical of how enforcement worked is the following account by a white landowner, contained in *Deep South*:

> There was one [colored tenant] out our way not long ago ... who was getting smart. I told my boys that if he didn't behave they ought to take him out for a ride, and tend to him, and tell him that if he didn't stop talking and acting so big, the next time it would be either a bullet or a rope. That is the way to manage them when they get too big—take them in hand before any trouble starts. (Davis, Gardner, and Gardner 1941, 394)

John Dollard, in *Caste and Class in a Southern Town*, places the violence within the context of the more generalized exploitation integral to the entire sharecropping system:

> Some owners ... juggle the accounts to keep the cropper in debt and thus hold him on the land.... [An] informant said that [when] the cropper is called to the accounting, the boss man sits at the desk, a forty-five caliber revolver beside him [and] roughly asks what the tenant wants. The tenant says he wants a settlement. "Yes," says the boss man. "You made fifteen dollars last year." The tenant cannot argue or dispute or the boss will grasp the gun and ask if he is going to argue. If he does, boom-boom. (1937, 125)

A crucial accomplishment of the civil rights movement thirty years later was the direct and physical confrontation of this terror, a strategy that would cost many lives. In the twenty years between the end of World War II in 1945 and the commencement of Freedom Summer in Mississippi in 1964 by the Student Non-violent Coordinating Committee, the great world "out there" entered these isolated communities through the electronic mass media. In *Blackways of Kent*, Lewis captures the process of change as he observed it under way in a Piedmont community in the late 1940s. First in importance was World War II, which drew three-quarters of black men between the ages of eighteen and forty into the ranks of the armed forces. When these men came home, they were armed for life with "important memories, different conceptions of themselves and their worth as human beings, and a more personal interest in national and world affairs" (1955).

In addition to following the crises of the early cold war, Lewis reports, these men followed President Truman's actions on civil rights with great care (Lewis 1955, 41).

A comparison of two scenes is instructive to show how change came to the Deep South after World War II. The first scene is taken from John Dollard's *Caste and Class in a Southern Town* (1937, 7, 8): One morning in the middle 1930s, John Dollard uneasily and quite publicly found himself merging his "observer" and "participant" roles when a black man came to call on the porch of the rooming house where Dollard was staying:

> One morning a Negro friend came to my boarding house and knocked on the *front* door. It was a crisis for him, for the family, and for me. Perhaps he felt a sense of his own dignity as a middle-class Negro, perhaps he felt that the house had become extra territorial to southern society because I was living there. He was left standing on the porch and the family member who called me seemed unhappy and reproachful. I had unwittingly aided in imposing a humiliation on my hosts. The interview on the porch was constrained on both sides. Small towns have eyes and ears, and Southerntown is strict in its policing of newcomers. My Negro friend brought still another Negro on the porch to meet me. Should we shake hands? Would he be insulted if we did not, or would he accept the situation? I kept hands in pockets and did not do it, a device that was often useful in resolving such a situation. My friend must have noticed this, but with genuine politeness, he gave no sign and even later seemed not to hold it against me. In point of fact, we were fortunate. He might have been sent away rudely, or told to go to the back door, or I might have been severely condemned. Still there was a strain in the social atmosphere of the house thereafter, a strain which informed me that Negroes might not change their behavior toward its occupants because I was a resident there. As a researcher in Southerntown one lives always with a sense of spiritual torsion, willing but unable to conform to the conflicting elements in the social pattern.

Scene two comes from the field research of Hylan Lewis in the late 1940s. Lewis is here recording the words of a "white official" (Lewis 1955, 297):

> Some of the niggers are getting mighty uppity, even around here. Every time a colored man has come to the house since I have been in Kent, he has come to the front door. Fortunately, I have never had to ask any of them into the house—I have always been able to finish my business with him on the porch.

World War II might have brought a new attitude to some in the rural South, but the research of E. Franklin Frazier during the 1930s in Louisville, Kentucky, and Washington, D.C., finds a spirit of resistance of which the boxer Joe Lewis was the most powerful unifying symbol. As Frazier argued in *Negro Youth at the Crossways*, "Joe Lewis enables ... many Negro youth and adults in all classes ... to inflict vicariously the aggressions they would like to carry out against whites for the discrimination and insults which they have suffered" (Frazier 1940, 179).

E. Franklin Frazier (1894–1962), a professor at Howard University for many years, is one of the leading American social scientists of the 20th century, and one of the closest students of African American life during the Great Depression. He is best known for his monograph, *The Negro Family in the United States* (1939), which became controversial in the 1960s and 1970s when its findings were interpreted by some as arguing that the structure of the African American family was significantly responsible for persistent inequality. (*Photographs and Prints Division, Schomburg Center for Research in Black Culture, The New York Public Library, Astor, Lenox and Tilden Foundations*)

So, what was it like to be "segregated against"? As they entered black homes and lives, these investigators were acutely sensitive to the fact that they operated within reality deeply layered with fear and suspicion. As Allison Davis and John Dollard made eloquently clear in *Children of Bondage*, their study of 123 families in Natchez, Mississippi, and New Orleans, Louisiana, the surface acceptance of caste relations by blacks was an illusion:

> Negroes in the Deep South are continually expressing to each other the sharpest antagonisms against whites and the deepest sense of frustration of their position in society. They verbalize these tabooed feelings only to their colored friends or to colored interviewers, and to Northern white men, that is, to members of those groups that will not punish them for such expressions. (Davis and Dollard 1941, 238)

In one case, study, Davis and Dollard tell of a young man who wanted blacks to arm themselves and fight back with violence, while admitting the impracticality of his solution. The key point is that the American caste system had little of the mutuality of caste, traditionally defined: Many whites, as Charles Johnson argued, no longer shared in the assumptions that supported the segregation script, and many blacks were "struggling against this [unequal status] rather than accepting it."

What was it like to be "black"? African Americans possessed deep and highly nuanced understanding of social etiquette: a clear understanding of the rationalizations behind segregation and the benefits that accrue to white people because their color. It is also assumed by some that, in the words of one Chicago businessman interviewed for a study of "Negro personality development" in Chicago headed by W. Lloyd Warner, "The greatest competition we have is the psychology of our [own] people. They have a tendency to believe even yet that what is white is best" (Warner 1941, 176).

It should come as no surprise that African-Americans might speculate and indeed wish for the experience of life on the other side of the color line. The evidence seems overwhelming that these feelings however, coexisted with stronger feelings of pride for how they and their racial group had survived in a society organized against them. There is no evidence that African Americans believed that a social order based on white supremacy was a reflection of the natural organization of humanity. The focus on race can also blind us to the strength of class as a factor. For a sense of how these themes shared psychic space in individual minds, consider the following statement received by Frazier from an "upper class youth of very fair complexion":

> Sometimes I feel all right.... At other times, I feel sorry because I am a Negro. There are many classes of us and many in those lower classes do not know how to conduct themselves; and yet white people class us all alike. I can't understand that, particularly since there are different classes in their group and they don't fail to make the distinction.... I'm proud of the fact that I am a Negro. Proud of the fact that my family represents the upper stratum of the race which I hope to perpetuate. I am proud of those of my group who have made good despite racial odds [*sic*], and I feel sorry for those stuck in the mite.... However, knowing that there are difficulties that confront us all as Negroes, if I could be born again.... I'd really want to be a white boy—I mean white or my same color, providing that I could occupy the same *racial and economic level* I now enjoy ... I realize ... that there are places where I can't go despite my family or money just because I happen to be a Negro. With my present education, family background, and so forth, if I was only white I could go places in life. A white face holds supreme over a black one despite its economic and social status. Frankly, it leaves me bewildered. I just don't understand. (Frazier 1940, 65–66)

A girl of mixed-race background from a lower-middle-class family had a similar reaction, expressed more dramatically. Allison Davis and John Dollard relay the encounter in *Children of Bondage*:

> In her relations with the white world, Julia feels the sting of systematic deprivation. She says that she wishes she were white "because white people got all the money." ... Julia is not a person to be controlled by force, or to accept rejection meekly. She fights back and returns hate for contempt. "I hate white

An African American man uses the "colored entrance" to a segregated cinema during the 1940s. The doctrine of segregation established by the U.S. Supreme Court case *Plessy v. Ferguson* (1896) determined the social landscape of separate facilities that persisted even after the landmark desegregation case of *Brown v. Board of Education* (1954). (*Library of Congress*)

> people,'' she repeats many times.... They don't like us, so I don't see why we should like them.'' (Davis and Dollard 1941, 42)

For some of their parents, who had seen the course of human events run far longer, the immediate bottom line, since equal treatment was impossible, was to be left unmolested by whites. One man put the matter directly:

> White folks are all right as long as a [black] man stays in his place. Down here in the South, a Negro ain't [*sic*] much better off than he was in slavery times. We work all the time but don't get nothing for it 'cept [*sic*] a place to live and a plenty to eat. Some can't get that [*sic*]. We all equal and ought to have a equal chance but we can't get it here [*sic*]. (Johnson 1941, 17)

For this man, and perhaps may others, the interaction with whites was but one part of a larger life:

> In this settlement there ain't [*sic*] no white folks ... so we don't have no trouble. Folks live peaceably here and tend to their own business so I consider it a good place to be. I don't know any place else I'd rather be. This suits me fine. (Johnson 1941, 17)

The declaration that ''This suits me fine'' seems a good place at which to end. These words both reveal the strength of the scholarship assembled here, and, at the same time, take us up to the limits of what it can tell us today—we are left wondering what we have been missing in the life lived beyond "participant observation."

The civil rights movement, which was indispensable to enacting the Civil Rights Act of 1964 and the Voting Rights Act of 1965, won its battle with political terror in the Mississippi Delta, although the battle against widespread poverty remains to be won there.

The startlingly incomplete quality of our reconstruction—and the extent to which slavery continues to leave an enduring social scar on the United States is conveyed by the fact that, according to Charles T. Clotfelter's careful study of the national experiment with desegregation, *After Brown: The Rise and Retreat of School Desegregation,* school segregation remained severe fifty years after the practice was first roundly denounced by the U.S. Supreme Court. In Sunflower County, Mississippi, the community John Dollard studied more than seventy years ago, 73 percent of the white children enrolled for the 1999–2000 school year attended private schools. This statistic, according to Clotfelter, is indicative of a larger continuity with the slavery past: "In … Deep South communities with high proportions of blacks, where relations between the races historically were marked by separation and inequality, private schools became—and continue to be—the primary means of maintaining segregation in schools (Clotfelter 2004, 113)."

The success of Barack Obama as a viable presidential candidate is a subtle reminder of the political work and political power that began nearly a century ago in Chicago's Bronzeville and, later, in all the other cities, North and South, East and West, where African Americans moved to start again. In these same cities today, Americans must address the urgent problems caused when political success cannot stop "deindustrialization" in the modern "rust belt." The positive changes of the last fifty years have been advanced within the political framework that, seventy-five years ago, both made possible the New Deal and limited its practical scope. That we continue to live in segregation, in fact if not in law, is, to large degree, because race and class remain only somewhat less thoroughly implicated in one another than they were then.

References

Banks, Vera J. 1986. *Black Farmers and Their Farms.* U.S. Department of Agriculture Rural Development Research Report No. 69. Washington, DC: United States Government Printing Office.

Cayton, Horace R., and George S. Mitchell. 1939. *The Black Worker and the New Unions.*Chapel Hill: The University of North Carolina Press.

Clotfelter, Charles T. 2004. *After Brown: The Rise and Retreat of School Desegregation.* Princeton: Princeton University Press.

Davis, Allison, and John Dollard. 1940, *Children of Bondage. The Personality Development of Negro Youth in the Urban South.* Washington, DC: American Council on Education.

Davis, Allison, John Dollard, Burleigh B. Gardner, and Mary R. Gardner. 1941. *Deep South: A Social Anthropological View of Caste and Class.* Chicago: University of Chicago Press.

Dollard, John. 1937. *Caste and Class in a Southern Town.* New Haven: Yale University Press.

Drake, St. Clair, and Horace Cayton. 1945. *Black Metropolis: A Study of Negro Life in a Northern City,* 2 vols. New York: Harcourt Brace and Company.

DuBois, W. E. B. 1899. The Philadelphia Negro. Cambridge: Harvard University Press.

Frazier, E. Franklin. 1940. *Negro Youth at the Crossroads: Their Personality Development in the Middle States.* Washington, DC: American Council on Education.

Greene, Lorenzo J. 1942. *The Negro in Colonial New England.*

Holloway, Jonathan Scott, and Ben Keppel, eds. 2007.*Black Scholars on the Line: Race, Social Science, and American Thought in the Twentieth Century.* Notre Dame: University of Notre Dame University Press.

Johnson, Charles S. 1938. *The Negro College Graduate.* Chapel Hill: The University of North Carolina Press.

———. 1941. *Growing up in the Black Belt: Negro Youth in the Rural South.* Washington, DC: American Council on Education.

Lewis, Hylan. 1955. *Blackways of Kent.* Chapel Hill: The University of North Carolina Press.

Raper, Arthur F. 1936. *A Preface to Peasantry: A Tale of Two Black Belt Counties.* Chapel Hill: The University of North Carolina Press.

Warner, W. Lloyd, Buford H. Junker, and Walter A. Adams. 1941. *Color and Human Nature: Negro Personality Development in a Northern City.* Prepared for the American Youth Council. Washington, DC: American Council on Education.

U.S. Department of Agriculture. 1986. *Social and Economic Environment of Black Farmers.* Washington, DC: U.S. Government Printing Office.

U.S. Department of Agriculture. 2002. *Black Farmers in America, 1865-2000.* Washington, DC: U.S. Government Printing Office.

Part 2

American Culture in the Age of the Great Depression

The Role of the Group in New Deal Planning

8

George T. McJimsey

Redefining the Group

Two notable features of the New Deal (1933–1939) have been its reputation for "planning" and for "experimentation." The first suggests a purposeful drive toward a predetermined objective; the second suggests a searching, by trail and error, that in the longer run might redefine objectives. This chapter seeks to find a place for both characteristics in the New Deal's approach to dealing with groups. It concludes that the New Deal sought specific objectives but that those objectives had their own indeterminate ends. Thus, between 1933 and 1939, the New Deal changed its approach to planning. At first its goal was to produce a kind of institutional commonwealth in which social groups consciously interacted with one another for the common good. But there was no way to guarantee that outcome. In the end, New Deal thinking focused on a kind of rights-based pluralist democracy that combined economic security with capitalist opportunity, facilitated by "flexible," "interactive" government administration.

The inspiration for New Deal planning was the Great Depression, the most widespread and devastating economic collapse in American history. Its motive force was a sense of urgency created by the collapse of major economic institutions, widespread unemployment and rural misery, and fear of social conflict. The means for planning came from the professional scholars that president-elect Franklin D. Roosevelt recruited to analyze the Depression's causes and to propose remedies. Those remedies were based on assumptions about the nature and function of social groups.

Since the late nineteenth century, social scientists (primarily sociologists) had turned away from the individualism that had characterized earlier social thinking and had begun to stress the "interdependence" of society's parts. At first scholars, business leaders, and public officials generally agreed that this insight justified centralized, hierarchical management (considered essential for "efficiency"), but by the late 1910s, the consensus was turning away from hierarchy and toward the idea that society's parts interacted in complex, ever-changing ways that were difficult to predict and thus difficult to manage centrally. Groups had different characteristics. Their parts might be similar or identical (as a "race" or an isolated community); or they might be dissimilar but interdependent so that in one or more respects they would have unity. All these groups would have a "center" that made up their "identity." All groups constantly faced new challenges; each action to solve a problem produced results that posed new problems.

Redefining the group meant redefining how it functioned. The idea of group leadership, for example, changed from the need for a strong, authoritative individual to the idea that a leader merely played a role in a group, and because the nature of groups was always changing and because these groups were facing different problems, many people could be leaders. The best leadership "facilitated" the course of group action instead of determining it. It inspired group members to common action or provided useful advice that the members could apply in ways most practical to their own circumstances. Thus, the group had a center, but its parts were separate, differentiated, decentralized. The essential function of a society that operated in this way was to achieve a "balance" among its parts so that its interdependence would benefit the largest number. The processes of a "good" society, then, were inclusive, integrating the largest number into a cooperative whole. Because of the complexity of social interactions, the resulting "whole" always would be different or greater than the sum of its parts.

Many current scholars of the New Deal take a cue from Roosevelt's address during the campaign of 1932 to the Commonwealth Club of San Francisco. In this address, Roosevelt announced what others would label the idea of a "mature economy." The traditional means of economic opportunity, Roosevelt declared, no longer existed. The nation's industrial plant had been built, and 600 corporations controlled two-thirds of it. The frontier of "free land" had been used up and the farm population was declining. The United States was no longer able to provide for immigrants. Indeed, "we are now providing a drab living for our own people."

In such conditions, Roosevelt declared the need for government and business to create "an economic declaration of rights, an economic constitutional order" (Rosenman 1938, vol. 1, 742–56).

> Every man has a right to life; and this means that he has a right to make a comfortable living. He may by sloth or crime decline to exercise that right, but it may not be denied him. We have no actual famine or dearth; our industrial and agricultural mechanism can produce enough and to spare. Our government formal and informal, political and economic, owes to every one an avenue to possess himself of a portion of that plenty sufficient for his needs, through his own work.
>
> Every man has a right to his own property, which means a right to be assured, to the fullest extent attainable, in the safety of his savings. By no

> other means can men carry the burdens of those parts of life which, in the nature of things, afford no chance of labor; childhood, sickness, old age. In all thought of property, this right is paramount; all other property rights must yield to it. If, in accord with this principle, we must restrict the operations of the speculator, the manipulator, even the financier, I believe we must accept the restriction as needful, not to hamper individualism but to protect it.

Roosevelt concluded that it was now necessary for economic groups to realize these rights by pursuing the public interest. "The responsible heads of finance and industry instead of acting each for himself, must work together to achieve the common end" (Roosevelt 1932).

Given what followed Roosevelt's election—the "Hundred Days" that inaugurated the legislative program of the New Deal—it is easy to interpret Roosevelt's remarks as a blueprint for the national government's planning a cooperative economic system based on individual rights. Many years ago, scholars referred to this approach as "Jeffersonian" ends (individual rights) secured by "Hamiltonian" means (national power). But the actual approach, in theory and practice, cannot be characterized so neatly. The ideas of Rexford Tugwell, one of the New Deal's early architects and a member of Roosevelt's "Brains Trust" that planned the early program of the New Deal before and following his election in 1932, illustrate this point.

In the spring of 1933, Tugwell published *The Industrial Discipline and the Governmental Arts*, a coherent statement of his ideas. Tugwell did not subscribe to the classical economic model of the rational individual. At the same time, however, he held that the individual was the proper base of social action. Groups were only the embodiment of individual desires. Groups came into existence because people identified their self-interest with them. They achieved their identity through action and through enforcing an internal discipline. Society was composed of groups that pursued their objectives in relative isolation, sometimes competing, sometimes cooperating. And because individual interests changed from time to time, groups were changeable, impermanent, and, Tugwell concluded, poor material for social analysis.

But Tugwell's purpose was not to dismiss group analysis; it was to place it in its proper context. Once he had established that groups were changeable, he had established a basis for reforming society. Reformers worked with the elements necessary for industrial advancement: research and invention, standardization of materials and production processes, and the clerical tasks of accounting and recordkeeping. They then fitted these elements into a rational plan to improve the economy; one that would save about a third of the costs currently incurred because of old habits and lack of competition. Tugwell called this process "series-unit" concentration, or closely linking together the various stages of production and distribution in a "continuous process." New techniques, devised by "experts" or "technicians," were developing to place persons in the jobs most suited to them. This served "democracy" by employing persons in jobs that engaged their minds as well as their bodies. Workers thus placed would see how their welfare benefited from greater efficiency and would become partners in the planning process. Although efficiency would in theory require leadership by one dominant group, the fact that each would use its dominant position to further its own interests led him to conclude that the best leadership would come from a combination of expertise, ownership, and labor—this, in turn, would be furthered by the growing associational character of economic and social life. Thus, efficiency would become a self-fulfilling process. By creating greater wealth and higher standards of living it would encourage all to cooperate to maintain it.

To attain this goal, Tugwell recommended "planning." The federal government should establish an agency to gather data that would be used to develop a plan for the efficient production and distribution of goods and should enable this plan by substituting federal incorporation law for state incorporation law and by using the taxing power to force surplus capital into the market for more efficient investments. A series of "associations," subordinate to a central "board," would study and make recommendations for various economic sectors. The central board would reconcile these recommendations with a plan submitted by the government for the allocation of capital and the regulation of prices. The goal would be to replace competition with cooperation and the overall integration of economic endeavor. The object was to create groups that disciplined individual self-interest to efficient effort for the common good.

Tugwell did not believe that the process would be rapid. Instead he called for a willingness to "experiment" in a long-term search for the best outcome.

This experimentation began in March 1933, during a special session of Congress called by President Roosevelt to deal with the banking crisis, but it stretched to 100 days to produce the most productive congressional session in American history and the legislative outline of the New Deal. The following discussion describes the New Deal's efforts to correct what it saw as certain structural weaknesses in the American economy by forming groups and conferring on them "rights" to create a "balance" among them. In an operational sense, this was New Deal "planning."

Corporate Enterprise: Group Formation by Interest Group Consensus

Corporate enterprise was born with the nation, but it assumed its modern form after the Civil War. Corporations made it possible for a large business to operate by putting its functions in the hands of "managers," who supervised its specific operations. Corporations operated in the market, but they tried to protect themselves from market pressure, notably by merging into larger units and consolidating management authority through "holding companies" that held shares in previously competing companies and operated them under the laws of especially tolerant states. By the mid-1920s, large concentrations of corporate enterprise dominated major economic sectors. These units sought further to protect themselves by forming trade associations that shared information and ideas about business practices. Still, most association members hesitated to give up power to larger units

A woman hangs a National Recovery Administration (NRA) poster in a restaurant window to show support for the government program. The NRA was considered the cornerstone of the New Deal and was often controversial in its regulation of industrial codes of competition. (*Franklin D. Roosevelt Presidential Library*)

that might be either too weak to enforce its policies on all members or might be strong enough to impose policies that would favor some members over others. In many ways, then, corporations continued to act as individual enterprisers in a competitive market instead of large organizations of economic production and distribution.

Such competitive behavior was intensified by the economic crisis of the Great Depression, which produced downward spirals of prices, production, and employment. By the time Franklin D. Roosevelt assumed office, many corporate executives and trade association leaders were calling for the federal government to protect them by enforcing rules of association.

The administration's response, crafted during the Hundred Days of the special session, was the product of various interests: financiers, trade association leaders, labor leaders, professional economists, and officials of the Department of Commerce. In May 1933, Congress produced a draft that a month later became the National Industrial Recovery Act (NIRA). The act permitted business associations to draft "codes" of practice that would govern their industry. The act offered something for everyone. Business received authority over production and prices, labor received the right to organize trade unions, professional economists and "planners" received the power to approve the codes, and the president, through a National Recovery Administration (NRA) received the power to enforce their terms.

The purpose of the NRA was, as one trade association executive observed, to "recognize the necessity of becoming 'group-minded' and accept some limitations of individual rights for the sake of promised enlarged practical advantage" (Hanke 1933). "Individual manufacturers cannot by independent action protect themselves from the affects of destructive competition brought about by causes beyond their control," declared the National Lumber Manufacturers Association. "Cooperative action with enforceable performance offers the only practicable solution" (Outline of Code 1933). Working under pressure to produce results rapidly, the administration allowed industrial groups to identify themselves as representing their entire industries. The result was that about between four and ten entities drew up each code. (The administration invited comment from outside groups, an offer that produced no results.)

The success of the NRA, then, depended on the New Deal's ability to create a group out of existing groups. Its original plan was to organize the ten major industrial groups that controlled the bulk of the nation's industrial employment. No one in the Roosevelt administration questioned the structure of corporate enterprise. They wanted to organize that structure into larger wholes in partnership with the federal government. When he signed the act on June 16, 1933, Roosevelt called on all interested parties to do their part.

In the same statement Roosevelt declared that the NRA's purpose was "to put people back to work—to let them buy more of the products of farms manufactories and start our business at a living rate again" (Roosevelt, statement, June 1933). The NRA was to improve the conditions of labor by establishing maximum hours, minimum wages, and a shorter work week to encourage more employment through job-sharing. These measures, the New Dealers hoped, would increase the national standard of living. Roosevelt made this clear in a conversation with representatives of the coal industry and the United Mine Workers union. The object of the meeting was to work out the details of the labor provisions of the coal industry code. After getting the owners to agree to rewrite the contract in language the miners would be able to understand, Roosevelt turned to the issue of the miners' compensation. He declared that Harry Hopkins, head of federal relief had

> given me many examples of a miner, because he's in debt to the company, not receiving any pay for his work—not a red cent. Legally, this may be one thing, but from a human point of view, it's quite another. If the country were told the facts tomorrow, there'd be an awful explosion. We have examples everywhere. I know of a case where a man has worked for two months and received nothing in cash. You can't explain that kind of thing away.
> (Elmhirst, notes on meeting, September 1933)

Raising living standards also meant holding down prices. News that many industries intended to use the codes to raise prices to increase profits lent urgency to this need. But the industries and their associations, dispirited by Depression-induced price drops, were determined to "stabilize" prices. By 1935 the overwhelming majority of industrial codes included some provision for price-fixing. Business also resisted unionization and the nation was plagued by protests and strikes.

In the end, New Deal industrial policy failed because the administration could find no way to enforce business to comply with its wishes. Roosevelt might want consensus and cooperation, but he could not have it on his own terms. Business was willing to cooperate but only on what made sense to it. In its industrial policy, the New Deal was better able to recognize groups than to create them. It could not create a group that represented the "larger" or "public" interest of business; it could only create larger business groups.

Amid complaints of price increases and price-fixing, the New Deal scrambled for a response. Some argued that higher prices were necessary for higher wages and more employment. Roosevelt himself had considered deflation a major ill of the Depression. Others declared that the government should step in and control prices. But NRA lawyers and Roosevelt's attorney general advised that the government had no constitutional way to enforce the codes. In the end, it was decided to create a group that would check the price spiral. This meant that the New Deal would create a category of consumers.

The Consumer and Federal Relief: Group Formation by Identifying Individual Need

In 1933, the idea of the consumer as an economic group was largely a figment of economists' imagination. One theory of the Depression, advanced by Tugwell and others, was "underconsumption," that the purchasers of industrial products, largely workers and farmers, had received too little income to buy the products that industry turned out. The New Deal attempted to correct this imbalance through the NRA codes and a program to increase farm income. But neither advocates for agriculture nor for labor articulated the cause of the consumer as effectively as the administrators of federal relief for the unemployed.

To provide emergency assistance to the destitute while its programs for industry and agriculture took effect, the New Deal created a Federal Emergency Relief Administration (FERA), which was empowered to make matching grants or emergency direct grants to the states to aid people who qualified, according to state and local standards, for "relief." When the industrial and agricultural programs failed to produce general prosperity and the nation faced an unemployment crisis for the winter of 1933–1934, Roosevelt created a Civil Works Administration (CWA) to employ people directly on federally funded projects. When the Depression continued through 1934, Roosevelt agreed to create a Works Progress Administration

(WPA) to expand work relief. This program would continue through the rest of the New Deal.

WPA operated like the NRA in that it took the groups in American society as they existed. It worked through state and local governments, which recommended projects that the WPA then funded and operated under federal guidelines. Relief director Harry Hopkins soon learned that, for work relief to achieve broad coverage, it would be necessary to categorize relief clients by group. Most of its project were in construction and employed men: roads, bridges, parks, and public buildings. For women, it set up projects for sewing, clerical work, and childcare. It also employed writers, musicians, actors, and artists. Because Congress severely limited its appropriation so that it could never care for more than a third of the unemployed, it was always acutely aware of the cost of living and how higher prices limited its mission. By the middle of 1934, FERA officials were noting that relief stipends had increased 12 percent while prices had increased 20 percent. Out of this concern, they developed a theory of prosperity through increased consumption.

Their theory was simply stated. Work relief enhanced both production and consumption. Because relief funds came from government appropriations, they showed how government could contribute to recovery by stimulating consumption. Thus, government would not need to control or regulate industry; it simply could stimulate a demand for the products of industry. The argument was elaborated in *An Economic Program for American Democracy*. Published in 1938, the book was jointly written by a number of economists who had worked in various New Deal agencies but who were coming to be associated with Harry Hopkins. The program called for government to spend for public works and aid to the elderly, ill, and unemployed. Financing would come from borrowing and from taxes collected from those best able to pay.

Overlying this program was developing the conception of what we can call "social citizenship." When he spoke on behalf of relief for the unemployed, Harry Hopkins referred to the needy as "citizens," and, as such, as people who deserved to be helped in hard times. Touring WPA projects, he asked his listeners to consider the projects and those who worked on them from their own experience, and to decide whether the projects were a value to the community and whether those who worked on them—often their friends, neighbors, or relatives—deserved to be helped.

By using the conception of citizenship, Hopkins formed the unemployed, who under work relief followed various work regimes, into an overall group that in many ways was larger than the sum of its parts. Franklin Roosevelt employed the same kind of large conception by speaking of work relief as part of the fight for democracy. In an address on federal relief, he declared: "More and more people, because of clearer thinking and a better understanding, are considering the whole rather than a mere part relating to one section or to one crop, or to one industry, or to an individual private occupation. That is a tremendous gain for the principles of democracy" (Hopkins, Radio Address, 1935; Rosenman 1938, vol. 4, 133).

Social Security: Group Formation by Social and Cultural Definition

At the same time Roosevelt was establishing the WPA for people on relief, he was formulating a program of "social insurance" for the elderly and unemployed. In 1935 Congress passed the Social Security Act. The act had three principal features: old-age assistance to retired persons, unemployment insurance, and aid to dependent children. Although the act had broad implications, some of its features and implementation caused it to conform to existing ideas about groups in society. Old-age assistance was potentially the most general, providing pensions to people age 65 and over. But old-age assistance contained restrictive provisions that targeted its benefits primarily to white males. It based assistance on a person's work history, granting larger pensions for longer times worked and amount of money earned. This approach benefited males, who ranked highest in these categories. By excluding agricultural laborers, it cut out the majority of African American males, who were still employed primarily on southern farms and plantations. The act also excluded people working in domestic service, thus cutting out almost all African American females. The act further restricted benefits to women by omitting coverage for workers in

New York City postal workers wave Social Security applications as they begin to deliver the forms in November 1936. More than 3 million forms were distributed in New York City alone. (*Library of Congress*)

religious and nonprofit organizations, cutting out teachers, nurses, and social workers.

Unemployment insurance took on a similar character. The program relied on the states to set standards for eligibility but encouraged them to meet federal guidelines by promising to pay up to 90 percent of the program costs if the states complied. Still, the states were allowed to determine eligibility in ways that benefited white men.

Aid to dependent children was modeled on "mother's pension" laws that many states had adopted a generation earlier. The law was directly aimed to benefit women, but it permitted standards of "eligibility" that restricted support to women of "good character."

Roosevelt took a dynamic view of the act, portraying social security as a means to advance democracy.

> We in America know that our own democratic institutions can be preserved and made to work. But in order to preserve them we need to act together, to meet the problems of the Nation boldly, and to prove that the practical operation of democratic government is equal to the task of protecting the security of the people.... Not only our future economic soundness but the very soundness of our democratic institutions depends on the determination of our Government to give employment to idle men. The people of America are in agreement in defending their liberties at any cost, and the first line of that defense lies in the protection of economic security. Your Government, seeking to protect democracy, must prove that Government is stronger than the forces of business depression. (Roosevelt, Message to Congress, 1938; Rosenman 1938, vol. 7, 221–33)

Labor and Agriculture: Group Formation by Majority Vote

The National Industrial Relations Act had sought to stabilize labor conditions by having the industrial codes include provisions for wages, hours, working conditions, and the right to form labor unions. The codes included these provisions but succumbed to management hostility to unions and to its customary desire to consider wages and hours as costs of doing business to be managed rather than as rights to be recognized. Hoping that management would voluntarily use the codes as an opportunity to treat labor fairly, Roosevelt refused to throw his support behind an independent labor movement. The result was that between 1933 and 1935 the New Deal struggled and dithered over its labor policy while industrial disputes and major strikes shook the nation.

The turning point came in the spring of 1935, when the Supreme Court declared the National Industrial Recover Act unconstitutional. It so happened that, at this moment, Congress was considering a bill sponsored by Senator Robert Wagner of New York to protect workers and labor unions. With the labor provisions of the NIRA no longer enforceable, Roosevelt gave Wagner's bill his full support. In July 1935, the Wagner Act became law.

Mrs. Elinore Morehouse Herrick had, in slightly more than a year, helped to resolve more than 450 disputes between management and labor. She was a hardworking New Dealer. She was the chair of the Regional Labor Board of the National Recovery Administration for the New York and Connecticut district. And how did she ascend to this important position?

She had much experience as a factory worker and manager. A single mother in Buffalo, New York, she took a series of factory jobs to support herself and her two young sons. She easily diagnosed and fixed factory machines, and even improved their speed and efficiency. After working in several departments at a rayon factory, she became production chief. In Buffalo, she supervised male workers of Polish and Italian background; many had difficulty accepting a woman as boss. But production quotas were met, and disputes were settled peacefully. When a new branch plant opened in Tennessee, she was transferred to chief of production there, where the workers were rural women with no factory experience. They found their new work environment, including the machines, intimidating. They had even more trouble accepting Mrs. Herrick as boss. She trained them to be good production workers. As before, quotas were met, and profits increased.

After six years, Mrs. Herrick quit factory work. She studied economics at Antioch College. She supported herself through a variety of means, including running a boarding house. She graduated and moved to New York City in 1929, where she became executive secretary of the Consumers League, for which she conducted research on labor problems in several industries. In 1933, because of her expertise, she became a member of the New York City Labor Mediation Committee, and in the fall, she won a spot on the Regional Labor Board. Six months later, she became chairman of that board. Together, she and her colleagues on the two boards adjudicated more than 600 disputes between employers and their laborers. Section 7(a) of the National Industrial Recovery Act stipulated that laborers belonging to a union could organize and bargain collectively. Almost every dispute she and her board colleagues were involved in had at its core management's opposition to section 7(a), the right of laborers to join a union and bargain collectively.

SOURCE: *New York Times*, March 25, 1934.

The Wagner Act's major feature was its encouragement of labor union organization. It declared the right of workers to form unions that were independent from management by a majority vote and listed "unfair" practices that management was not permitted to do to inhibit them. It established a National Labor Relations Board (NLRB) to supervise and enforce its terms.

More important, the Wagner Act breathed life into a labor movement weakened and demoralized by unemployment and employer hostility. Because the act's provisions were not self-starting and because management often refused to cooperate with it pending challenges in court, workers and union officials had to take the initiative to make organization a reality. This they accomplished in a number of ways: protests and threats, shop-floor slowdowns, and strikes. In Akron, Ohio, tire and rubber workers engaged in the first "sit-down" strike, during which they stopped work and refused to leave the factories, in effect taking control of the property. However they chose to act, the motive behind it was their belief that the national government was on their side.

Indeed, as Professor Lizabeth Cohen has shown in her book about industrial workers in Chicago, *Making a New Deal* (1990), the New Deal's programs for work relief, banking reform, and home mortgage credit had encouraged the workers not only to believe that the government was on their side but also to expect that it would be on their side. The New Deal had inspired them to believe they had the rights of social citizenship.

That citizenship they would confirm by voting to form unions that would be independent of management and would be empowered by law to bargain with management. During the first eighteen months under the Wagner Act, three-fourths of workers voted to form independent unions, approximately the proportion that had voted for them under the NIRA. But under the Wagner Act, less than half as many voted to form company unions that would be part of the management structure. In 1938, union membership made up 27 percent of all wage and salaried workers, up from 11 percent in 1933.

The Roosevelt administration intended to empower American agriculture more directly. In 1933 approximately 20 percent of American workers were in agriculture. Believing that low crop prices and farm income had been a major cause of the Depression, the administration had pushed through an Agricultural Adjustment Act. The act identified major commodity groups and promised farmers in those groups to subsidize their income if they reduced their production. Less production, the New Dealers reasoned, would lead to higher prices that in turn would reduce the need for subsidies.

To put this policy into operation, the act created an Agricultural Administration (AAA) to organize farmers to sign production and price support contracts. To act quickly, it worked through the Extension Service, which the U.S. Department of Agriculture operated in cooperation with state land grant colleges. Extension Service agents organized local committees that encouraged farmers to sign the contracts. In effect, by signing the contract, a farmer voted for the program. Initial signings covered 75 to 95 percent of crop acreage, but not always the majority of farmers.

Participation in the agriculture programs enhanced their political support. Members of Congress were not inclined to vote against a program that most of their farmer constituents favored. Representatives from the cities were inclined to go along, not wanting to lose farm state support for legislation in their interest. Realizing this, the AAA provided members with data on program participation, and Congress scheduled their own votes on the program until after the farmers had voted on participation.

Functionally, the New Deal farm programs were less "democratic" because they worked through the local committees. These were usually made up of the most "prominent" or "successful" farmers. This meant that the democratic nature of the agriculture program depended on the democratic nature of the local social structure. Here, the most conspicuous failing was in the southern states, primarily those of the former

Confederacy. There, as in Civil War times, cotton and tobacco were the principal cash crops, land ownership was concentrated, and tenancy was particularly widespread. Often the landowner shared little or nothing of the benefit payment with the tenant. Over time, the AAA tried to correct this situation by requiring the owner to share the proportion of the payment that the tenant had produced. Thus, if the owner and tenant had agreed to share half the crop, the tenant should receive half of any benefit payment. The local committees usually agreed to these terms and then ran them to suit their own interests.

The Tennessee Valley Authority: Group Formation by Regional Planning

An important feature of the social science formulation of the interdependent society was ''regionalism''—that is, the idea that certain geographic areas shared common economic, social, and cultural characteristics that could be brought together to achieve a better life for all. Achieving this, however, would require some kind of guidance, or ''planning.''

Many, including President Roosevelt, saw a rich opportunity for the planning approach in the Tennessee River Valley. Carved by a river that rambled through seven southern states, the valley was characterized by rural poverty, aggravated by the river's persistent flooding. The key to taming the river and advancing the region's prosperity existed at the northern Alabama town of Muscle Shoals in the form of the Wilson Dam built to provide electric power to produce munitions for American troops in World War I. Following his election, Roosevelt visited Muscle Shoals and promised to make the valley a laboratory for social planning, ''tying industry and agriculture and forestry and flood prevention ... into a unified whole over a distance of a thousand miles so that we can afford better opportunities and better places for millions yet unborn to live in the days to come'' (Roosevelt, speech, January 1933; Rosenman 1938, vol 1, 887). During the Hundred Days, Congress gave him the chance to realize his promise.

The act that Roosevelt signed created a Tennessee Valley Authority (TVA) and gave the president the power to appoint a board of directors. Roosevelt chose a three-person board that represented the major thrusts of the project: social planning, agricultural development, and electric power production. TVA's first major project was constructing a dam near Knoxville. The dam would produce electricity for the area. The nearby town of Norris would become an ideal community of small, comfortable houses and residents employed in various cooperative businesses.

The community ideal represented the thinking of Arthur Morgan, whom Roosevelt chose to chair the TVA board. Morgan had a vision of a region of small towns, each with its own diversity of small industries and cooperative businesses. But his counterparts, Harcourt Morgan, an agricultural scientist and president of the University of Tennessee, and David Lilienthal, an attorney who specialized in public utility regulation and who headed TVA's production of electric power, had difference ideas.

Greenbelt, Maryland, was the New Deal's most famous attempt in community planning. The idea was a self-sufficient co-operative community that would relieve the area's housing shortage, create jobs, and constitute a model of urban development. In 1935, Congress appropriated $200 million to the United States Resettlement Administration, demanding that the money be spent to relieve unemployment within eighteen months. Planning and building proceeded furiously. Abandoned tobacco fields near the District of Columbia became Greenbelt's location. Construction began on an artificial lake, pathways, and roads. Eventually 574 masonry townhouses, 306 garden apartments, and 5 prefabricated detached houses were built. Community facilities included a school, a town center with shops and a theater, underpasses, walkways, parks, and playgrounds. Functional art deco was the design, with curving lines and glass brick inserts. Homes were concentrated in superblocks. There was a system of interior walkways that permitted residents to walk from home to town center without crossing a major street. Foot and vehicular traffic were kept apart. There were two major curving streets; these

Morgan and Lilienthal became natural allies. Morgan subscribed to the "integrated," "interdependent" approach to reviving the valley, but he proceeded from the vantage point of agricultural reform. He began with a program of soil conservation and enrichment from diversified plantings. This approach would be supplemented by damming the river to produce electric power for phosphate fertilizers and rural electrification, converting it from a raging torrent into an avenue of commerce. The resulting farm prosperity would balance agriculture and industry by creating a market for manufactured goods, especially appliances now made affordable by cheap electricity. Soon Lilienthal was making speeches stressing how electricity would benefit farm families by enabling them to have electric lights, ranges, water heaters, and refrigerators, as well as water pumps and other labor-saving devices. Lilienthal continually emphasized that low electric rates alone would not create "an electrified America"—only large-scale distribution of electric appliances could achieve that goal.

Thus TVA's electric power and fertilizer programs became its principal thrusts. Local businessmen ecstatically supported the prospect of new industries and jobs, as did their congressional representatives. This tended further to confirm Lilienthal's advantage. Under Lilienthal's guidance, TVA developed the idea of widely distributing its power and using its rates as a "yardstick" to judge the fairness of the rates charged by private power companies. To meld power development with social and economic development, TVA created the Electric Home and Farm Association, which provided inexpensive electric appliances to valley residents.

As TVA developed, many of its plans for social reconstruction faded away. Engineers cooperated to integrate flood control, navigation, and recreation. The Authority built more dams and bought others from private power interests, selling the electricity to local cooperatives. Local farmers, fertilizer manufacturers, and agricultural extension agents experimented were laid out on and below a crescent-shaped natural ridge. Community facilities—shops, school, ball fields, and community buildings—were located in the crescent's center. Miss Elizabeth Hofflin declared that she and her colleagues at the U.S. Resettlement Administration had made a success of Greenbelt. We "made the furniture to fit the small rooms of these low-rent units"; residents furnished their homes for less than $240. These were frugal times indeed.

Greenbelt was for whites only, and lower income working class or middle class, thus reflecting key New Deal voting constituencies. Residents had to create community life from scratch, quickly founding Maryland's first city manager and the county's first kindergarten, but also a citizens' association, a community newspaper, and clubs too numerous to enumerate. Interdenominational religious services took place in the town center. In 1939 the community acquired sufficient funds to start a community cooperative, which operated a food store, gas station, pharmacy, barber shop, movie theater, and several other "necessary" stores.

SOURCE: Cathy D. Knepper, *Greenbelt, Maryland. A Living Legacy of the New Deal* (Baltimore: Johns Hopkins University Press), 2001.

with types of crops and farming practices. By 1947 average income in the valley had increased from 40 percent of the national average to 60 percent. Instead of becoming a community of cooperative enterprise, Norris became a bedroom suburb of Knoxville, and its residents were content to aspire to the middle-class life of the "average American." This was the essential course of New Deal planning.

The New Deal Focuses Its Vision

In the end, the course of New Deal planning followed the course of the TVA. Increasingly, the New Deal turned to special solutions and aid to targeted groups. Unable to have industrial codes that would be fair to large and small business alike, it approved the Robinson-Patman Act that limited the ability of big retailers to undersell small retailers. The New Deal regulated securities markets, broke up utility holding companies, and threatened big business with antitrust prosecution. Unable to cover all workers under Wagner Act unionization, it sponsored the Fair Labor Standards Act that set a standard for minimum wages and maximum hours. Unable to provide for all the poor and isolated Americans through regional planning, it set up individual communities like "Arthurdale" in West Virginia and the "greenbelt communities" near Washington, D.C. For the rural poor excluded from the benefits of the AAA, it set up the Resettlement Administration and the Farm Security Administration. More broadly and effectively, it distributed electric power to rural America by selling power to cooperatives via the Rural Electrification Administration. Congress also passed legislation specifically limiting cotton and tobacco production.

Tennessee Valley Authority (TVA) employees string transmission lines. The TVA, a program covering the entire Tennessee Valley and parts of Alabama and West Virginia, was established during the New Deal administration of President Franklin D. Roosevelt to control flooding and use dams to provide power. (*Franklin D. Roosevelt Presidential Library*)

The Transformation of "Planning"

By the end of the decade, the New Deal had moved away from large, essentially static solutions of the NIRA. From the "cooperative commonwealth," it had taken up what we can call "pluralist democracy." This was the belief that by granting "social rights" to different groups of people it would spread the American middle-class ideal. It would be "democratic" not just because persons were voting to join programs and to form institutions that would advance their social status but also because it would enlist them as partners in the further development of American society. Americans would retain their different identities, but they would have the rights of equal citizens, entitled to a secure existence and a proper claim on their country's protection and support.

The New Deal moved from seeking to integrate different parts of society to identifying the central identity and conferring upon it benefits in line with the "rights" it wished to confer. The ultimate consequences would be worked out through historical processes to which government would have to respond but which it could not control. Still, by conferring rights on various groups, the New Deal had tried to direct that development. Because such rights are universal and because New Deal programs aimed to increase incomes and standards of living, it sought to homogenize society around a middle-class, capitalist ideal. This ideal would be the basis on which cooperation, toleration, interdependence, and "democracy" would stand.

This was a turning away from the idea of the "mature economy" toward an emphasis on economic growth, toward bringing more of the nation's resources into production to increase the standard of living. Now government was charged not to create a cooperative commonwealth but to facilitate the prosperity of a complex, diverse, decentralized society. This meant that it needed to be "flexible" to adjust to changing conditions, that it needed to be "responsive" or "interactive" to maintain contact with the American people and advance American "democracy," and that it needed to promote the common good by reconciling the conflicts that inevitably arose in a complex, ever-changing society.

This was the reality that New Deal planning eventually discovered. During the course of Roosevelt's first two terms, his administration established a series of planning agencies. The National Planning Board became the National Resources Board and, in 1935, the National Resources Committee (NRC). In 1939 this organization (soon to assume its final form as the National Resources Planning Board) produced a comprehensive study, *The Structure of the American Economy*. The NRC had gathered its information by a decentralized method, in which its field service worked with regional, state, and local planning staffs and with consultants that advised on specific matters. It further employed specialized administrative divisions, project advisory committees, and a technical research staff.

This complex structure produced a complex analysis. The NRC study identified five different kinds of corporate organization, eight major economic concentrations, and eleven connections among these eight. The key feature in identifying these concentrations was control. Determining this required knowledge of the history of the corporation and knowledge of the persons who controlled it. Quantitative or "objective" definition was not possible. Similarly, the study identified five types of trade unions, four types of collective bargaining agreements, and ten subjects of negotiation and methods of enforcement "of too great variety to be discussed in detail" (National Resources Committee 1939). The report identified geographic areas of economic specialization, examined their historical development and potential for further expansion, and discussed their financial elements. All this it presented with the understanding that structure and operating policies were subject to constant change and interactions that might be beneficial or frictional. Invention, shifting consumer wants, new forms of business organization and management, and shifting balances in labor-management relations all would influence the structure.

But no amount of complexity should obstruct the search for improving the nation's economic performance. The potential existed vastly to improve living standards, but it was not being realized. Too many workers and factories were idle. Too many wants were going unmet. The report warned that nothing less than the "maintenance of democracy requires that an adequate solution be found to the problem of keeping resources fully employed."

Finding a "democratic" solution would be neither short nor simple. It would require "many minds working through a period of years." Nor did the report provide more than a "frame of reference" for seeking a solution. "It must be left to the reader," the report concluded, "to combine these separate aspects in his own mind into a unified conception of the national economy as a whole" (National Resources Committee 1939).

The report summarized lessons learned. Tugwell's prescription for long-term solutions achieved by experimentation remained, but his confidence in the leadership of experts had disappeared. Now the expert merely played a role in the larger group, while each member of the larger group was instructed to seek their own solutions. At some future time, the New Dealers seemed to hope, these solutions would restore the nation's economic well-being by "democratic" means.

Sooner than any of the authors believed, the nation's well-being was restored, but by war. Massive spending combined with forced saving to achieve New Deal objectives and to validate New Deal democracy. Pluralist democracy became the order of the day. It now seemed possible that everyone could aspire to the middle-class ideal and melt into a homogeneous society. Economists discovered that United States was blessed with a "mixed" economy, sociologists discovered that most Americans considered themselves "middle class," and social critics saw the country plagued by the pervasive blandness of a middle-class consumer culture. Others found that culture to be reassuring. Dr. Benjamin Spock encouraged the worried mother-to-be to "trust yourself," school children were encouraged to be "leaders" and to develop a variety of skills (to become "well rounded"), and African Americans acquired new energy through equal rights. Between 1946 and 1966, the present author's mother, Harriet McJimsey, taught home economics students how to classify their physical features so each of them could be "well dressed."

New Deal planning had formed groups and identified them as worthy members of society. In the 1946 Christmas holiday film *It's a Wonderful Life*, surely the most enduring expression of New Deal pluralism, actor James Stewart portrayed George Bailey, a building and loan executive who loans money to low-income citizens so they can live in clean and comfortable surroundings. Thereby, he affirms their value and gives them security and the chance to become useful, contributing middle-class members of society. When the town banker, Sherman Potter (played by Lionel Barrymore) "the richest and the meanest man in town," derides Bailey for loaning money to "rabble," Bailey responds:

> Doesn't it make them better citizens? Doesn't it make them better customers? You—you said—what'd you say a minute ago? They had to wait and save their money before they even ought to think of a decent home. Wait? Wait for what? Until their children grow up and leave them? Until they're so old and broken down that then.... Do you know how long it takes a working man to save five thousand dollars? Just remember this, Mr. Potter, that this rabble you're talking about ... they do most of the working and paying and living and dying in this community. Well, is it too much to have them work and pay and live and die

in a couple of decent rooms and a bath? Anyway, my father didn't think so. People were human beings to him. But to you, a warped, frustrated old man, they're cattle. Well, in my book he died a much richer man than you'll ever be.

References

Cohen, Lizabeth. 1990. *Making a New Deal: Industrial Workers in Chicago, 1919–1939*. Cambridge, MA: Harvard University Press.

Elmhirst, Leonard K. 1933. Notes on meeting, September 6, 1933, President's Personal File, Franklin D. Roosevelt Presidential Library, Hyde Park, New York.

Hanke, A. P. 1933. Managing Director, National Association of Furniture Manufacturers, May 31, 1933, Papers of Morris L. Cooke, Franklin D. Roosevelt Presidential Library, Hyde Park, New York.

Hopkins, Harry. 1935. Radio Address. In: Franklin D. Roosevelt, "Radio Address," April 28, 1935; Rosenman, vol. 4, 133.

National Resources Committee. 1939. *Part One, The Structure of the American Economy*. Washington, DC: Government Printing Office.

Outline of Code of Fair Competition in the Lumber Industry. 1933. Papers of President's Official File, Franklin D. Roosevelt Library, Hyde Park, New York.

The Roosevelt addresses below are available in: Rosenman Samuel, 1938, *Public Papers and Addresses of Franklin D. Roosevelt, 1933–1945;* 13 volumes. New York: Random House.

Roosevelt, Franklin D. 1932. Commonwealth Club Address, San Francisco, California, September 23, 1932. Available online at: http://teachingamericanhistory.org/library/index.asp?documentprint=447. Rosenman, vol.1, 742–56.

Roosevelt, Franklin D. 1933. Address at Muscle Shoals, Alabama; January 21. Rosenman, vol.1, 887.

Roosevelt, Franklin D. 1935. Radio Address, April 28. Rosenman, vol.4, 133.

Roosevelt, Franklin D. 1938. Message to Congress, April 14. Rosenman, vol.7, 221–33.

When Numbers Failed: Social Scientists, Modernity, and the New Cities of the 1920s and 1930s

9

Alan I Marcus

From Social Reform to Social Science

In the late 1920s and 1930s, American social scientists and others began to turn away from statistical analyses and data sets in their examination of cities. In lieu of mathematical rigor, they began to gather vignette, story, and analogy to explain and explore the urban milieu. Flight from the sort of numerical precision that had come to define social science is startling. It would be incorrect not to note, of course, that some scholars still found numerical analysis useful. But the kind of detailed statistical forays into the minutiae of social class and economic arrangement—the kind of statistical analysis that Adna Weber brought to his study of cities in the late nineteenth century—virtually disappeared from cutting-edge social science work.

Social scientists in the late 1920s and 1930s almost always recognized their radical departure from traditional social science practice. In fact, these scholars often used introductions to their studies or first chapters of long works to stake out the reasons for their sudden abandonment of numerical analyses. Invariably they argued that what numbers failed to provide or even measure were exactly what social scientists now wanted and needed to know. Vignette, tale, and discussion represented more important information and information in a more appropriate manner than social statistics. To these men and women as well as many of their fellow Americans, the reason for the shift from numbers to verbal exposition was clear: cities in the 1920s and 1930s seemed something quite different than they previously had been considered.

What was this new city? What did social scientists describe, and how did they account for their verbal portraits? Almost to a person, commentators pinned their transition from mathematical to verbal explanations on the creation of a new social reality; cities of the late 1920s and 1930s were

William Foote Whyte

In February 1937, William Foote Whyte, a twenty-three year old junior fellow at Harvard University, moved into a third-story room in Boston's North End, then one of the city's worst slums, and began the research that would eventually make him a world-famous sociologist. As a junior fellow, he could take any course he wanted to, and he persuaded Harvard officials to permit him to research a book on the North End's well-known Italian-American youth gangs, then a subject of great social interest among social scientists and laypersons alike. His advantages and experiences growing up prepared him for this challenge. The only son of a professor of German, John Whyte, and of his wife, Caroline Van Sickle, William lived in places where education was favored, including the Bronx, in New York City, and in Bronxville, New York, where as a high school student he wrote well-researched essays for the town newspaper on the local schools as well as many news stories for the *Bronxville Press*. After spending a year with his father in Germany, he enrolled in Swarthmore College, where he majored in economics and graduated in 1936.

Whyte spent more than a year living in the North End, staying with the Orlandi family, who owned and operated the Capri, a neighborhood restaurant. He hung out with gang members. He watched them gamble. He observed their arguments and fights. He studied how the boys flirted with the girls, and, for that matter, how the girls led on (or did not lead on) the boys. He noted the differences between the neighborhood boys and the college boys in every conceivable kind of thought and deed, noting that this was the dividing line, so to speak, between the community's past and its future—the former belonged to gangs, due to their dismal employment prospects, and the latter, who had that most precious attribute,

new creatures, the product of new or recent social forces that had rendered conventional numerical analysis obsolete.

Robert E. Park, dean of what would become known as the Chicago School of Sociology to later generations of scholars, put the matter bluntly: "The city is not ... a physical mechanism and an artificial construction." While those types of arrangements could be counted, parsed, and examined through appropriate statistical means, Park understood them as inadequate measures for cities. To Park, cities lacked an absolute social reality outside the human imagination and intellect. The city was nothing more than "a state of mind, a body of customs and traditions." The city's only reality and only defining characteristics were those that its inhabitants and others posited upon it. An individual city was a particularistic entity, locked in time, place, and space. Each city is "involved in the vital processes of the people who compose it," Park maintained. Like an individual human being, each city was "the product of nature, and particularly of human nature." This intersection between nature—physical reality—and its constituent humans theoretically differed from place to place because the environment and human populations differed from place to place. To examine a city, social scientists needed to learn the uniqueness of its attendance at college, or perhaps, even a degree, and who were therefore marked for movement out of the community and into the suburbs once they found steady white collar work. Clearly the Depression was accentuating conflicts and competition within the North End, not to mention the city and the state. He also helped the youth to organize marches, parades, and demonstrations to prod City Hall into spending more money in the neighborhood.

Whyte called his approach "participatory action research." By this, he meant that he could have his cake and eat it too; he could maintain his objectivity and yet gently nudge those he studied down the path of social amelioration and uplift. In short, he combined the two main traditions of social science then: the dispassionate student of society but also the social reformer, the not-so-giddy partisan of a better tomorrow. Given the times in which he lived as a young man—the Great Depression—this was an attitude to be expected. He married his sweetheart in May, 1938, and two years later his book, *Street Corner Society*, was accepted as his dissertation for the Ph.D. in sociology at the University of Chicago. That book eventually was one of the greatest best sellers in sociology, selling more than 270,000 copies, and was translated into Chinese, Japanese, German, French, Italian, and Spanish. Whyte contracted polio in 1943, but this did not stop him from having both a satisfying family life and a stellar academic career, mainly at Cornell University. He wrote over twenty books and was an outspoken advocate of liberal causes. His life during the Age of the Great Depression illustrated many important trends about American life and the social scientists who studied it.

SOURCE: *New York Times*, "William Whyte, a Gang Sociologist, Dies at 86", July 20, 2000, B8.

inhabitants' attitudes. As Park put it, to learn about the lower North Side of Chicago, social scientists had to conduct an "investigation of the customs, beliefs, social practices, and general conceptions of life prevalent in Little Italy." To understand Greenwich Village, he continued, required similar sorts of "recording the more sophisticated folkways of the inhabitants" of that area as well as "the neighborhood of Washington Square." He continued, "Every separate part of the city is inevitably stained with the particular sentiments of its population." What without people was "a mere geographic expression" is transformed into "a locality with sentiments, traditions, and a history of its own." He needed to see life as lived (Park and Burgess 1967 [1925], 1–3).

Park knew where he might find a model of how to study the ways and means of urban groups. He suggested that the emergent discipline of anthropology could provide guidance. In particular, he urged urbanologists to adopt the "same patient methods of observation which anthropologists like [Franz] Boas and [Robert] Lowie have expended on the study of the life and manners of the North American Indian." Social scientists need to conduct field work to learn the culture of early twentieth-century American urbanites. Analysis of that type required social scientists to interview and

Robert Park exerted a major influence on the development of American sociology. A professor at the University of Chicago in the 1920s, he became a leader of the "Chicago school" of sociology and pioneered in the study of race and ethnic relations. (*UPI-Bettmann/Corbis*)

even live as participant observers with the subjects of their studies. Understanding the minutiae of custom, tradition, and habit as it was practiced by one group in a particular locale necessitated a virtual total immersion in that neighborhood. Cold numbers never could explain the rich detail that characterized social existence (Park and Burgess 1925, 3).

But that was not all. Park saw that cities each were made up of several populations, of several neighborhoods, each with its own unique character. This, he argued, complicated and enriched matters. Cities were webs of interactions between people and places—neighborhoods—none of which could be studied or dissected without harming the teeming living mass. As Park put it, the modern city "is a living entity." And each modern "city has a life of its own." The vast complexity of these living social organisms not only reflected the habits, culture, and customs of the groups that comprised them but caused them to become something different and more. The modern city lays "bare to the public view in a massive manner all the human characters and traits which are ordinarily obscured and suppressed in smaller communities." The cultural interaction within the neighborhoods of modern cities "shows the good and evil in human nature in excess." Because of this persistent, intense interaction, the modern city serves as "a laboratory or clinic in which human nature and social processes may be conveniently and profitably studied" (Park and Burgess 1925, 1, 4, 6, and 36).

The area in which Ernest W. Burgess, Park's associate at Chicago, focused his attention—urban growth—seemed rather straightforward, certainly ameliorable to numerical analysis. Certainly Burgess paid tribute to Max Weber and the other earlier statistical sociologists. But he prized their work because it identified populations distinct from those populating rural environs, not for its ability to analyze how those new populations behaved within the urban milieu. In fact, he complained that the "only aspect of growth [that Weber] adequately described was the rather obvious process of the aggregation of urban population." To Burgess, the key facet of a large urban mass was how the groups constituting that mass acted and interacted. That placed the emphasis directly on urban expansion, the geographic extension of the city rather than its numerical increase. Analyzing geographic expansion was not some mere measure of population density or some such thing. Burgess described that type of "urban growth as a resultant of organization and disorganization analogous to the anabolic and katabolic process of metabolism in the body." As the city expanded both numerically and geographically, every facet of its "soul" changed. Old neighborhoods declined, evolved, or were transformed. New areas were integrated into other neighborhoods as well as the city generally. Growth was a process of concentration and decentralization; it never stopped. Things were constantly in motion, decaying, reviving, and being incorporated in what to Burgess was truly a dynamic process. Growth was not a neighborhood phenomenon, even if it simply occurred within a neighborhood. It was a citywide phenomenon because every other place felt the effect of change on any number of levels. Growth bubbled through the modern city and stressed parts and areas of the city in new, different ways. From those new stresses emerged crime, juvenile delinquency, poverty, and wealth. The modern city then was a living cauldron of simultaneous organization and disorganization (Park and Burgess 1925, 48, 53).

Robert Lynd also eschewed statistical analysis when he undertook his classic study of Muncie, Indiana. His *Middletown: A Study in Modern American Culture* (1929)explicitly sought the science and objectivity of traditional predecessors. But it purposely dismissed numerical techniques as inadequate, even pernicious. Despite the fact that he chose to investigate "a small American city" rather than a metropolis, like Chicago, Lynd understood modern urban life in a manner familiar to Park and Burgess. There the "different aspects of civilization interlock and intertwine, presenting—in a word—a continuum." A modern city, regardless of size, was simply "a unit complex of interwoven trends of behavior." His goal was "to study synchronously the interwoven trends that are the life" of the municipality (Lynd and Lynd 1929, 1–3).

Investigating such a template required a creative mind. Lynd further insisted that what he learned remain beyond reproach (a claim of the old numbers crowd who called their data "empirical"), a stipulation that focused entirely on his methodology. His initial starting point was to reject any attempt to prove or disprove a hypothesis; he claimed that his study would not attempt "to prove any thesis." He underscored "the old error of starting out, despite oneself, with emotionally weighted presuppositions and consequently failing ever to get outside the field one set out so bravely to objectify and study." His method to secure "maximum objectivity and ... some kind of orderly procedure" was simply to divide the community into broad, life-related tasks. This functional anthropology approach was "simply as a methodological expedient." Lynd claimed that they had no intrinsic "merit" other than lifting things "to an impersonal plane" (Lynd and Lynd 1929, 1–3).

Nothing could have been further from the truth. Part of the functionalist anthropology project was the notion that "an outstanding characteristic of the ways of living of any people at any given time [was] that they are in the process of change." Like the Chicagoists, Lynd would write about the urban process, Middletown in motion, building and decaying. To demonstrate the minutiae of process, Lynd chose to ground his study in 1890, a time before "the industrial revolution ... descended upon villages and towns." Simply, Lynd's technique revolved around contrasting the present with what he believed had been. Lynd argued that by selecting a striking counterpoint, he could examine points of intersection and discuss change with "a degree of detachment indispensable for clearer vision." The present state of affairs would be delineated by the factors "by which it is conditioned." The present, to Lynd, was nothing more than "the most recent point in a moving trend" (Lynd and Lynd 1929, 1–3).

Only "a dynamic, functional study of the contemporary life of this specific American community in the light of the trend of changing behavior observable in it during the last thirty-five years" could adequately explain Middletown's present. That goal forced Lynd to rely on data not suitable to mathematical manipulation. He soon championed vignette, interview, or tale, no matter how commonplace, unsophisticated, or imprecise that sort of data seemed. To Lynd, it was neither the pristineness, definitiveness, or rigorousness of each or any piece of data that truly mattered. Pieces of data only assumed critical importance because of "their inter-relatedness in a specific situation." It was the interrelationship between data where precision was meaningful. The context—what it was juxtaposed against and what it was in conjunction with—informed each iota of data, at least in part. Data was only meaningful as it interacted, impacted, and was impacted upon in a given instance or situation; its integrity—its raw value or precision—was never the issue. Its ability to influence and affect virtually every other aspect of the city—its context—gave it critical meaning. And that was much too complex for the kind of statistical analysis regularly used by late nineteenth- and early twentieth-century social scientists. Only by carefully observing the interaction, interdependence, and diffusion of phenomena could a social scientist counter urban problems. Their "stubborn resistance" of these problems to amelioration, argued Lynd, stemmed in part from the "common habit of piecemeal attack on them" (Lynd and Lynd 1929, 1–3).

Clark Wissler, Franz Boas's successor at the American Museum of Natural History and a prominent anthropologist in his own right, agreed with Lynd's assessments. In his introduction to *Middletown,* Wissler took pains to declare that "experience with social phenomena is bringing us nearer and nearer to a realization that we must deal directly with life itself, that the realities of social science are what people do." Little could be gained by the "gathering of intimate statistics as to wages, living conditions, etc.... Masses of individuals ... live and function in communities." It is the interaction of the various peoples, activities, processes, institutions, conventions, traditions, and customs—lives and functions—that defines and makes the city. And because these variables are continually shifting and influencing each other, the city is constantly in flux even as it might appear stable or static to the outside eye. Understanding the dynamic nature of American cities "will not be complete until these communities [themselves] are made objects of study." To Wissler, a city is "a social phenomenon," a "community affair." Analysis of community interactions, often through vignette, anecdote, or interview, must become "the objective methods" to study cities "that are collectively American" (Lynd and Lynd 1929, v–vii).

Caroline Ware's classic study of Greenwich Village sounded the same themes. The historian moved into the village, establishing an office where she resided during her two-year study. Ware felt it imperative to immerse herself in village life and culture. Only through that endeavor could she study "the dynamic interrelations within this community." To rely on social statistics would raise "the danger of oversimplifying what is, by definition, a complex situation." She found it an "impossibility of isolating for laboratory study factors whose essential quality is their interplay with others." Rather than neatly discrete variables, Ware found messiness, disorder, and disorganization. Life in Greenwich Village failed to fit "a coherent pattern" and "conduct [did] not fit traditional categories." Categories proved meaningless when each facet of life and custom affected and was affected by every other custom or activity (Ware 1965 [1935], 3–8).

Ware certainly recognized that the constituents of that village life differed from those found in most modern cities. Bohemians, reprobates, Italian immigrants, and others all worked, lived, and played in proximity. The village was the refuge for those at war with traditional values and practices. Yet despite that acknowledgment, Ware thought village life was representative of the forces influencing modern cities nationwide. The birth communities of Greenwich Village residents had undergone the same annihilation of traditional early and mid-nineteenth-century American culture as she detected in their new home. What made them special was that they actively sought a new American urban ethos. And what made village existence so relentlessly depressing was their failure to find or create one. The village offered, she lamented, "no solution to the cultural problems which drove people to the area. Escape it offered but not solution." Village life "contributed no new [cultural patterns] to take their place. In the fact of cultural disintegration, it either fostered escape or erected the individual as psychological entity into an end itself." Ware found "no social cement [that] bound into a social whole the fragments of" the various cultures found in the village. "Nor were there any distinguishable signs that forces were at work to shape new cultural patterns out of the fragments of the old." There existed "no evidence that the direction of social evolution in this community was toward a society for the twentieth-century American." The only clear movement was "away from the social orders of the past" (Ware 1965 [1935], 422–424).

This remarkably damning assessment of village and American urban life Ware laid directly on industrialization. Emerging in the late nineteenth century, that pervasive monster killed bucolic America and left only cultural vapidness or devastation in its wake. In her identification of a new force entered into the cultural stew, she differed from the Chicago sociologists. Their causal agent was the automobile, which they recognized as altering expectations and patterns of activity. Automobiles inserted into urban life a dimension it lacked previously. Mobility and distance combined to rearrange urban living.

If any sort of analysis called out for number crunching, it would have been that of the Chicagoists or Ware. Certainly, automobiles could be counted and graphs created to demonstrate potential triggers or other points of action. Similarly, industrialization (or at least what might have made up its constituents) could have been counted, dissected, pinpointed, and quantified. Ware was not alone in selecting industrialization as a new urban variable. Lynd's entire methodology of tracing Middletown over 35 years incorporated the notion that the effects of industrialization could be seen and identified as they caused Middletown's culture to build and decay. That none of these urbanologists, nor most of their leading contemporaries, opted for statistical analyses was not a matter of ignorance but intent. What was important to each and every one of them was that they identify a force new to the urban social milieu. And that was important precisely because of how they understood urban culture.

From Static to Dynamic Cities

The problem of cities in the late 1920s and 1930s was not a question of numbers but rather the introduction of a new variable that caused massive perturbations within what had been urban culture and life. Whether the automobile, industrialization or something else, the new force destroyed the static equilibrium that had characterized the city and replaced it with a dynamic equilibrium that redefined and reidentified all elements of the urban milieu. Industrialism or automobiles changed the character of everything they touched, causing old forms to decay and new forms of activity and association to rise.

Ware maintained that she did not know what new social equilibrium would emerge from the introduction of the social force of industrialization. Her historical colleague, Arthur Schlesinger, Sr., claimed to have no such trepidations. His *Rise of the City* (1933) contended that a new, vibrant form of

Street in Bethlehem, Pennsylvania, 1935. Photo by Walker Evans. (*Library of Congress*)

living accompanied industrialism, that of urban life. Unlike Ware, Schlesinger saw urban existence as a concomitant of industrialism; industrialism and immigration caused cities to rise and exert their influence within American culture. Industrialism caused "the momentous shift of the center of national equilibrium from the countryside to the city." Schlesinger realized that "the process was painful and confusing," but he also saw that it meant "the release of energies and ambitions." In any case, he was certain that "the city had come and ... it had come to stay" (Schlesinger 1933, 120, 435).

Yet even Schlesinger worried that the rise of the city, optimistic though he remained, might result in an America less open to initiative, innovation, and participation than its rurally dominated predecessor. Was this new city culture's "mission to be that of a new Jerusalem or of ancient Babylon?" That the new urban-based America remained in flux constituted "the chief unfinished business of the departing generation" (Schlesinger 1933, 435–436).

Schlesinger and Ware in their ways saw industrialism as destabilizing elements within American society, especially its impact on urban living. Lewis Mumford, the noted writer and cofounder of the Regional Planning Association of America, went further. He saw the events of the previous hundred years—the era of industrialism—as an unmitigated disaster. What had occurred, Mumford maintained in his *Culture of Cities*, was "disurbanization." He noted that "[m]isbuilding and malformation, dissociation and disorganization'' characterized this period as city structures, cultures, and societies decayed. To Mumford, this was especially troublesome because it was atypical. Cities throughout history had been beacons of culture, ''the form and symbol of an integrated social relationship.'' There ''human experience is transformed into viable signs, symbols, patterns of conduct, systems of order'' (Mumford 1938, 3–13).

Cities then were an inextricably interrelated interaction of things human—forces, structures, ideas, habits, and customs. A new powerful force entered the mix in the later nineteenth century to upset the dynamic equilibrium. The ''machine ideology''—industrialism or, as Mumford called it, ''the will to profit''—caused ''the fact of disintegration'' of urban society. ''Perversities and evils spread more quickly'' as in the ''stones of the city, these anti-social facts become embedded.'' This ''crystallization of chaos ... hardened uncouthly in metropolitan slum and industrial factory districts'' and forced people to flee the city proper, thereby ''widen[ing] the area of social derangement.'' A ''civic nucleus'' was a casualty of this ideology as ''parasitic and predatory modes of life'' overcame the city's traditional ''effective symbiosis, or co-operative living together'' (Mumford 1938, 3–13).

Numerical analysis played no essential part in Mumford's determinations. Contemporary cities suffered a crisis of elemental proportion; it was the elements of urban existence that had changed. That was the crux of Mumford's concern. Mumford and the others who eschewed statistical analysis defined cities in a remarkably similar way. To this group of social scientists and historians, cities were composed of elements so interdependent that each within the city took at least some of its definition and meaning from the other elements; none of the elements within the city stood or had an integrity entirely its own. Numbers were unnecessary to make that case and meaningless to change the situation. Only by varying the elements—by adding, subtracting, or reshaping one or more—could amelioration take place. Even that activity, moreover, was not subject to mathematical assessment. Again, that these elements literally modified each other meant that numerical precision—or exact prediction—was impossible. Only through manipulation—trial and error, hardly the signposts of systematic inquiry—could an appropriate equilibrium point be reestablished.

Herbert Hoover's ''Research Committee on Social Trends'' had more direct policy implications. The committee was nothing less than a grand attempt to engage the federal government in understanding the presumed consequences of modernity. Created in 1929 soon after his election, Hoover established the committee to examine ''emerging problems.'' Ever the good engineer, the new president appointed a wide variety of experts in social arrangements (social scientists) to gather the information, identify the new problems, and plot potential means to ameliorate them. The committee itself acknowledged its landmark social science significance. ''For the first time,'' the committee intoned, ''the head of the Nation has called upon a group of social scientists to sponsor and direct a broad scientific study of factors of change in modern society.'' The committee's comprehensive approach was its virtue. It refused to overlook the ''intricate relations'' behind the whole panoply of emerging issues because it knew that what "appears to be a satisfactory solution of a single problem ... [would] likely produce new problems by putting that solution into practice" (McKenzie 1967 [1933], v–vi).

It was that understanding it took into its analysis of cities. To head that investigation, the committee chose R. D. McKenzie, who had worked with the Chicago sociologists in the mid-1920s. True to his roots, McKenzie discussed in his 1933 final report the "limitations of the statistical data." He insisted that "to show in an objective and verifiable manner some of the basic changes" brought on by modernity, he "not infrequently" would "resort to the case procedure to suggest developments" of even a general character (McKenzie 1967 [1933], 3–7). Interview, vignette, and case study would be the means to demonstrate modernity's influence on cities.

McKenzie focused on motor transport as the telling new force that disrupted traditional urban arrangements. He argued that the automobile "has erased the boundaries and bridged the distances which formerly separated urban from rural territory and has introduced a type of local community entirely without precedent in history." This was a "new type of supercommunity organized around a dominant focal point and including a multiple of differentiated centers of activity, characterized by "complexity ... and the mobility of its population." McKenzie claimed that this supercommunity, which he also called a "metropolitan community," was "not confined to the great cities" but stood as "the communal unit of local relations throughout the entire nation." Indeed, the "vast amount of rearrangement of populations and institutions" involved in these new supercommunities meant that interactions among their various parts were "still far from having attained an equilibrium." Everywhere were "territorially differentiated, yet interdependent, units of settlement." Each supercommunity had "a constellation of centers, the interrelations of which are characterized by dominance and subordination." At the heart rested "a central city or focal point of dominance in which are located the institutions and services that cater to the region as a whole and integrate it with other regions." A new supercommunity was nothing less than a "economic and social organism" (McKenzie 1967 [1933], 3–7).

Diagrams of the City

McKenzie then had outlined an urban model far larger in scope and jurisdiction than a city. But despite the size of the unit and his absolute devotion to the automobile as causal agent, McKenzie advocated a social arrangement consistent with that posited by the other urbanologists of his generation. Whatever their locus of concern—neighborhood, city, or nation—the models they envisioned were composed of discrete yet interdependent parts—structures, people, groups, and facilities. It was the interactions among these various entities that mattered.

To these scholars, the automobile, industrialism, or the will to profit was the element that radically disturbed the dynamic milieu that had seemed to function so successfully for so long. This new force upset the ecological-cultural balance. In the mid-1920s and after, Mumford's Regional Planning Association of America (RPAA) aimed to approximate the restoration of the previous ecological-cultural equilibrium. They did not want to fix contemporary environments; contemporary environments and the premises upon which they were based were to these scholars obsolete; they were the problem. Cities as they had grown in the late nineteenth and early twentieth centuries had to be replaced by units consonant with the events, practices, and ambitions of the 1920s and 1930s. Through numerous writings and plans, the group advocated a type of living arrangement that would foster traditional cultural values, yet suitable for the modern age. This regional planning was by definition multidisciplinary; the RPAA was composed of foresters, sociologists, architects, economists, housing reformers, and other specialists, each of whom recognized that their own expertise was insufficient to reorganize urban life effectively to accommodate modernity. Only by pooling their talents and skills could these scholars, philanthropists, and planners design a satisfactory form for urban life in the second quarter of the twentieth century.

Indeed, the membership of the RPAA mimicked its understanding of the nature of contemporary urban life. Because society was a dynamic system in which each facet—structures, cultures, traditions, inventions—materially influenced and modified every other facet, any attempt to render assistance required a similarly diverse and complicated amalgam of persons adept at any number of specific enterprises. Their hubris (and an explanation for the appeal to activism) was that they thought that they could artificially construct an environment that would facilitate cultural blending and mingling and foment human happiness, that somehow an environment properly constructed would be the most important variable in modern social arrangements. It could shape whatever forces and situations its varied human inhabitants brought to it; humanity and its institutions would adapt to the environmental particulars.

That environmental determinism led the RPAA to agree that contemporary geopolitical jurisdictions did not match actual living patterns; neighborhoods, cities, suburbs, and rural areas all seemed interdependent and should not be arbitrarily separated. Each affected the others, making place-based action ineffective, perhaps even pernicious. Only by breaking down existing jurisdictional units and erecting a central authority based on a principle quite different than "the will-to-profit" could living be reconstituted on a humane basis. To the RPAA, the means to structure contemporary society existed: Automobiles, electricity, and airplanes promised to overcome the grime, congestion, and dirt of contemporary cities; to annihilate distance as they brought suburbs into more intimate connection; and to restore a bucolic aspect missing from urban life. The first step in incorporating the best features of traditional American village life and the excitement of the modern era was establishing a single geopolitical entity consistent with that transformation. In this case, a properly constructed government entity would be able to fine-tune—to legislate and proscribe as seemed necessary—social arrangements to encourage a healthy, yet dynamic equilibrium among the various portions of the new regional community.

A kind of social homeostasis was the RPAA's goal. Its artificially constructed environment would be suitable for the modern age yet appear to be built around and to reinforce traditional cultural values. The patina of modernity would shelter an otherwise wholesome, small-town existence. Traditional values and practices might be visually transcendent but at the same time the environment would enable its residents to pursue the American dream of a middle-class existence and all the modern amenities that went with that station. A modern life, replete with all the material and emotional advantages as well as the best of traditional small-town America, seemed to these scholars an achievable goal.

The RPAA worked at the fringes of governments in the 1920s and 1930s to encourage state and local governments to adopt its recommendations. A number of its members curried political influence and lobbied for positions from which to launch initiatives consistent with the organization's vision. They certainly agitated to convince their fellow social scientists of the validity of their diagnosis. As early as 1925, RPAA members wrote essay after essay touting the idea of regional planning for a special issue of *Survey Graphic* as they urged lawmakers and others to accept a Regionalist model. A few years later, they brought their criticisms to bear on a new plan for metropolitan New York and carried out a heated and extensive exchange in the pages of the *New Republic*.

Perhaps the most significant attempt to create a new environment for the modern era occurred during the Roosevelt administration. His Brain Trusters, many of them social scientists, explicitly expected to use social scientific insight to resolve America's problems and drew on then-contemporary social science models to design federal programs to refashion society. Cities quite quickly received their scrutiny.

Roosevelt's Resettlement Administration, its name reflective of its goals, tackled the city question straight on. Created by executive order in 1935, it was administered by Columbia University Economics Professor, Rexford Tugwell. Through "the establishment, maintenance, and operation" of "communities in rural and suburban areas," the agency aimed to create new living arrangements to overcome the emergent problems of urban and rural poverty (Executive Order No. 7027, 1935). By virtue of what the Resettlement Administration proposed, it diagnosed both situations as a matter of environment; the modern age had rendered traditional urban and rural environments dysfunctional. The Resettlement Administration championed single-family home ownership, mixed-income residential areas, and comprehensive planned living spaces. Ample roadways would join residential unit clusters with other places, leaving broad greenbelts in between. Numerous electric power lines would provide clean energy to these residential enclaves as social scientists planned what amenities would give the residential area a communal character. Schools were an obvious necessity, but the social scientists insisted on a community center, library, and a shopping district as critical institutions in melding together urban and rural poor. Separate traffic routes for motorists and

Houses in Greenbelt, Maryland, were built in large blocks, with pedestrian and automobile traffic separated. Greenbelt was established in 1937 as one of three "greenbelt" communities planned by President Franklin D. Roosevelt's Resettlement Administration. (*Library of Congress*)

pedestrians were constructed and issues as seemingly inconsequential as whether residents should be allowed to smoke cigarettes were discussed.

Although only three of these new residential communities were actually built—$31 million in federal funding was spent—the agency initially planned to erect 3,000 such communities. Each would house between 10,000 and 30,000 residents, the land for which would be leased to cooperatives of local residents. Equally telling was Tugwell's explanation of the process of community building. The Resettlement Administration would go, he claimed, "outside centers of population, pick up cheap land, build a whole community and entice people into it." Then the agency would "go back into the cities and tear down whole slums and make parks of them" (Gelfand 1975, 133).

Tugwell's explanation and his prescription that slums be turned into parks, coupled with the agency's devotion to smoking bans, libraries, and shopping districts as appropriate facets of these greenbelt communities, reflected just how imperative creating the right environment seemed to agency social scientists. To these men and women, an appropriate environment became the sine qua non of social renovation. Only by erecting and mandating institutions, practices, and customs that favored a healthful, happy, prosperous society could one manufacture the possibility of achieving that end. In this framework, individuals not only brought certain habits, traits, and abilities that defined them and their cohort, but they also had the capacity to be shaped and modified by the environment—a certain plasticity characterized modern American men and women. As important, the social engineers understood that a properly sculpted environment would eliminate or diminish certain kinds of behavior that were unsuccessful in the social milieu and therefore unproductive. Over time, new successful behavior and customs—behaviors and customs increasingly successful within this particularly shaped environment—would flourish and become ingrained within the body politic. The result would be a society and social order consistent with modernist principles.

That social science formulation extended this emergent evolutionary synthesis into the social sphere. Environments within this new synthesis were deterministic in the sense that behaviors and other factors catered for favor within that particularistic milieu. To many of these social scientists, the environment was virtually predictive, a means to inculcate communalism. Within a perfected environment, the struggle for social existence would be one sided. Behaviors that were functional would be rewarded in the environment, whereas those that failed to further community cohesion—dysfunctional behaviors—would be excised. Put simply, the environmentalism of the period amounted to a social determinism in which persons, places, customs, and things that could adapt to the environment would be favored and therefore strengthened. An appropriate environment would enable good things to flourish.

This social scientific theory required no statistical measures. It needed little more than common sense and the will and power to create "modern" environments, the kind of environments spelled out in the various social science literature of the period. Indeed, this environmental determinism accounted for the passionate embrace of any of a number of residential models that placed people, places, institutions, and the like in most intimate connection. It also indicated the depth of disappointment with established forms of urban governance and life. It was not simply that the old way hampered progress. Rather, persistence of the old way ended virtually any opportunity for revision and success. The failed status quo guaranteed the persistence of the emergent problems of modernity.

Not content to merely refashion urban environs, New Deal social scientists and their supporters also tried to "modernize" opinion. The Resettlement Administration sponsored photography of common folk and the Regionalist art of Grant Wood as it campaigned to convince others of the wisdom of its proposals by using methods then prevalent in modern advertising. The Resettlement Administration also pressed for documentary movies as an effective means to make its case. Tugwell initially proposed the making of eighteen such films. Two in fact were made. Both *The Plow that Broke the Plains* (1936)—about the Dust Bowl—and *The River* (1939)—about the TVA—provided visual images tailored to make the case for the creation of new federally financed and actuated environs.

Roosevelt was so pleased by the efforts that he created the U.S. Film Service in 1938 and tapped Pare Lorentz, who had conceived and supervised the Resettlement Administration's films, to be its head. Before he left, however, Lorentz sketched out what would have been the Resettlement Administration's third film, which called for creation of a modern urban environment. That movie would be known as *The City* (1939) and Lorentz would serve as producer.

A diverse collection of humanists, social scientists, and other do-gooders from inside and outside the federal government joined Lorentz in making this film. The American Institute of Planners, spearheaded by several RPAA members, sponsored the effort and the Rockefeller Foundation and Carnegie Corporation of New York funded it. Mumford wrote most of the narrative. Ralph Steiner and Willard Van Dyke, U.S. Department of Agriculture (USDA) photographers and cameramen on *The Plow* and *The River*, directed and photographed the visually stunning effort. Aaron Copland, composer of such Regionalist pieces as *Appalachian Spring* (1944) and *Rodeo* (1942), as well as *Quiet City* (1939), wrote the score.

The film opened at the 1939 New York World's Fair, whose theme was "Building the World of Tomorrow." It proved an instant hit, a quite sophisticated integration of words, visuals, and music. The film contrasted the rustic New England past, a time of joy and "communitarianism" in which humans were in touch with nature and with the industrial city (Pittsburgh was used). There blight, smoke, hopelessness, and poverty reigned. The metropolis—New York City—was portrayed as an impersonal place where breakneck speed was the norm—jostling on sidewalks and automated pancake and toast machines gone out of control were the pertinent images—and danger lurked around every corner. Attempts at relaxation, such as going to the beach at the Jersey shore, were thwarted by massive traffic jams, flat tires, overheated vehicles, screaming children, and congestion-related automobile accidents.

In *The City*, greenbelt communities restored an environment gone terribly wrong. Here the visuals were from Greenbelt, Maryland, a Resettlement Administration greenbelt community. Hydroelectric power, glass, steel, and automobiles produced a bright, new environment, sensitive to integrating humanity, the soil, and the machine. This was an environment fit for modern life and living.

The visuals and Copland's adept score dominated the film. But while words were sparse, those written by Mumford focused on children, on the next generation of Americans, and how the modern age could lay waste to the depressing present. In the New England past, there existed "lasting harmony between soil and people, the town was us, and we were part of it." But then the industrial city emerged.

> Smoke makes prosperity, they tell you here, no matter if you choke on it. There are prisons where a guy for doing wrong can get a better place to live than we can give our children.... Can we afford all this disorder, the hospitals, the jails, the reformatories, the wasted years of childhood? These are future citizens, voters, lawmakers, mothers, fathers (*The City* 1939).

In the metropolis, "people count the seconds and lose the days."

Greenbelt cities were different. They were explicitly designed for modern humankind. So said the seductive words in the film's narration: "Science takes flight at last for human goals"—as compared to the will for profit—as the new cities were as appropriate for "human wants as a plane is shaped for speed." "All we know about machines, soils, and raw materials and human ways of living is waiting." This "new city is organized to make cooperation possible between machines and men and nature." It "works for modern living as once it did for the old New England town." "Here boys and girls achieve a balanced personality, ready to build and meet a many sided world" (*The City*, Parts 1 & 2, 1939).

A New Paradigm

The huge success of this motion picture suggests just how central a nerve its message hit. But even as it was being released, the social science thrust that gave it its momentum was under attack. Louis Wirth, a student of Park's at Chicago, used the lead article in the *American Journal of Sociology*, the journal of record in his field, to urge his colleagues to go back to numbers. In a nutshell, his argument was that without numbers and the definitions made real by them, sociologists would not be able to come to bear on the problems of modernity. Without a common definition of qualities and conditions of modernity, quantities and deviations from those definitions could not be measured. Wirth's basic premise was simple. Modernity made what he called urbanism the way of life; cities and especially aggregations of peoples in the modern world influenced not simply their environs but entire countries and even the world's population. If that were the case, then it became incumbent upon sociologists to recognize that fact and then to elicit the degree and type of influence felt or recorded, and that required measurement, precision, and exactitude. What was necessary, according to Wirth, was "a comprehensive body of compendent hypotheses which may be derived from a set of postulates implicitly contained in a sociological definition of the city, and from our general sociological knowledge which may be substantiated through empirical research"—research that generated measurable, countable numbers. Even these hypotheses would require "ample and exact verification" (Wirth 1938, 6–8, 18–19, 20–23).

Wirth knew that the entire matter hinged on theory. "By means of a body of theory," he claimed that "the complicated and many-sided phenomena of urbanism" could be reduced to "a limited number of basic categories"—things that could be quantified or measured. A cogent statistics-dependent theory would give "the sociological approach to the city" an "essential unity and coherence enabling the empirical investigator" to treat urban life "in a more integrated and systematic fashion." Since what "passes as an 'urban sociology' ... at present" lacked such a tool, Wirth decided to produce one. With attendant subdivisions and caveats, Wirth maintained that "urbanism as a characteristic model of life may be approached empirically from three interrelated perspectives"—as a "physical structure," as a "system of social organization," and as "a set of attitudes

In 1941, Constance Warren, president of Sarah Lawrence College in Bronxville, New York, was excited that faculty and students had conducted a social survey that would pave the way for a federally financed slum clearance project in nearby Tuckahoe. This would bring prestige to this decade-old woman's college, for, as President Warren believed, a science education and calling would do more to emancipate women than anything else. It finally paid off with a grant of $325,000 from the United States Housing Authority for the Tuckahoe project. In colonial times, Tuckahoe began as a farming community. In the 1810s, settlers discovered large lodes of beautiful marble; Tuckahoe was radically transformed into a working-class community of Irish immigrants and African Americans. Tuckahoe carried its heritage proudly, but as the marble quarries petered out, so did the village's economic fortunes. The Depression almost trebled unemployment there.

In 1938, the Yonkers Family Aid Society had asked the College to help with a survey of a depressed section in Tuckahoe. In that survey, the professor and her students framed the questionnaires and calculated, correlated, and tabulated data on such questions as race, occupation, income, housing conditions, and costs. The survey's results provided the rationale for the local application to the United States Housing Authority for new housing funds—about $1,000,000. The million-dollar grant for Tuckahoe village was not approved, but in March 1941, $325,000 was approved. Old-time "social survey" social science, complete with college women aspiring to be social workers providing the work, their professors as guides and experts, and the New Deal, with its federal to state to local grant in aid programs, had carried the day.

SOURCE: *New York Times*, March 23, 1941.

and ideas." Wirth understood that his definition/theory contained severe flaws and gross limitations. He felt compelled to offer it because "it is only so far as the sociologist has a clear conception of the city as a social entity and a workable theory of urbanism that he can hope to develop a unified body of reliable knowledge." His theory of urbanism would be "elaborated, tested, and revised in the light of further analysis and empirical research"—each number-dependent. Theory would enable "the miscellaneous assortment of disconnected information which has hitherto found its way into sociological treatises on the city"—the studies of the previous fifteen years when numbers had failed—to be "sifted and incorporated into a coherent body of knowledge" (Wirth 1938, 6–8, 18–19, 20–23).

Wirth's prescription was direct. It overturned discrete sets of living arrangements—cities, neighborhoods, towns, rural—for a single theory of modernity, which he termed a theory of urbanism; urbanism was modern. This theory facilitated measurements from place to place and from time to time. It restored numbers to a central place in what had been urban social science. Wirth had restored order to the chaos that his mentor, Park, had created in the late 1920s, but at the expense of doing away with cities as a category or living arrangement. What mattered to Wirth and his descendants was not the uniqueness of social arrangements but rather how they compared to a de facto artificially established normal. Wirth's approach established that normal as the base and made problem resolution simply an attempt to get matters to conform to the hypothetical normal. It established the model as normal, which meant that every time the model was "refined," normal in fact changed. The situation became one of relative truth in which problem solving reflected only the application of the newest social science model. It established a situation both in theory and in practice in which the theoretical world displaced reality.

Wirth himself keenly recognized the desire to achieve the appearance of stability and meaning in an otherwise indeterminate world. He wrote, "Only by means of some such theory will the sociologist escape the futile practice of voicing in the name of sociological science a variety of often unsupportable judgments concerning [social] problems." He realized that social scientists "cannot solve any of these practical problems," but if each "discovers his proper function," they will have "an important contribution to make to [problem] comprehension and solution." Opportunities for social scientists to improve the social weal, Wirth concluded, "are brightest through a general, theoretical, rather than through an ad hoc approach." Numbers would provide certainty to urbanologists in the modern world, even if only relatively so (Wirth 1938, 24).

In the years after Wirth's essay, urban social scientists resurrected their precious numbers. That act denigrated other forms of evidence—the case study, vignette, anecdote—that had proliferated in the late 1920s and 1930s. Downplaying nonnumerical material signaled a rejection of interest in the uniqueness of experience, life as lived. Urbanologists in the very late 1930s and after opted almost exclusively for a sterile, mathematically precise approximation of reality and proceeded as if it were real. That decision held very real consequences. By substituting measuring deviance from a hypothetical and idealized point for an exact description of a particular situation at hand, they traded an end—coming to bear on "social" issues—for an understanding of the unique interplay among the various forces, people, and customs in a particular place. Model building and data fitting came to dominate modern urban social science.

References

American Institute of Planners. 1939. *The City*, Parts 1 and 2. 50 min. Documentary film. Producer, Pare Lorentz; narrator, Lewis Mumford; musical score, Aaron Copeland.

Copeland, Aaron. 1939. *The Quiet City. Incidental music.*

Copeland, Aaron. 1942. *Rodeo.* Musical composition.

Copeland, Aaron. 1944. *Appalachian Spring.* Musical composition.

Executive Order No. 7027, 1935. Establishing the resettlement administration, May 1.

Gelfand, Toby. 1975. *A Nation of Cities: The Federal Government in Urban America, 1933–1965.* New York: Oxford University Press.

Lynd, Robert S., and Helen Merrell Lynd. *Middletown: A Study in Modern American Culture* New York: Harcourt, Brace and World, 1929.

McKenzie, R. D. *The Metropolitan Community.* New York: The Macmillan Co., 1967 [1933].

Mumford, Lewis. *The Culture of Cities.* New York: Harcourt, Brace, 1938.

Park, Robert E., and Ernest W. Burgess. *The City.* Chicago: The University of Chicago Press 1967 [1925].

Schlesinger, Arthur M. *The Rise of the City, 1878-1898.* New York: Macmillan, 1933.

Ware, Caroline F. *Greenwich Village 1920-1930. A Comment on American Civilization in the Post-War Years.* New York: Harper and Row, 1965 [1935].

Wirth, Louis. 1938. "Urbanism as a Way of Life." *American Journal of Sociology*, 1–23.

Spectacle, Symbol, Strain, and Showpiece: American Technology in the 1930s

10

Amy Sue Bix

Technology Takes Hold

In 1928, American voters elected Herbert Hoover to the presidency, giddy with his confident assertion that upcoming years would bring continued increases in national prosperity. Herbert Hoover, who trained as an engineer at Stanford University and made a fortune in the mining business, embodied the faith that many observers of the 1920s placed in America's new machine age. Indeed, as secretary of commerce in the early 1920s, Hoover had personally promoted the expansion of commercial aviation, development of radio, and even experiments with television.

For Americans of the roaring twenties, especially middle-class consumers, modern technology seemed to be the ultimate guarantee of national prosperity. Manufacturing output practically doubled during that decade. More middle-class families were able to acquire (often on credit) automobiles with annual model changes, radios, new kitchen equipment, and other exciting products. Major firms, such as AT&T, General Electric, and DuPont, had established corporate research laboratories, harnessing chemistry and engineering innovation to bring to market new plastics, appliances, and consumer services. Thanks to the efficiencies of assembly-line development, supply-chain integration, and other mass production techniques, Henry Ford was making 1.5 million cars a year in the 1920s. Americans could buy a Model T for less than $300.

Yet behind headlines touting the soaring stock market, signs of trouble loomed. Slowdowns in consumer spending and construction led to excess manufacturers' inventories, threatening layoffs and a downward spiral of economic trends. The great crash of 1929 shook up easy rhetoric about modern science and technology ensuring national wealth. Over subsequent months, industry and construction slowed, banks closed, and farmers blockaded roads to protest low crop prices. National unemployment rose above 25 percent, and some cities experienced even worse difficulty. Detroit's economy imploded, as vehicle production plunged from more than 5 million in 1929 to just over 1 million in 1931. The world's biggest factory, Henry Ford's 11,000-acre River Rouge plant, laid off 75 percent of its workforce, leaving large numbers of families without any support and facing eviction. In March 1932, labor organizers led an estimated 3,000 autoworkers and their families in a "Ford Hunger March" to protest layoffs and demand union recognition. Ford's private security force and local police attempted to block this protest with tear gas and fire hoses, then opened fire on the crowd, killing five.

Desperately seeking to explain the Great Depression, some Americans began to question the gospel of machine age progress. Critics suggested that rather than guaranteeing the growth of prosperity, rapid technological change might have contributed to economic disaster as industrial mechanization led to the elimination of jobs.

Yet even as middle-class Americans read newspaper stories and heard lectures about the threat of technological unemployment, people also witnessed continued technological milestones. Despite the Depression, construction of bridges, dams, and record-setting skyscrapers continued, symbolizing man's triumph over nature. Pilots thrilled onlookers by breaking aviation records, while the development of new airplanes promised the conquest of geographic limitations.

More than that, President Franklin Delano Roosevelt's New Deal relied on technological development as a tool to revive the country's economy and a symbol for progress. His plans for rural electrification, hydroelectric power, and infrastructure building promised to transform entire regions, opening up opportunities for poorer or isolated Americans to share the comforts of new consumer technologies. While economic disaster forced families to cut back spending on luxuries, many considered cars, radio, and movies to be modern necessities, providing both reassurance and escapism. New technology in the form of streamlined trains and nylon stockings generated widespread excitement and represented the hope of continued technological progress. Exhibits at the New York World's Fair of 1939 made this promise tangible, that over the long run, science, engineering and business working together would pull the United States out of Depression and ensure its consumers the world's best standard of living.

Technology as Spectacle: Engineering Megaprojects and Aviation

The sheer size of Depression-era construction megaprojects and continued technical developments in aviation commanded people's attention. Although many building plans had originated back in the 1920s before the Depression hit, their spectacular completion symbolized the hope of restoring American greatness. Technical innovations in large-scale concrete work and materials handling facilitated construction, while population growth, especially in the West, prompted concern for infrastructure development.

Thousands of unemployed American workers rushed to the big engineering projects to seize the job opportunities they offered. Erector™ Sets, toy construction kits complete with metal beams and small gears, were a popular toy for boys, who could dream about becoming grown-up civil and mechanical engineers designing skyscrapers, dams, bridges, and railways.

Among this era's most exciting engineering projects was Boulder Dam (later renamed Hoover Dam). The construction, begun in 1931, formed a massive reservoir out of rough desert and set the stage for continued development to reshape the land and economy of the American West. Especially across southern California, this modern engineering transformed inhospitable territory into new residential environments, industrial opportunity, and valuable agribusiness. One of the most dramatic technical challenges arose right from the start, as builders proceeded to divert the powerful Colorado River. Crews raced each other as they drilled and dynamited four tunnels, fifty feet in diameter, into the canyon wall, and then constructed a giant cofferdam out of tons of rock to redirect the entire river. Before starting the dam itself, workers had to dig away centuries-old sediment to reach bedrock, while building major networks of rail lines, cables, and pulleys to carry heavy material to the site.

With up to 5,000 men on the project, simply providing temporary housing posed logistical nightmares, as did supplying the mess hall where workers consumed twelve tons of vegetables and fruit, five tons of meat, and more than two tons of eggs each week. Dehydration, electrocution, carbon-monoxide poisoning, and falls posed constant threats, as did the blistering summer heat. More than 100 men were killed and hundreds more seriously injured. "High-scalers" undaunted by heights (supposedly including former circus acrobats and sailors, along with many Native Americans) dangled along canyon walls to clear debris.

The dam's scale, more than 700 feet tall, raised further complications; calculations showed that the vast heap of concrete would take over a century to cool naturally, and resulting stresses would risk cracking the dam. Accordingly, engineers devised an ingenious system of integrating pipe coils into dam blocks that could run cold water through the structure. The entire project, including powerhouses, intake towers, and overflow spillways, was finished under budget and in less than five years, two years ahead of schedule. Tourists poured in to see what became upon completion the world's tallest dam and the world's largest hydroelectric facility, supplying electricity to seven states. Hard labor and powerful engineering had overcome heat, danger, and technical challenges to reshape nature to human needs, continuing America's conquest of the Western frontier.

Another structural icon created during the 1930s was San Francisco's Golden Gate Bridge. Many engineers had long insisted such a structure would be impossible to build for anything less than $100 million. Bridge designer Joseph Strauss promised an affordable construction and began aggressively promoting his vision to local politicians, along with cannily distributed bribes. Civic leaders realized that with the city blocked on three sides by water, future geographic expansion depended on securing better automobile access to open areas on the north. The already-overcrowded ferry system could not handle more traffic, though owners whipped up an intense but futile campaign to block bridge plans. Lured by the promise of jobs amid headlines about the growing Depression, Bay Area voters in 1930 overwhelmingly agreed to a $35 million bond issue, pledging their counties' property and individual homes, ranches, and businesses as collateral.

After reassurances that construction would not hamper civilian shipping or military harbor operations, the U.S. War Department, which owned land on either side of the strait, gave the go-ahead. Excavators moved more than 3 million cubic feet of dirt and stone in 1933 before pouring the massive concrete anchorages. Divers fought tricky currents to lay blast charges for the southern tower's base, working blindly in murky ocean and risking "the bends" from decompressing too fast under the tight work schedule. While Strauss initially proposed an awkward cross between a suspension and cantilever structure, designers ultimately dared build what became the world's longest main suspension span, 4,200 feet between the two towers. The bridge was calculated to flex and sway as much as twenty-seven feet in strong Pacific gales. The 7,659-foot-long cables would absorb the brutal wind stress, each more than three feet in diameter, the biggest ever made. Technological innovations speeded up the onsite spinning of the cables; each bundled together more than 27,000 individual strands, enough wire to circle the equator three times. Bridge architects gave the structure a distinctiveness to match the dramatic setting, with its elegant Art Deco style and vibrant "international orange" paint. The bay's freezing fog and sixty-mile-per-hour wind gusts made the slippery metal catwalks and girders incredibly treacherous for the high-steel workers. Conventional expectations projected that for each million dollars spent on a major bridge, one death would occur. Strauss insisted that workers don an early version of the modern hardhat and use safety lines, while spending more than $130,000 to sling a safety net beneath the entire span. This net caught nineteen men who otherwise would have fallen to their death, survivors subsequently nicknamed the "Halfway to Hell Club." Showboating workers had to be dissuaded from jumping into the net for thrills. The admirable safety record of months without a single fatality was shattered when an unsafe scaffold collapsed and tore the net loose, killing ten workers.

Following more than four years of construction (but ahead of schedule and under budget), the Golden Gate Bridge opened in May 1937. On the first day, reserved for pedestrian traffic, approximately 200,000 people came to walk (or run, roller-skate, and even tap-dance) across the city's new icon and enjoy the spectacular view from its road. Five hundred airplanes flew over the bridge; the battleship *Pennsylvania* led a fleet sailing under the bridge, while the city celebrated with spectacular fireworks, parades, and a pageant titled, "The Span of Gold." Counties on the north side immediately began marketing redwood forests and other natural attractions to visitors.

On the East Coast, the Depression failed to halt New York City skyscraper-builders' race for record height. In May 1930, the seventy-seven-story Chrysler Building became the first to pass the 1,000-foot mark.

Wanting a bold architectural statement representing the essence of modernity, Walter Chrysler gave his new headquarters a dramatic Art Deco crown. Gargoyles resembled Chrysler hood ornaments; other building decorations were modeled after car radiator caps, while the finial was covered in a new form of steel that gleamed in the sunlight. After announcing the intended height, the architect ensured that his building would top its competitor, the Bank of Manhattan, by secretly altering his plans to add a 180-foot-tall spire. That needle was dramatically hoisted into position from inside the spire in just ninety minutes at the end of construction, making the Chrysler the world's tallest building—for less than a year.

When President Herbert Hoover threw a ceremonial switch in Washington, D.C., on May 1, 1931 to officially open and light up the new Empire State Building, that 102-story tower took the title of the world's tallest building. Construction had finished in just thirteen months, sometimes as fast as one story per day, and under budget at $25 million. In the Depression-era labor market when other projects had ground to a standstill, foremen had their pick of the city's best ironworkers, stonemasons, carpenters, plasterers, brick workers, concrete workers, and electricians, almost 3,500 workmen who were grateful to earn almost $2 an hour. Trucks hauling more than 50,000 tons of structural steel practically still hot from Pennsylvania mills, plus Italian marble, Indiana limestone, and granite, drove right into the building's basement. Their loads were immediately hoisted onto small temporary railroads, specially built on each floor, which carried materials directly to workers.

Lewis Hine, whose well-muscled blue-collar heroes concentrated fearlessly on their expert work, immortalized the drama of skyscraper construction in photographs. A classic Hine photo titled "Icarus" showed one of these "sky boys" suspended gracefully on midair cables, trusting in experience and balance rather than on safety harnesses or other protective equipment (one dozen men were killed on the project). The tower was capped with a steel and glass mooring-mast for dirigibles, but strong winds and lack of room eliminated any prospect of having airships dock there regularly. Making the building usable required sixty-seven elevators, traveling up to 1,000 feet per minute, plus a giant water-pumping system with tanks every twenty floors. Upon completion, thousands of visitors each day flocked to its observation decks, but the Depression put a damper on office rentals, generating the nickname of the "Empty State Building." Still, the building instantly became a symbol of New York and, by extension, American greatness, featured in the dramatic climax of the original *King Kong* movie (1933). Writer E. B. White later commented that the Empire State "managed to reach the highest point in the sky at the lowest moment of the Depression" and "shot 1,250 feet into the air when it was madness to put out as much as six inches of new growth" (*New York Times*, April 23, 2006). After destruction of the World Trade Center on September 11, 2001, the Empire State Building again became New York City's tallest building.

Americans who flocked to watch the Hoover Dam being built, gawk at the rising Empire State Building, or walk across the Golden Gate Bridge

Lewis Hine's photograph, *Icarus*, showing a worker fastening steel cable to hold a derrick in place prior to lifting steel girders and other steel parts at the top of the Empire State Building. (*Bettmann/Corbis*)

also remained fascinated by aviation. The Wright brothers' pioneering experiments at Kitty Hawk, North Carolina, in 1903 had inspired rapid development of airplane engineering and flight skill in both the United States and Europe, leading up to the dog fighting and aerial reconnaissance of World War I. The postwar surplus of affordable planes encouraged enthusiasts to learn to fly, while thousands visited air shows to gasp and scream at the rolls, dives, and other stunts performed by barnstormers. Government support for airmail, airports, and nighttime flying encouraged improvement of aviation, as did federally funded research on airplane engineering. Nevertheless, through most of the 1920s, U.S. passenger air service remained irregular; widely publicized accidents meant most people remained more comfortable traveling by train.

Despite the Depression, the 1930s became a golden age of American aviation, a time of significant advances in airplane technology and business. Perfection of all-metal, single-wing designs symbolized modernization, replacing the World War I era wood and fabric construction that proved inadequate for commercial airline growth. Famous Notre Dame football coach Knute Rockne was among the passengers killed in a 1931 TWA crash; investigations showed that the wooden structure of the widely used Fokker Trimotor was prone to delamination, that is, midair wing separation. Poor design also meant that drag prevented older planes from reaching more than 100 miles per hour. For profitability, airlines required a faster plane that would provide pleasant passenger service.

In 1936, Douglas Aircraft introduced the all-metal monoplane DC-3, one of the most significant and successful airplanes in history. Known as the first modern airliner, the DC-3 dominated the commercial aviation market within just six years and supported airline growth around the world. Thanks to easy maintenance and aerodynamic innovations that engineers said almost let the plane fly itself, the DC-3 made passenger routes profitable. Its impressive safety record accelerated public acceptance of air travel, while its ceiling of more than 20,000 feet let pilots rise above bad weather. With soundproofing, passengers could even hold conversations without shouting, impossible in earlier planes. A sleeper model held luxurious berths for fourteen passengers, allowing American Airlines to offer a seventeen-hour Newark-to-Los Angeles service, substantially speeding up transcontinental routes that previously took more than twenty-four hours. United introduced the first stewardesses, required to be under twenty-five, single, and registered nurses, who could tend to airsick or nervous passengers. Almost 11,000 civilian and military versions of the DC-3 were manufactured, and hundreds were still flying in the year 2000, for both passenger and cargo service.

But the real glamour of 1930s aviation came from Pan American Airlines (Pan Am), whose "China Clippers" carried mail and passengers more than 8,000 miles between the U.S. mainland and Hawaii or the Philippines. Before opening these new routes, Pan Am had to build new long-distance communication systems, set up radio towers, and develop direction-finding navigation systems with greater range. Pan Am built and expanded remote bases on Midway and other Pacific islands, dynamiting lagoons and chopping down jungles to clear areas for refueling and to build hotels for passenger stopovers. The biggest Pan Am "flying boats" could carry up to seventy-four passengers or provide overnight sleeper service for thirty-six. At a round-trip cost of almost $1,500, passengers received luxury treatment meant to match the extravagance of the finest ocean liners, with armchairs and full dinners served on good china. Crossing the Pacific by steamship required three weeks, while Clipper service from San Francisco to the Philippines took just sixty hours, stretched over seven days. Glamorous advertisements showed well-dressed passengers disembarking under Hawaiian palm trees, welcomed by beautiful native girls offering leis. Though such extravagance was almost unimaginable for Depression-era middle-class Americans, transoceanic Clipper service symbolized romantic adventure as well as the new global reach of technology.

Other observers in the early 1930s thought that the future success of long-distance passenger service would depend on lighter-than-air vessels. Germany led the world in developing airship technology, stemming from its World War I use of dirigibles; its *Graf Zeppelin* made a round-the-world flight in 1929. To prove the Reich's technical and political superiority, the Nazi government proceeded to build the largest rigid airship ever.

Philippine Clipper in flight over the Golden Gate Bridge, 1936. Pan American Airlines had three M-130's in the 1930s: the *China Clipper*, *Philippine Clipper*, and the *Hawaii Clipper*. (*Library of Congress*)

Emblazoned with swastikas, the *Hindenburg* made a spectacular appearance at the 1936 Berlin Olympic Games. Crowds gathered to watch the *Hindenburg*take off for its ten successful transatlantic Europe-U.S. flights the first year, at a time when no such commercial airplane service was available. Even amid the Depression, the *Hindenburg* sold virtually every seat; its round-trip price of $720 and speeds over eighty miles an hour were faster and less costly than ocean liners. Passengers enjoyed luxurious cabins as well as a fancy dining room, library, lounge (complete with a lightweight aluminum baby-grand piano) and even a specially protected smoking room.

On May 6, 1937, after arriving from Germany on that season's first transatlantic flight, the *Hindenburg* burst into flame and crashed within seconds. A radio announcer watching passengers and crew jumping to escape screamed into his microphone, "Oh, the humanity!" (Van Riper 2003, 119). Sixty-two out of ninety-seven passengers and crew actually survived (with one member of the ground crew killed). Immediately, ongoing controversy arose over the cause; conspiracy theorists suggested sabotage aimed at embarrassing Hitler's regime, while others speculated that lightning or static electricity from nearby storms had ignited the more than 7 million cubic feet of hydrogen. Later investigations linked the disaster to the highly flammable nature of the *Hindenburg*'s skin covering. The shocking accident, combined with spreading military aggression that diverted government attention, ended optimistic hopes for extensive commercial lighter-than-air passenger transport.

During this era, aviation heroes continued to grab headlines, and the danger of flying only added to its intrigue. Pilots pushed the limits in aiming to break records; several died in attempts to cross the Atlantic Ocean in nonstop flights. On May 21, 1927, airmail pilot Charles Lindbergh captured world adoration after completing the first solo nonstop airplane flight between Europe and North America, reaching Paris thirty-three hours after leaving New York in his *Spirit of St Louis*.

Almost from the beginning of aviation, a handful of women had mastered the new technology, defying conventional gender expectations and frequently garnering the scorn of male pilots. While the daring of all aviation celebrities elicited awe, women flyers carried an extra curiosity value and air of glamour. Among the most famous female pilots was Amelia Earhart, a tomboy fascinated by air shows who acquired her pilot's license in 1921. In 1932, marking the fifth anniversary of "Lucky Lindy's" flight, Earhart overcame mechanical difficulties and icy winds to cross from Newfoundland to Ireland in just under fifteen hours. As the first woman to fly solo across the Atlantic, Earhart displayed immense courage and aviation sense in the days when long-distance flying remained incredibly risky. She was immediately nicknamed "Lady Lindy," and Congress rewarded Earhart with the Distinguished Flying Cross, the first time that award was presented to a woman. Just three months later, Earhart became the first woman to fly solo nonstop from one U.S. coast to the other, then broke her own record time with a second cross-country flight the following year. Earhart worked to popularize aviation, publishing books about her flights, going on national speaking tours, and serving as aviation editor for *Cosmopolitan* magazine, even writing articles promoting the excitement of flying for women.

In 1935, Earhart became the first aviator, male or female, to solo the 2,400 miles from Hawaii to the U.S. mainland, yet already had in sight an even more ambitious goal. While previous pilots had completed round-the-world flights, Earhart aimed for the longest distance, at the equator. Heading east from Miami in June 1937, Earhart and navigator Fred Noonan successfully covered more than 22,000 miles, roughly two-thirds of the journey. On July 2, the pair headed out of New Guinea on the most difficult leg, with the navigational challenge of trying to locate tiny Howland Island after crossing 2,500 miles of empty Pacific Ocean. Assistants in a waiting Coast Guard cutter listened helplessly to Earhart's final radio messages declaring that her fuel was running low. The tragedy captured international headlines, as did the ensuing futile search. Almost immediately, rumors spread that Earhart's flight had been cover for a secret American spy mission against the Japanese, who then shot down and captured her. Speculations surrounding Earhart's mysterious disappearance have continued to multiply over the years. Intriguing clues (including discovery of a woman's shoe and airplane parts similar to those of Earhart's Lockheed Electra) may suggest a crash landing on a nearby island, but no definitive proof has emerged. The drama of 1930s aviation, even its apparent accidents and failures, only underlined the significance of conquering the skies.

Technology as Symbol: New Deal Transformation and Machine Age Beauty

With Roosevelt's inauguration speech declaring that "the only thing we have to fear is fear itself" (Black 2003, 270), the president started a whirlwind of activity that committed the federal government to dealing directly with Depression problems. Among the resulting "alphabet soup" of New Deal agencies, the Civilian Conservation Corps, the Public Works Administration, and the Work Progress Administration supported major construction projects around the country. Millions of jobless men earned paychecks by building roads, parks, airports, schools, telephone lines, and New York City's Lincoln Tunnel, which today remains the world's busiest vehicle tunnel. Such infrastructure development was just one way that Roosevelt's administration embraced technology as a tool for initiating major social and economic changes.

President Roosevelt was particularly interested in leveling inequalities faced by rural families by using technology to improve farm work, modernize backward homes, spur industrial development, and correct environmental problems. Eager social science experts in the new administration felt confident that by combining skilled government planning with large-scale engineering, they could transform entire regions. In 1933, Roosevelt set up the ambitious Tennessee Valley Authority (TVA) project, aimed at alleviating poverty and improving lives across seven states by building an integrated system of dams and hydroelectric plants along the Tennessee River. The undertaking aimed to solve many of the area's problems simultaneously, controlling devastating floods, improving navigation, and providing employment. Idealistic project managers hoped that by generating massive amounts of cheap power, TVA would bring the benefits of modernization to thousands of rural residents who never had electricity before and also stimulate regional industrial development. While private power companies protested against this government-sponsored competition, the courts upheld TVA's legality. Engineers tackled the challenges of designing Norris Dam and the TVA's other enormous water-control projects, while planners built (white-only) model communities nearby to house workers, complete with schools and hospitals. Agriculture experts set up demonstration farms to promote fertilizer use and reforestation to help residents salvage eroded and depleted soil, while health workers distributed vaccinations against smallpox and typhoid.

With creation of the Rural Electrification Administration (REA), Roosevelt expanded this principle of using technology as an economic and social catalyst to reshape an even larger area of the country. By the early 1930s, electric light and power were available to most city residents (outside the poorest neighborhoods), but to only about 10 percent of rural Americans. Country dwellers appeared increasingly out of touch with modern technological life, experts warned, enticing young people to leave family farms. Promoters promised that electrification would raise both living standards and profits for farmers. State fair exhibits touted the wonders of electric threshing machines, butter churns, and wood splitters. Agricultural experiment stations published evidence that hens surrounded by electric light laid more eggs, while cows drinking continuously pumped fresh water produced more milk. Although a few farmers installed windmills or dammed streams to generate their own electricity, private utilities judged it prohibitively expensive to extend distribution lines to remote areas with low population density. In 1935, New Deal government stepped in to remedy that situation, constructing almost 75,000 miles of electric lines in just two years and helping to establish more than 400 electric cooperatives. Within five years, one-quarter of rural households had been electrified, along with rural stores, churches, and schools. REA agents offered farmers government loans for buying electric corn huskers to speed up harvesting, electric stoves to ease housework, and radios to bring news and entertainment into isolated homes. REA publicity contrasted photos of a woman using her new electric washing machine to pictures of her with an old-fashioned hand wringer. Such images underlined the optimistic message that technology could give rural Americans all the modern consumer lifestyle benefits already enjoyed by their urban counterparts.

Prominent Depression-era artists conveyed admiration for the sheer power and beauty of electricity and other technology in their work. In 1932, Mexican Marxist painter Diego Rivera came to the Detroit Institute of Arts to paint a large mural (commissioned by Henry Ford's son Edsel) to comment on the relationship between humans and modern technology. Rivera, who had been fascinated by machinery as a child, spent weeks studying and sketching Ford's world-famous River Rouge plant and its equipment, along with workers' faces, homes, and neighborhoods. The "Detroit Industry" frescos revealed Rivera's admiration for American industrial might. His detailed depictions conveyed the harmonious design and impressive capacity of steam turbines, stamping presses, and blast furnaces. Rivera painted Ford's multiracial workforce making molds for engine blocks, stacking them on conveyor belts, and pouring molten metal, muscle, and machinery that combined harmoniously in valuable productivity. As a socialist, Rivera admired engineers and prized technology's potential to create a better world. But other parts of his twenty-seven-panel mural showed modern science and technology as dualities of creation and devastation, contrasting the horrors wrought by chemical weapons and warplanes to the benefits brought by vaccination and innovative passenger aircraft.

Charles Sheeler spent much of the 1930s trying to capture the visual appeal of modern machinery and industrial architecture. Back in 1927, the Ford Motor Company hired Sheeler to photograph River Rouge for a promotional campaign, and he produced dramatic images of how the giant complex transformed coal, lumber, iron ore, and other material into a steady stream of finished product. Sheeler's photos made conveyor belts look as graceful as cathedral arches, with a modern rhythmic geometry. Sheeler turned a number of his photographs into paintings that he called part of a new American art movement, Precisionism. While earlier artists painted the splendor of waterfalls, fields, and other natural features,

It would appear that there was still a chance for the amateur or hobbyist inventor to invent, even in the age of the Great Depression, when it seemed that large-scale industry and "big" technology had precluded such possibilities. Thus, in November 1930, two young New York musicians, Leopold Mannes and Leo Godowsky, Jr., sold their processes of color photography to the Eastman Kodak Company in Rochester, New York. Leopold and Leo, both thirty years old, were the sons of famous New York musicians, the one a conductor and violinist, the other a pianist and composer.

Both Leopold Maines and Leo Godowsky worked on developing a simple process for making color photographs as handily as black and white ones. They met when they were fifteen years old. They soon understood they were trying the same techniques. Hence, they combined efforts, even as they studied to be musicians, and established a laboratory as partners in 1920 in New York City. At that time, both had graduated from college, Leopold Maines from Harvard in physics, and Leopold Godowsky from the University of California, and each continued to pursue a musical career while also maintaining a scientific and technological partnership with the other to develop their desired simple process for making color photographs. In this work, they were self-taught, mainly through reading and in their experiments in their laboratory. What started as an adolescent hobby had grown into a full business and technological partnership. The arrangement they made with Eastman Kodak provided that they sold their research to the company but would continue to work on their process as Kodak employees, initially in their laboratory, eventually in Rochester. In the meanwhile, they continued their careers as members of New York City's musical gentry. Leopold Godowsky, for example, had just married Frances Gershwin, daughter of Mr. and Mrs. I. B. Gershwin of New York City, and a sister of the composer George Gershwin.

SOURCE: *New York Times*, November 6, 1930.

Precisionists treated the twentieth-century's manmade and urban environment as equally attractive and important. Artists such as Sheeler and George Demuth concentrated on depicting material objects such as water towers, gasoline pumps, ocean liners, or elevated trains, making function attractive with sharp detail. Many Precisionist images contained no human presence at all, while others showed a few scattered people as machine tenders, their minimal appearance serving to emphasize the grand scale of industry. In 1938, commissioned by *Fortune Magazine*, Sheeler began six paintings of steam turbines, hydroelectric machinery, dams, and other technology to glorify the theme of "power." Similarly, for the first issue of *Life* in 1936, editors chose a cover photo by Margaret Bourke-White showing the Fort Peck Dam under construction, its imposing walls looming like castle ramparts.

During the 1930s, manufacturers worked to make technology even more attractive. In previous decades, industrial engineers had introduced scientific management principles and efficiency goals to optimize production rates. Depression-era businesses hoped to stimulate buying through what might be called consumption engineering. To differentiate their products from competitors and provoke consumer interest, the new field of

Diego Rivera seated in front of a mural depicting American "class struggle," 1933. (*Library of Congress*)

industrial design focused on style, giving objects a modern look. This psychology created a Depression-era craze for streamlining, the rounded corners, smooth surfaces, and sweeping horizontal lines inspired by the sleek Douglas DC-3.

Railroads exemplified the era's obsession with streamlining, competing with each other to promote the most modern-looking designs. The most famous was the 1934 Burlington Zephyr, which had articulated joints between its stainless-steel cars to make the train (soon nicknamed "the silver streak") resemble an unbroken bolt of lightning. Wherever the Zephyr went, crowds gathered along rail lines to watch it break old speed records. Ridership rose, as advertising urged people to "see America streamlined" and promoted railroads' "fleet of modernism" (Porter 2002, 58). For passenger comfort, in contrast to the nineteenth century's ornately decorated Pullman cars, the Zephyr had sophisticated furniture, air-conditioning, and radio music. In contrast to the old images of coal-fired locomotives as disgustingly dirty, the streamliners were clean symbols of the twentieth century, compared to wingless airplanes on tracks.

Yet Detroit engineers discovered that it was possible to stretch the streamlining fad too far. Designers began to take aerodynamic testing seriously and after wind-tunnel testing, decided to give the 1934 Chrysler Airflow a curved roof, a broad flat nose, and headlights integrated into the hood. This dramatic switch from the boxy cars of just several years before proved too radical. Advertisements pictured the Airflow alongside the era's gorgeous streamlined trains, and resulting excitement stimulated a record number of initial orders. But the Airflow's unusual design, with a specially engineered new suspension system promising a smoother ride, proved difficult and expensive to manufacture. The first to reach market acquired a bad reputation owing to serious production defects, and Chrysler culture shifted back to a conservative style.

Technology as Strain: Labor Tensions and Unemployment

While Sheeler and other machine-age artists painted factories as modern temples, the reality of Depression-era industry proved unhappier. With dark humor, Charlie Chaplin's 1936 film *Modern Times* captured the grim physical and mental stresses of assembly-line labor. The film's boss, leisurely sipping coffee, ordered conveyor belts accelerated to full speed, making it impossible for Chaplin's character to pause in his bolt tightening even to pause to scratch an itch. Chaplin drew on real-life horror stories of Ford spying on his own workers and showed workers affected by what today's doctors call repetitive-stress syndrome, arms involuntarily jerking after making the same movements for hours. The film showed Chaplin's character driven mad by the unrelenting pace, running wildly through the plant destroying machinery and diving headfirst into the equipment, literally getting caught in its huge gears.

The 1930s proved to be a showdown time for auto-industry labor relations. In 1936, members of the United Auto Workers (UAW) mobilized to force General Motors (GM), the world's biggest automaker, to negotiate with the union. In response to wage cuts and production speedups, the UAW mounted a series of work stoppages and then its famous sit-down strikes. Members brought production at Flint, Michigan's Fisher Body Plant to a standstill by refusing to leave and barricading doors with car bodies and steel. Workers stayed warm and dry rather than enduring the miseries of December picketing, while their occupation of the plant reinforced union solidarity and made it impossible for management to bring in scabs. When police and company security tried to storm the plant with teargas and guns, strikers drove them back by throwing metal parts. Workers formed internal committees to keep the plant clean and held daily exercises and classes to keep up morale, while their wives organized and defied police intimidation to deliver food supplies. After forty-four days, GM capitulated and signed a contract giving workers the right to support the union openly. In a subsequent wave of union militancy during early 1937, workers across the country organized more than 100 sit-down strikes, not just in auto plants but also in lumberyards, meatpacking plants, and even laundries and department stores. Major companies such as United States Steel were forced to grant wage increases and union agreements. But although UAW membership soared to half a million, the Ford Motor Company remained a stubborn holdout, obsessed with blocking unionization. In the 1937 "Battle of the Overpass," Ford thugs beat up outnumbered labor organizers (including women from the UAW Ladies' Auxiliary) who had received a city permit to distribute leaflets on public property near the River Rouge factory gates. Newspaper photographs of the vicious attack drew national attention, and after a bitter strike, Ford was forced to recognize the UAW in 1941.

As Depression woes deepened, Americans expressed growing concern that increasing workplace mechanization had contributed significantly to displacing industrial, agricultural, and service labor. Talk of "technological unemployment" filled union meetings, government offices, and economic conferences. While economists had long analyzed the theoretical relationships between mechanization and employment, the Depression moved such questions out of abstract economic textbooks and into frontpage headlines. The fear was that modern technological change operated too fast for society to keep up, setting off destabilizing consequences in many areas of employment simultaneously, and threatening to render workers obsolete faster than they could be retrained. Roosevelt's 1940 State of the Union address warned that the United States faced a crisis of "finding jobs faster than invention can take them away. We have not yet found a way to employ the surplus of our labor which the efficiency of our industrial processes has created" (Israel 1967, 2853–2854).

Reviewing economic data, government experts confirmed that technological unemployment was a real problem affecting broad segments of American workers. Milwaukee's A. O. Smith factory used electric cranes and conveyors to produce 10,000 automobile frames daily with almost no floor labor; critics denounced the company's "quest for 100% mechanization" as "an iron bouncer" (Bix 2001, 151). Inventions had seemingly revolutionized entire industries almost overnight; one lightbulb-making machine increased production from forty per day to 73,000, supposedly replacing more than 900 workers. Railroad unions claimed that more than 28,000 workers had been displaced since the 1920s by the introduction of automatic loading machines and electric track circuits. Steelworkers complained that new continuous-strip mills had reduced man-hour-per-ton labor requirements by 36 percent since 1923. The United Mine Workers blamed the loss of 78,000 jobs on technological change; one miner's wife wrote President Roosevelt, "The bosses made the men take their tools out of the mine and they are letting coal-loading machines do all the work" (Elderton 1931, 80–81). In agriculture, a 1939 government report estimated that the use of wheat combines requiring only three men to perform tasks formerly requiring ten had displaced some 100,000 farmworkers. John Steinbeck's 1939 *Grapes of Wrath* dramatized agricultural labor's complaints of being "tractored out." Even white-collar jobs seemed threatened; telephone switchboard work had formerly offered an attractive employment option for thousands of women, but with the introduction of new automatic-dial systems, the phone company needed fewer operators. Of course, new machines still required some operatives and repairmen, but as labor leader William Green said, "[A] man laid off in a steel mill where new machinery has just been installed cannot tomorrow take up work as a barber" (Green 1930).

Yet it was not clear that labor could block technological change. Hollywood's Depression-era embrace of sound films reportedly cost almost

10,000 musicians their theater jobs playing the accompaniment for silent movies. The American Federation of Musicians mounted a $500,000 public relations push to convince audiences to reject scratchy "talking pictures" and insist on beautiful live music; the campaign fizzled within three years. When mine workers called for the elimination of mechanical coal loaders, union leader John L. Lewis blocked the motion, declaring, "You can't turn back the clock and scrap all modern invention. We must see to it that we share in the benefits of the machine in the form of reduced working time and increased compensation" (Lewis 1934, 189–191).

Fears of technological change permeated Depression culture. Cartoonists drew monstrous robots yanking tools out of workers' hands, painting signs reading "No Help Wanted," and literally sweeping workers off the payroll. Science fiction stories, such as John Campbell's *Twilight* (1934) pictured a future when robot domination rendered humans superfluous or even extinct. Even in children's literature, *Mike Mulligan and the Steam Shovel* (1939) told the story of how nobody needed the beautiful steam shovel Mary Anne and her forlorn operator, after powerful new gas, electric, and diesel shovels came along.

Desperation spurred the growth of Technocracy, a small political and intellectual movement that called for shifting from the free market to a managed economy run by engineers, who would make policy decisions purely on the grounds of technical priorities and efficiency. Collecting data in a 1932 "energy survey," director Howard Scott announced that the nation had reached a crucial juncture. Comparing the pre-1900 American economy with gradual technical change to a slow-moving ox cart, Scott declared that just three decades later, the economy had become a racecar about to spin out of control. Since industrialists were determined to speed up assembly lines and embrace mechanization, Scott warned, Americans were locked into a self-destructive cycle of advancing technology and declining employment. Rather than halting change, he decreed, the United States needed to revamp its entire economic structure to fit the rapid pace. Technocracy sneered at mainstream economists for clinging to outdated ideas such as price and profit, calling for a new machine-age economic system centered on calories, foot-pounds, and thermodynamic balance. For a few months, Technocracy attracted significant attention in the popular press, but it quickly lost most of its appeal after mainstream economists challenged Scott's vague gibberish and revealed that he had lied about his background.

America's business community maintained that complaints about technological unemployment were entirely mythical. The Machinery and Allied Products Institute poked fun at complaints that steam shovels replaced 100 men using hand shovels, saying one might equally well argue that machinery had replaced 10,000 men digging with teaspoons. Henry Ford insisted that, in the near future, corporate research and development laboratories would create entirely new industries to both provide new employment for workers and exciting new products for consumers. An extensive 1937 General Electric public relations campaign declared that technological progress allowed middle-class women to buy "two new dresses for the price of one."

Implying that fears of technological unemployment were not only pessimistic but also unpatriotic, ads showing a couple driving a sporty roadster proclaimed that even in the Depression-era United States, "millions of people are wealthy" (General Electric 1937, 357, 454).

In 1927, public concern about the increasing destructiveness of military technology had spurred talk of placing a temporary moratorium on scientific research. Depression-era engineers and scientists feared that the outcry over labor displacement might encourage more calls for a "science holiday." In 1936, Roosevelt told the Society of Arts and Sciences, "I suppose that all scientific progress is, in the long run, beneficial, yet the very speed and efficiency of scientific progress in industry has created present evils, chief among which is unemployment" (Roosevelt 1936). The president's qualified phrase "I suppose," along with the directness of his link between efficiency and unemployment, shocked scientists and engineers, who felt that their life's work was becoming the scapegoat for economic disaster. Caltech physicist Robert Millikan declared flatly, "There is no such thing as technological unemployment," while MIT president Karl Compton added, "The idea that science takes away jobs is contrary to fact, based on ignorance, vicious in its possible social consequences, and yet has taken an insidious hold on the minds of many people" (Compton and Millikan 1934, 297–309).

While controversy over technological unemployment raged throughout the Depression, Americans never approached the point of stopping scientific and engineering work. A type of technological determinism dominated the debate, the notion of innovation as a natural force that could not and should not be restrained. Technological change would come, and society would need to adjust, a conviction reflected in the motto of Chicago's 1933–1934 Century of Progress Exposition, "Science Finds—Industry Applies—Man Conforms."

Technology as Showpiece: Consumer Products and the New York World's Fair

Despite alarm about technological unemployment, the Depression led middle-class Americans to appreciate the benefits of consumer technology more than ever, particularly with regard to entertainment. Radio's technical origins came from the late 1800s, and at first, the power of the "wireless telegraph" to pull sounds from hundreds of miles away out of thin air seemed almost magical. During the 1920s, the number of commercial stations broadcasting skyrocketed. Listening became such a popular sensation among middle-class Americans that Westinghouse and other manufacturers had difficulty keeping up with demand for new sets. By the 1930s, radio's novelty had worn off, yet the Depression only underscored the continued value Americans attached to this new medium of communication. During winter evenings, approximately 40 percent of households would turn on the radio. Roosevelt was the first president to make effective use of radio to share his ideas and promote his agenda of trying to win

A new industry was born—commercial television—on the campus of the 1939 New York World's Fair on April 30, at 12:30 p.m. sharp, when President Franklin Delano Roosevelt opened the Fair with a speech telecast 8 miles away. It took almost two decades for television to become a technically feasible medium. There were scientists and engineers working on television technology in several countries. The technical problems were not simple. How to capture a visual image and transmit it—that required an army of researchers and much trial and effort.

The activities of two Russian immigrants, Vladimir Kosma Zworykin, an engineer, and David Sarnoff, a Russian Jewish immigrant who developed the Radio Corporation of America (RCA) mattered the most. Zworykin was born in 1889, in a small river town, where his father ran a fleet of boats. In 1912, he earned a degree in electrical engineering at the St. Petersburg Institute of Technology; his mentor there insisted that the future of television rested with the cathode ray tube and not the contemporary belief in

public and Congressional support for new programs such as Social Security. His fireside chats brought the president's voice into every living room on a regular basis for the first time, with a powerful immediacy that created a personalized impression of Roosevelt reaching out to ordinary citizens in a common cause. Of course, radio also supplied a vehicle for Roosevelt's critics and demagogues, such as Detroit-based "radio priest" Charles Coughlin, whose demagogic rants against international bankers attracted numerous followers.

In Depression-era radio, music accounted for the majority of programming, giving isolated or poorer Americans the opportunity to hear concerts they could not have attended, enjoying this culture at home in ease and privacy. Stations played everything from classical music and opera to hymns and country music, but radio's accessibility particularly facilitated the spread of jazz music, especially the danceable swing of Benny Goodman and Duke Ellington. Roughly 24.5 million Americans owned at least one radio during the Depression years, providing a ready mass audience for advertisers, who inserted product plugs and jingles into the drama, comedy, suspense, or children's shows that they sponsored. Humorist Jack Benny greeted his audience with the words, "Jell-O, everyone" (Douglas 1999, 121).

The era's most notorious example of the power of radio came with brilliant director Orson Welles's 1938 broadcast of the science-fiction classic *War of the Worlds,* featuring simulated news bulletins about aliens invading New Jersey. Reports suggested that as many as 1 million listeners began packing up to flee or simply panicked, after they missed the identification of the realistic-sounding broadcast as fiction or heard rumors from neighbors. While some historians have since suggested that accounts of mass alarm were sensationalized, Welles did hold a press conference the day following his show to apologize, and the episode became a legendary part of radio history.

Movies emerged from the late nineteenth century primarily as a novelty and cheap amusement for working-class people and non-English-speaking mechanical systems of capturing and projecting images. During World War I, Zworykin served as an officer in the Czar's army and fled the Bolshevik revolution, settling in the United States in 1919. In the 1920s, he worked for Westinghouse and, eventually, for the Radio Corporation of America; in his spare time he toiled on many inventions, especially on making a viable cathode ray television picture tube. He and Sarnoff met in 1928, when the latter was president of RCA. Zworykin, ever the inventor, told Sarnoff that it would take only $100,000 and a few months to perfect television as a commercial industry. Sarnoff, ever the entrepreneur, found that it took fifty millions and eleven years to finish the job. By 1939, television was technologically feasible; New York City had several hundred subscribers, and London, England, about 14,000. By 1939, television was born and developed after World War II.

SOURCE: *New York Times*, April 30, 1939, August 1, 1982.

immigrants. But by the 1920s, star-laden features gave films new respectability that increasingly attracted middle-class audiences, as did the glamorous "movie palaces." The Depression cut weekly movie attendance rates by about one-third, and numerous theaters closed. However, construction of more than a dozen grand palaces around the country continued, with their elaborate Art Deco, exotic Orientalist, or Middle Eastern ornamentation designed to make movie-going a thrilling sensory experience. Technological innovations in 1930s films also drew attention; 1927 brought *The Jazz Singer*, the first feature-length "talking picture," and Hollywood continued to experiment with sound over subsequent years. While a few color movies had been made in earlier decades (some with hand-painted frames), refinement of Technicolor processes encouraged studios to produce an increasing number of color features during this era, including Walt Disney's hit *Three Little Pigs* (1933).

Car culture, the ultimate symbol of American consumer well-being and freedom, survived a Depression-era slump. New car sales fell from 4.4 million in 1929 to a low of 1.1 million in 1932; sales rebounded to 3.9 million by 1937, only to plunge again to 2 million as recession hit during the following year. The Depression forced many small automobile manufacturers out of business, leaving the "big three" (Ford, Chrysler, and GM) to dominate the market. Meanwhile, some Americans who owned cars could no longer afford to maintain or drive them and let their registrations lapse. Nevertheless, people continued to prize cars, even used Model T's, as both necessity and pleasure. Between 1929 and 1932, gasoline sales actually increased more than 15 percent, while millions hit the road for family vacations. Many bought trailers to make travel more affordable, while campgrounds did impressive business, as did motel, tourist cottages, roadside restaurants, and other businesses catering to auto travelers.

While the Depression forced many Americans to ration their movie-going, delay purchasing a new car, or otherwise cut back on consumer spending, advertisements promised that technological progress under the control of corporate enterprise would soon bring a future of fabulous abundance. The business world made such dreams tangible at the 1939–1940 New York World's Fair, where 45 million people came to tour "The World of Tomorrow." Displays entertained visitors with mechanical ingenuity and promises of new consumer goods, overwhelming them enough to preempt any questions about the relationship between technology and unemployment. For example, AT&T enticed visitors by offering free long-distance calls. A gee-whiz demonstration of "What Happens When You Dial" used flashing lights to help crowds trace the path of a call being automatically connected. Switchboard operators who blamed the introduction of the dial system for eliminating their jobs had no such prominent venue to plead their case.

Other fair exhibits drove home the message that, despite unemployment, Americans should be grateful that technological progress already

Poster featuring the Trylon and Perisphere at the 1939 New York World's Fair. The structures at the fair were designed around a futuristic theme. (*Library of Congress*)

had given them the world's highest standard of living. At DuPont's "Wonder World of Chemistry" offering "better things for better living," "Miss Chemistry" posed in an entire outfit of manmade fibers. Male guests were particularly enraptured by the "leg show" when the girl lifted her skirt to display DuPont's new nylon stockings. "Fabricated from coal, water, and air ... as strong as steel, as fine as a spider's web," DuPont declared, this artificial substance was an improvement on nature (Fenichell 1996, 135). Models at the exhibit played tug-of-war with nylons to demonstrate their miraculous durability, stronger and more affordable than silk, more sheer and sexy than wool or cotton. When nylons hit the market in May 1940, women lined up at department stores before dawn, and although buyers were restricted to one pair each, DuPont's 5 million pairs were gone by evening. Unscrupulous dealers even pretended that silk stockings were nylon, to cash in on the frenzy.

Women coming to New York's Fair enjoyed the Westinghouse homemakers' race, the "Battle of the Centuries," in which "Mrs. Modern" simply loaded the latest dishwasher and pushed the start button, while poor "Mrs. Drudge" covered herself in soapsuds and sweat, washing a sinkful of dishes by hand. RCA's display showing off experimental television broadcasting was mobbed, though it would be years before middle-class families would have their own living-room sets. Further technological astonishment came from Elektro the "moto-man," a humanoid robot who astonished audiences by moving forward on command and counting on his fingers.

The ultimate technological excitement came from GM's "Futurama," where famous designer Norman Bel Geddes carried visitors on a simulated airplane trip over an American city of 1960, showing its triple-deck, fourteen-lane divided superhighways able to keep cars flowing at 100 miles per hour. Twenty-seven million visitors waited two hours or more to enter this technological utopia, where they received souvenir pins reading, "I Have Seen the Future."

As events turned out, Americans would have to wait longer for the automobiles of the future, and it would be more than a decade before television entered middle-class homes. World War II interrupted the promised flow of new consumer goods made possible through the wonders of technology and science. River Rouge and other factories stopped manufacturing new cars for the duration, converting practically overnight to run overtime, producing bombers and tanks. Engineers and scientists left universities to work on top-secret projects such as the development of radar, proximity fuses, and, of course, the atom bomb. The TVA, conceived during Depression, proved vital to defense industry mobilization. TVA electricity supplied the power to run giant aluminum-making factories and nitrate plants crucial for munitions manufacture, as well as the Oak Ridge, Tennessee, laboratory that was busy purifying uranium and producing plutonium for the Manhattan project. Advocates felt sure that American engineering and science would provide the essential edge for an Allied victory, underlining the Depression-era message that technology was what defined modern life.

References

Bix, Amy Sue. 2001. *Inventing Ourselves Out of Jobs? America's Debate over Technological Unemployment,* 1929–1981. Baltimore: Johns Hopkins University Press.

Black, Conrad. 2003. *Franklin Delano Roosevelt: Champion of Freedom.* New York: Public Affairs.

Burton, Virginia Lee. 1939. *Mike Mulligan and His Steam Shovel.* Boston: Houghton Mifflin.

Compton, Karl, and Robert A. and Millikan. 1934."The Contributions of Science to Increased Employment." *Scientific Monthly* 38:297–309.

Douglas, Susan J. 1999. *Listening In: Radio and the American Imagination.* New York: Random House.

Elderton, Marion, ed. 1931. *Case Studies of Unemployment.* Philadelphia: University of Pennsylvania Press.

Fenichell, Stephen. 1996. *Plastic: The Making of a Synthetic Century.* New York: HarperCollins.

General Electric Company. 1937. *Survey Graphic* (June). Advertisement, 357; *Survey Graphic* (September). Advertisement, 454.

Greene, William. 1920."Labor versus Machines. An Employment Puzzle." *New York Times,* June 1.

Lewis, John L. 1934. Proceedings of the Thirty-Fourth Constitutional Convention of the United Mine Workers of America. January 23–31, 189–91.

Page, Max. 2006. "Crashing to earth, again and again." *New York Times* April 23.

Porter, Glenn. 2002. *Raymond Loewy: Designs for a Consumer Culture.* Wilmington, DE: Hagley Museum and Library.

Roosevelt, Franklin D. 1936. Letter to Carl Byoir, May 20, 1936, file PPF 700 "Science." Franklin Delano Roosevelt Presidential Library, Hyde Park, New York.

Roosevelt, Franklin D. 1940. State of the Union message, January 3, 1940, in Fred Israel, Ed. *The State of the Union: Messages of the Presidents,* vol. 3, 1905–1966. New York: Chelsea House, 2853–54.

Van Riper, A. Bowdoin. 2003. *Imagining Flight: Aviation and Popular Culture.* College Station: Texas A&M University Press.

Hollywood Movies and the American Community 11

Charles M. Dobbs

Depression-Era Movies and Values

During the 1930s, Hollywood movies helped define and also reflected broad American social, cultural, and political values. The United States was one of the few industrial countries that did not lurch dramatically to the right during the Great Depression, and it is interesting to speculate on plausible explanations. Some historians have written about "the genius of American politics" (Boorstin 1953) and have suggested that Americans simply do not gravitate toward extremes. Others have suggested that such fascist movements existed in America but lacked ongoing charismatic leadership to equal Hitler in Germany, Mussolini in Italy, and the militarists in Japan, among others. But popular movies produced for a mass audience helped explain the Depression, offered relief and escape, and, after 1933, promoted values supportive of the status quo.

Hollywood benefited from a largely homogenous audience. In *The Search for Order,* Robert Wiebe found that, in the immediate years after the Civil War, America was "a nation of loosely connected islands," that is, isolated communities, and late nineteenth-century industrialization, urbanization, and immigration threatened to overwhelm the older order. Before World War I, the United States was a nation of so-called hyphenated Americans, for example, German-Americans and Polish-Americans, and our differences in language, culture, and religion were as great as the factors that united us. There were great culture wars over a national "language," religion, alcohol and prohibition, the women's right to vote, and other so-called wedge issues.

This homogeneity developed from the rise of mass culture in the 1920s, which helped create a broad American language to overcome differences in ethnicity, religion, and culture. World War I brought what had been a divided an American people together with a common language and

The cast of the 1939 MGM production of *The Wizard of Oz* stand together during a scene from the movie, circa 1939. From left to right are: Judy Garland as Dorothy; Bert Lahr as the Cowardly Lion; Jack Haley as the Tinman; and Ray Bolger as the Scarecrow. Along with *Gone with the Wind*, the *Wizard of Oz* was one of the most famous movies of the 1930s. (*Bettmann/ Corbis*)

shared values. Doughboys and marines had fought well on the Western Front and had impressed the German enemy with their irrepressible courage. Soon thereafter, in the 1920s, mass culture helped replace individual ethnic culture as radio, mass circulation magazines, professional and college sports, and movies, for example, became dominant means of recreating and also releasing anger and frustration at the inhumanities of an increasingly urbanized, industrialized, and impersonal society.

By the 1930s, Hollywood-produced movies were the dominant popular culture in America. The coming of sound to film, which was in the vanguard of a host of technical improvements, and the rise of the production system that ensured a steady stream of quality films for what were largely movie production–owned theaters meant audience satisfaction and steady profits. Hollywood stars dominated the cultural landscape, and when, in 1934, Clark Gable took off his shirt and revealed he was not wearing an undershirt in *It Happened One Night*, cotton producers and manufacturers were aghast. Gable soon starred in advertisements extolling the virtues of cotton T-shirts.

Clark Gable and actress Claudette Colbert in a scene from Columbia Pictures' 1934 film *It Happened One Night*, directed by Frank Capra. (*Bettmann/ Corbis*)

Such images and themes may help explain the improvement from the popular despair of the Hoover years to the greater hope of the Roosevelt years. Hoover tried to maintain morale without dramatically changing American politics or economics. Sadly, the depth of the Depression overwhelmed his measures—including the Reconstruction Finance Corporation, initial construction on what became Hoover Dam, and other projects—and such phrases as a Hoover "blanket" (a newspaper used to cover a homeless person) and a Hoover "flag" (an empty pants pocket turned inside out)—entered common language. Roosevelt seemed an irrepressible warrior, and his optimism and energy seemed to improve the mood of the American people. But, as we shall see, movie themes created an environment in which Americans could forget their troubles for several hours and emerge better prepared to face the situation about them.

Popular culture had risen to dominance in the 1920s. Radio, mass circulation magazines, Madison Avenue advertising for a consumer society, sports, and movies all helped create mass culture and provide entertainment and escape to an ever-increasing audience. Their common images, language, and catch phrases created a common culture that helped bring the American people together. Radio broadcasting began in 1920 at KDKA in Pittsburgh, Pennsylvania, and by 1922, there were more than 600 stations, and by 1930, 60 percent of American families had radios around which they gathered for nighttime entertainment. Radio stations broadcast music, sporting events, newscasts and weather reports, and commentary of interest to the listening audience. After the end of World War I, mass circulation magazines largely moved from muckraking to consumerism, and advertising became so entrenched that the phrase "Madison Avenue" as a synonym for advertising companies entered the daily lexicon. *Time* began publishing in 1923, and new tabloid-size newspapers such as *The New York Daily News* gained large circulations. Advertising benefited from and was critical to the growth of such mass circulation publications. Advertisements for soft drinks, home appliances, automobiles, cigarettes, clothing, and hundreds of other items became standard fare in such outlets. Under the leadership of commissioner (and former federal judge) Kenesaw Mountain Landis, baseball recovered from the "Black Sox" scandal and entered a golden age symbolized by Babe Ruth who moved to the New York Yankees and became one of baseball's greatest homerun hitters. Jack Dempsey and Gene Tunney's heavyweight bout in 1926, watched by tens of thousands and listened to by a huge radio audience, exemplified the popularity of boxing; their rematch in 1927 became famous as "The Long Count Fight." Bobby Jones led a dramatic increase in the number of golfers and also in golf courses. College football came of age in the 1920s, and new stadiums were modeled after ancient Greek stadiums and the Roman Coliseum. Attendance at games doubled during the decade, and commercial radio broadcasts helped involve fans in teams many miles away.

An "Exceptional" American Movie Industry

In America, the movie industry developed quite differently from Europe.

From the outset, European filmmakers appealed to an elite audience and charged ticket prices equivalent to other fine arts performances. American filmmakers appealed to immigrant masses seeking distraction from the stresses of adjusting to a new society and urban life. Prices were low and theaters were initially small rooms with a white sheet hanging against a wall serving as the movie "screen." While movie production began in New Jersey perhaps reflecting Thomas Edison's pioneering role, it eventually centralized in Los Angeles because labor prices were lower, sunshine was abundant (important because so many sets, both indoor and outdoor, were outdoors), and diverse locations from mountains to oceans were within a short drive.

Movie themes in the 1920s changed in mid-decade as the audience diversified from mostly lower-class, frequently first-generation urban residents to a broader, more middle-class audience. In the early 1920s, Charlie Chaplin spoke directly to a lower-class audience facing daily challenges in the struggle for life. His "Little Tramp" character survived overbearing authority with dignity and humor. Many other actors were similarly slight of build—Buster Keaton and Harold Lloyd—symbolizing their unequal battle against larger forces. Thereafter, movies began to play up themes of the roaring twenties—speakeasies, Prohibition, easier relations between young men and women, and a fascination with aspects of urban life—as movies began to appeal to middle-class audiences. As movies increased in popularity, movie stars became the definition of attractiveness, and Americans sought to look and dress like their favorite celluloid figures. Bigger audiences generated greater profits, and movie companies constructed grand theaters with thousands of seats in major American cities. Middle- and upper-class Americans admired the chandeliers, the art work, and the luster of these palaces.

Sadly, beneath the veneer of the roaring twenties was a shaky economic foundation. World War I was ruinously expensive and added to the death and destruction of the conflict were nearly 20 million deaths from the so-called Spanish Flu soon after the war ended. Instead of helping revive the world economy, the U.S. government passed a series of increasingly higher tariff bills making it difficult for foreign goods to sell competitively in America, thus harming the rebuilding economies. At the same, the U.S. government limited its influence over the domestic economy by reducing expenditures and taxes, while the relatively new Federal Reserve Board did not fully grasp its powers to control the economy and moderate cycles through the discount rate and other tools it possessed. Income was too concentrated in the upper classes; the broad middle class, the bedrock of a consumer economy, arose later during World War II. The speculative mania of the 1920s reached its zenith in stock market investments. By 1929, some companies were using assets to purchase shares of other companies, rather than expand their own businesses, because stock purchasing seemed a surer route to corporate profits. In a well-documented sequence of events in late October 1929, the market, heavily dependent on margin loans, began to contract, and the pressure to sell to meet margin "calls" soon began a panic and the market continued to decline into 1932.

The stock market crash, while not causing the Depression, put more pressure on the U.S. economy. The crash destroyed economic optimism, soaked up investment capital, and gradually companies and individuals had to pay for years of borrowed money. With increasing speed, the economy worsened in 1930 and 1931 and dropped off precipitously in 1932. President Herbert Hoover believed it was a temporary down phase of the traditional economic cycle, and avoided profoundly dramatic steps that would alter American values. Despair increased as more and more people lost jobs—perhaps 25 percent of the population—and others feared loss of their jobs. Prices fell, loan payments—whether for business, agriculture, or personal—were difficult to make, thus threatening the banking system, and many people looked for someone or something to blame.

Into this void stepped the motion picture industry. By 1932, Walter Gifford, the head of President Hoover's Organization on Unemployment Relief, "advocated the distribution of free movie tickets to the poor," ranking movies only behind food and clothing as necessities. In 1929, Warner Brothers studio premiered *The Jazz Singer,* a mostly silent film with four talking interludes. Audiences reacted favorably: "Jolson sings!" The excitement led to a doubling of weekly paid admissions, and Hollywood introduced sound into thousands of theaters across America at a cost of millions of dollars. The relatively rapid move to sound greatly affected the movies and its audience appeal. Adjusting to the requirements of sound caused

In the 1930s, many Americans were excited about movie stars. Fan magazines did much to stir the pot. Even the self-professed cynics who wrote for the fan magazines could succumb to star appeal. Thus one such writer, Katherine Albert, gushed excitedly in print about her discovery of Johnny Weissmuller, the swimmer turned "Tarzan" actor in the movies. Weissmuller was "swell," she declared. She confessed that she had seen *Tarzan, the Ape Man* four times. At first, Katherine could not understand what all the excitement about Johnny Weissmuller was about; all through the first reel of *Tarzan, the Ape Man* she thought this was so much hokum, just a lot of leftover animals from a kid movie. "All Johnny had to do was to yell 'Yoo-hoo, yoo-oh-oh-oh' and leap down out of a tree on a tiger's back, and home, mother, and the little kiddies waiting for me were forgotten," she wrote. When the movie came to town, the magazine's office was womanless; all had seen the movie, and they swooned and raved about his physique.

Work stopped in *Photoplay*'s office when Weissmuller strode inside. Three girls fainted. Katherine Albert rushed after him, to interview him; he sat down, saying he was

many actors from the silent era to retire early—foreign accents, high voices, or unappealing mannerisms ended the careers of many—and a generation of actors trained on the stage to travel west to Los Angeles. Movie directors had to learn how to handle microphones and to permit the camera to glide about noiselessly filming the action. Moving the camera led to greater depth in sets, and hence more complex scenes, and that too added to the appeal of movies.

Sound obviously increased the cost of movie production almost precisely as America fell into the depths of Depression. Initially, talking movies helped Hollywood survive, and profits in 1931 exceeded those of 1930. But income and profits fell in 1932 and 1933, causing movie studios and the eastern investment syndicates that financed them to close studios and movie theaters—some 30 percent of them, to lay off thousands of employees, and to cut pay of others. At the same time, Hollywood lowered the price of most movies from $0.30 to $0.20 and provided various giveaways all to maintain a shrinking audience. Hollywood carefully focused on films that would draw audiences to the theaters, and so films sought to follow trends in the larger society. Profit rather than art was the key.

Until 1933–1934, movies appealed to a broad audience while offering a distinct and absolutely inaccurate explanation of the Great Depression. It was the heyday of "corruption and depression" as movie themes, although the Depression really resulted from speculation in the markets, inadequate income distribution, tariffs inhibiting international trade, and little effective action by government to direct and moderate economic cycles. As Robert Sklar wrote, "movies called into question sexual propriety, social decorum and the institutions of law and order." The goal was to maintain the audience as the Depression worsened. Equally important, as Martin Quigley and Robert Gertner wrote, "movies did much to maintain flagging morale as the country and the world sank deeper and deeper into the Depression" (Quigley and Gertner 1970, 39).

bewildered by all the female attention he was getting because the movie's producers all thought that *Tarzan, the Ape Man* was a movie for kids only, and no great shakes at that. And Johnny was not the Hollywood type. He was shy, a bit ill at ease at cocktail parties, and embarrassed by all the female fans who had crushes on him. In fact, Johnny was more at home swimming and being with his wife than anything else, even though *Tarzan, the Ape Man* broke box office records all over the country. He had other things on his mind besides Hollywood and being the "top-notch heart flutterer of the year," as Katherine put it. He liked to swim and play golf. He was in love with his wife. "She's a swell kid," he says. "She likes swimming almost as much as I do, and she swims under water too, hanging onto my belt and sputtering like a seal," Weissmuller explained.

Here was pure fan adulation, Depression-era style.

SOURCE: Katherine Albert, "Hey! Hey! Here Comes Johnny!" *Photoplay*, 42 (June 1932), 28–29, 118–119.

Gangster films help establish this world of ''corruption and depression.'' Edward G. Robinson starred as Caesar Enrico Bandello in *Little Caesar* (1930) and, as Rico, he rises through his criminal organization to achieve supreme power. Jimmy Cagney mesmerized audiences as Tommy Powers—an obvious play on the tommy gun, associated with gangsters in the 1920s—and as someone who took great pleasure in killing and mistreating women—the famous scene where he shoved a grapefruit half into the face of actress Mae Clarke—in *The Public Enemy* (1931). Cagney's character contrasted with his brother, Mike, who joined the Marines. Paul Muni played a fictionalized Al Capone—Tony Comonte—in *Scarface* (1932); unlike Robinson's Rico, he was not particularly intelligent, and unlike Cagney's Powers, he was not particularly shrewd. Rather, his violent ways caused other mobsters to turn on him, and fearing an outbreak of gang warfare, the police eventually killed him in a beautifully filmed final scene. But Paul Muni in *I am a Fugitive from a Chain Gang* (1932) best symbolized the despair of the era; at the film's end, standing in the shadows outside his home, he answered his wife's question, ''How do you live?'' with ''I steal,'' and then disappeared into the darkness. In all, the chaos in the lives of the principal characters reflected the more general chaos in American life, and thus these films resonated with the moviegoing audience in these years who were suffering chaos in their own lives.

Government and society collapsed under the Hollywood criminal onslaught. In *Lawyer Man* (1932), William Powell played a corrupt attorney who, when his secretary tried to open an office window for fresh air, closed it to keep in the corruption and filth. In *The Secret Six* (1931), a group of six masked gunmen—all prominent citizens—acted outside the law as vigilantes to bring crime boss Ralph Bellamy to justice because the system was so corrupt and broken. In *Corsair* (1931), the hero took the law into his hands chartering his own ship to seize the cargoes of bootleggers bringing illegal booze on shore.

If men became gangsters, women had a worse fate. In *Faithless* (1932), Tallulah Bankhead was forced to engage in prostitution. The same fate awaited Dorothy MacKaill in *Safe in Hell* (1931). In each case, the women sold their bodies, the only work they could find in the Hoover Depression years, to obtain needed funds to help their respective men. In *Susan Lennox, Her Fall and Rise* (1931), Marlene Dietrich underwent an amazing ordeal. She prostituted herself to a wealthy politician, played by Cary Grant, to raise money for her husband's radiation poisoning treatments; her husband cast her out when he learned what she had done, and she migrated south to a flophouse and whorehouse in New Orleans, in a sense mimicking a decent into Hell. Somehow she traveled to France where she used her body to rise to the top, but in the end, begged her husband to forgive her and to accept her. Woman's lot was bad in the Depression, perhaps a payback of a sort for the wild times during the roaring twenties.

These films glorified criminals and frequently degraded those with whom they interacted. They also seemed to speak to the American people, offering a deep social critique about the failure of government and the allure of criminals. They served as a safety valve, allowing people worried about the future to purge themselves of anger and relieve their stress in the darkness of a movie palace rather than by demonstrating in the streets.

Comedy films exposed flaws in the existing social and moral order. Director Ernest Lubitsch challenged society's mores in such films as *Trouble in Paradise* (1932) in which two lovers, actors Herbert Marshall and Miriam Hopkins, robbed each other as they professed their affection for one another. That is, Lubitsch suggested that all love was grounded in great deceit—a fine value system on which to construct a society based on family life. W. C. Fields made four short films for Paramount in 1932–1933, *The Dentist, The Pharmacist, The Barber Shop,* and *The Fatal Glass of Beer,* and attacked pillars of small town society in each one. For example, Fields, the pharmacist, wrapped stamps in paper bags—a picture of great incompetence—and Fields, the barber, strapped patrons into barber chairs and then dropped blazing towels on their faces—a picture of sadism. In destroying these minor pillars of society, Fields and Director Mack Sennett provided no substitutes—it was nihilist and reflected the despair of many Americans at the seeming failure of our representative democracy and capitalist economy.

The Marx Brothers made the most sustained attack on language, relations between men and women, and the existing social order. In *Cocoanuts* (1929), based on their successful stage play, the Marx Brothers critiqued the great Florida land boom of the mid-1920s that died in the great hurricane; until that moment, there were more real estate agents in Miami than there were other residents. Groucho's exchange with brother Chico about crossing the viaduct—"why a duck, why a no chicken?"—was a moment of supreme silliness. In *Animal Crackers* (1930), Groucho single-handedly destroyed the image of adventurers challenging themselves against untamed and unknown nature. In *Horsefeathers* (1932), the brothers attacked the sanctity of college, as Groucho moved from a teaching position to the college presidency, making fun of fellow faculty, football, students, alumni, and all those involved in higher education. In one of the film's funnier

Harpo Marx displays the extremes in dog actors with "Mite" and "Mighty," who work with him in the Marx Brothers' Paramount comedy, *Horse Feathers*, 1932. (*Bettmann/Corbis*)

moments, he and his brother Chico seek entry into a speakeasy and cannot remember the password, ''Swordfish.'' Critically, in 1933 they filmed *Duck Soup,* which played in many theaters in 1934. Groucho played Rufus T. Firefly, the president of Freedonia, and engaged in a pointless war with neighboring Sylvania. He asked long-time foil Margaret Dumont how her husband died, and eventually she answered that ''he died in my arms'' to which Groucho commented, ''so, it was murder!'' During a Cabinet meeting, Groucho stated the report was so clear that a four year could understand it, and then turned to his brother, Zeppo, and said ''get me a four year old.'' At another point, he and Chico tell brother Harpo that ''while you're out there risking life and limb, we'll be safe in here thinking what a sucker you are.'' So much for bravery, patriotism, and self-sacrifice. But the film played after Franklin Roosevelt became president, New Deal measures generated vast amounts of energy, and public attitudes were shifting, and making such fun of national leaders, even fictional ones, no longer fit the

American attitude. Thereafter the brothers declined in stature as they filmed *A Night at the Opera* (1935) and eight other films, leaving the heights of national leadership to those better qualified to lead.

Out with Nihilism, In with Optimism

Musical films were frequently tied to the stage and often with the Depression outside the theater. Musicals were still in their infancy, the only genre really to arise with the coming of sound (imagine musicals—singing and dancing—during the silent era!). The great musical *42nd Street* (1933) typified musicals during the Hoover presidency. "Julian Marsh" (played by actor Warren Baxter), a successful Broadway director, produced a new show. The show's principal backer was an old man in love with the show's star; the star, "Dorothy Brock." She broke her ankle the night before the premier, and Marsh pressed "Peggy Sawyer," famed dancer Ruby Keeler, a mere dancer in the chorus to take the lead. As the orchestra began playing the prelude, Marsh gave Sawyer a pep talk clearly tying the film to the Depression outside the movie theaters where the audience sat:

> Now Sawyer, you listen to me and you listen hard. Two hundred people, two hundred jobs, two hundred thousand dollars, five weeks of grind and blood and sweat depend upon you. It's the lives of all these people who have worked with you. You've got to go on, and you have to give and give and give. They've got to like you, they've got to. Do you understand? You can't fall down. You can't, because your future is in it, my future and everything all of us have is staked on you. All right now, I'm through. But you keep your feet on the ground and your head on those shoulders of yours and go out—**and Sawyer, you're going out a youngster, but you've *got* to come back a star** [emphasis in his speech].

Of course, she succeeded, but the musical clearly was set in Depression-era America, and the musical numbers needed a stage to unfold, that is, they existed apart from the film rather than advancing its plot line through song and dance.

Meanwhile, Western movies all but disappeared, relegated when made to hour-long B films aimed at children. In the 1920s, Westerns were so popular that, in this silent era when film could more easily move across national borders (simply change the "dialogue" cards), they were the most popular films in Japan. But with films glorifying the roaring twenties, the West of Tom Mix and others—of heroes and villains, of good and bad—faded, and in the early Depression years, few Americans seemingly wanted to relive the great story of unfolding civilization across the harsh frontier.

When Franklin Roosevelt became president, and the New Deal exhibited great energy if not a great turnaround in the U.S. economy, Hollywood movie themes changed. Roosevelt remarked in 1934 that "when the spirit of the people is lower than at any other time during this Depression, it is a splendid thing that for just 15 cents, an American can go to a movie and look at the smiling face of a baby [Shirley Temple] and forget his troubles.'' Roosevelt sought to buck up the American people, thinking that in part the Depression was a state of mind and thus he famously stated during his Inauguration on March 4, 1933, that ''the only thing we have to fear is fear itself.'' Hollywood helped fill the gap, providing inexpensive relief and entertainment that those affected by the Depression could turn for escape. To be sure, movie theaters gave away dishes and ovenware several times a week to lure audiences, lowered ticket prices, and slashed costs, but the movie industry fared at least as well as any industry in these years. Still, Will Hays, who became the head of the Motion Picture Producers Association, stated that ''no medium has contributed more greatly than the film to the maintenance of the national morale during a period featured by revolution, riot and political turmoil in other countries.'' As Terry Cooney wrote in *Balancing Acts,* ''whether films offered visions of order restored, affirmations of work-centered values, or celebrations of a culture rooted in the mythic American village, they also held out images of competing worlds that might be entered through mimicry or consumption'' (Cooney 1995, 39). Or, put differently, the characters portrayed in films of the late 1930s lived in a world of fancy furniture and highly polished floors, of expensive suits and elegant gowns, of nightclubs redolent with cigarette smoke, fine champagne, and modern music, all of which had little in common with the world in which the majority of the audience lived; however, the opportunity to live a better life vicariously was well worth the $0.25 cost of admission.

People's spirits seemed to revive. Historians have always recounted events with a degree of amazement. When he became president, Roosevelt announced a banking holiday as net outflows of dollars threatened a general bank failure. Several days later Roosevelt announced the banking system was once again sound long before the federal government could meet the challenge with the Glass-Steagall Banking Act of 1933, and three-quarters of a billion dollars returned to bank accounts. Fireside chats, exhortations to action, and the activity of the first Hundred Days combined to raise spirits if not improve the economy.

Hollywood movie themes changed, and it seemed they helped account for the return of hope in America. Movies during the Hoover presidency emphasized the Depression, and glorified gangsters and crime, denigrated law enforcement and politics, showed economic catastrophe hanging over musicals, and suggested if women left comfortable home and hearth their alternatives were severely curtailed. Perhaps a sincere desire to help improve the national mood, an effort to reach out to the new Democratic administration, and recognition of the need to self-police themes to avoid federal legislation—the so-called Breen Code—combined to change movie themes from despair to hope.

Gangster films largely disappeared, although actors and themes would reemerge toward the end of the decade as Nazi spies and agents, for example, *Confessions of a Nazi Spy* (1939). The 1935 film, *G-Men,* symbolized the change as the bland FBI agent became the hero, while the gangster was neither glamorous nor victorious. To forestall federal legislation, the movie industry hired Will Hays, a former postmaster general under Warren

Harding, to administer a movie production code that required movies not lower the morals of the viewing audience. Since gangster films helped lower respect for law and order, there was pressure to restructure plots. Equally important, repeal of the 18th Amendment in December 1933 ended Prohibition, and gangsters lost some of their attractiveness to the general public. In *G-Men,* James Cagney starred as a ruthless FBI agent determined to infiltrate criminal gangs operating in the Midwest. While Cagney's character was every bit as violent as the gangster characters of several years earlier, he worked to uphold the law. First National Pictures, which released *G-Men,* claimed in a press release that it "performed a patriotic service by showing how one branch of the government's law enforcement agencies will wipe out gangland"—perhaps a bit of an overstatement but good for drawing in audiences. In *Bullets or Ballots* (1936), Edward G. Robinson went undercover and joined a criminal organization, to bust it. In *Angels with Dirty Faces* (1938), James Cagney became a criminal condemned to execution while childhood friend Pat O'Brien played a priest who convinced Cagney to act as a coward on the walk to the execution chamber so impressionable young men who idolized him would not follow him into a life of crime. Cagney agreed, and his walk had the desired effect. In each case, the films upheld the existing order, suggesting it was well-intentioned and contrasted favorably with the violence and brutality of the criminal world. Cagney's turnabout became complete in 1942 with the great musical, *Yankee Doodle Dandy,* in which he played, sang, and danced as great George M. Cohan, uplifting spirits during the dark days of World War II. Comedy films underwent a spectacular change, from the deceit of Ernst Lubitsch and the anarchy and nihilism of the Marx Brothers to the feel-good films of Frank Capra and other directors of screwball comedies. Robert Sklar wrote that screwball comedies were used "to support the status quo" and that they were "romantic comedies whose purpose was to show how imagination, curiosity and cleverness could be channeled into support of things as they are" (Sklar 1975, 187). The key to these films was a series of juxtapositions—of educated and uneducated, rich and poor, intelligent and stupid, honest and dishonest, and, most important, of male and female. Sharp language and frequently silly situations—the screwball, and the hope that the lead actor and actress would, indeed, fall in love—drove the plot and drew audiences. These films included *My Man Godfrey* (1936), *Bringing Up Baby* and *Holiday* (both 1938), and *The Philadelphia Story* and *His Girl Friday* (both 1940). The characters were typically wealthy and the films demonstrated that the rich were funny, loveable, and harmless. In *Bringing Up Baby,* Cary Grant played against his suave and sophisticated image as a somewhat bookish and unworldly scholar studying dinosaur skeletons who became caught up in the madcap world of Katherine Hepburn, and after she thoroughly destroyed his carefully constructed existence, he of course fell madly in love with her. In *Holiday,* again starring Grant and Hepburn, Grant told his girlfriend, Hepburn's younger, greedy sister, and her father, a wealthy investment banker, that he was in business only long enough to make money to escape. The younger sister rejected him because he rejected her world, but Hepburn found herself reborn, and the two of them ran off together.

Audiences likely lessened their resentment of the wealthy as they observed that the wealthy were as troubled and stressed as they were, and that money, in the old cliché, did not buy happiness.

A Happy Ending Trumps All

Frank Capra created his own world of screwball comedies. In his first great film, *It Happened One Night* (1934), Clark Gable, the hard-nosed reporter, and Claudette Colbert, a somewhat scatterbrained socialite, met, settled their differences, and fell in love to the ultimate joy of everyone involved. In one famous scene, Gable engaged in a long explanation of the art of using one's thumb to secure a ride—hitchhiking—but he failed. Colbert showed him, raising the hem of her skirt, and the very next vehicle screeched to a halt. Such films were profoundly, socially conservative. As Sklar wrote, "for women, especially, the messages were persistent: romantic love is better than gold digging, marriage better than a career or divorce" (Sklar 1975, 187, 188). As for Capra, he was sentimental and sought to revitalize the nation's old communal myths, and thus many of his films—for example, *Mr. Deeds Goes to Town* (1936) and *Mr. Smith Goes to Washington* (1939) ended with the scene in which all the disparate elements of the society portrayed in the film came together to celebrate the wisdom and insight of the protagonist, in the former, Gary Cooper, and in the latter film, Jimmy Stewart. Film historians have commented that Capra's films extolled the basic goodness of human nature and show the value of unselfishness and hard work.

Musical films entered their Golden Age. Faster film, improved sound, and deeper focus camera boxes improved the quality of musicals. Sound quality obviously helped determine movie quality, and new film stock helped accentuate the contrast of black and white, which was a staple of the grand sets in the famous Astaire-Rogers musicals. Faster film helped keep pace with swiftly moving stars, while the so-called deep focus cameras allowed great depth in scenes so dancers, for example, could effortlessly glide from center front to the far corners of the set and remain in focus.

Unlike earlier musicals, the Depression rarely appeared in the frothy escapist films of Fred Astaire and Ginger Rogers. Fred was resplendent in his signature tuxedo—top hat, white tie, and tails—while Ginger stunned in a variety of gowns. They traveled in exclusive circles, and money—or its lack thereof—rarely was an issue. Instead, moviegoers focused on the classic tale of boy meets girl, boy loves girl, boy chases girl, and after various fits and starts, boy gets girl, and fadeout, in which the songs helped advance the plot and the plot—such as it was—helped support the singing and dancing. Astaire and Rogers made nine films for RKO Pictures, and *Top Hat* (1935) was in many ways their signature movie. After a decade's hiatus, they made *The Barkleys of Broadway* (1949), which was the least successful. As *The Literary Digest* reported in 1936, "the 80,000,000 persons who weekly jam the motion picture theaters of the United States by this time are divided into two clearly defined groups: There are approximately 60,000,000 who can't keep away from a Ginger Rogers-Fred Astaire

Ginger Rogers and Fred Astaire in a scene from *Carefree*, 1938. (*Bettmann/Corbis*)

picture, only 20,000,000 who won't be drawn to see one." As the publication noted, "they arrive at a happy ending." Technically, Astaire insisted the camera shoot the entire dancer, and dance numbers flowed logically from the story and helped further it; meanwhile, the movies featured great music by such outstanding composers as George Gershwin and Jerome Kern (*Literary Digest* 1936, 17–18).

Success of the Astaire-Rogers films helped popularize movie musicals. Shirley Temple was but five years old in 1934 when Paramount released *Little Miss Marker.* In the film, her father committed suicide, and a gambler played by Adolph Menjou married his girlfriend, played by Dorothy Dell, to adopt Temple. She made some 20 films in the decade, all with tear-jerker stories, in which she sang and danced, and audiences could forget their troubles while admiring her precociousness. In 1938, 20th Century Fox released *Alexander's Ragtime Band,* where twenty-eight Irving Berlin tunes formed the basis of a movie about a band that started in San Francisco and eventually enjoyed great success capped by an appearance at Carnegie Hall in New York.

Interestingly, the swashbuckler, staple of the mid-1920s, returned, every bit as unrealistic but inspiring as its predecessor. Errol Flynn almost single-handedly defined the genre. Whether it was the *Captain Blood* (1935), *The Adventures of Robin Hood* (1938), or *The Sea Hawk* (1940), Flynn initially appeared as an everyman, wronged by the system, who fought back according to his own rules, triumphed over adversity, and won the hand of beautiful Olivia de Havilland. Adventure films showed heroes fighting impossible odds, defeating evil, winning the hand of the fair maiden, and eventually restoring goodness where there was chaos and problems.

The swashbuckler was always tall, handsome, virile, brave, and victorious—a great contrast to the gangster-villains of a few years earlier. In *Captain Blood,* Flynn played physician Peter Blood sentenced to deportation to the Caribbean and a life of a slave on a sugar plantation. He was but one of many, many desperate men condemned to that island, and he organized them, escaped, seized a ship, and preyed on English shipping to extract his revenge. After a brief alliance with a French brigand played with great panache by Basil Rathbone, a frequent Flynn foil, Blood returned to the fold, helped secure British control over the Caribbean, and in turn, was appointed by the King as governor of the island—a kind of Robin Hood story. In *The Adventures of Robin Hood,* Flynn played Sir Robin of Locksley, who ran afoul of evil Prince John and escaped to Sherwood Forest where he attracted other desperate men and women. They formed a community and financed their activities by robbing the rich and sharing it among the poor. While stopping and robbing Sir Guy of Gisbourne and the Sheriff of Nottingham, Robin spied the beautiful Maid Marian and, of course, fell instantly in love. He was willing to risk all to save her, and in the end he stabbed Gisbourne, rescued Marion, and helped restore "good" King Richard to the English throne after his return from the Crusades and imprisonment. In turn, with an honest, caring, and efficient government restored, King Richard exiled his brother, Prince John and restored Robin to his lands. Robin and Marian ran off, presumably to marry and start their own personal adventure.

Clark Gable helped define the genre in *Mutiny on the Bounty* (1935), based on the true story of a crew mutiny on the H.M.S. *Bounty* in the late eighteenth century. As the mutineers put ship captain Charles Laughton (Captain Bligh) and several loyal crewmen onto a small boat, Laughton yelled, "Well, you're *wrong,* Christian! I'll take this boat, as she floats, to England if I must. I'll live to see you—*all* of ya—hanging from the highest yard arm in the British fleet!" In *Anthony Adverse* (1936), actor Fredric March in the title role eventually learned that his father killed his mother's lover and gave him to a convent; along the way he battled adversity—hence the film's title—that in many ways made the travails of the Depression seem rather minor. Of course, in the end he triumphed.

Perhaps the greatest spectacular of the 1930s deserves its own special section. On December 15, 1939, after two years in the making, *Gone With the Wind* premiered in Atlanta, Georgia. Georgia Governor Eurith Rivers declared a state holiday and former President Jimmy Carter remembered it as "the biggest event to happen in the South in my lifetime." Based on Margaret Mitchell's novel, the movie told a story of the South framed by the tumultuous relationship of Scarlett O'Hara (actress Vivien Leigh) and Rhett Butler (Clark Gable). It moved from the eve of the Civil War and life in the South through the devastation at Tara and the burning of Atlanta, and ends with Scarlett promising that she would persist. It was prejudiced and racist, and certainly favored a white Southern view of slavery and the war. But its acting, directing, set design, script, and overpowering images

Movies diverted Americans from their economic woes. So involved were many that they wrote letters to fan magazines, giving the impression of a cult. Many things got people to write, although there two kinds of fan letters.

The first illustrated the movies' influence as trendsetters. Thus, an Ohio woman wrote that telephone companies reported a huge demand for French telephones as seen in the movies. A California fan became a nurse because *Arrowsmith* convinced her to help others. A Louisiana fan wrote that the movies taught women to know themselves, thus doing more for women's emancipation than anything else. A Seattle writer insisted that reading the book from which the movie was made first made the characters more authentic. A high school football player confessed *Touchdown* made him a better person by realizing he had to play for the team, not just himself. A Georgia schoolteacher declared the movies stimulated schoolchildren to imagine what they read. An Ohio beauty shop owner said having *Photoplay* for the customers helped them imagine new hairstyles and improved her business.

And some fans weighed in on their favorite or not so favorite stars. Here was the

made it, based on the number of paid admissions, the most popular American film in history. These adventure films created a world in chaos, similar to the United States during the Depression, and argued that one good and strong-minded man—and it had to be a man and not a woman—could restore order and happiness, perhaps like President Franklin Roosevelt and his New Deal.

Westerns returned in the mid-1930s. In explaining the appeal of the western, Thomas Schatz has written that "the Western depicts a world of precarious balance in which the forces of civilization and savagery are locked in a struggle for supremacy." Cecil B. DeMille, the great silent film director, shot *The Plainsman* (1937) and reminded Hollywood of the power of the myth of the West. Gary Cooper as Wild Bill Hickok and Jean Arthur as Calamity Jane battle a crooked arms dealer, the Native Americans who receive the guns, and each other. As they work out their sometimes-tortuous relationship, Custer and his men die at the Little Big Horn because of the guns the Indians received from Lattimer, the arms dealer. The utter lack of historical accuracy contrasted with the exercise in myth-making, and as the newspaper editor later said in *The Man Who Shot Liberty Valance* (1967), "this is the West, sir. When the legend becomes fact, print the legend." John Ford's classic, *Stagecoach* (1939) subjected the inhabitants of a stagecoach ride from Tonto to Lordsburg, Arizona, representing the disparate elements of society, to various pressures. They included a righteous sheriff, the stagecoach driver as comic relief, a prostitute with a heart of gold, an alcoholic doctor, a bank executive who just embezzled the bank's assets, a whiskey salesman, a gambler who is a refined killer, a cavalry commander's wife who is pregnant and searching for her husband, and the hero, John Wayne, as "the Ringo Kid," who is both an escaped criminal and a brother bent on avenging his brother's death. In the end, the Ringo Kid kills those who killed his brother and rode off with Dallas, the prostitute (Clare Trevor) second type of fan letter: praise, trash, or in other ways comment on the stars. Clark Gable was just becoming famous—and controversial—in early 1932. Thus, a Massachusetts matron reported she gotten an autographed studio picture of him back for her fan letter and surely would be "a Gable admirer long after feminine bosoms have ceased to heave whenever he comes into view". An Ohio fan, wrote, "Don't pluck your eyebrows, Clark Gable. Only sissies do that. You should remain the he-man you are." A New York moviegoer insisted that Robert Montgomery had infinitely more talent than Gable would ever have. Gable was hardly the only actor who drew comments. In just two issues, *Photoplay* printed letters praising or criticizing Greta Garbo, Joan Crawford, Eric von Stroheim, Leslie Howard, Joan Blondell, Norma Shearer, Wallace Beery, Frank Fay, and Gloria Swanson, to name but a few. That the movies could provide release and fantasy in troubling times was indeed the case, provoking diverse responses.

SOURCE: "What the Audience Thinks," *Photoplay* 41 (February, 1932) and (March, 1932).

to restart society, now freed of the shackles of its value judgments. Westerns told an epic tale of good and evil, where good eventually triumphed and values from the civilized East did not matter. The same year Errol Flynn and Olivia de Havilland starred in *Dodge City*. It contained all the elements of a classic western, save for an Indian attack. Flynn helped make a wild frontier town safe as a terminus of the cattle trails from Texas, rids the town of its bad elements, and of course wins the hand of de Havilland.

Walt Disney began a series of extremely popular full-length cartoon features with *Snow White and the Seven Dwarfs*. It premiered on December 21, 1937, and amazed audiences. Disney was politically conservative, and *Snow White* told a traditional tale of a young man, Prince Charming, having adventures, while a young woman, having to flee a wicked stepmother, lives with seven dwarfs, and falls into a deadly sleep after eating a poisoned apple only to be reawakened when the prince kisses her. *Snow White* stood as moral counterpoint to films of the roaring twenties in which men and women cavorted equally together.

Finally, there were the great biopics. In the early Depression years, Hollywood focused on the violent and those who lived at the margins of society. In the Roosevelt Depression years, Hollywood offered a series of movies about great individuals, including Abraham Lincoln, who each made a great difference in human existence. John Ford directed Henry Fonda as *Young Mr. Lincoln* (1939) and again Raymond Massey in *Abe Lincoln in Illinois* (1940). Paul Muni moved from *Scarface* to acting out *The Story of Louis Pasteur* (1936) and *The Life of Emile Zola* (1937). In the first, he told the story of the French scientist who found a cure for anthrax and for whom pasteurization is name; in the second, he acted out the life of the French writer who fought hypocrites who denounced his novel, *Nana*, and defended a French army officer Louis Dreyfus, who was a victim of anti-Semitism in French society.

Spencer Tracy won back-to-back Oscars (not equaled until Tom Hanks in 1993 and 1994) for *Captains Courageous* (1937) and *Boys Town* (1938). In the first, he played a wise Portuguese fisherman who saved a boy who fell off an ocean liner and amid great adventure on the high seas taught him, very much against his will, how to live a life. In the latter, he played Father Flanagan who started Boys Town west of Omaha, Nebraska, to create a place to save boys ruined by life in Depression America's cities. In all these movies, great men made a great difference. Lincoln saved the Union; Pasteur dramatically advanced our knowledge of germ theory; Zola fought for justice; the old fisherman passed on wisdom; Father Flanagan saved troubled boys. At dark times in the past, great men and occasionally great women helped save troubled societies.

Social Change and the Movies

What was the relationship between popular American film and the American people? Dick Cavett perhaps said it best in a documentary, *Hollywood: The Dream Factory* (1972). He noted that, whether Hollywood created American values, reflected such values, or ignored them, film left a rich legacy of images that drew Americans into movie theaters during the Great Depression.

This relationship hit its peak during World War II. While wartime spending ended the Great Depression, the vicissitudes of a worldwide war created a need for escape, and Hollywood provided it. Movie attendance peaked at 110 million weekly paid admissions in a nation of 140 million people (and with 12.8 million in the armed forces). Hollywood continued with the themes of the later 1930s to which it added war films, most of rather dubious quality and accuracy, and a new genre, presaging some of the doubts that the postwar era would bring—*film noir,* including such great movies as *The Maltese Falcon* (1944), *The Postman Always Rings Twice* (1946), *Double Indemnity* (1944), and *Force of Evil* (1948). In each case, action is reflected in shadows; the audience rarely sees all that is occurring, and a woman is usually more threatening to the hero than the more obvious villains, perhaps reflecting American life as veteran returned home and society tried to force women back into an updated cult of domesticity.

Thereafter, the breaking of the vertically integrated industry, and more important, the socioeconomic complex of suburbia, the baby boom, and the rise of television pushed movies to the edge of popular culture to be replaced by television and popular music. In 1947, the U.S. Supreme Court ruled that the system in which movie studios also owned movie theaters was illegal, and broke the cozy world. Separately, Olivia de Havilland won her suit over long-term contracts, and movie production companies cut back salaried actors, moved production offshore (frequently to Europe where the dollar went further), and reduced the number of movies produced each year. This blow to the movie production system likely mattered less than the key trend of the postwar era. The baby boom lasted from 1946 to 1964, and millions of American couples left cities to move to new, mass-produced homes in brand new suburbias, often moving in before construction of schools, stores, and other essential services. Leaving grandparents behind, parents of small children were less likely to go out, and movie attendance suffered. Television viewing increased dramatically, and many B-movie stars and character actors migrated to television production. Gross income from movies fell below $1 billion in 1947, a figure not reached again until *The Graduate* and *Herbie, the Love Bug* tapped both ends of the baby boom generation some twenty years later.

References

Boorstin, Daniel J. 1953. *The Genius of American Politics*. Chicago: University of Chicago Press.

Cooney, Terry. 1995. *Balancing Acts: American Thought and Culture in the 1930s*. New York: Twayne Publishers.

Quigley, Martin, and Richard Gertner, Jr. *Films in America, 1929–1969*. New York: Golden Press, 1970.

Literary Digest. 1936. "Sixty Million: Three Fourths of America's Film Fans Like Rogers-Astair Dancing Team." *Literary Digest*, September 12, 17–18.

Schatz, Thomas. 1981. *Hollywood Genres*. New York: Random House.

Sklar, Robert. *Movie-Made America: A Cultural History of American Movies*. New York: Random House, 1975.

Primary Documents

Documents of American Society in the Age of the Great Depression

These documents illuminate what sort of social, political, and economic regime ordinary Americans lived under during the Great Depression and what changes came about that affected their daily lives. The documents are all public, even government and political, in character. As such, they illustrate the point that whatever the New Deal was able to do, everything was open and an integral part of civic society. Members of all groups in society were influenced, to a greater or lesser extent, by these (and related) political acts. We may look back from today's perspective and say that American society was still racially segregated, that the free flow of immigration from around the world had been cut off in the previous decade, and that the status of women had barely changed in the past thirty years, save for the vote. On the other hand, the New Deal did establish the beginnings of the modern social entitlement state in the United States. Each one of these documents illustrates a government activity or program that potentially influenced many ordinary Americans, including many members of the groups highlighted in this book.

President Franklin D. Roosevelt's First Inaugural Address, March 4, 1933

It was a cold, blustery Saturday morning. Franklin D. Roosevelt had assembled all his cabinet designates to pray at St. John's Episcopal Church, located near the White House. The mood was somber, at 1 P.M., as roughly 100,000 persons gathered on the Capitol grounds, and another 400,000 throughout the city for the new president's inaugural address. And many millions more turned on their radios to listen in, and, indeed, it was the speech that was heard all over Europe and Latin America. The next day, Roosevelt was wheeled into his office, and found it empty of paper, pencils, or any other kind of equipment to start governing. He had to shout for assistance from the next room. And so the New Deal began, with neither a bang nor a whimper, but a bellow. Soon, however, there was a public reaction that was no less than a tidal wave. Almost half a million Americans wrote letters to their new chief executive about his address in the next several days. Many were thrilled, excited; some were apprehensive and anxious about the future. Never had there been such a deluge in the history of the presidency.

This is preeminently the time to speak the truth, the whole truth, frankly and boldly. . . . This great Nation will endure as it has endured, will revive and will prosper. So, first of all, let me assert my firm belief that the only thing we have to fear is fear itself—nameless, unreasoning, unjustified terror which paralyzes needed efforts to convert retreat into advance. . . .

our common difficulties. . . . concern, thank God, only material things. Values have shrunken to fantastic levels; taxes have risen; our ability to pay has fallen; government of all kinds is faced by serious curtailment of income; the means of exchange are frozen in the currents of trade; the withered leaves of industrial enterprise lie on every side; farmers find no markets for their produce; the savings of many years in thousands of families are gone.

More important, a host of unemployed citizens face the grim problem of existence, and an equally great number toil with little return. . . .

Yet our distress comes from no failure of substance,. . . Nature still offers her bounty and human efforts have multiplied it. Plenty is at our doorstep, but a generous use of it languishes in the very sight of the supply. Primarily this is because rulers of the exchange of mankind's goods have failed through their own stubbornness and their own incompetence, have admitted their failure, and have abdicated. Practices of the unscrupulous money changers stand indicted in the court of public opinion, rejected by the hearts and minds of men. . . . They have no vision, and when there is no vision the people perish.

Happiness lies not in the mere possession of money; it lies in the joy of achievement, in the thrill of creative effort. The joy and moral stimulation of work no longer must be forgotten in the mad chase of evanescent profits. These dark days will be worth all they cost us if they teach us that our true destiny is not to be ministered unto but to minister to ourselves and to our fellow men.

Restoration calls, however, not for changes in ethics alone. This Nation asks for action, and action now.

Our greatest primary task is to put people to work. This is no unsolvable problem if we face it wisely and courageously. It can be accomplished in part by direct recruiting by the Government itself, treating the task as we would treat the emergency of a war. . . .

We face the arduous days that lie before us in the warm courage of national unity; with the clear consciousness of seeking old and precious moral values; with the clean satisfaction that comes from the stem performance of duty by old and young alike. We aim at the assurance of a rounded and permanent national life.

In this dedication of a Nation we humbly ask the blessing of God. May He protect each and every one of us. May He guide me in the days to come.

Source: Samuel Irving Rosenman, The Public Papers and Addresses of Franklin D. Roosevelt. Volume 2. New York: Random House, 1938, pp. 11–16.

Federal Emergency Relief Act, May 12, 1933

In the three months between Roosevelt's inauguration and the adjournment of the 73rd Congress in mid-June, the president asked for, and got, fifteen major laws passed by Congress, designed to address the Depression's problems. The so-called Hundred Days program has been something of a benchmark for succeeding administrations. Space prohibits its publication here; the major laws took the country off the gold standard, vastly strengthened banking and securities regulation, addressed the problems of factory, store, and countryside, and provided relief for the unemployed. Below is one of the more successful and far-reaching laws, establishing (for two years) an agency that would distribute federal monies to states and localities for unemployment relief. The funds came from the Reconstruction Finance Corporation, initially.

To provide for cooperation by the Federal Government with the several States and Territories and the District of Columbia in relieving the hardship and suffering caused by unemployment, and for other purposes.

Be it enacted by the Senate and House of Representatives of the United States of America in Congress assembled, that the Congress hereby declares that the present economic depression has created a serious emergency, due to widespread unemployment and increasing inadequacy of State and local relief funds, resulting in the existing or threatened deprivation of a considerable number of families and individuals of the necessities of life, and making it imperative that the Federal Government cooperate more effectively with the several States and Territories and the District of Columbia in furnishing relief to their needy and distressed people.

Source: United States Statutes at Large, "Federal Emergency Relief Act," Volume 48, Part 1. 73rd Congress, pp. 55–58.

The Tennessee Valley Authority Act, May 18, 1933

Another of the pieces of legislation passed during the Hundred Days, the Tennessee Valley Authority (TVA) reflected the New Deal's penchant for regional planning and development. The idea was to provide for the multifaceted development of a structurally impoverished region—and an important constituency of the Democratic Party—to end that region's troubled economic structure permanently. Some idea of the audacity behind the TVA can be appreciated in the excerpt, below. It was no small irony that it took seven years for the TVA's governing board to resolve its differences and begin operations.

To improve the navigability and to provide for the flood control of the Tennessee River; to provide for reforestation and the proper use of marginal lands in the Tennessee Valley; to provide for the agricultural and industrial development of said valley; to provide for the national defense by the creation of a corporation for the operation of Government properties at and near Muscle Shoals in the State of Alabama, and for other purposes.

Be it enacted by the Senate and House of Representatives of the United States of America in Congress assembled, that for the purpose of maintaining and operating the properties now owned by the United States in the vicinity of Muscle Shoals, Alabama, in the interest of the national defense and for agricultural and industrial development, and to improve navigation in the Tennessee River and to control the destructive flood waters in the Tennessee River and Mississippi River Basins, there is hereby created a body corporate by the name of the "Tennessee Valley Authority" (hereinafter referred to as the "Corporation"). This Act may be cited as the "Tennessee Valley Authority Act of 1933."

SEC. 4. the Corporation

. . . (f) May purchase or lease and hold such real and personal property as it deems necessary or convenient in the transaction of its business and may dispose of any such personal property held by it. . . .

(h) Shall have power in the name of the United States of America to exercise the right of eminent domain,. . .

(i) Shall have power to acquire real estate for the construction of dams, reservoirs, transmission lines, power houses, and other structures, and navigation projects at any point along the Tennessee River, or any of its tributaries,. . .

(j) Shall have power to construct dams, reservoirs, power houses, power structures, transmission lines, navigation projects, and incidental works in the Tennessee River and its tributaries, and to unite the various power installations into one or more systems by transmission lines.

SEC. 5. The board is hereby authorized

(a) To contract with commercial producers for the production of such fertilizers or fertilizer materials as may be needed in the Government's program of development and introduction in excess of that produced by Government plants. . . .

(b) To arrange with farmers and farm organizations for large scale practical use of the new forms of fertilizers under conditions permitting an accurate measure of the economic return they produce.

(c) To cooperate with National, State, district, or county experimental stations or demonstration farms, for the use of new forms, of fertilizer or fertilizer, practices during the initial or experimental period of their introduction.

(d) The board in order to improve and cheapen the production of fertilizer is authorized to manufacture and sell fixed nitrogen, fertilizer, and fertilizer ingredients at Muscle Shoals by the employment of existing facilities, . . .

(h) To establish, maintain, and operate laboratories and experimental plants, and to undertake experiments . . . to furnish nitrogen products for military purposes, and nitrogen and other fertilizer products for agricultural purposes. . . .

(l) To produce, distribute, and sell electric power, as herein particularly specified. . . .

SEC. 10. The board is . . . to sell the surplus power . . . to States, counties, municipalities, corporations, partnerships, or individuals, . . . it shall give preference to States, counties, municipalities, and cooperative organizations of citizens or farmers, not organized or doing business for profit, but primarily for the purpose of supplying electricity to its own citizens or members: . . . to promote. . . the fullest possible use of electric light and power on farms within reasonable distance of any of its transmission lines the board shall . . . construct transmission lines to farms and small villages that are not otherwise supplied with electricity at reasonable rates, . . . the board is hereby authorized and directed to make studies, experiments, and determinations to promote the wider and better use of electric power for agricultural, and domestic use, or for small or local industries, and it may cooperate with State governments, or their subdivisions or agencies, with educational or research institutions, and with cooperatives or other organizations, in the application of electric power to the fuller and better balanced development of the resources of the region.

SEC. 11. . . . the policy . . . [is] to distribute and sell the surplus power generated at Muscle Shoals equitably among the States, counties, and municipalities within transmission distance. . . . the projects herein provided for shall be considered primarily as for the benefit of the people of the section as a whole and particularly the domestic and rural consumers to whom the power can economically be made available, and accordingly that sale to and use by industry shall be a secondary purpose, to be utilized principally to secure a sufficiently high load factor and revenue returns which will permit domestic and rural use at the lowest possible rates and in such manner as to encourage increased domestic and rural use of electricity. . . .

Source: United States Statutes at Large, "Tennessee Valley Authority Act." Volume 48, Part 1. 73rd Congress, pp. 58–72.

National Housing Act, June 27, 1934

This was the first important piece of New Deal legislation designed to solve the nation's housing problems. It had three functions. It was to make possible more housing construction, to elevate construction standards, and to provide, through the Federal Housing Authority (FHA), a reliable and affordable system of financing for residences by insuring mortgages issued by private lenders. It encouraged the upgrading of farm and small business properties and created a fund of three billion dollars to insure mortgages in its initial operations.

To encourage improvement in housing standards and conditions, to provide a system of mutual mortgage insurance, and for other purposes. . . .

TITLE I-HOUSING RENOVATION AND MODERNIZATION
CREATION OF FEDERAL HOUSING ADMINISTRATION

SECTION 1. The President is authorized to create a Federal Housing Administration, all of the powers of which shall be exercised by a Federal Housing Administrator (hereinafter referred to as the "Administrator"), who shall be appointed by the President, by and with the advice and consent of the Senate, shall hold office for a term of four years, and shall receive compensation at the rate of $10,000 per annum. In order to carry out the provisions of this title and titles II and III, the Administrator may establish such agencies, accept and utilize such voluntary and uncompensated services, utilize such Federal officers and employees, and, with the consent of the State, such State and local officers and employees, and appoint such other officers and employees as he may find necessary, and may prescribe their authorities, duties, responsibilities, and tenure and fix their compensation, without regard to the provisions of other laws applicable to the employment or compensation of officers or employees of the United States. The Administrator may delegate any of the functions and powers conferred upon him under this title and titles II and III to such officers, agents, and employees as he may designate or appoint, and may make such expenditures (including expenditures for personal services and rent at the seat of government and elsewhere, for law books and books of reference, and for paper, printing, and binding) as are necessary to carry out the provisions of this title and titles II and III, without regard to any other provisions of law governing the expenditure of public funds. All such compensation, expenses, and allowances shall be paid out of funds made available by this Act.

Source: United States Statutes at Large, "National Housing Act," Volume 48, Part 1. 73rd Congress, pp. 1246–1265.

Franklin Roosevelt's Annual Message to the Congress, January 4, 1935

In this address, Roosevelt announced his epochal program of reform, which has often been dubbed by historians the "Second New Deal," meaning that the Hundred Days legislation was the first New Deal, and focused on recovery, not reform. His three major goals were (1) security of livelihood through better use of national resources, (2) security against unemployment and old age, and (3) slum clearance and better housing. He also endorsed a national works program to absorb the unemployed as a part of his plan to secure against unemployment. All of these goals were met.

Mr. President, Mr. Speaker, Members of the Senate and of the House of Representatives:

We have undertaken a new order of things; yet we progress to it under the framework and in the spirit and intent of the American Constitution.

We have proceeded throughout the Nation a measurable distance on the road toward this new order. Materially, I can report to you substantial benefits to our agricultural population, increased industrial activity, and profits to our merchants. Of equal moment, there is evident a restoration of that spirit of confidence and faith which marks the American character. . . .

As the various parts in the program begun in the Extraordinary Session of the 73rd Congress shape themselves in practical administration, the unity of our program reveals itself to the Nation. The outlines of the new economic order, rising from the disintegration of the old, are apparent. We test what we have done as our measures take root in the living texture of life. We see where we have built wisely and where we can do still better. . . .

We find our population suffering from old inequalities, little changed by past sporadic remedies. In spite of our efforts and in spite of our talk, we have not weeded out the overprivileged and we have not effectively lifted up the underprivileged. Both of these manifestations of injustice have retarded happiness. No wise man has any intention of destroying what is known as the profit motive; because by the profit motive we mean the right by work to earn a decent livelihood for ourselves and for our families.

We have, however, a clear mandate from the people, that Americans must forswear that conception of the acquisition of wealth which, through excessive profits, creates undue private power over private affairs and, to our misfortune, over public affairs as well. In building toward this end we do not destroy ambition, nor do we seek to divide our wealth into equal shares on stated occasions. We continue to recognize the greater ability of some to earn more than others. But we do assert that the ambition of the individual to obtain for him and his a proper security, a reasonable leisure, and a decent living throughout life, is an ambition to be preferred to the appetite for great wealth and great power.

I recall to your attention my message to the Congress last June in which I said: "among our objectives I place the security of the men, women and children of the Nation first." That remains our first and continuing task; and in a very real sense every major legislative enactment of this Congress should be a component part of it.

In defining immediate factors which enter into our quest, I have spoken to the Congress and the people of three great divisions:

1. The security of a livelihood through the better use of the national resources of the land in which we live.
2. The security against the major hazards and vicissitudes of life.
3. The security of decent homes.

I am now ready to submit to the Congress a broad program designed ultimately to establish all three of these factors of security—a program which because of many lost years will take many future years to fulfill. . . .

Source: Samuel Irving Rosenman, The Public Papers and Addresses of Franklin D. Roosevelt. Volume 4. New York: Random House, 1942, pp. 15–25.

Emergency Relief Appropriations Act, April 8, 1935

With this joint resolution, Congress left direct relief to the states, thus creating a federal program that would funnel federal monies to the states. Roosevelt and his aides, especially Harry L. Hopkins, who came to run the Works Progress Administration (WPA), the program's key agency, were especially concerned that the unemployed would lose morale if they lost their sense of individual autonomy and pride. About 85 percent of WPA funds went directly into wages and salaries; by 1943, when the WPA was terminated, it had employed at least 8.5 million persons on 1.4 million projects at a cost of about 11 billion dollars.

Resolved by the Senate and House of Representatives of the United States of America in Congress assembled, that in order to provide relief, work relief and to increase employment by providing for useful projects, there is hereby appropriated, out of any money in the Treasury not otherwise appropriated, to be used in the discretion and under the direction of the President, to be immediately available and to remain available until June 30, 1937; the sum of $4,000,000,000 . . . shall be available for the following classes of projects, and the amounts to be used for each class shall not, except as hereinafter provided, exceed the respective amounts stated, namely: (a) Highways, roads, streets, and grade-crossing elimination, $800,000,000 (b) rural rehabilitation and relief in stricken agricultural areas, and water conservation, transmountain water diversion and irrigation and reclamation, $500,000,000; (c) rural electrification, $100,000,000; (d) housing, $450,000,000; (a) assistance for educational, professional and clerical persons, $300,000,000; (f) Civilian Conservation Corps, $600,000,000; (g) loans or grants, or both, for projects of States, Territories, Possessions, including subdivisions and agencies thereof, municipalities and the District of Columbia, and self-liquidating projects of public bodies thereof, where, in the determination of the President, not less than twenty-five per centum of the loan or the grant, or the aggregate thereof, is to be expended for work under each particular project, $900,000,000; (h) sanitation, prevention of soil erosion, prevention of stream pollution, sea coast erosion, reforestation, forestation, flood control, rivers and harbors and miscellaneous projects, $350,000,000. . . .

Source: United States Statutes at Large, "Emergency Relief Appropriations Act of 1935." Volume 49, Part 1, Section 1. 74th Congress. pp. 115–119.

The First ''Fireside Chat'' of 1935. ''Fear Is Vanishing, Confidence Is Growing, Faith Is Being Renewed in the Democratic Form of Government,'' April 28, 1935

Roosevelt was the "radio President' par excellence; neither of his immediate predecessors, Calvin Coolidge nor Herbert Hoover proved nearly as effective and successful as he. In his first two terms, Roosevelt broadcast no less than sixteen "fireside chats," and these triggered literally millions of letters, almost all positive, in response. As is clear from this example, Roosevelt established himself as "I," and his audience as "you," thus creating an intimacy that was instrumental to his political objectives—and reduced the need for personal appearances, which, given his disability, were always awkward and difficult to manage. This chat was distinctive for its explanation of the New Deal's expansive political theories. The chat was, of course, an outline of his "Second New Deal" as announced in Franklin Roosevelt's Annual Message to the Congress, January 4, 1935. It is important to understand that these programs, especially Social Security, left out minorities and made aid to dependent children a parsimonious, skinflint program for years to come.

In the many weeks since my Annual Message to the Congress . . . [it] has devoted itself to the arduous task of . . . making distinct progress [in] formulating legislation necessary to the country's welfare.

Before I come to any of the specific measures, however, I want to leave in your minds one clear fact. The Administration and the Congress are not proceeding in any haphazard fashion in this task of government. Each of our steps has a definite relationship to every other step. The job of creating a program for the Nation's welfare is, in some respects, like the building of a ship. At different points on the coast where I often visit they build great seagoing ships. When one of these ships is under construction and the steel frames have been set in the keel, it is difficult for a person who does not know ships to tell how it will finally look when it is sailing the high seas.

It may seem confused to some, but out of the multitude of detailed parts that go into the making of the structure, the creation of a useful instrument for man ultimately comes. It is that way with the making of a national policy. The objective of the Nation has greatly changed in three years. Before that time individual self-interest and group selfishness were paramount in public thinking. The general good was at a discount.

Three years of hard thinking have changed the picture. More and more people, because of clearer thinking and a better understanding, are considering the whole rather than a mere part relating to one section, or to one crop, or to one industry, or to an individual private occupation. That is a tremendous gain for the principles of democracy. The overwhelming majority of people in this country know how to silt the wheat from the chaff in what they hear and what they read. They know that the process of the constructive rebuilding of America cannot be done in a day or a year, but that it is being done in spite of the few who seek to confuse them and to profit by their confusion. Americans as a whole are feeling a lot better—a lot more cheerful than for many, many years.

My most immediate concern is in carrying out the purposes of the great work program just enacted by the Congress. Its first objective is to put men and women now on the relief rolls to work and, incidentally, to assist materially in our already unmistakable march toward recovery. . . . many millions more people have private work today than two years ago today or one year ago today and every day that passes offers more chances to work for those who want to work. . . . we have come to recognize the possibility and the necessity of certain helpful remedial measures. . . . The first is to make provisions intended to relieve, to minimize, and to prevent future unemployment; the second is to establish the practical means to help those who are unemployed in this present emergency. Our social security legislation is an attempt to answer the first of these questions; our Works Relief program, the second.

The program for social security now pending before the Congress is a necessary part of the future unemployment policy of the Government. . . . We must begin now to make provision for the future. . . . our social security program proposes. . . . by means of old-age pensions, to help those who have reached the age of retirement to give up their jobs and thus give to the younger generation greater opportunities for work and to give to all a feeling of security as they look toward old age.

The unemployment insurance part of the legislation will not only help to guard the individual in future periods of lay-off against dependence upon relief, but it will, by sustaining purchasing power, cushion the shock of economic distress. Another helpful feature of unemployment insurance is the incentive it will give to employers to plan more carefully in order that unemployment may he prevented by the stabilizing of employment itself.

Provisions for social security, however, are protections for the future. Our responsibility for the immediate necessities of the unemployed has been met by the Congress through the most comprehensive work plan in the history of the Nation. Our problem is to put to work three and one-half million employable persons now on the relief rolls. It is a problem quite as much for private industry as for the Government.

. . . For many months preparations have been under way. The allotment of funds for desirable projects has already begun. The key men for the major responsibilities of this great task already have been selected. . . .

Our responsibility is to all of the people in this country. This is a great national crusade to destroy enforced idleness which is an enemy of the human spirit generated by this depression. Our attack upon these enemies must be without stint and without discrimination. No sectional, no political distinctions can be permitted. . . .

It is time to provide a smashing answer for those cynical men who say that a Democracy cannot be honest and efficient. If you will help, this can be done. I, therefore, hope you will watch the work in every corner of this Nation. Feel free to criticize. Tell me of instances where work can be done better, or where improper practices prevail. Neither you nor I want criticism conceived in a purely fault-finding or partisan spirit, but I am jealous of the right of every citizen to call to the attention of his or her Government examples of how the public money can be more effectively spent for the benefit of the American people.

Never since my Inauguration in March, 1933, have I felt so unmistakably the atmosphere of recovery. But it is more than the recovery of the material basis of our individual lives. It is the recovery of confidence in our democratic processes and institutions. We have survived all of the arduous burdens and the threatening dangers of a great economic calamity.

We have in the darkest moments of our national trials retained our faith in our own ability to master our destiny. Fear is vanishing and confidence is growing on every side, faith is being renewed in the vast possibilities of human beings to improve their material and spiritual status through the instrumentality of the democratic form of government. That faith is receiving its just reward. For that we can be thankful to the God who watches over America.

Source: Samuel Irving Rosenman, The Public Papers and Addresses of Franklin D. Roosevelt. Volume 4. New York: Random House, 1942, pp. 132–140.

National Labor Relations Act, July 5, 1935

The National Labor Relations Act gave workers the right to organize and bargain collectively under the constitutional authority of the commerce clause. This was one of the most important pieces of legislation of the "Second New Deal" inasmuch as it led to the development of strong craft and industrial unions over the next several years. It has been rightly called "Labor's Magna Charta," meaning its conferral of basic rights. The National Labor Relations Board became a federal agency dedicated to the collective rights of working men and women. The organization of the mass industries—the auto and steel industries, for example—did not come without strikes and violence, but come it did. By 1945, with the end of World War II, business and labor had come to recognize each other's rights and to pass on higher labor costs to consumers. In 1937, the U.S. Supreme Court surprisingly upheld the law, 5–4, in *NLRB v. Jones & Laughlin* (301 U.S. 1).

FINDINGS AND POLICY

SECTION 1. The denial by employers of the right of employees to organize and the refusal by employers to accept the procedure of collective bargaining lead to strikes and other forms of industrial strife or unrest, which, have the intent or the necessary effect of burdening or obstructing commerce by (a) impairing the efficiency, safety, or operation of the instrumentalities of commerce; (b) occurring in the current of commerce; (c) materially affecting, restraining, or controlling the flow of raw materials or manufactured or processed goods from or into the channels of commerce, or the prices of such materials or goods in commerce; or (d) causing diminution of employment and wages in such volume as substantially to impair or disrupt the market for goods flowing from or into the channels of commerce.

The inequality of bargaining power between employees who do not possess full freedom of association or actual liberty of contract and employers who are organized in the corporate or other forms ownership association substantially burdens and affects the flow of commerce, and tends to aggravate recurrent business depressions, by depressing wage rates and the purchasing power of wage earners in industry and by preventing the stabilization of competitive wage rates and working conditions within and between industries.

Experience has proved that protection by law of the right of employees to organize and bargain collectively safeguards commerce, from injury, impairment, or interruption, and promotes the flow of commerce by removing certain recognized sources of industrial strife and unrest, by encouraging practices fundamental to the friendly adjustment of industrial disputes arising out of differences as to wages, hours, or other working conditions, and by restoring equality of bargaining power between employers and employees. It is hereby declared to be the policy of the United States to eliminate the causes of certain substantial obstructions to the free flow of commerce and to mitigate and eliminate these obstructions when they have occurred by encouraging the practice and procedure of collective bargaining and by protecting the exercise by workers of full freedom of association, self-organization, and designation of representatives of their own choosing, for the purpose of negotiating the terms and conditions of their employment or other mutual aid or protection. . . .

SECTION 7. Employees shall have the right to self-organization, to form, join, or assist labor organizations, to bargain collectively through representatives of their own choosing, and to engage in concerted activities, for the purpose of collective bargaining or other mutual aid or protection.

SECTION 8. It shall be an unfair labor practice for an employer

(1) To interfere with, restrain, or coerce employees in the exercise of the rights guaranteed in section 7. . . .

SECTION 16. This Act may be cited as the "National Labor Relations Act."

Source: United States Statutes at Large, "National Labor Relations Act." Volume 49, Part 1, Section 1. 74th Congress, pp.449–457.

Social Security Act, August 14, 1935

A landmark piece of the "Second New Deal," this law created the Social Security Board and Administration that in turn established a cooperative federal-state social entitlement system, with fairly uniform provisions and benefits for unemployment compensation, old-age assistance, and other welfare purposes, including aid to the blind and to dependent children. The law also created financing provisions by installing taxes on employers and workers. It remains today as the framework for the nation's entitlement system, much expanded and far more generous in its benefits.

To provide for the general welfare by establishing a system of Federal old-age benefits, and by enabling the several States to make more adequate provision for aged persons, blind persons, dependent and crippled children, maternal and child welfare, public health, and the administration of their unemployment compensation laws; to establish a Social Security Board; to raise revenue, and for other purposes.

Be it enacted by the Senate and House of Representatives of the United States of America in Congress assembled,

TITLE I. GRANTS TO STATES FOR OLD-AGE ASSISTANCE
APPROPRIATION

SECTION 1. For the purpose of enabling each State to furnish financial assistance, as far as practicable under the conditions in such State, to aged needy individuals, there is hereby authorized to be appropriated for the fiscal year ending June 30, 1936, the sum of $49,750,000, and there is hereby authorized to be appropriated for each fiscal year thereafter a sum sufficient to carry out the purposes of this title. . . .

TITLE III. GRANTS TO STATES FOR UNEMPLOYMENT
COMPENSATION ADMINISTRATION
APPROPRIATION

SECTION 301. For the purpose of assisting the States in the administration of their unemployment compensation laws, there is hereby authorized to be appropriated, for the fiscal year ending June 30, 1936, the sum of $4,000,000, and for each fiscal year thereafter the sum of $49,000,000, to be used as hereinafter provided.

TITLE IV. GRANTS TO STATES FOR AID TO DEPENDENT CHILDREN
APPROPRIATION

SECTION 401. For the purpose of enabling each State to furnish financial assistance, as far as practicable under the conditions in such State, to needy dependent children, there is hereby authorized to be appropriated for the fiscal year ending June 30, 1936, the sum of $24,750,000, and there is hereby authorized to be appropriated for each fiscal year thereafter a sum sufficient to carry out the purposes of this title. . . .

TITLE V. GRANTS TO STATES FOR MATERNAL
AND CHILD WELFARE
PART 1. MATERNAL AND CHILD HEALTH SERVICES
APPROPRIATION

SECTION 501. For the purpose of enabling each State to extend and improve, as far as practicable under the conditions in such State, services for promoting the health of mothers and children, especially in rural areas and in areas suffering from severe economic distress, there is hereby authorized to be appropriated for each fiscal year beginning with the fiscal year ending June 30, 1936, the sum of $3,800,000. . . .

PART 2. SERVICES FOR CRIPPLED CHILDREN
APPROPRIATION

SECTION 511. For the purpose of enabling each State to extend and improve (especially in rural areas and in areas suffering from severe economic distress), as far as practicable under the conditions in such State, services for locating crippled children, and for providing medical, surgical, corrective, and other services and care, and facilities for diagnosis, hospitalization, and aftercare, for children who are crippled or who are suffering from conditions which lead to crippling, there is hereby authorized to be appropriated for each fiscal year, beginning with the fiscal year ending June 30, 1936, the sum of $2,850,000. . . .

PART 3. CHILD-WELFARE SERVICES

SECTION 521. (a) For the purpose of enabling the United States, through the Children's Bureau, to cooperate with State public welfare agencies in establishing, extending, and strengthening, especially in predominantly rural areas, public-welfare services (hereinafter in this section referred to as "child-welfare services") for the protection and care of homeless, dependent, and neglected children, and children in danger of becoming delinquent, there is hereby authorized to be appropriated for each fiscal year, beginning with the fiscal year ending June 30, 1936, the sum of $1,500,000. Such amount shall be allotted by the Secretary of Labor for use by cooperating State public-welfare agencies on the basis of plans developed jointly by the State agency and the Children's Bureau, to each State, $10,000, and the remainder to each State on the basis of such plans, not to exceed such part of the remainder as the rural population of such State bears to the total rural population of the United States. . . .

PART 4. VOCATIONAL REHABILITATION

SECTION 531. (a) In order to enable the United States to cooperate with the States and Hawaii in extending and strengthening their programs of vocational rehabilitation of the physically disabled, and to continue to carry out the provisions and purposes of the Act entitled "An Act to provide for the promotion of vocational rehabilitation of persons disabled in industry or otherwise and their return to civil employment" approved June 2, 1920, as amended (U.S.C., title 29, ch. 4; U.S.C., Supp. VII, title 29, secs. 31, 32, 34, 35, 37, 39 and 40), there is hereby authorized to be appropriated for the fiscal, years ending June 30, 1936, and June 30, 1937, the sum of $841,000 for each such fiscal year in addition to the amount of the existing authorization, and for each fiscal year thereafter the sum of $1,938,000. . . .

TITLE VI. PUBLIC HEALTH WORK
APPROPRIATION

SECTION 601. For the purpose of assisting States, counties, health districts, and other political subdivisions of the States in establishing and maintaining adequate public-health services, including the training of personnel for State and local health work, there is hereby authorized to be appropriated for each fiscal year, beginning with the fiscal year ending June 30, 1936, the sum of $8,000,000 to be used as hereinafter provided. . . .

TITLE X. GRANTS, TO STATES FOR AID TO THE BLIND
APPROPRIATION

SECTION 1001. For the purpose of enabling each State to furnish financial assistance, as far as practicable under the conditions in such State, to needy individuals who are blind, there is hereby authorized to be appropriated for the fiscal year ending June 30, 1936, the sum of $3,000,000, and there is hereby authorized to be appropriated for each fiscal year thereafter a sum sufficient to carry out the purposes of this title. . . .

Source: United States Statutes at Large, "Social Security Act." Volume 49, Part 1, Section 1. 74th Congress. pp. 620–648.

The Second Inaugural Address. ''I See One-Third of a Nation Ill-Housed, Ill-Clad, Ill-Nourished,'' January 20, 1937

Here again is Franklin Roosevelt, that master political leader, with his second inaugural address, a considerably more chipper, indeed optimistic speech than his first inaugural; he was obviously delighted over his landslide reelection to the presidency and the progress, thus far, of his legislative program to solve the Great Depression's serious problems. His main point was that as far as the nation had come in recovery and reform, there was still a long road ahead to travel.

When four years ago we met to inaugurate a President, the Republic, single-minded in anxiety, stood in spirit here. We dedicated ourselves to the fulfillment of a vision—to speed the time when there would be for all the people that security and peace essential to the pursuit of happiness. We of the Republic pledged ourselves to drive from the temple of our ancient faith those who had profaned it; to end by action, tireless and unafraid, the stagnation and despair of that day. We did those first things first.

Our covenant with ourselves did not stop there. Instinctively we recognized a deeper need—the need to find through government the instrument of our united purpose to solve for the individual the ever-rising problems of a complex civilization. Repeated attempts at their solution without the aid of government had left us baffled and bewildered. For, without that aid, we had been unable to create those moral controls over the services of science which are necessary to make science a useful servant instead of a ruthless master of mankind. To do this we knew that we must find practical controls over blind economic forces and blindly selfish men. We of the Republic sensed the truth that democratic government has innate capacity to protect its people against disasters once considered inevitable, to solve problems once considered unsolvable. We would not admit that we could not find a way to master economic epidemics just as, after centuries of fatalistic suffering, we had found a way to master epidemics of disease. We refused to leave the problems of our common welfare to be solved by the winds of chance and the hurricanes of disaster. . . .

Four years of new experience hold out the clear hope that government within communities, government within the separate States, and government of the United States can do the things the times require, without yielding its democracy. Our tasks in the last four years did not force democracy to take a holiday. . . .

In fact, in these last four years, we have made the exercise of all power more democratic; for we have begun to bring private autocratic powers into their proper subordination to the public's government. The legend that they were invincible—above and beyond the processes of a democracy—has been shattered. They have been challenged and beaten. . . .

Old truths have been relearned; untruths have been unlearned. We have always known that heedless self-interest was bad morals; we know now that it is bad economics. Out of the collapse of a prosperity whose builders boasted their practicality has come the conviction that in the long run economic morality pays. We are beginning to wipe out the line that divides the practical from the ideal; and in so doing we are fashioning an instrument of unimagined power for the establishment of a morally better world. . . .

I see a great nation, upon a great continent, blessed with a great wealth of natural resources. Its hundred and thirty million people are at peace among themselves; they are making their country a good neighbor among the nations. I see a United States which can demonstrate that, under democratic methods of government, national wealth can be translated into a spreading volume of human comforts hitherto unknown, and the lowest standard of living can be raised far above the level of mere subsistence.

But here is the challenge to our democracy: In this nation I see tens of millions of its citizens—a substantial past of its whole population—who at this very moment are denied the greater part of what the very lowest standards of today call the necessities of life.

I see millions of families trying to live on incomes so meager that the pall of family disaster hangs over them day by day.

I see millions whose daily lives in city and on farm continue under conditions labeled indecent by a so-called polite society half a century ago.

I see millions denied education, recreation, and the opportunity to better their lot and the lot of their children.

I see millions lacking the means to buy the products of farm and factory and by their poverty denying work and productiveness to many other millions.

I see one-third of a nation ill-housed, ill-clad, ill-nourished.

It is not in despair that I paint you that picture. I paint it for you in hope—because the Nation, seeing and understanding the injustice in it, proposes to paint it out. We are determined to make every American citizen the subject of his country's interest and concern; and we will never regard any faithful, law-abiding group within our borders as superfluous. The test of our progress is not whether we add more to the abundance of those who have much; it is whether we provide enough for those who have too little. . . .

Source: Samuel Irving Rosenman, The Public Papers and Addresses of Franklin D. Roosevelt. Volume 6. New York: Random House, 1944, pp. 1–6.

United States Housing Act, September 1, 1937

This law—another integral part of the "Second New Deal"—was intended to provide assistance to upgrade housing conditions (slums were the operational concept) for low-income groups. It created the U.S. Housing Authority (USHA), in the Department of the Interior, to extend low-cost, long-term loans to local housing authorities to construct new residential construction for low-income citizens. By the beginning of 1941, the USHA had completed loan contracts for 511 low-rent public housing projects, with a total of 161,162 dwelling units at an estimated cost of $767.5 million. During World War II, the USHA contributed to defense housing, and after the war, it facilitated "urban renewal" and slum clearance in many American cities.

To provide financial assistance to the States and political subdivisions thereof for the elimination of unsafe and insanitary housing conditions, for the eradication of slums, for the provision of decent, safe, and sanitary dwellings for families of low income, and for the reduction of unemployment and the stimulation of business activity, to create a United States Housing Authority, and for other purposes. . . .

DECLARATION OF POLICY

SECTION 1. It is hereby declared to be the policy of the United States to promote the general welfare of the Nation by employing its funds and credit, as provided in this Act, to assist the several States and their political subdivisions to alleviate present and recurring unemployment and to remedy the unsafe and insanitary housing conditions and the acute shortage of decent, safe, and sanitary dwellings for families of low income, in rural or urban communities, that are injurious to the health, safety, and morals of the citizens of the Nation.

DEFINITIONS

SECTION 2. When used in this Act

(1) The term "low-rent housing" means decent, safe, and sanitary dwellings within the financial reach of families of low income, and developed and administered to promote serviceability, efficiency, economy, arid stability, and embraces all necessary appurtenances thereto. The dwellings in low-rent housing as defined in this Act shall be available solely for families whose net income at the time of admission does not exceed five times the rental (including the value or cost to them of heat, light, water, and cooking fuel) of the dwellings to be furnished such families, except that in the case of families with three or more minor dependents, such ratio shall not exceed six to one.

(2) The term "families of low income" means families who are in the lowest income group and who cannot afford to pay enough to cause private enterprise in their locality or metropolitan area to build an adequate supply of decent, safe, and sanitary dwellings for their use.

(3) The term "slum" means any area where dwellings predominate which, by reason of dilapidation, overcrowding, faulty arrangement or design, lack of ventilation, light or sanitation facilities, or any combination of these factors, are detrimental to safety, health, or morals.

(4) The term "slum clearance" means the demolition and removal of buildings from any slum area.

(5) The term "development" means any or all undertakings necessary for planning, financing (including payment of carrying charged), land acquisition, demolition, construction, or equipment, in connection with a low-rent-housing or slum-clearance project, but not beyond the point of physical completion. Construction activity in connection with a low-rent-housing project may be confined to the reconstruction, remodeling, or repair of existing buildings. . . .

Source: United States Statutes at Large, "United States Housing Act," 79th Congress, Volume 50, pp. 888–899.

Fair Labor Standards Act, June 25, 1938

This legislation, again a part of the "Second New Deal," at least in spirit, established for the first time minimum national standards for wages and hours for workers engaged in interstate commerce, but with many exclusions (including farm workers, domestic servants, and professionals). The U.S. Supreme Court upheld its constitutionality in *U.S. v. Darby Lumber Co.* (312 U.S. 100). By the end of World War II, hundreds of thousands of workers were protected by this legislation at some minimal standard.

FINDING AND DECLARATION OF POLICY

SECTION 2. (a) The Congress hereby finds that the existence, in industries engaged in commerce or in the production of goods for commerce, of labor conditions detrimental to the maintenance of the minimum standard of living necessary for health, efficiency, and general well-being of workers (1) causes commerce and the channels and instrumentalities of commerce to be used to spread and perpetuate such labor conditions among the workers of the several States; (2) burdens commerce and the free flow of commerce; (3) constitutes an unfair method of competition in commerce (4) leads to labor disputes burdening and obstructing commerce and the free flow of goods in commerce; and (5) interferes with the orderly and fair marketing of goods in commerce.

(b) It is hereby declared to be the policy of this Act, through the exercise by Congress of its power to regulate commerce among the several States, to correct and as rapidly as practicable to eliminate the conditions above referred to in such industries without substantially curtailing employment or earning power. . . .

MINIMUM WAGES

SECTION 6. (a) Every employer shall pay to each of his employees who is engaged in commerce or in the production of goods for commerce wages at the following rates—

(1) during the first year from the effective date of this section, not less than 25 cents an hour,

(2) during the next six years from such date, not less than 30 cents an hour

(3) after the expiration of seven years from such date, not less than 40 cents an hour, or the rate (not less than 30 cents an hour) prescribed in the applicable order of the Administrator issued under section 8, whichever is lower, and

(4) at any time after the effective date of this section, not less than the rate (not in excess of 40 cents an hour) prescribed in the applicable order of the Administrator issued under section 8.

(b) This section shall take effect upon the expiration of one hundred and twenty days from the date of enactment of this Act.

MAXIMUM HOURS

SECTION 7. (a) No employer shall, except as otherwise provided in this section, employ any of his employees who is engaged in commerce or in the production of goods for commerce

(1) for a workweek longer than forty-four hours during the first year from the effective date of this section

(2) for a workweek longer than forty-two hours during the second year from such date, or

(3) for a workweek longer than forty hours after the expiration of the second year from such date, unless such employee receives compensation for his employment in excess of the hours above specified at a rate not less than one and one-half times the regular rate at which he is employed.

(b) No employer shall be deemed to have violated subsection (a) by employing any employee for a workweek in excess of that specified in such subsection without paying the compensation for overtime employment prescribed therein if such employee is so employed. . . .

CHILD LABOR PROVISIONS

SECTION 12. (a) After the expiration of one hundred and twenty days from the date of enactment of this Act, no producer, manufacturer, or dealer shall ship or deliver for shipment in commerce any goods produced in an establishment situated in the United States m or about which within thirty days prior to the removal of such goods therefrom any oppressive child labor has been employed. . . .

(b) The Chief of the Children's Bureau in the Department of Labor, or any of his authorized representatives, shall make all investigations and inspections under section 11 (a) with respect to the employment of minors, and subject to the direction and control of the Attorney General, shall bring all actions under section 17 to enjoin any act or practice which is unlawful by reason of the existence of oppressive child labor, and shall administer all other provisions of this Act relating to oppressive child labor.

Source: United States Statutes at Large, "Fair Labor Standards Act," Volume 52. 75th Congress, pp. 1060–1069.

Executive Order No. 8802, June 25, 1941

By early 1941, the wartime economic recovery was proceeding apace. A. Philip Randolph, president of the Brotherhood of Sleeping Car Porters and a leading African American trade union leader, organized a protest march on Washington, D.C., to force the Roosevelt administration to provide for fair employment for African Americans in companies that had contracts with the federal government. Roosevelt was strongly opposed to the threat of perhaps fifty or one hundred thousand demonstrators in the nation's Capitol, and feared of alienating southern Democratic leaders and voters. On the day before the march was to begin, Roosevelt signed the epochal Executive Order No. 8802, which forbade racial discrimination in employment by companies with federal contracts and created a Fair Employment Practices Committee (FEPC) to investigate reported cases of employment discrimination.

Although it could be argued that Roosevelt's order accomplished less than met the eye, the episode marked a turning point in that African Americans found that demonstrations, or the threat thereof, were an effective tool to advance their civil rights, more so, perhaps than the lawsuits which the National Association for the Advancement of Colored People had fancied. That makes this document a fitting conclusion to this section, for it suggested that, in the future, politics and reform would be even more determined by ordinary citizens than by the professional elite, which thus far had been the case through the twentieth century.

Whereas it is the policy of the United States to encourage full participation in the national defense program by all citizens of the United States, regardless of race, creed, color, or national origin, in the firm belief that the democratic way of life within the Nation can be defended successfully only with the help and support of all groups within its borders; and whereas there is evidence that available and needed workers have been barred from employment in industries engaged in defense production solely because of consideration of race, aced, color, or national origin, to the detriment of workers' morale and of national unity:

Now, therefore, by virtue of the authority vested in me by the Constitution and the statutes, and as a prerequisite to the successful conduct of our national defense production effort, I do hereby reaffirm the policy of the United States that there shall be no discrimination in the employment of workers in defense industries or government because of race, creed, color, or national origin, and I do hereby declare that it is the duty of employers and of labor organizations, in furtherance of said policy and of this Order, to provide for the full and equitable participation of all workers in defense industries, without discrimination because of race, creed, color, or national origin;

And it is hereby ordered as follows:

s. All departments and agencies of the Government of the United States concerned with vocational and training programs for defense production shall take special measures appropriate to assure that such programs are administered without discrimination because of race, creed, color, or national origin;

a. All contracting agencies of the Government of the United States shall include in all defense contracts hereafter negotiated by them a provision obligating the contractor not to discriminate against any worker because of race, creed, color, or national origin;

b. There is established in the Office of Production Management a Committee on Fair Employment Practice, which shall consist of a Chairman and four other members to be appointed by the President The Chairman and members of the Committee shall serve as such without compensation but shall be entitled to actual and necessary transportation, subsistence, and other expenses incidental to performance of their duties. The Committee shall receive and investigate complaints of discrimination in violation of the provisions of this Order and shall take appropriate steps to redress grievances which it finds to be valid. The Committee shall also recommend to the several departments and agencies of the Government of the United States and to the President all measures which may be deemed by it necessary or proper to effectuate the provisions of this Order.

Source: Samuel Irving Rosenman, The Public Papers and Addresses of Franklin D. Roosevelt. Volume 10. New York: Random House, 1943, pp. 233–237.

Reference

Agape A word from the Greek meaning *union* came to stand for creating community among especially liberals in the Depression.

Agricultural Adjustment Act (May 12, 1933) Sought to restore the ability of agricultural producers to participate in the economy by cutting back on the supply of commodities, thus hoping to raise prices, and the development of parity prices for designated farm commodities, to support agricultural production. The parity price levels were the high point of agricultural prices in the period 1909–1914. This was in effect a subsidy program. The law established the Agricultural Adjustment Administration to run the program within the Department of Agriculture. It was ruled unconstitutional by the U.S. Supreme Court in ***U.S. v. Butler* (1935)**.

Agricultural Adjustment Act of 1938 (February 16, 1938) An administration-sponsored scheme to replace the ineffectual **Soil Conservation and Domestic Allotment Act of 1936** with a constitutionally sanctioned version of the 1933 **Agricultural Adjustment Administration (AAA),** which enabled the Secretary of Agriculture to set marketing quotas, work with farmers via referenda for such quotas, and established parity prices for crops. The measure also created the **Federal Crop Insurance Corporation (FCIC)** with an initial capitalization of $100 millions to insure wheat crops initially against losses from unavoidable disasters, such as floods, drought, hail, and so on.

Andy Hardy film series Starring child actor Mickey Rooney, portrayed normal, happy, fun-loving adolescents from stable middle-class families in small town America, in such films as ***A Family Affair* (1937)** and ***Love Finds Andy Hardy* (1938)**.

"Aunt Jemima" Both a brand name and a series of real African American women playing the role of promoter of ready mix pancake mixes. This tradition stretched back to the 1830s, when a slave woman first donned the Aunt Jemima costume to promote the processed food. In 1926 the Quaker Oats Company bought the Aunt Jemima Mills Company, and in 1933 the company's public relations people brought the Aunt Jemima persona back for the Chicago World's Fair. They hired an African American woman, Anna Robinson, described as a large, friendly person with a sweet face, and she traveled the country promoting the Aunt Jemima line until she died after World War II. Aunt Jemima was a cultural icon of slightly less significance than Betty Crocker.

Beer-Wine Revenue Act (March 22, 1933) Legalized the sale of wine, beer, lager beer, and ales to 3.2 percent alcoholic content, to raise revenues, thus making the campaign song of the Democrats the previous year, "Happy Days Are Here Again," come true.

"Betty Crocker" A fictional person, and cultural icon, and a brand name and trademark of the General Mills company of Minneapolis, Minnesota. The name was first developed in 1921 to give a personalized response to consumer questions; "Betty" was chosen because it seemed a cheerful, all-American name, and "Crocker" was the surname of an important director of the original company. In 1929, Betty Crocker coupons were introduced, inserted in bags of flour, and redeemable for reducing the cost of Oneida flatware; the program became so popular during the Depression that whole sets of flatware were offered and coupons were printed on boxes of company products. During the Depression, General Mills published and distributed Betty Crocker cookbooks; in 1945 ***Fortune*** magazine named Betty Crocker as the second-most-popular American woman, only Eleanor Roosevelt bested her at number one.

Civilian Conservation Corps Reforestation Relief Act (March 31, 1933) An employment scheme that established the Civilian Conservation Corps (CCC) was authorized to provide work for 250,000 unemployed males between the ages of 18 and 25 in reforestation, road construction, prevention of soil erosion, and projects in national parks and flood prone areas. The CCC set up work camps; the young men received $30.00 per month, all but $5.00 of it went home to their parents or dependents. As many as 2 million young men had worked for the CCC by December 1941.

The culture theory Promoted by American anthropologist Franz Boas of Columbia University and his professional allies, meant that each people has its own distinctive history and that all such human groups or populations have equal potentiality for cultural achievement in politics, economy, the arts and sciences, and other human endeavors. This theory, which had roots in British and German social thought, had been developed before the 1930s but came into its own in the Depression decade.

The Dust Bowl During the decade in the Southern Plains, and throughout the Great Plains more generally, severe weather conditions of drought, wind, and dislocated topsoil devastated large parts of Colorado, New Mexico, Kansas, Oklahoma, and Texas as well as the Dakotas, in a large, oval-shaped territory that drove many hundreds of thousands of rural people off the land, often to California, thus inspiring the young California writer John Steinbeck to write the great epochal novel ***The Grapes of Wrath* (1939)**.

Empire State Building A 102-story Art Deco skyscraper in New York City at the intersection of Fifth Avenue and West 34th Street. When completed in 1931, it was the tallest building in the country. Construction took less than fifteen months, but, thanks to the Depression, it was not a profitable property until 1951. In the 1930s, New York wits sometimes referred to it as the "Empty State Building," a play on the building's name, which was taken from the nickname for New York State. It cost $40,0948,99 to build. On May 1, 1931, President Herbert Hoover signaled the building's opening ceremony by pushing a button in the nation's capital, but the first use of the building's tower lights came to mark the victory of Franklin D. Roosevelt over Hoover in the election of November 1932.

Fair Labor Standards Act (June 23, 1938) Applied to enterprises in interstate commerce and provided certain minimum wages and maximum hours of work; its constitutionality was upheld by the U.S. Supreme Court in ***U.S. v. Darby Lumber Company*** **(1941)**.

Farm Credit Act (June 16, 1933) Facilitated short-term and medium-term credits for agricultural production and marketing, with the effect of refinancing farm mortgages at a low rate of interest for a much longer term.

Farm Holiday Association (spring and summer of 1932) Iowa farmer Milo Reno organized to boycott the distribution and sale of farm commodities, especially in the Middle Western Corn Belt, because of the ruinously low prices of said commodities. There were some instances of violence, and threats of violence, of farmers against other farmers and marketers.

William Faulkner A brilliant Mississippi writer who wrote a series of novels in the decade that explored the dark secrets of southern society, including ***As I Lay Dying*** **(1930)** and ***Sanctuary*** **(1931)**.

Federal Emergency Relief Act (May 12, 1933) Created the **Federal Emergency Relief Administration (FERA)** and authorized an appropriation of $500 millions; half went to direct relief aid to the states, the other half was spent on a $1 federal match for every $3 in state and local money for relief. These were outright grants, not loans, as had been true in the previous administration. State and local entities were to apply for relief, and a federal relief administrator, Iowa-born **Harry L. Hopkins (1890–1945),** a professional social worker, became that administrator.

Game theory Invented in the late 1930s by John von Neumann, a mathematician, and Oskar Morgenstern, an economist, at the Institute for Advanced Study and Princeton University, respectively, although their magnum opus, ***Theory of Games and Economic Behavior*** was not published until 1944. They claimed to have found a calculus for the social sciences, and clearly established the "decision sciences," with important implications for war games and military strategy, as well as economic regulation, in the years to come.

Golden Gate Bridge A giant suspension bridge connecting San Francisco, California, and Marin County, immediately north across the San Francisco Bay, was one of the engineering marvels of the decade. Construction began in January 1933 and finished in April 1937, at a cost of more than $35 millions, but $1.3 million under budget. The stock market crash and the Depression delayed construction from 1929 to late 1932, when finally the Bank of America, a San Francisco bank, agreed to purchase all the construction bonds to help the local economy.

Gone With the Wind (1936) Atlanta native Margaret Mitchell's highly popular historical novel from which the most popular Hollywood film of the decade was made, a sentimental romance of the Old South and what happened to its "ideal" characters during the horrors of the Civil War. The novel and the motion picture both represented a popular thirst for history, for nostalgia, and for constructing a "useful past" for the American nation.

Gone With the Wind (1939) The cinematic version of the novel was directed by Victor Fleming, who also directed in the same year *The Wizard of Oz*. The film had its premier in Atlanta just two weeks before Christmas 1939 and starred Vivien Leigh as the manipulative femme fatale, Scarlett O'Hara, and Clark Gable as the raffish Rhett Butler, who carried on a tumultuous and high-profile love affair in the South during the Civil War and Reconstruction.

Ernest Hemingway Iconic novelist of the interwar years, whose ***To Have and Have Not* (1937),** was one of the major novels of the decade.

"Hobos" Referred to (usually) unemployed men and women who had no regular homes and who begged or worked for food and board on a daily basis throughout the country.

Homeostasis The doctrine, in medical and biological science, that the body is a network of systems that are self-regulating and that it is the duty of the physician or biologist to facilitate those processes. Walter Bradford Cannon, a professor at Harvard University Medical School, made this doctrine famous in ***The Wisdom of the Body* (1932)**.

Home Owners Refinancing Act (June 13, 1933) Created the Home Owners Loan Corporation with a capital stock of $200 million and an additional $2 billion in bonds to refinance home mortgages in arrears and prevent foreclosures.

Hooverville The popular name for a shanty town for poor people during the Depression. It was Charles Michelson, publicity chief of the Democratic National Committee, who contributed the term to Depression-era language. These settlements were usually on empty land in urban areas. The homes for these unemployed men were constructed from whatever materials were at hand, including wood, cardboard, and metal scraps—and some men lived in sewer mains. There were long-term Hoovervilles in many cities, including New York, the District of Columbia, Seattle, Brooklyn, and St. Louis, the longest-lasting one, with a population of more than 1,000 persons.

Democrats came up with more terms, all to punish Herbert Hoover for the Depression, including "Hoover blanket" for old newspaper used as a blanket outdoors; a "Hoover flag" for an empty pants pocket turned inside out; "Hoover leather" for cardboard deployed to replace a worn out shoe sole; and, last but not least, a "Hoover wagon" for a car with horses to pull it, to show the owner had no money for gasoline—possibly a political stunt.

"The Hundred Days" (March 9–June 16, 1933) Refers to the fifteen major pieces of legislation that President Roosevelt asked the Congress to pass in that first three months of the new administration to help solve the Depression.

Mickey Mouse A comic animal cartoon character first created by Walt Disney and his associate Ub Iwerks in 1928; by 1930, they had produced more than a dozen cartoon short features. Mickey evolved in many respects, but in the Depression decade, he was always the little guy, the average fellow, who was able by cleverness and nimbleness to defeat opponents who appeared to be much larger and stronger than he, thus representing, in a sense, the average American fighting against the large odds of the Depression.

NLRB v. Jones and Laughlin Steel Company (1938) In which the U.S. Supreme Court upheld the National Labor Relations Act by a 5–4 vote by interpreting "stream of commerce" more broadly than ever before, thus bringing union activities under the interstate commerce clause of the U.S. Constitution.

National Housing Act (June 28, 1934) Intended to stimulate the housing market, the act established the **Federal Housing Authority (FHA)** to insure loans made by banks, trust companies, savings and loan associations, and other lending institutions; it also made possible the expansion of small businesses, farms, and other commercial as well as residential construction.

National Industrial Recovery Act (June 16, 1933) Called the NIRA, the act was supposed to revive economic activity by industrial self-regulation by creating the **National Recovery Administration (NRA)** to administer the fair trade codes used for many industrial and trade associations during World War I. This soon ran into violations of agreement, or nonagreements, and the U.S. Supreme Court declared the NRA unconstitutional in ***Schechter Poultry Corp. v. U.S.* (1935)**.

National Labor Relations Act (July 5, 1935) Created a new National Labor Relations Board to enforce appropriate collective bargaining arrangements between management and labor, including enabling laborers to bargain collectively through organizations of their own choosing.

National Youth Administration, NYA (June 26, 1935) Established under executive order by the president to provide a work relief and jobs program for people between the ages of 16 and 25 from families on relief and no longer in school, although it also was available for needy students in secondary and postsecondary schools and colleges. Millions finished their education, especially members of minority groups. The program was terminated in 1943.

Resettlement Administration, RA (May 1, 1935) Established by President Roosevelt by executive order, with Rexford Guy Tugwell as administrator, the

RA was intended to help impoverished rural people find new opportunities who were not helped by the Agricultural Adjustment Administration. While it made grants to poor farmers to improve their situations—flood drainage, soil conservation, and the like, ironically its most famous accomplishments were the founding of three "greenbelt" towns, as demonstrations of the garden city idea, in which middle-class persons would live and work in the same community; these small suburbs were founded near Washington, D.C., Cincinnati, Ohio; and Milwaukee, Wisconsin. In 1937 the **RA**'s functions were absorbed by the **Farm Security Administration**.

"Riding the rails" Refers to the widespread practice, especially of young people during the Depression, of traveling as stowaways on trains from place to place in the country.

Rural Electrification Administration, REA (May 11, 1935) Which the president established by executive order, lent the cost of extending and distributing electrical power to isolated rural areas not served by private utilities. It facilitated the electrification of large parts of the countryside.

Scottsboro Boys In 1931, nine young African American men riding on the rails in Alabama were accused of having raped two white women and spent the next twenty years fighting for their freedom, even when one of the women repudiated her own testimony and the medical evidence of rape was nonexistent. The affair was an example of Southern white segregationists' belief that any question of an African American sexually molesting a white female was unacceptable, punishable by death. Collectively the nine young men spent over one hundred years in jail for their "offense."

Second New Deal (January 4, 1935) **President Roosevelt** announced in his annual message to Congress a program of social reform of security of livelihood, security against unemployment and other vagaries of economic life, and better housing.

Snow White and the Seven Dwarfs (1937) Released on December 21, the first full-length animated film produced by the Disney Studios marked a genuine milestone in cinematic art—and popular appeal.

Social Security Act (August 14, 1935) Created a Social Security Board to administer a wide-ranging federal entitlement program related to old-age security, unemployment assistance, and other benefits through a system of new federal taxes on payrolls.

Soil Conservation and Domestic Allotment Act (February 29, 1936) Created to replace the **Agricultural Adjustment Administration,** which the Supreme Court had ruled unconstitutional in ***U.S. v. Butler* (1935)**. Instead of authorizing controls of crop production, farmers received benefit payments for soil conservation in cooperation with government programs. This proved ineffectual and was replaced in 1938 by a reformed **Agricultural Adjustment Act of 1938**.

John Steinbeck California novelist, wrote a series of novels in the Depression, including ***Tortilla Flat* (1935)**, ***Of Mice and Men* (1937)**, and his epochal novel of the Dust Bowl, ***The Grapes of Wrath* (1939)**.

"Swing music" Came to be teen music by the midpoint of the decade, which featured large bands with a section to "anchor" rhythm that in turn supports a lead section with various soloists, either singers or instrument players. The music was derived from jazz, especially African American jazz of the previous decades. Among the famous bandleaders of swing were the African American genius "Duke" Ellington and the white Jewish leader Benny Goodman, who presented contrasting styles of symphonic harmony versus edgy, almost twitchy, jazz.

The synthetic theory of evolution Worked out in the 1930s by American and British scientists, the theory sought to bring together Darwin's theory of natural selection with proofs of micromutations and with the paleontological evidence of evolution, thus unifying nineteenth- and twentieth-century evolutionary theory.

Tennessee Valley Authority (May 18, 1933) A major New Deal program to provide modern benefits to an impoverished area of the South, bringing flood control, land reclamation, prevention of soil erosion, forestation, hydroelectric dams, the development of aluminum, fertilizer, and other industrial products, and to enable a class of poor whites to raise themselves to a more comfortable middle-class existence.

Wall Street Stock Market Crash (commencing on October 24, 1929) The crash in which 13 million shares traded, and five days later another 16 million shares traded, created an unprecedented panic, which in turn set off the crash.

The Wizard of Oz (1939) A musical film, in color, directed by Victor Fleming and taken from L. Frank Baum's children's novel, *The Wonderful Wizard of Oz*. The film featured Judy Garland, as Dorothy Gale, a Kansas farm girl swept away by a tornado to the magical land of Oz where she has a variety of adventures—many songs in the picture entered into the mainstream of popular culture, especially Garland's rendition of "Somewhere Over the Rainbow." The movie was a critical success and a modest commercial success—especially considering its fantastic production costs at that time.

Grant Wood An Iowa regionalist painter whose style of painting did not take on a celebration of the Midwestern region until the Great Depression. His most famous paintings were ***Dinner for Threshers*** and ***American Gothic,*** both of which were executed while he was both a professor of art at the University of Iowa in Iowa City and the head of an artist colony in nearby Stone City, Iowa.

Works Progress Administration (April 8, 1935) Called the **Works Projects Administration (WPA)** starting in 1939, was the major federal agency for the distribution of federal matching assistance to states and localities for large-scale national works programs for the unemployed and Harry

L. Hopkins became its chief. The WPA helped administer federal relief programs, employing millions every month; by 1943, when it was terminated, the WPA or its allied agencies, such as the **Civilian Conservation Corps** or the **National Youth Administration,** had hired more than 8.5 million different individuals on more than 1.4 million specific projects; had spent about $11 billion on 651,087 miles of highways, roads, and streets; and had constructed or repaired 124,031 bridges, 125,110 public buildings, 8,192 parks, and 853 airport landing fields.

Bibliography

Angelou, Maya. *I Know Why the Caged Bird Sings.* New York: Random House, 1969.

Baker, Russell. *Growing Up.* New York: Signet Publishing, 1982.

Baldwin, Sidney. *Poverty and Politics: The Rise and Decline of the Farm Security Administration.* Chapel Hill: The University of North Carolina Press, 1968.

Balio, Tino. *Grand Design: Hollywood as a Modern Business Enterprise, 1930–1939.* New York: Charles Scribner's Sons, 1993.

Ballderrama, Francisco E., and Raymond Rodriguez. *Decade of Betrayal: Mexican Repatriations in the 1930s.* Albuquerque: University of New Mexico Press, 1995.

Banks, Vera J. *Black Farmers and Their Farms.* U.S. Department of Agriculture, Rural Development Research Report No. 69. Washington, DC: U.S. Government Printing Office, 1986.

Baydo, Gerald R., ed. *The Evolution of Mass Culture in America, 1877 to the Present.* St. Louis: The Forum Press, 1971.

Bergman, Andrew. *We're in the Money. Depression America and Its Films.* New York: New York University Press, 1971.

Berry, Chad. *Southern Migration, Northern Exiles.* Urbana: University of Illinois Press, 2000.

Bilstein, Roger E. *Flight in America: From the Wrights to the Astronauts,* 3rd ed. Baltimore: Johns Hopkins University Press, 2001.

Bix, Amy Sue. *Inventing Ourselves Out of Jobs: America's Debate over Technological Unemployment, 1929–1981.* Baltimore: Johns Hopkins University Press, 2001.

Borth, Christy. *Pioneers of Plenty: The Story of Chemurgy.* Indianapolis, New York: Bobbs-Merrill, 1942.

Breitman, Richard, and Alan M. Kraut. *American Refugee Policy and European Jewry, 1933–1945.* Bloomington: Indiana University Press, 1987.

Caro, Robert A. *The Power Broker: Robert Moses and New York.* New York: Alfred A. Knopf, 1975.

Carter, Dan T. *Scottsboro: A Tragedy of the American South.* Rev. ed. Baton Rouge: Louisiana State University Press, 1979.

Cayton, Horace R., and George S. Mitchell. *The Black Worker and the New Unions.* Chapel Hill: The University of North Carolina Press, 1939.

Clotfelter, Charles T. *After Brown: The Rise and Retreat of School Desegregation.* Princeton: Princeton University Press, 2004.

Cochrane, Willard W. *The Development of American Agriculture: A Historical Analysis.* Minneapolis: University of Minnesota Press, 1979.

Cohen, Lizabeth. *Making a New Deal: Industrial Workers in Chicago, 1919–1939.* Cambridge, MA: Harvard University Press, 1990.

Conklin, Paul K. *Tomorrow a New World: The New Deal Community Program.* Ithaca, NY: Cornell University Press, 1959.

Corn, Joseph. *The Winged Gospel: America's Romance With Aviation.* New ed. Baltimore: Johns Hopkins University Press, 2002 [1983].

Daniels, Roger. *Guarding the Golden Door: American Immigration Policy and Immigrants Since 1882.* New York: Hill and Wang, 2004.

———. "Immigration Policy in a Time of War: The United States, 1939–1945." *Journal of American Ethnic History* 25 (2006): 108–116.

Davis, Allison, and John Dollard. *Children of Bondage; The Personality Development of Negro Youth in the Urban South.* Washington, DC: American Council on Education, 1940.

Davis, Allison, John Dollard, Burleigh B. Gardner, and Mary R. Gardner. *Deep South: A Social Anthropological View of Caste and Class.* Chicago: University of Chicago Press, 1941.

Detholoff, Henry C., and Irwin M. May, eds. *Southwestern Agriculture: Pre-Columbian to Modern.* College Station: Texas A&M University Press, 1982.

Divine, Robert A. *American Immigration Policy, 1924–1952.* New Haven: Yale University Press, 1957.

Dollard, John. *Caste and Class in a Southern Town.* New Haven: Yale University Press, 1937.

Dooley, Roger B. *From Scarface to Scarlett: American Films in the 1930s.* New York: Harcourt, Brace, Jovanovich, 1981.

Douglas, Susan J. *Inventing American Broadcasting.* Baltimore: The Johns Hopkins University Press, 1989.

———. *Listening In: Radio and the American Imagination.* New York: Random House, 1999.

Downs, Linda Bank. *Diego Rivera: The Detroit Industry Murals.* New York: W.W. Norton, 2000.

Drake, St. Clair, and Horace Cayton. *Black Metropolis: A Study of Negro Life in a Northern City,* 2 vols. New York: Harcourt Brace and Company, 1945.

Dubofsky, Melvin, and Stephen Burwood, eds. *Women and Minorities during the Great Depression.* New York: Garland Publishers, 1990.

Early, Steven C. *An Introduction to American Movies.* New York: New American Library, 1978.

Elder, Glen H. *Children of the Great Depression.* Boulder, CO: Westview Press, 1998.

Frazier, E. Franklin. *Negro Youth at the Crossroads: Their Personality Development in the Middle States.* Washington, DC: American Council on Education, 1940.

Fell, John C. *A History of Films.* New York: Holt, Rinehart, and Winston, 1979.

Fenichell, Stephen. *Plastic: The Making of a Synthetic Century.* New York: Harper Collins, 1996.

Gilbert, Richard V., et al. *An Economic Program for American Democracy.* New York: The Vanguard Press, 1938.

Grant, H. Roger, and L. Edward Purcell, eds. *Years of Struggle: The Farm Diary of Elmer G. Powers, 1931–1936.* Ames: Iowa State University Press, 1976.

Gregory, James N. *The Southern Diaspora: How the Great Migrations of Black and White Southerners Transformed America.* Chapel Hill: The University of North Carolina Press, 2005.

Grey, Michael R. *New Deal Medicine: The Rural Health Program of the Farm Security Administration.* Baltimore: The Johns Hopkins University Press, 2002.

Gilmore, Glenda, *Defying Dixie: The Radical Roots of Civil Rights, 1919–1950* New York: W.W. Norton and Co., 2008.

Goodman, James. *Stories of Scottsboro.* New York: Pantheon, 1994.

Grubbs, Donald. *''Cry From the Cotton'' The Southern Tenant Farmers Union and the New Deal.* Chapel Hill: University of North Carolina Press, 1971.

Hagood, Margaret. *Mothers of the South.* Chapel Hill: The University of North Carolina Press, 1939.

Hahamovitch, Cindy. *The Fruits of Their Labor: Atlantic Coast Farmworkers and the Making of Migrant Poverty, 1870–1945.* Chapel Hill: University of North Carolina Press, 1997.

Harris, William H. *Keeping the Faith: A Philip Randolph, Milton P. Webster, and the Brotherhood of Sleeping Car Porters, 1925–1937.* Urbana; University of Illinois Press, 1977.

Hapke, Laura. *Daughters of the Great Depression: Women, Work, and Fiction in the American 1930s.* Athens: The University of Georgia Press, 1995.

Himmelberg, Robert F. *The Great Depression and the New Deal.* Westport, CT: Greenwood Press, 2000.

Hine, Lewis W., and Freddy Langer. *Lewis W. Hine: The Empire State Building.* New York: Prestel Publishers, 1998.

Hine, Thomas. *The Rise and Fall of the American Teen Ager.* New York: Avon Books, 1999.

Hooker, Nancy H., ed. *The Moffat Papers: Selections from the Diplomatic Journals of Jay Pierrepont Moffatt, 1919–1943.* Cambridge, MA: Harvard University Press, 1956.

Holloway, Jonathan Scott, and Ben Keppel, eds. *Black Scholars on the Line: Race, Social Science, and American Thought in the Twentieth Century.* Notre Dame: University of Notre Dame University Press, 2007.

Hoppe, Robert A., et al. *The Economic and Rural Development of Black Farmers.* Agriculture and Rural Economics Division, Economic Research Service, U.S. Department of Agriculture, Rural Development Research Report 61. Washington, DC: United States Government Printing Office, 1986.

Hurt, R. Douglas. *American Agriculture: A Brief History.* Ames: Iowa State University Press, 1994.

———. *Problems of Plenty: The American Farmers in the Twentieth Century.* Chicago: Ivan R. Dee, 2002.

Jerome, Harry. *Migration and Business Cycles.* New York: National Bureau of Economic Research, 1926.

Jones, James H. *Bad Blood: The Tuskegee Syphilis Experiment.* New York, Basic Books, 1981.

Johnson, Charles S. *Shadow of the Plantation.* Chicago: University of Chicago Press, 1934.

———. *The Negro College Graduate.* Chapel Hill: The University of North Carolina Press, 1938.

———. *Growing up in the Black Belt: Negro Youth in the Rural South.* Washington, DC: American Council on Education, 1941.

Judd, Richard M. *The New Deal in Vermont: Its Impact and Aftermath.* New York: Garland Publishing Co., 1978.

Karl, Barry D., and Charles E. Merriam. *Executive Reorganization and Reform in the New Deal, The Genesis of Administrative Management, 1900–1939.* Cambridge, MA: Harvard University Press, 1963.

———. *The Study of Politics.* Chicago: University of Chicago Press, 1974.

Keiler, Allan. *Marian Anderson: A Singer's Journey.* Urbana: University of Illinois Press, 2002.

Kett, Joseph. *Rites of Passage: Adolescence in America, 1790 to the Present.* New York: Basic Books, 1977.

Komarovsky, Mirra. *The Unemployed Man and His Family: The Effect of Unemployment Upon the Status of the Man in Fifty-nine Families.* New York: The Dryden Press, 1940.

Kyvig, David E. *Daily Life in the United States, 1920–1940: How Americans Lived Through the 'Roaring Twenties' and the Great Depression.* Chicago: Ivan R. Dee, 2002.

Lane, James B., and Edward J. Escobar, eds. *Forging a Community: The Latino Experience in Northwest Indiana, 1919–1975.* Chicago: Cattails Press, 1987.

Laqueur, Walter Z. *The Terrible Secret: Suppression of the Truth about Hitler's ''Final Solution.''* Boston: Little, Brown, 1980.

Levine, Lawrence W., and Cornelia R. Levine. *The People and the President: America's Conversation with FDR.* Boston: Beacon Press, 2002.

Lewis, Hylan. *Blackways of Kent.* Chapel Hill: The University of North Carolina Press, 1955.

Lilienthal, David E. *TVA: Democracy on the March.* New York: Harper & Brothers, 1944.

Low, Ann Marie. *Dust Bowl Diary.* Lincoln: the University of Nebraska Press, 1984.

Lowitt, Richard. *The New Deal and the West.* Bloomington: Indiana University Press, 1984.

Lowitt, Richard, and Maurine H. Beasley, eds. *One Third of a Nation: Lorena Hickock Reports on the Great Depression.* Urbana: University of Illinois Press, 2000.

Lubove, Roy. *Community Planning in the 1930s.* Cambridge, MA: Harvard University Press, 1963.

Lucic, Karen. *Charles Sheeler and the Cult of the Machine.* Cambridge, MA: Harvard University Press, 1991.

Lynd, Robert S., and Helen Merrell Lynd. *Middletown: A Study in Modern American Culture* New York: Harcourt, Brace and World, 1929.

Lynd Robert S., and Helen Merrell Lynd. *Middletown in Transition: A Study in Cultural Conflicts.* New York: Harcourt, Brace, and Company, 1937.

MacGowan, Kenneth. ''When the Talkies Came to Hollywood.'' *The Quarterly of Film Radio and Television* 10 (Spring 1956): 288–301.

Martin, Charles H. *The Angelo Herndon Case and Southern Justice.* Baton Rouge: Louisiana State University Press, 1979.

Marcus, Alan I., and Howard P. Segal. *American Technology: A Brief History,* 2nd ed. San Diego: Harcourt, Brace, and Jovanovich, 1989.

McCluskey, Audrey Thomas, and Elaine M. Smith., eds. *Mary McLeod Bethune: Building a Better World.* Bloomington: Indiana University Press, 1999.

McElvaine, Robert A., ed. *Down and Out In the Great Depression. Letters from the ''Forgotten Man.''* Chapel Hill: The University of North Carolina Press, 1983.

McElvaine, Robert S. *The Great Depression: America, 1929–1941.* Pittsburgh: Three Rivers Press, 1993.

McKenzie, R. D. *The Metropolitan Community.* New York: The Macmillan Co., 1967 [1933].

McJimsey, George T. *Harry Hopkins: Ally of the Poor and Defender of Democracy.* Cambridge, MA: Harvard University Press, 1987.

———. *The Presidency of Franklin D. Roosevelt.* Lawrence: University Press of Kansas, 2000.

McWilliams, Carey. *Factories in the Field: The Story of Migratory Labor in California,* 4th ed. Berkeley and Los Angeles: University of California Press, 2000.

Meier, August, and Elliott Rudwick. *Black Detroit and the Rise of the UAW.* New York: Oxford University Press, 1979.

Melendy, H. Brett. *Asians in America: Filipinos, Koreans, and East Indians.* Boston: Twayne, 1973.

Meikle, Jeffrey L. *Twentieth Century Limited: Industrial Design in America, 1925–1939.* Philadelphia: Temple University Press, 1979.

Mintz, Steven. *Huck's Raft: A History of American Childhood.* Cambridge, MA: Harvard University Press, 2004.

Mitchell, George T., *Dr. George: An Account of the Life of a Country Doctor.* Carbondale: Southern Illinois University Press, 1994.

Mitchell, H. L. *Mean Things Happening in This Land.* Montclair, NJ: Allanheld, Osmun, 1979.

Mumford, Lewis. *The Culture of Cities.* New York: Harcourt, Brace, 1938.

Naison, Mark. *Communists in Harlem during the Depression.* Urbana: University of Illinois Press, 1983.

National Resources Committee. *Part One, The Structure of the American Economy.* Washington, DC: Government Printing Office, 1939.

Nelson, Paula M. *The Prairie Winnows Out Its Own: The West River Country of South Dakota in the Years of Depression and Dust.* Iowa City: University of Iowa Press, 1996.

Nixon, Edgar B., ed. *Franklin D. Roosevelt and Foreign Affairs.* Cambridge, MA: Harvard University Press, 1969.

Ogilvie, Sarah A., and Scott Miller. *Refuge Denied: The St. Louis Passengers and the Holocaust* Madison: University of Wisconsin Press. 2006.

Paine, Jeffrey. *The Simplification of American Life: Hollywood Films of the 1930s.* New York: Arno Press, 1972.

Palladino, Grace. *Teenagers: An American History.* New York: Basic Books, 1996.

Park, Robert E., and Ernest W. Burgess. *The City.* Chicago: The University of Chicago Press, 1967 [1925].

Parrish, Michael E. *Anxious Decades: America in Prosperity and Depression, 1920–1941.* New York: W.W. Norton, 1992.

Podolsky, Scott H. "The Changing Fate of Pneumonia as a Public Health Concern in 20th Century America and Beyond." *American Journal of Public Health* 95 (December 2005): 2144–2155.

Porter, Glenn. *Raymond Loewy: Designs for a Consumer Culture.* Wilmington, DE: Hagley Museum and Library, 2002.

Posadas, Barbara M. *The Filipino Americans.* Westport, CT: Greenwood Press, 1999.

Quigley, Martin, and Richard Gertner, Jr. *Films in America, 1929–1969.* New York: Golden Press, 1970.

Raper, Arthur F. *A Preface to Peasantry: A Tale of Two Black Belt Counties.* Chapel Hill: The University of North Carolina Press, 1936.

Reiman, Richard. *The New Deal and American Youth: Ideas and Ideals in a Depression Decade.* Athens: University of Georgia Press, 1993.

Rich, Doris. *Amelia Earhart: A Biography.* Washington, DC: Smithsonian Books, 1989.

Riney-Kehrberg, Pamela. *Rooted in Dust: Surviving Drought and Depression in Southwestern Kansas.* Lawrence: University of Kansas Press, 1994.

Roosevelt, Eleanor. *It's Up to the Women.* New York: Frederick Stokes and Company, 1933.

Rutland, Robert Allen. *A Boyhood in the Dust Bowl, 1926–1934.* Niwot, CO: University Press of Colorado, 1995.

Salmond, John A. *The Civilian Conservation Corps 1933–1942: A New Deal Study.* Durham: Duke University Press, 1967.

Salutos, Theodore. *The American Farmer and the New Deal.* Ames: Iowa State University Press, 1982.

Schapp, Jeremy. *Triumph: The Untold Story of Jessie Owens and Hitler's Olympics.* Boston: Houghton Mifflin, 2007.

Schatz, Thomas. *Hollywood Genres.* New York: Random House, 1981.

Schlesinger, Arthur M. *The Rise of the City, 1878–1898.* New York: Macmillan, 1933.

Schwartz, William B. *Life Without Disease: The Pursuit of Medical Utopia.* Berkeley and Los Angeles: University of California Press, 1998.

Sharpless, Rebecca. *Fertile Ground, Narrow Choices. Women on Texas Cotton Farms, 1900–1940.* Chapel Hill: University of North Carolina Press, 1999.

Sklar, Robert. *Movie-Made America: A Cultural History of American Movies.* New York: Random House, 1975.

Sitkoff, Harvard. *A New Deal for Blacks: The Emergence of Civil Rights as a National Issue: The Depression Decade.* New York: Oxford University Press, 1978.

Soule, George. *The Planned Society.* New York, Macmillan, 1933.

Stevens, Joseph E. *Hoover Dam: An American Adventure*. Norman: University of Oklahoma Press, 1988.

Stewart, Barbara McDonald. *United States Government Policy on Refugees from Nazism, 1933–1940*. New York: Garland, 1982.

Stock, Catherine McNicol. *Main Street in Crisis: The Great Depression and the Old Middle Class on the Northern Plains*. Chapel Hill: The University of North Carolina Press, 1992.

Sullivan, Patricia. *Days of Hope: Race and Democracy in the New Deal Era*. Chapel Hill: University of North Carolina Press, 1996.

Tauranac, John. *Empire State Building: The Making of a Landmark*. New York: Scribner, 1995.

Taylor, Brenda Jeannette. "The New Deal and Health: Meeting Farmers' Needs in Ropesville, Texas, 1933–1943." *Journal of the West* 36 (January 1997): 38–46.

Terkel, Studs. *Hard Times: An Oral History of the Great Depression*. New York: Pantheon Books, 1970.

Thomas, Gordon, and Max Morgan Witts. *Voyage of the Damned*. New York: Stein and Day, 1974.

Tobey, Ronald C. *Technology as Freedom: The New Deal and the Electrical Modernization of the American Home*. Berkeley: University of California Press, 1996.

Thomson, David. *America in the Dark. The Impact of Hollywood Films on American Culture*. New York: William Morrow & Company, 1977.

Tugwell, Rexford G. *The Industrial Discipline*. New York: Columbia University Press, 1933.

Uys, Errol Lincoln. *Riding the Rails: Teenagers on the Move During the Great Depression*. New York: Routledge, 2003.

Van Der Zee, John. *The Gate: The True Story of the Design and Construction of the Golden Gate Bridge*. New York: Simon & Schuster, 1987.

Van Riper, A. Bowdoin. *Imagining Flight: Aviation and Popular Culture*. College Station: Texas A&M University Press, 2003.

Wade, Wyn Craig. *The Fiery Cross: The Ku Klux Klan in America*. New York: Simon and Schuster, 1987.

Ware, Caroline F. *Greenwich Village 1920–1930. A Comment on American Civilization in the Post-War Years*. New York: Harper and Row, 1965 [1935].

Ware, Susan. *Beyond Suffrage: Women in the New Deal*. Cambridge, MA: Harvard University Press, 1981.

———. *Holding Their Own: American Women in the 1930s*. Boston: Twayne Publishers, 1982.

———. *Still Missing: Amelia Earhart and the Search for Modern Feminism*. New York: W.W. Norton, 1993.

Warner, W. Lloyd, Buford B. Junker, and Walter A. Adams. *Color and Human Nature: Negro Personality, Development in a Northern City*. Washington, DC: American Council on Education, 1941.

Watkins, T. H. *The Hungry Years: A Narrative History of the Great Depression in America*. New York: Henry Holt, 1999.

Webster, Charles. "Health, Welfare, and Unemployment During the Depression." *Past and Present* 109 (1985): 104–130.

Weiss, Nancy J. *Farewell to the Party of Lincoln: Black Politics in the Age of FDR*. Princeton, NJ: Princeton University Press, 1983.

Westin, Jean Eddy. *Making Do: How Women Survived the '30s*. Chicago: Follett Publishing, 1976.

Willis, Carol, ed. *Building the Empire State*. New York: W.W. Norton, 1998.

Wilson, Richard Guy. *The Machine Age in America, 1918–1941*. New York: Harry N. Abrams, 1986.

Winokur, Mark. *American Laughter: Immigrants, Ethnicity, and 1930s Hollywood Film Comedy*. New York: St. Martin's Press, 1996.

Wolters, Raymond. *Negroes and the Great Depression: The Problem of Economic Recovery*. Westport, CT: Greenwood Publishers, 1970.

Wood, Michael. *America in the Movies*. New York: Basic Books, Inc., 1975.

Wyman, David S. *Paper Walls: America and the Refugee Crisis*. Amherst: University of Massachusetts Press, 1968.

Young, William H., and Nancy Young. *The 1930s*. Westport, CT: Greenwood Press, 2002.

Zim, Larry, Mel Lerner, and Herbert Rolfe. *The World of Tomorrow: The 1939 New York World's Fair*. New York: Harper & Row, 1988.

Note: The editor thanks the authors for their valuable suggestions; he has added a few favorite resources of his own.

Index